Democracy, Markets, and Structural Reform in Latin America:

Argentina, Bolivia, Brazil, Chile, and Mexico

D0107155

North·South Center
UNIVERSITY OF MIAMI

Democracy, Markets, and Structural Reform in Latin America:
Argentina, Bolivia, Brazil, Chile, and Mexico

Edited by

William C. Smith, Carlos H. Acuña,
and Eduardo A. Gamarra

Transaction Publishers
New Brunswick (U.S.A.) and London (U.K.)

The mission of the North-South Center is to promote better relations among the United States, Canada, and the nations of Latin America and the Caribbean by providing a disciplined intellectual focus for improved relations, commerce, and understanding in the hemisphere, wherein major political, social, and economic issues are seen in a global context. The Center conducts policy-relevant research and programs of education, training, cooperative study, and public outreach and engages in an active program of publication and dissemination of information on the Americas. The North-South Center fosters linkages among academic and research institutions throughout the Americas and acts as an agent of constructive change in the region.

Library of Congress Cataloging-in-Publication Data

Democracy, markets, and structural reform in contemporary Latin
    America: Argentina, Bolivia, Brazil, Chile, and Mexico / edited
    by William C. Smith, Carlos H. Acuña, Eduardo A. Gamarra.
        p.   cm.
At head of title: North-South Center, University of Miami.
    Includes index.
    ISBN 1-56000-721-4 (pbk.)
    1. Latin America — Economic conditions — 1982 – 2. Latin America
— Economic policy. 3. Democracy — Latin America. 4. Latin America —
Politics and government — 1980 –   I. Smith, William C., 1946-
II. Acuña, Carlos (Carlos H.)   III. Gamarra, Eduardo.
HC125.0444 1993
338.98—dc20   93-44980
                                                                              CIP

    ISBN-1-56000-731-1 (paper)
    Printed in the United States of America

    00 99 98 97 96 95 94 7 6 5 4 3 2 1

Contents

Contributors

Carlos H. Acuña teaches comparative politics at the Universidad de Buenos Aires and is an associate researcher at the Centro de Estudios de Estado y Sociedad (CEDES) in Argentina. He is the author of *La burguesía industrial como actor político en la Argentina* (forthcoming), editor of *El nuevo sistema político argentino* (forthcoming), and coeditor with William C. Smith and Eduardo A. Gamarra of *Latin American Political Economy in the Age of Neoliberal Reform: Theoretical and Comparative Perspectives* (1994) and with Catalina Smulovitz of *Los militares como actor político en las nuevas democracias del Cono Sur* (forthcoming).

Antônio Barros de Castro teaches economics at the Universidade Federal de Rio de Janeiro in Brazil. He has served as president of the Banco Nacional de Desenvolvimento Econômico e Social (BNDES). Among his books are *7 Ensaios sobre a Economia Brasileira* (1971) and *O Capitalismo Ainda É Aquele* (1979). He is coauthor with Francisco Eduardo Pires de Souza of *A Economia Brasileira em Marcha Forçada* (1985).

Adolfo Canitrot is senior researcher at the Instituto Torcuato Di Tella in Buenos Aires, Argentina. He has served as Argentina's vice minister of economy. He is the author of many studies of the Argentine economy, including *La viabilidad de la democracia: Un análisis de la experiencia peronista, (1975), Teoría y práctica del liberalismo* (1975). *Política antiinflacionaria y apertura económica en la Argentina* (1981), and *Orden social y monetarismo* (1982).

Eduardo A. Gamarra teaches Latin American politics at Florida International University and is a member of the editorial staff of *Hemisphere*. He is the coauthor with James Malloy of *Revolution and Reaction: Bolivia, 1964-1985*

(1988) and coeditor with William C. Smith and Carlos H. Acuña of *Latin American Political Economy in the Age of Neoliberal Reform: Theoretical and Comparative Perspectives* (1994), and with A. Douglas Kincaid of *Seguridad ciudadana y seguridad nacional: La policía y relaciones cívico militares en América Latina.* (forthcoming).

Manuel Antonio Garretón is senior researcher at the Facultad Latinoamericana de Ciencias Sociales (FLACSO) in Santiago, Chile. He has authored numerous books, including *El proceso político chileno* (1983), *Dictaduras y democratización* (1984), *La Unidad Popular y el conflicto político en Chile* (1993), and *Reconstruir la política: Transición y consolidación democrática en Chile* (1987). He is coeditor with Marcelo Cavarozzi of *Muerte y resurreción: Los partidos políticos en el autoritarismo y las transiciones en el Cono Sur* (1989), and with Juan E. Corradi and Patricia Weiss Fagen of *Fear at the Edge: State Terror and Resistance in Latin America* (1992).

Blanca Heredia teaches international relations and comparative politics at the Instituto Tecnológico Autónomo de México (ITAM) in Mexico City. She is the author of numerous articles and chapters on business and politics in Mexico and on processes of economic reform. Her most recent article is "Mexican Business and the State: The Political Economy of a 'Muddled' Transition," forthcoming in Earnest Bartell and Leigh Payne, eds., *Business Elites and Democracy in Latin America.*

Juan Antonio Morales teaches economics at the Universidad Católica Boliviana and has served as minister of economy in the Bolivian government. He is the author of many studies of the Bolivian economy, including "Bolivia's Economic Crisis" with Jeffrey Sachs, in *Developing Country Debt and Economic Performance* (1990). He is also a coauthor of *Bolivia: Ajuste estructural, equidad y crecimiento* (1991).

Jaime Ros teaches economics at the University of Notre Dame where he is also a researcher at the Kellogg Institute of International Studies. He is one of several coauthors of *La organización industrial en México, Siglo XXI* (1990), the editor of *La edad de plomo del desarrollo latinoamericano* (1993) and *MODEM: Un modelo macroeconómico para México* (1985), and is coeditor with Roberto Bouzas of *Economic Integration in the Western Hemisphere: Issues and Prospects for Latin America* (1994).

Lourdes Sola teaches political science at the Universidade de São Paulo. She is the author of many articles, including "Gestão da Economia e Mudança de Regime" (1985) in *Ciências Sociais Hoje* and "Heterodox Shock in Brazil: Técnicos, Politicians, Democracy" (1991) in the *Journal of Latin American Studies*. She is the editor of *O Estado da Transição: Política e Economia na Nova República* (1991) and *Estado, Mercado, Democracia: Política e Economia Comparada* (1993).

William C. Smith teaches Latin American politics at the University of Miami and is director of the Task Force on Democratization at the North-South Center. He is the author of *Authoritarianism and the Crisis of the Argentine Political Economy* (1989) and coeditor with Carlos H. Acuña and Eduardo A. Gamarra of *Latin American Political Economy in the Age of Neoliberal Reform: Theoretical and Comparative Perspectives* (1994), and with Lars Schoultz and Augusto Varas of *Security, Democracy, and Development in U.S.-Latin American Relations* (1994).

Pilar Vergara is senior researcher at the Facultad Latinoamericana de Ciencias Sociales (FLACSO) in Santiago, Chile. She is the author of numerous books and articles on the state and Chilean social policy, including *Auge y caída del neoliberalismo en Chile* (1985) and *Políticas hacia la extrema pobreza en Chile, 1973-1988* (1990).

Preface and Acknowledgments

The unraveling and collapse of models of accumulation based upon import-substitution industrialization in Latin America during the 1970s and 1980s were accompanied by profound transformations in relations among the state, civil society, and the economy. The postauthoritarian regimes that emerged in Latin America over the past decade have achieved a degree of democratic consolidation, but they continue to confront severe political and economic challenges. Stable and sustainable growth remains an elusive goal for many countries, despite the modest successes of neoliberal strategies of market-oriented restructuring in achieving external adjustment, taming hyperinflation, and disciplining public sector finance. Sharp declines in per capita income in many countries have exacerbated poverty and worsened already egregious patterns of inequality and concentration of wealth and control over productive resources. Moreover, the often autocratic implementation frequently associated with stabilization and structural adjustment policies has shown a disturbing tendency to undermine representative institutions and the conditions for deepening democratic politics, particularly in the broadening of citizenship rights beyond the electoral arena.

Understanding these social and economic transformations and their implications for democracy demands a fundamental rethinking of many central issues in Latin American political economy. This is obviously not the first time shifts in prevailing political and economic models in Latin America have provoked theoretical and methodological debates among social scientists or prompted calls for new paradigms better equipped to capture the elusive reality of rapidly changing circumstances; one has only to recall the fervor that informed still simmering debates between structuralists and monetarists or between the defenders of theories of development and modernization and those advocating perspectives privileging questions of external dependency and the region's peripheral or semiperipheral insertion in the world economy. This volume is motivated by a more modest goal. We harbor no illusion of having discovered a new paradigm. Rather, we seek to articulate a perspective that eschews conventional approaches and the theoretico-methodological reductionisms that consider one or the other set of variables, be they political or economic, as "exogenous" or as merely "contextual" to the object of analysis. In this spirit, we hope to offer interpretations of sociopolitical processes in the region that advance beyond the old antimony between "economics" and "politics."

The many themes analyzed first emerged in the individual research agendas of the editors. Early discussions about the tensions among democracy, markets, and economic reform between Bill Smith and Eduardo Gamarra led to a project supported by the External Grants Office of the North-South Center at the University of Miami. This endeavor was soon enriched by the incorporation of Carlos Acuña into the discussions. Collective brainstorming, in turn, evolved into a conference held in March 1992 in Buenos Aires. During three, highly stimulating, albeit exhausting days, more than two dozen political scientists and economists from both Latin America and the United States, plus several dozen invited guests from various Buenos Aires research institutions, engaged in collective debate early in the morning and, as is the habit among the *porteños*, recessed only in the early hours of the following morning.

The Buenos Aires symposium was followed by editors' requests to the participants for extensive revisions of their original *ponencias*. The resulting chapters were originally planned for one volume, whose heft caused the editors to refer to it as the *ladrillo*, or "brick." One evening, after a long day's labor on the manuscript, and stimulated by an excellent cabernet sauvignon, it dawned upon us that we really had produced two books, rather than one, with each book capable of standing alone — the present volume consists of careful case studies of the five countries selected for analysis, while the other provides theoretical and comparative perspectives on democracy, markets, and economic restructuring. Readers of this volume may wish to consult the theoretical arguments advanced in *Latin American Political Economy in the Age of Neoliberal Reform.*

---

* The topics and contributors to this volume include Market-Oriented Reform and Democratization in Latin America: Challenges of the 1990s (Eduardo A. Gamarra); The Political Economy of Structural Adjustment: The Logic of Support and Opposition to Neoliberal Reforms (Carlos H. Acuña and William C. Smith); Convergence and Dissension: Democracy, Markets, and Structural Reform in World Perspective (Aldo C. Vacs); Growth and Structural Reform in Latin America: Where We Stand (José María Fanelli, Roberto Frenkel, and Guillermo Rozenwurcel); Politics: A Key for the Long Term in Latin America (Marcelo Cavarozzi); On the State, Democratization, and Some Conceptual Problems (A Latin American View with Glances at Some Post-Communist Societies) (Guillermo O'Donnell); and Economic Reforms in New Democracies: A Social-Democratic Approach (Luiz Carlos Bresser Pereira, José María Maravall, and Adam Przeworski).

This volume opens with an examination by Bill Smith and Carlos Acuña of the options and strategies available to elites and societal actors confronting the uncertainties inherent in the construction of democratic politics in the context of traumatic economic reform. Smith and Acuña analyze four alternative politico-economic scenarios — "organic crisis"; fragmented and exclusionary democracy with neoliberal economics; inclusionary democracy, strong actors, and an activist state; and dualistic democracy — and then evaluate the probability of various future outcomes for Argentina, Bolivia, Brazil, Chile, Mexico, Peru, and Venezuela. Their discussion raises many of the theoretical, methodological, and strategic political issues underlying contemporary debates of Latin American political economy. The remaining chapters are organized in five matched pairs of case studies by a political scientist and an economists of Argentina, Bolivia, Brazil, Chile, and Mexico.

In Chapter 2, Carlos Acuña analyzes why the future of Argentine politics "no longer is what it used to be," explaining how the Carlos Menem government has been able to implement a far-sweeping package of market-oriented reforms by means of a "Hobbesian" strategy vis-à-vis the political opposition, the armed forces, the entrepreneurial class, and organized labor. Adolfo Canitrot in Chapter 3 examines the "destruction of the state" initiated during the post-1976 military regime and continued following the return to democratic government in 1983 and the hyperinflationary crisis of 1989. His basic thesis is that the Argentine state itself is a root cause of the crisis. Both Acuña and Canitrot give particular emphasis to Menem's economic and public-sector reforms culminating in the "Convertibility Plan" launched in 1991 by Economy Minister Domingo Cavallo. Canitrot argues that the emergent model resembles a modernized version of the old authoritarian project envisioned by the military in the post-war years. In Canitrot's view, whether this project can be compatible with uncorrupted democracy is still unknown. Acuña, in contrast, avers that democracy in Argentina has been effectively consolidated, although he also notes that the economic model is exclusionary and socially regressive.

The advent of neoliberal reform in Bolivia is treated in Chapter 4 by Eduardo Gamarra, who focuses on the crafting of support for stabilization and structural adjustment. Both Víctor Paz Estenssoro, who initiated the "New Economic Policy," and Jaime Paz Zamora, his successor, relied heavily on elite pacts engineered by the executive in order to insulate change teams from the exigencies of competitive politics. Chapter 5, by Juan Antonio Morales, examines the abandonment of dirigiste assumptions and lays bare the economic logic underlying neoliberalism in Bolivia. Morales concludes that relatively poor economic performance in terms of growth, employment, wages, and access to public services probably may be contested with future challenges likely to come from electoral populism and pressures for greater democratization of the political system.

Brazil is the region's laggard in enacting stabilization and adjustment policies. In Chapter 6, Lourdes Sola dissects the serious distortions in parliamentary representation and the "incomplete federalism" established by Brazil's 1988 Constitution, showing how they combine to perpetuate a deepening fiscal crisis of the state eroding democratic governability. In Chapter 7, Antônio Barros de Castro offers a provocative interpretation of the rise and demise of what he calls Brazil's "renegade" model of development based on the dynamism of public sector enterprise. Barros de Castro's diagnosis parallels and reinforces Sola's interpretation of the Brazilian crisis, with both authors underscoring the importance of administrative reform and strengthening state capacity, without which successful economic restructuring and the transition to a new pattern of development would be impossible.

The experiences of Mexico and Chile, where market-oriented reforms were initiated by authoritarian elites *before* significant political liberalization and democratization, differ significantly from the rest of the region. In Chapter 8, Manuel Antonio Garretón examines the specifically political dimensions of democracy and structural reform in Chile. Opposing perspectives that attempt to understand politics on the basis of a structural logic rooted in the economy, Garretón examines profound transformations of the "classical matrix" characteristic of Chilean society, economy, and polity and analyzes the still inchoate emergence of new relations among the state, the system of political representation, and societal actors in the 1990s. In Chapter 9, Pilar Vergara examines social policies implemented since the mid-1970s and questions the ability of the current model of social welfare to reconcile the goals of economic growth and greater social equity with the effective democratization of Chilean society. Vergara concludes that the restoration of an activist state role in coordinating and promoting development is needed to ensure that the priority assigned to growth and macroeconomic equilibria does not stand in the way of a more equitable and inclusive social welfare system and the establishment of democratic control of markets and societal control of the state.

In Chapter 10, Blanca Heredia critiques conventional interpretations of policy reform and demonstrates that in Mexico the formal and informal institutions through which political power is generated and reproduced are of fundamental importance. Heredia argues that economic liberalization was greatly facilitated in Mexico by a structure of authority based on hierarchical patronage networks and by an extraordinary degree of elite cohesion, both mitigating against collective action on the part of negatively affected sectors of the population. According to Heredia, it is less the struggles between economic winners and losers than the realm of elite dynamics that will be crucial in shaping Mexico's political future. Jaime Ros, in Chapter 11, argues that factors such as competent policy management, political structure, or geopolitical advantage are insufficient to explain Mexico's relative success in applying the radical market reforms of the "Washington Consensus." Identifying singular features rooted firmly in the country's macroeconomic structure, Ros develops a political economy model to explain the acceleration of the reform drive during the presidency of Carlos Salinas de Gortari. Rather than focusing on the merits frequently imputed to market reform policies, Ros argues for macroeconomic policy trade-offs as the keys to the sustainability of the restructuring process. One important implication, Ros observes, is that the Mexican experience may not be very relevant to economic reformers elsewhere.

* * *

On behalf of all the participants in this symposium, we wish to express our great appreciation to those who made this project possible. For the necessary financial support, as well as for continued advice and friendship, we owe special thanks to the North-South Center and its director, Ambassador Ambler H. Moss, Jr., and to Mary Uebersax, in charge of the External Grants Program, and Robin Rosenberg, who oversees research and studies at the Center. In later stages of the project, the involvement of other Center staff, including Richard Downes, Kathy Hamman, Jayne Weisblatt, Diane Duys, Mary Mapes, and Stephanie True Moss, was essential to the preparation of the manuscript for publication. Robert Barros did a magnificent job translating from the originals. We are also grateful to Patricia Rosas, at the University of California at San Diego, who helped bring a sense of clarity and style to the sometimes opaque prose of the editors and contributors.

This project would not have been possible without the collaboration of our respective institutions, colleagues, students, and staff. At Florida International University, the assistance of Francine Bard and René Ramos of the Latin American and Caribbean Center and the Department of Political Science is gratefully acknowledged. In Buenos Aires, Mercedes Laplace, then at the Centro de Estudios de Estado y Sociedad, was responsible for the organization and smooth operation of the symposium. We also thank Torcuato Di Tella for making available the conference facilities at the Fundación Simón Rodríguez. The countless hours of cheerful and dedicated work in translating and editing manuscripts and managing endless reams of paperwork on the part of Vanessa Gray, Erick Bridoux, Mariela Córdoba, and Pamela Mulder, students at the University of Miami's Graduate School of International Studies, are deeply appreciated. Finally, we happily recognize the patience and inspiration received from María de Lourdes and Gabriela, Elsa and Malena, and Terry and Jackie.

Although the project was originally conceived by Smith and Gamarra, the order of names simply reflects Bill Smith's overall leadership and responsibility for editing the final product. In every way, this book reflects a collective effort on the part of editors and authors.

William C. Smith
Carlos H. Acuña
Eduardo A. Gamarra
Coral Gables, Florida
January 15, 1994

Democracy, Markets, and Structural Reform in Latin America:

Argentina, Bolivia, Brazil, Chile, and Mexico

Chapter One

Future Politico-Economic Scenarios for Latin America

William C. Smith
Carlos H. Acuña

Introduction

Latin America is in the midst of a complex historical transition. Overcoming deeply rooted authoritarian legacies — which, in some cases, encompassed prolonged periods of military tutelage over civilian governments — the region has embarked upon a path that hopefully will lead to more liberal, competitive, and participatory democracies. Concomitantly, equally profound transformations initiated during the 1980s are rapidly dismantling state-centric and populist modes of regulation associated with import-substitution industrialization (ISI) in semi-closed economies (Cavarozzi 1992a, 1994). Projects of neoliberal restructuring[1] are rapidly redrawing the boundaries between the state and the market, as well as forging new forms of insertion into the global economy. Making sense of these two transitions — toward democratic consolidation[2] and toward the hegemony of marketplace logic — obliges us to rethink the relationship between politics and economics.[3]

The external shock of the debt crisis and ensuing economic reforms advocated by the U.S. government and international financial institutions led to the implementation of policies with strong common elements — trade liberalization and promotion of foreign investment, privatization of state enterprises, deregulation of markets, fiscal reforms, macroeconomic equilibrium, and so on — along the lines of the so-called "Washington Consensus."[4] Structural adjustment frequently has reinforced already pronounced tendencies toward the concentration of power in the executive branch and the exclusion of the popular sector from participation in the formulation and implementation of social and economic policies. These policies also exacerbated tensions between the executive and other branches, resulting in the weakening of parliamentary and judicial institutions. The disarticulation of

1

social actors, particularly those of the subaltern sectors, also has been a common consequence of structural adjustment. Given these important political and economic similarities, can we speak of a single, or common, Latin American political model? Is it legitimate to infer from the narrowing of feasible economic options a convergence in the region toward a common future in which differences among countries will be merely a matter of degree? And finally, what do these similarities tell us about the future of democracy and about the welfare of the people of Latin America?

This chapter argues that the specific institutional characteristics and the social bases of post-transition democratic regimes in Latin America in the 1990s probably will vary considerably and that the emergence of a single, modal pattern is not very likely. In fact, as the region is transformed by the exigencies of market-oriented restructuring, it may become progressively less useful to think of a common future for Latin American societies. Different societies are now embarked upon developmental paths leading toward not one but several possible future scenarios combining market reform and democratic consolidation.

Analysis of future scenarios for Latin America should consider the specificities of each society in order to identify the alternatives that best resonate with the different historical trajectories observed in the region. This discussion is not an exercise in "scientific futurism." Rather, we want to talk politics. We are specifically interested in examining the options and strategies available to elites and societal actors confronted with the uncertainties intrinsic in the construction of democratic politics in an era of wrenching economic restructuring. In this sense, our discussion of the politico-economic future of Latin America is necessarily grounded in a combination of empirical knowledge, a dash of conceptual rigor, and a measure of speculation.

Alternative Politico-Economic Scenarios[5]

Let us begin with a few brief observations concerning the relationship between economic performance (inflation, wages, investment, growth, and so on) and sociopolitical conflict. Contrary to the conventional wisdom, which predicts that economic hard times aggravate sociopolitical conflict, we have argued elsewhere[6] that there are moments in the process of neoliberal restructuring when *worsening* economic conditions tend to go hand-in-hand with *declining* sociopolitical tensions. Moreover, at the first sign that economic conditions are *improving*, rational individuals and collective actors may step up their revindicative behavior, thus initiating a cycle characterized by *rising* sociopolitical tensions.

In the context of economic improvement, the consistent minority, that in every Latin American society has from the very beginning opposed governmental projects for market-oriented reform "no matter what," will acquire more resources for collective action and become more militant. As inflation is controlled and growth begins again, this militant minority will be joined by a second group, who had previously adopted a risk-averse, wait-and-see attitude. Pro-government groups, who from the very beginning had always supported economic reform "no matter what," will find themselves increasingly isolated. Consequently, an opposition majority that threatens the continuation of the process of neoliberal restructuring will tend to emerge. Moreover, the emergence of an oppositional majoritarian coalition will generally occur *before* any significant increase in investment has taken place; thus, economic reactivation may not be sustainable in the long run, and redistributional policies may lead to inflationary consequences and the abortion of reform.

Figure 1
Latin American Politico-Economic Scenarios

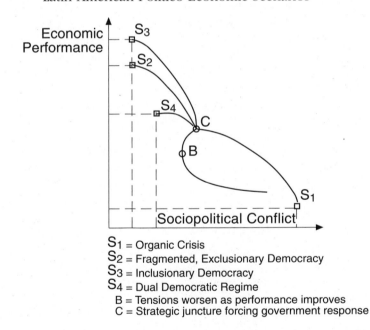

S_1 = Organic Crisis
S_2 = Fragmented, Exclusionary Democracy
S_3 = Inclusionary Democracy
S_4 = Dual Democratic Regime
B = Tensions worsen as performance improves
C = Strategic juncture forcing government response

Once the crystallization of a potential anti-reform majority is recognized by governments, at point C in Figure 1, the survival of economic reform policies will, to a great extent, depend on the political capacity and strategies of policy makers and opposition actors. At point C, governments and economic teams face two basic political alternatives: 1) either economic policy making can incorporate political processes as *endogenous* to the model, and the government will undertake negotiations (perhaps leading to social or political pacts); or 2) policy makers can stubbornly continue to justify their models with a discourse alleging "irrational," "shortsighted," and "selfish" behavior on the part of the social actors they confront.[7] This latter option opens the way for the unilateral imposition of "Hobbesian solutions"[8] to the problem of reconciling growth and sociopolitical harmony. Point C is, therefore, a politico-economic strategic moment, because the actions undertaken at this particular location on the curve will determine differential probabilities for subsequent trajectories that, in turn, will have radically different evolutionary paths. This logic is reflected in our analysis of alternative scenarios (S_1, S_2, S_3, or S_4).

We are interested in two types of politico-economic scenarios. The first scenario (S_1) represents one type and presents a *tendency* toward zero-sum, increasingly conflictive outcomes (where tensions increase and economic performance declines). This scenario does not constitute an equilibrium and is thus inherently unstable and transitory. The other three scenarios (S_2, S_3, S_4) represent alternative democratic "end states" of self-reproducing relative stability. The particular set of institutions and the structure of conflict in each of these alternatives combine so that none of the main politico-economic actors has sufficient incentive to deviate from the rules of the game if other actors also refrain from deviating. Each of these latter scenarios should thus be considered as a distinct mode of democratic consolidation.[9]

If a democratic government enacts an exclusionary style of policy design and implementation, it can succeed or fail in imposing its will on the sociopolitical opposition, alternatives that determine the consideration of our first two scenarios (S_1 and S_2). On the other hand, if a democratic government responds to increasing sociopolitical tensions at point C by reducing the degree of Hobbesianism and exclusion in the policy-making process, the possible outcomes are described in the last two scenarios (S_3 and S_4).

First Scenario: "Organic Crisis" Revisited

If a government fails in its attempt to restructure the economy, performance probably will falter and sociopolitical tensions will increase, thus unleashing a tug-of-war among social and political actors. With the socioeconomic reform effort half completed, S_1 becomes the most probable outcome. In this unstable and stagflationary situation, domestic social actors find themselves in a zero-sum relationship, although the differential structural position of capitalists and workers empowers the former to defend their profits more effectively than wage earners can protect their income, a property of capitalism that is at the core of the inflationary spiral. The tendency is toward regressive redistribution in the context of a stagnant or even declining national income base. In this situation, only monopolies or those firms that can effectively play the financial game reap increased profits.

This first scenario usually includes an unresolved, and increasingly critical, external debt crisis (soon reproduced domestically in the form of uncontrollable fiscal deficits) that may force the economic authorities to suspend — with or without an explicit unilateral moratorium — interest payments owed to external creditors. This prospect places international challenges at the center of the government's problems. The typical dilemma is either to reject the demands of multilateral institutions and the foreign private banks (a defiant heterodoxy) or to yield and adjust social and economic policies accordingly to meet external conditionalities.[10] In this first scenario, renewed politico-economic crisis tempts rulers to embark upon even harsher attempts to impose Hobbesian solutions. This might take the form of alternative political outcomes ranging from a new economic policy (implemented by the same economic team in an attempt to impose new economic "packages"), a new team of economists, the government's replacement, or even a crisis of the regime, its downfall, and the threat of an authoritarian regression. Any of these events could lead to a new "starting point," although probably one with higher levels of sociopolitical tension and poorer economic performance than at t_0, when the previous crisis prompted the first efforts at economic adjustment. Political stalemate, escalating distributional conflict, and serious difficulties in capital accumulation combine to produce an "organic crisis" of the society as a whole.

Second Scenario: Fragmented and Exclusionary Democracy with Neoliberal Economics

For a democratic government to implement a full-blown variant of neoliberal restructuring, a series of preconditions must be met. The maintenance of a majoritarian political coalition (both in elections and in congress)[11] in support of governmental policies is necessary but not sufficient. Neutralization of the opposition may be achieved by repression and dismantling the institutional framework that facilitated these actors' capacity for strategic behavior. This entails the progressive disarticulation of social networks and the erosion of collective identities and political solidarities.[12] In a nutshell, the democratic regime's capacity for political domination is based on the "silence of civil society" resulting from the fragmentation of the social actors and the exclusionary design and implementation of social and economic policies.

What we observe in these cases is the accelerated enactment of radical neoliberal reforms abolishing or rolling back laws and regulations related to neocorporatist decision-making institutions, workers' organizations, and collective bargaining. Thus, the deepening of market-oriented reforms may gradually transform traditional societal cleavages and lead to a renovated party system reflecting emergent social and economic realignments. Depoliticization of policy debates, along with competition for electoral advantage within the institutional parameters of the incipient neoliberal order, are also part of this process. Seen from this perspective, the efficient use of the government's majoritarian political support (although this support will probably decline in the interval between points B and C) is necessary to disarticulate the organization and political presence of social actors in a successful Hobbesian strategy for achieving better economic performance while simultaneously controlling sociopolitical tensions.

The consolidation of this second scenario implies that the government has managed to control the external debt by renegotiating its reduction (historical experience has placed these reductions at approximately 35 percent), that many state enterprises have become private monopolies, that the economy is opened to world trade (with average tariffs hovering at approximately 10 percent), and, above all, that the market has become the main mechanism of resource allocation. These successes reinforce stability, and fiscal reforms may oblige the bourgeoisie to pay more taxes than before the debt crisis, although the lack of state coordination and a state-induced growth strategy may well entail slow and erratic economic expansion, particularly if pragmatism is eschewed and orthodoxy is strictly observed.[13] Also the weakening of social actors, particularly of labor unions via the marketization of capital-labor relations, will produce a new distributional equilibrium below the pre-1980s historical average. Therefore, successful realization of this scenario implies emergence (and possible crystallization) of a new politico-economic matrix in which neoliberal economic reforms are accompanied by neoliberal political transformations, resulting in the consolidation of a fragmented and exclusionary democracy.

Third Scenario: Inclusionary Democracy, Strong Actors, and an Activist State

At point C in Figure 1, it is conceivable that the executive could choose to abandon Hobbesian strategies. To do so would imply the reformulation of the decision-making process by strengthening the fundamental social actors and incorporating them more fully into the process of policy design and implementation. This more inclusionary strategy represents an attempt to base democratic stability on sociopolitical pacts that would assure major collective actors their interests would not be seriously hurt by neoliberal reforms. It also implies some sort of redistribution of political and economic resources acceptable to all parties to the pact. If this strategy is successful, the logic underlying democratic consolidation coincides with the "social democratic" proposal made by Luiz Carlos Bresser Pereira, José María Maravall, and Adam Przeworski (1993, 1994), as well with Przeworski's analysis of democratic class compromise (Przeworski 1985a, 1985b).

The institutional framework and political dynamics associated with this alternative closely resemble neocorporatism (Schmitter 1974; Schmitter and Lehmbruch 1979; Crepaz 1992). This framework implies negotiations of socioeconomic policies at the national level among the state and peak associations of workers and capitalists,[14] as well as parliamentary oversight of neocorporatist pacts to minimize the costs transferred to those actors (consumers, students, feminists, and so on) and public interests (such as the environment) excluded from tripartite negotiations. Three preconditions for the success of this alternative are 1) the organization of the membership of each class with a national leadership capable of obliging its rank-and-file to comply with the terms of negotiated agreements, 2) high institutionalization of capital-labor relations and sufficient state capacity to monitor and sanction breaches of agreements, and 3) low levels of risk and uncertainty for investment required for future higher employment, higher wages, and long-term economic expansion.[15]

Successful pact-making with key collective actors would, as in S_2, lead to a politico-economic equilibrium with lower sociopolitical tensions and better economic performance than at point C. Also as in S_2, important economic reforms are completed (privatization, opening of the economy, control over fiscal deficits). Nevertheless, S_3, which envisions more active state participation in the implementation of social policies and growth inducement than does the "Washingtonian" version of economic adjustment, should produce a similar stable macroeconomic equilibrium, but at a *higher* growth rate (see S_3 in Figure 1). Historical comparisons and the expected consequences of labor union participation in the decision-making process make distributional properties of this third scenario less regressive than in the neoliberal model S_2. Better economic performance with more equitable distribution of income and wealth, plus the abandonment of Hobbesian postures, implies a relative deepening of democracy, with respect to the other scenarios considered.

The problem is that in Latin America this *maximalist* version of democratic class compromise is clearly unfeasible. The fundamental preconditions for democratic class compromise are unlikely to be fully achieved by any Latin American country. Nevertheless, it is politically and theoretically important to underscore the possibility of a *minimalist* version of this scenario under conditions prevailing in Latin America. A more flexible, minimalist version of S_3 would require the *initiation* of closely interrelated, long-term transformations that would point in the direction of maximalist objectives: state reform, negotiation with and strengthening of collective actors, politico-institutional reforms reinforcing parliamentary mechanisms, and the expansion of citizenship rights.

If state reform is to lead toward more just and equitable outcomes under democracy, it is crucial that in the long run the relationship between state capacity and societal actors not be seen a zero-sum game. In this sense, there is a need for an explicit commitment by political and bureaucratic elites to strengthen and incorporate societal actors into the process of formulation and implementation of public policies. In order to generate confidence in the government's sincerity, particularly skillful and courageous "reform-mongering" (probably with unmistakable "populist" and "clientelist" overtones) must broaden the scope of negotiations beyond the narrow parameters of social pacts with organized labor and business associations or of political pacts limited to deals with party elites. The incorporation of a broader array of social actors, along with strong measures to reinforce the legal system, would be necessary to combat what Guillermo O'Donnell (1994) refers to as impoverished "brown spots" and "low-intensity citizenship." Prospects for a minimalist S_3 scenario might be enhanced by changes in constitutional frameworks, such as the introduction of parliamentarism (and certainly enhanced technical expertise and oversight capacity by elected representatives) and extensive reforms of rules governing elections and the party system, as well as a new fiscal pact among the national, state, and local governments.[16]

Although this minimalist project is somewhat more likely than the original maximalist version of S_3, it still confronts important domestic and international obstacles. In addition to the reconstruction of state institutions needed to guarantee the enforcement of pacts, it will not be easy to unify the "voice" of both workers and capitalists. The main obstacles to reducing sociopolitical tensions are rooted in the risks involved for all leaders (state, business, and labor) in carrying out institutional reforms while simultaneously confronting conflicts over substantive issues (such as the exchange rate or wage rates).[17] Finally, the international obstacles to be faced extend well beyond the obvious limitations imposed by the debt crisis and the vagaries of international capital flows to include the more subtle forms of veto power over national policies wielded by multilateral financial institutions, transnational corporations and banks, and the United States government, which still generally view reformist strategies as dangerously "populist" or "leftist" and the cause of economic inefficiency, corruption, and political instability. A governmental leadership able to win the "confidence" of the international community could expand the reform space required for the success of this minimalist scenario.

If progress is made in advancing this agenda of reforms, admittedly ambitious, given conditions currently prevailing in Latin America, it is possible that a trajectory of democratic deepening could be initiated. The key would be a tendency toward a rearticulation of state and societal actors such that elected officials accumulate sufficient political and administrative capacity to sanction transgressors who violate social agreements (on wages, prices, investment levels, and so on). Greater embeddedness of state institutions in civil society would also endow elected officials with the capacity to act gradually to reduce the risks of investment and to provide the incentives required to convince social actors to abandon strategies of confrontation in favor of cooperative strategies tending to institutionalize distributional conflicts within the emergent democratic order. Here a reinvigorated, moderate democratic Left must play an essential role.[18]

A minimalist S_3 could conceivably, over a sufficiently lengthy period, undergo metamorphosis and emerge as a more genuine democratic and more socially just alternative (maximalist S_3). On the other hand, a minimalist S_3 scenario could "fall short" and constitute an equilibrium by itself, albeit probably a weak equilibrium. In view of the alternatives, "medium-intensity citizenship," modest redistribution, and reasonable economic growth are not to be disdained.

Fourth Scenario: Dual Democratic Regimes

In the fourth scenario (S_4), state elites seek to establish an alliance with a strategic minority of the opposition for the purpose of excluding the majority of the remaining social actors by disarticulating and neutralizing their capacity for collective action. Political and economic stability in this scenario is facilitated by a dual logic of state power (respect for the organization of the allied minority and disarticulation of the rest) and unequal distribution of resources (benefits are extended only to allied sectors of business and organized labor). The particularly elitist character of this logic of governability defines the dual democratic regimes that emerge in S_4. Of course, all regimes manifest this dual character to some extent because every strategy of inclusion necessarily implies exclusion. The high ratio of exclusion to inclusion, the dependence of the regime's stability on this ratio, and the intention of the main political actors to maintain it is what differentiates dual democratic regimes from others.

As O'Donnell points out (1994), widespread poverty, massive social and economic inequalities, and the weakness of the "state as law" perversely reinforce one another to (re)produce despotic and archaic social relations and what he calls "low-intensity citizenship." O'Donnell's depiction of "delegative democracy," with concentration of power in the executive and inherent hostility to accountability and the institutionalization of mechanisms of representation, also resonates with the syndrome of traits exemplified in S_4.[19]

Economic performance under S_4 will be less dynamic than in S_2 or S_3. Mediocre performance is a likely consequence of inefficiencies and distortions in the allocation of resources stemming from the subsidies and privileges awarded by the government to minority allies in exchange for their political support. But performance will surpass that which is possible under S_1 because the government will have achieved sufficient control over the principal macroeconomic variables to assure at least medium-term stability. On the other hand, although higher than in S_2 and S_3, sociopolitical tensions in S_4 will be lower than in S_1 because the dual logic of power and unequal distribution has been imposed on most of the population. Tensions will be higher than in S_2 because the minority of strategic actors incorporated into the dominant alliance means that a few important actors retain, and will use, their capacity for collective action to pressure the government. Sociopolitical tensions will also be higher than S_3 because the objective of the dominant alliance is not only to disarticulate "the others" but also to restrict the participation of the allied minority as much as possible in the negotiation of "macro" issues, thus setting the stage for constant zig-zags and recurrent confrontations with the opposition.

Relationships Among Scenarios

State elites and societal actors generally do not embark upon the fourth scenario as a consequence of rational calculation. Rather, this scenario usually emerges as the result of the failure of more ambitious elite initiatives (to achieve objectives related to S_2 or S_3) or as the result of the conviction by elites of their own political weakness (S_4 is preferable to the disaster of organic crisis S_1). Each of the paths to the other scenarios thus contains a possible route to S_4. We will examine each path briefly.

Given conditions of organic crisis in scenario S_1, state elites may opt to abandon maximalist objectives with respect to market-oriented reform and economic performance. Instead of a full-fledged Hobbesian strategy to restructure society and the political economy, or a risky option of strengthening and negotiating with societal actors, governing party politicians may select a few representatives from among opposition party elites or among corporate actors (labor unions and entrepreneurial associations) as interlocutors; the precise allies selected will depend on the support required to fashion a minimum winning coalition capable of disarticulating the rest of the society. This divide-and-conquer strategy might succeed, although the cost may be high: the potential members of the privileged minority will only be willing to enter into an alliance with the government in exchange for institutional arrangements that safeguard their own vital interests and capacity for collective action in the future. The obvious risk for the potential allies is that once the government has used their support to neutralize the "others," they themselves could then be "dealt with" by the exclusion of minority allies from the dominant alliance.

From the attempt to achieve S_2 the road is different. At point C in Figure 1, the government may decide to radicalize and deepen its Hobbesian strategy. But the government will be obliged to accept small concessions to strategic minorities, whose support provides the critical margin for success in negotiating specific reform issues (e.g., the privatization of public enterprises where unions could jeopardize the endeavor or the approval of legislation pertaining to the flexibilization of capital-labor relations). However, "partial success" only with respect to some specific aspects of neoliberal restructuring may undermine the long-term consolidation of S_2 and thus may favor the emergence of S_4. For example, the contradictions and ambiguities required by concessions to minority allies (e.g., clauses exempting them from the costs entailed in the approval of certain laws) means that partial reforms may well fall substantially short of the more drastic liberalizing measures typical of the initial period of crisis. As a result, in comparison with S_2, piecemeal economic reforms result in poorer economic performance and higher levels of conflict, because of the greater level of organization and capacity for collective action on the part of opposition actors. This determines a different point of equilibrium than the one initially sought by neoliberal reformers.[20] S_4 is thus a probable outcome in the event of the failure of an S_2 project.

The transition from attempting S_3 and ending up in S_4 results from a failed effort to strengthen and incorporate societal actors into the decision-making process. At this point, negotiations with minority interests might be initiated with the intention of "waiting out" the crisis in the hope of retaking the original path toward S_3 at some point in the future. Nevertheless, prolongation of the "emergency" and the "circumstantial" exclusion of majoritarian actors might eventually lead to an equilibrium from which none of the organized participants want to depart and the majority would thus be excluded permanently. On the other hand, the government might reason that its attempt to achieve S_3 (whether in its maximalist or minimalist version) faces insuperable obstacles and thus conclude that a progressive reform strategy in these circumstances might imply a level of sociopolitical conflict incompatible with its economic objectives. Governing party politicians and government bureaucrats might also realize that the balance of power between state and societal actors required for a radical change in direction toward the full-fledged neoliberal version of S_2 is unattainable. Therefore, in this case, S_4 is preferred as the only feasible alternative.

The failure to achieve S_3, or the political dynamics to assure the implementation of a series of partial, "micro" reforms needed to attempt S_2, and the risk of remaining or of falling into S_1 are alternative origins for the emergence of S_4 as a stable equilibrium. But some scenarios are simply not present as viable alternatives in many societies. In fact, in a given society certain scenarios may not even form part of the actors' historical conscious-ness, or even their imaginations. Nevertheless, and beyond the fact that no modal pattern can be inferred for the region as a whole, the properties and prerequisites for each scenario, as well as the relationships among the scenarios, suggest that dual democracies (S_4) are the most probable future in most cases.

An Overview of Seven Latin American Cases

We now turn to a brief, schematic overview of seven Latin American countries, including the five countries analyzed in this volume — Argentina, Bolivia, Brazil, Chile, and Mexico — along with Peru and Venezuela. These brief sketches are meant to illustrate how elements from the recent past and present of these societies may unfold in the future.[21]

Argentina

Raúl Alfonsín of the Radical party assumed the presidency in Argentina in 1983 with a rhetorical commitment to a "politics of individual citizens" in a crusade against the "corporations" (rejection of S_3) and an attempt to implement a neo-Keynesian, state-led economic strategy.[22] This liberal option was transformed and deepened with the implementation of the heterodox anti-inflationary Austral Plan in the direction of a clear-cut Hobbesian attempt of state-imposed macroeconomic policies without negotiation with business or labor. The result was a series of unsuccessful adjustments (S_1) and progressively more orthodox economic measures focusing on state reform and opening of the economy. Simultaneously, efforts were made to reverse the erosion of governmental power by negotiating with strategic entrepreneurial and union minorities to confront majoritarian dissatisfaction and increasing tensions (S_4). The failure of these measures in early 1989 led to hyperinflation (a new return to a worse S_1), with economic collapse, a dramatic increase in sociopolitical tensions, and Alfonsín's decision to hand the government over to Carlos Menem and the Peronists six months prior to the date established in the constitution.

Menem assumed the presidency in July 1989 with inflation raging at a monthly rate of more than 200 percent. Menem warned his fellow citizens to prepare for a "tough, costly, and severe adjustment" requiring "major surgery without anesthesia." With the collapse of the new government's first economic plan (a brief attempt at S_2), a new round of virulent hyperinflation resumed in early 1990 (S_1 once again) and was followed by period of "hyper-recession." Regressive income distribution and declining standards of living for the majority of the population enriched upper-income strata, while the growing concentration of control over productive assets benefitted local *grupos económicos* and their transnational partners. Despite the high social costs entailed, victory over hyperinflation and monetary stability were achieved by the "Convertibility Plan" enacted in March 1991 by Economy Minister Domingo Cavallo (see Chapter 3 by Adolfo Canitrot in this volume). The combination of idle productive capacity and rising aggregate demand resulted in striking growth rates of above 8 percent in 1991 and 1992, with the annual inflation rate falling below 10 percent.

The Menem government clearly pursued a strategy (S_2) based on an aggressive effort to disarticulate collective actors in order to facilitate the implementation of radical neoliberal reforms. However, as Carlos Acuña indicates (Chapter 2), relative economic success (the B-C portion of the curve in Figure 1) led to renewed demands from unions, entrepreneurial interests, and other social actors. In view of Peronism's populist heritage, some might fear a disastrous return to stagflation (S_1), while others might predict a neocorporatist response (S_3). However, this latter possibility seems foreclosed in the near-term future, although more-vigorous-than-expected economic expansion could conceivably, at some point in the future, provide the material basis for a possible project resembling a minimalist version of neocorporatism (S_3). However, it is more probable that the stable consolidation of a dual system of fragmented and exclusionary democracy will be accompanied by relatively slow economic growth (S_4), as argued in Canitrot's analysis (Chapter 3) of the consequences of market-oriented reform.

Bolivia

The implementation of neoliberal policies in Bolivia gathered steam when Hernán Siles Zuazo (1982-1985) abandoned failed heterodox policies. The pace of market-oriented reform accelerated rapidly under Víctor Paz Estenssoro (1985-1988) and his successor, Jaime Paz Zamora (1989-1993). Paz Estenssoro initiated his presidency with high levels of sociopolitical unrest and with inflation raging at 26,000 percent (S_1). He responded by using presidential decree powers to implement the "New Economic Policy" (NEP), which rapidly brought inflation under control and paved the way for the introduction of state and market reforms. Eight years and two governments later, the continuity in the implementation of the NEP is noteworthy, as revealed by Juan Antonio Morales' analysis (Chapter 5 in this volume). Public sector reforms, such as privatization, however, have proceeded at a slow pace. Moreover, antiinflationary programs and the "bottom of the barrel" stabilization since 1985 have produced only modest growth at best.

As Eduardo Gamarra shows (Chapter 4 in this volume), what stands out about the Bolivian case is the crafting of political pacts, such as the *Pacto por la Democracia* and the *Acuerdo Patriótico*, which served to both control labor unrest and overcome impasses with the legislature. In Bolivia, political pacts have indeed become an institutionalized feature of the political system. A Hobbesian solution vis-à-vis social and economic actors combined with executive-dominated pacts with the party elites point to S_4. Governmental hostility to social and political mobilization of subaltern groups and reluctance to enter into negotiations with strategic actors in an impoverished and extremely heterogenous society also strengthen the probability that Bolivia is moving toward the consolidation of a fragmented and exclusionary dualism. Nevertheless, if it proves impossible to consolidate this scenario, the second most probable outcome for Bolivia is a return to organic crisis and higher levels of economic instability and sociopolitical tension (S_1).

Peru

Peru is not represented among our case studies, but it dramatically exemplifies the sequence of events leading to organic crisis (S_1). Initial efforts toward free-market reforms under Fernando Belaúnde Terry (1980-1985) were interrupted by the heterodox administration of Alan García (1985-1990), only to be imposed with a new vengeance in the form of the "Fujishock" enacted by Alberto Fujimori following his surprise 1990 election victory (Conaghan, Malloy, and Abugattas 1990; Pastor and Wise 1992). The manifold tensions between democratic governance and radical neoliberalism came to a crisis in April 1992 with Fujimori's abrogation of constitutional rule and closure of parliament and the judiciary. Although the struggles against drug trafficking and *Sendero Luminoso* have received more comment, one key motive for the military-backed coup was revealed in Fujimori's broadsides against congress and the opposition parties — and by implication against democracy itself — for blocking the executive's radical economic reforms.

The civil-military coup in Peru constitutes an extreme example of a disquieting trend in the central Andes toward regimes of "strong presidentialism" with unmistakably authoritarian overtones (Conaghan 1992). If all democratic scenarios face serious obstacles, the prospects of authoritarian consolidation are not much better. In the case of Peru, the probability is for repeated economic and political crises (coincident with S_1), with an oscillation between brief democratic interludes marked by an impotent state's fleeting attempts at economic liberalization (S_2 and S_4) and authoritarian episodes during which inconclusive attempts at reform are attempted by executive fiat.

A more inclusionary formula (S_3 in its maximalist or minimalist versions) is simply not a viable option in contemporary Peru. Organic crisis (constant iteration of S_1) could pave the way for a genocidal bloodbath in the context of a tragic civil war, although international pressures probably would prevent Peru's dismemberment as a nation-state. In this stark panorama, a return to the formalities of democratic rule (an extremely fragile variant of S_4) would be a notable achievement. In short, a return to democratic rule in a context of continued economic instability, social tensions, and political violence represents Peru's most probable future scenario (S_1), although there may exist some possibility of achieving democratic stability through systematic exclusion of the great majority of the population (S_4).

Brazil

In Brazil, the period of strong economic expansion in 1984-1985 aggravated distributional conflicts and rising rates of inflation. The failure of heterodox efforts (Cruzado I and II, Bresser Plan, Summer Plan) returned policy making to S_1 and to repeated changes in the economic team and multiple economic "packages," all to no avail. The brief hyperinflationary debacle (another return to S_1, but with escalating tensions and declining performance) at the end of José Sarney's term in office (1985-1990) was followed by the autocratic policy style of the government of Fernando Collor de Mello, which resorted frequently to the abuse of so-called "provisional measures" of dubious constitutionality. The Collor government failed to achieve stabilization, while privatization efforts and trade liberalization were plagued by the opposition of certain business interests, bureaucratic incompetence, and allegations of pervasive official corruption involving the president and his entourage. The failure of the Collor I and Collor II economic plans (another return to S_1), evident in the resurgence of inflation to monthly rates of 20 to 25 percent, sharply eroded the government's initial popularity.

Finally, in October 1992, in the context of significant popular mobilization, the Chamber of Deputies approved impeachment charges alleging corruption, thereby forcing Collor's resignation and exit from the presidential palace. Collor's ouster through constitutional means, rather than a military coup, was a sign of the growing resiliency — and consolidation — of Brazil's emergent democratic institutionality. The future is unclear, however, particularly in view of the legacy of past "chaotic adjustments" and Brazil's failure, so far, to embrace the neoliberal formula fully. During its first year in office, the weak government headed by Itamar Franco vacillated between timid, piecemeal reforms and flirtations with a "pact of governability" in pursuit of more comprehensive economic restructuring. Meanwhile, monthly inflation rates neared 35 percent.

In the Brazilian context, a viable neocorporatist alliance (S_3) probably is not possible in view of the weakness of the parties and parliamentary institutions and the difficulties of negotiating with the major collective actors, with labor split regarding its economic and political strategy and with some powerful capitalist interests opposed to a full-blown neoliberal model. Lourdes Sola's discussion (Chapter 6 in this volume) of the serious distortions in parliamentary representation and the "incomplete federalism" established by the 1988 Constitution, which combine seriously to undermine central government finances, pinpoints the tremendous political obstacles to the implementation of the administrative and fiscal reforms without which successful economic restructuring is impossible. Antônio Barros de Castro's provocative depiction (Chapter 7 in this volume) of the demise of the "renegade" model, based on the dynamism of public-sector enterprise, points to the same difficulties in making the transition to a new pattern of development. Consequently, some variant of democratic continuity based on erratic macroeconomic performance (Brazil seems capable of 4 to 5 percent growth rates despite fiscal crisis and high inflation), together with a dualist fragmentation and massive social and economic exclusion of the majority of the population (S_4), is Brazil's most probable long-term scenario. If the dual democratic formula proves unstable, then a return to chronic crisis, with slowed economic growth, even higher inflation, and even higher levels of distributional conflict, emerges as the second most probable scenario (S_1).

Venezuela

Venezuela is not among the cases examined in this volume, although it is of particular interest for reasons of comparative analysis. The advent of Venezuelan neoliberal policies came from an unlikely source, namely the return in 1989 for a second presidential term of erstwhile populist big-spender Carlos Andrés Pérez of the social democratic *Acción Democrática* party. Fueled by tremendous petroleum wealth, which generated a large revenue base for Venezuela's rent-seeking state, the country's democracy has long combined elements of a neocorporatist class compromise with an oligopolistic system of two-party competition (McCoy 1989; Hellinger 1991; Karl 1987).

Democratic consolidation was achieved by the mid-1970s with a party structure and a dominant political discourse resembling the class compromise scenario (maximalist S_3), although Venezuela's socioeconomic structure and pattern of political exclusion present stronger affinities with the features of scenario S_4. In the context of slow unraveling of this petroleum-fueled compromise, and pressured by the U.S. government and Venezuela's international creditors, the Pérez government adopted free-market reforms. Although rapid economic growth above 9 percent was achieved in 1991 and 1992, the obvious enrichment of a powerful minority and deepening social cleavages combined to fan the widespread perception of corruption in high places in the government, the state apparatus, and among business elites.

Mounting political tensions erupted in 1992 in two attempted military coups with right-wing populist overtones. Although quickly quashed, these military rebellions and mounting popular pressure to abandon economic reforms are indicative of the havoc that neoliberal policies may wreak upon even long-institutionalized political systems. The resiliency of the political system was, nevertheless, demonstrated in the impeachment proceedings against Pérez in mid-1993. Although significant levels of sociopolitical conflict and more mediocre economic performance are certainly possible, a major economic collapse (scenario S_1) is doubtful because of Venezuela's petroleum wealth. Scenario S_2 is also not likely because of the high level of repression against the parties and popular sectors that would be required in order to produce a "Chilean" outcome. Venezuela's most probable trajectory, therefore, may be a deepening of poverty, inequality, and the disarticulation of most collective actors (S_4). However, in view of Venezuela's relatively well-consolidated two-party system and "social democratic" tradition, there is some possibility that the wealth generated by petroleum rents and inherited politico-institutional arrangements might eventually lead toward a limited version of inclusionary democracy (a minimalist S_3).[23]

Chile

The path has been quite different when neoliberal economic reforms have been implemented under military auspices. The political dynamics associated with reforms under authoritarian aegis are well illustrated in Chile, where neoliberalism was imposed by the force of arms under the Augusto Pinochet dictatorship *before* significant political liberalization was achieved (Silva 1992, 1993). Consequently, the Pinochet dictatorship enjoyed a particularly wide range of options (and greater political resources) when it reached the point of increasing sociopolitical tensions in spite of improving economic performance.[24] The regime retained the initiative in a complex political exchange in which coercion, preemptive use of social policies directed at marginal sectors, and threats to reverse the liberalization process were strategically employed in bargaining with the social and political opposition.

This Hobbesian strategy, reinforced by unforeseen political contingencies such as a failed assassination attempt against General Pinochet, stalled popular mobilization against the regime and divided the democratic opposition. These circumstances were crucial to the success of market-oriented reforms in the second half of the 1980s. As Manuel Antonio Garretón (Chapter 8 in this volume) points out, this set the stage for a "pacted" political transition resulting in Pinochet's authoritarian constitution and the institutional straightjacket constraining democratically elected governments. The armed forces and other "authoritarian enclaves" (e.g., the Supreme Court, unremovable senators appointed by Pinochet) wield significant veto power over the government of President Patricio Aylwin of the Christian Democratic party, which raises at least some questions regarding the democratic character of the regime.[25] These authoritarian residues, together with the strength of the "economic right" and the presence of strong right-wing parties with considerable electoral support, have militated against major innovations in macroeconomic policies.

Rapid economic expansion in the late 1980s and early 1990s, including growth above 10 percent in 1992, plus the continuation and modest expansion of targeted social policies initiated under the military regime (see Chapter 9 by Pilar Vergara in this volume), bolstered the first postauthoritarian civilian government by permitting it to reap the benefits of Pinochet's reforms. As a consequence, Chile appears to have embarked on a trajectory leading to the consolidation of a neoliberal scenario S_2, in which the emergence of a "Latin American dragon" has gone hand-in-hand with the consolidation of a fragmented and exclusionary democracy under significant military condition-ality.[26] In this context, significant departures from the S_2 equilibrium could increase uncertainty for all actors. Opposition by powerful conservative forces to a more inclusionary project (S_3), or a return to systemic crisis (S_1), could conceivably initiate a process leading to a more dualistic scenario of democratic consolidation (S_4).

Mexico

While less dramatic than in Chile, the relative success of Mexican reform efforts is also closely related to authoritarianism but, in this case, to the peculiar characteristics of a long-lived civilian authoritarianism. As in Chile, authoritarian rule gave the Mexican state a broad range of options in managing sociopolitical conflicts in the wake of the debt crisis and the first stages of economic liberalization. Indeed, the government of Carlos Salinas de Gortari (1988-1994) of the Institutional Revolutionary Party (PRI) has carried out significant economic reform by means of pacts with business and organized labor. The combination of limited repression and rigged electoral procedures forestalled serious challenges. Also crucial in ameliorating tensions has been the government's National Solidarity Program (PRONASOL) consisting of compensatory social programs directed at the urban and rural poor, who have been obliged to pay most of the cost of structural adjustment (Dresser 1991).

Fundamental priorities of the Salinas government have been the pursuit of a new and more durable macroeconomic equilibrium and renegotiation of the external debt, with the privatization of state enterprises and promotion of foreign investment also vigorously pursued (see Chapter 11 by Jaime Ros in this volume). The centerpiece of Mexican financial and trade liberalization policy is the North American Free Trade Agreement (NAFTA) with the United States and Canada. Modest economic reactivation and sharply reduced inflation have been attained, but at the price of widening socioeconomic and regional disparities. As Blanca Heredia convincingly demonstrates (see Chapter 10 in this volume), governability has certainly been strengthened, but the implications of neoliberal reform for the political liberalization of Mexican authoritarianism remain ambiguous. Heredia points out that one of the unexpected consequences of these reforms has been the partial dismantling of the microfoundations of the pyramidal structure of authoritarian domina-tion in Mexico. A process of construction of citizens has thus been initiated, and this process, no matter how embryonic and regardless of its neoliberal origins, is a necessary, although obviously insufficient, condition for the emergence of democracy.

In terms of the scenarios under consideration, the emergence of a center-right political party with major bourgeois support, the *Partido de Acción Nacional* (PAN), firmly committed to marketization and to the NAFTA, provides a strong guarantee of continued economic reform. The presence of a center-left coalition led by Cuauhtémoc Cárdenas and the *Partido de la Revolución Democrática* (PRD) also attenuates the hegemonic nature of the party system long-dominated by the PRI. Continued liberalization of authoritarian rule thus seems probable, an outcome that will probably be strengthened by economic integration with the United States in the context of NAFTA.

Economic success and political liberalization might foreshadow the consolidation of a fragmentary and exclusionary variant of neoliberal democracy (S_2). However, the crucial presence of neocorporatist actors (urban workers, controlled by the *Confederación de Trabajadores Mexicanos* — CTM, and rural labor, under the tutelage of the *Confederación Nacional Campesina* — CNC) linked to the PRI and the state apparatus militates against this outcome. But a full-blown neocorporatist scenario (S_3) is also unlikely, given the impact of neoliberal restructuring in deepening already egregious social and economic inequalities. Some variant of a dual democratic regime (S_4) with strong presidential leadership and extensive corporatist arrangements is the most probable outcome of political liberalization with marketization of the economy. On the other hand, deepening integration with the U.S. market will probably imply a steady inflow of foreign investment and an increase of manufactured exports eliciting increases in domestic investment. If relatively low risks for investment are achieved and are coupled with greater democratization of the electoral arena, and the old corporatist system reformed to give greater voice to subaltern groups (as in many postwar European societies), Mexico could conceivably initiate a trajectory leading toward a minimalist S_3, although the probability of this scenario is lower than that for an S_4 outcome of dual democracy.

Conclusions: Assessing Future Scenarios

In another article (Acuña and Smith 1994a), we have argued on theoretical grounds that the most probable scenario for most Latin American societies leads to dualistic democracies (S_4). We now confront that general conclusion with an assessment of the tendencies visible in several countries. Our discussion is recapitulated in the following table.[27] The purpose of this classification is to indicate which scenarios we judge as highly probable and to distinguish between the most probable outcomes (assigned a value of 1) and the second most probable outcomes (indicated by a value of 2) for each of the countries analyzed. Except when explicitly stated, we do not imply that other scenarios are impossible, merely not very likely.

Table 1

Probability of Alternative Scenarios
for Selected Latin American Countries

	"Organic Crisis" S_1	Fragmented-Exclusionary Democracy S_2	Inclusionary Democracy S_3	Dual Democracy S_4
Argentina			2	1
Bolivia	2			1
Brazil	2			1
Chile		1		2
Mexico			2	1
Peru	1			2
Venezuela			2	1

Neoliberal restructuring with democratic consolidation is not Latin America's most probable politico-economic future. Successful neoliberal revolution in the context of a *fragmented and exclusionary democracy* (S_2) will most likely be an exception in the region. Full-fledged market-oriented reform, with economic and sociopolitical stability, combined with strongly unequal income distribution and relatively low levels of organization and contestation on the part of collective actors, is the most probable future scenario only for Chile. This approximation to neoclassical utopia is not even the second most probable outcome for any of the other cases. In fact, our analysis concludes that the dominant trend is toward market-oriented structural reform that, without fully completing the neoliberal agenda, combines some degree of economic growth and sociopolitical conflict with *dual democracies*. S_4 is, thus, the most probable scenario for five countries (Argentina, Bolivia, Brazil, Mexico, and Venezuela) and the second most probable for the remaining two countries (Chile and Peru). This scenario, it will be remembered, is characterized by executive-centered politics, high levels of political and economic exclusion, and "low intensity" citizenship in which dominant coalitions include a few of the more organized actors within the popular sectors, while disarticulating most majoritarian actors.

S_1 is the most probable scenario for one case (Peru) and the second most probable for two other countries (Brazil and Bolivia). In this scenario, political stalemate and *organic crisis* prevail, while liberalization and marketization reforms are not completed, resulting in mediocre and erratic economic performance. Although not very likely in most of the region, this outcome warns the rest of Latin America of the chaotic and authoritarian threats that may accompany attempts to move from the relative stability of their most probable scenarios.

Last, a minimalist S_3 scenario is the second most probable outcome for three cases (Argentina, Mexico, and Venezuela). A few Latin American societies could conceivably achieve stability by strengthening the state's role in enacting market-oriented structural reform. The politico-economic process in this scenario could gradually strengthen the organization and promote the political incorporation of those interests initially excluded. This trajectory does not fully meet the preconditions for a democratic class compromise (in the sense of a maximalist S_3), although such an outcome could eventually crystallize in some distant future. Democratic consolidation, even without full class compromise, might take place in the context of a more modest, minimalist politico-economic equilibrium. It is suggestive that among the countries considered, only three scored at least a "second-most-probable" chance of a minimalist S_3 outcome. Argentina, Mexico, and Venezuela, regardless of the authoritarian or democratic tendencies of their past regimes, are the countries with the highest level of working class organization linked to the state and coupled with a single party (Peronism, PRI, *Acción Democrática*) capable of winning elections. Evidently, this distinguishing characteristic is crucial in historical trajectories tending toward democratic class compromise. A scenario of gradual democratic deepening, expanded citizenship rights, modest income redistribution, and reasonable economic growth merits further attention, particularly in view of the poor prospects offered by the other democratic scenarios.

Notes

1. Neoliberalism refers to more or less far-ranging market-oriented reforms of the sort defended by contemporary followers of the post-1920s "purists" (Friedrich Hayek, Ludwig von Mises, Wilhelm Röpke) who go beyond the defense of balanced budgets, unregulated markets, and attacks on state intervention to criticize the pernicious effects of state collusion with monopoly and oligopoly private sector interests and organized labor. For an extensive discussion, see Nylen (1992).

2. According to Guillermo O'Donnell (1992, 48-49), one of the key requirements for democratic consolidation is that "...democratic actors no longer have as one of their central concerns the avoidance of a (sudden or slow) authoritarian regression, and consequently do not subordinate their decisions (and omissions) to such a concern." He also highlights the "habitual nature" of practices compatible with the reproduction of democratic institutions and the requirement that the "procedural consensus" be consistent with the "extension of similarly democratic (or at least non-despotic and non-archaic) relations into other spheres of social life." Adam Przeworski's discussion of consolidation is similar but also underscores that "democracy is consolidated when compliance — acting within the institutional framework — constitutes the equilibrium of the decentralized strategies of all the relevant political forces" (1991, 26).

3. See Acuña and Smith (1994a) for an effort to address some of the central issues in rethinking the relationship between politics and economics. A major collaborative effort at rethinking theories of development is currently under way under the leadership of Marcelo Cavarozzi, Manuel Antonio Garretón, Jonathan Hartlyn, Gary Gereffi, Julio Labastida Martín del Campo, and Peter Cleaves. See Feldman and McCarthy (1993).

4. See Williamson (1990) for the original statement of the "consensus." For a critique and an argument that these reforms may trigger an "explosive path" of adjustment without necessarily generating stable economic growth, see Fanelli, Frenkel, and Rozenwurcel (1994) and Bresser Pereira, Maravall, and Przeworski (1994).

5. With some slight modification, this section is taken from Acuña and Smith (1994a).

6. See Acuña and Smith (1994a) for a detailed critique of conventional notions and the elaboration of an alternative perspective of the impact of structural limitations and imperfect information on the relationship between performance and sociopolitical tensions at different moments of the process of neoliberal restructuring.

7. Rasmusen (1992, 133) notes that the economist's new generic answer when facing "someone who brought up peculiar behavior that seemed to contradict basic theory" is to say that there "...must be some kind of asymmetric information." It is often the case that most economists in the role of reformers or occupying posts as high-ranking state administrators tend to forget political theory (although it seems that many just never learned this) and resort to fairly shallow politico-economic assumptions when confronting political contestation.

8. In game theory, a "Hobbesian" solution may be found through the presence of a hegemon, operating above and beyond the game to assure the Pareto optimal outcome by acting authoritatively to redefine the payoff structure so as to neutralize the costs of cooperation and reduce the benefits of defection.

9. Our use of "end state" in describing modes of democratic consolidation coincides with the definition of a Nash equilibrium. More technically oriented readers should take into account that of the second, third, and fourth scenarios we discuss, only the maximalist version of the third is a Pareto-efficient Nash equilibrium. In other words, no politico-economic scenario other than *inclusionary democracy with strong actors and an activist state* increases the payoff of one actor without decreasing that of any other actor. Finally, the scenarios we discuss below are not meant to be mere "labels" ranking alternative options faced by the actors from "most" to "least" desirable. Rather, these scenarios — and the genesis of different equilibria — are profoundly rooted in each society's legacies from the past, as well as shaped by contemporary structural constraints that inform specific national conjunctures. Situations of equilibrium reflect the shifting contingencies of political struggles among contending actors. In this sense, equilibria are relatively stable resolutions of tensions between memories of the past and perceptions of feasible alternatives on the part of actors set in specific historical struggles.

10. The Austral Plan (Argentina 1985) exemplifies a case in which it was still possible to attempt economic heterodoxy with the agreement of the U.S. government and the international financial institutions. Once the "Washington Consensus" crystallized its stabilization/structural reform agenda (circa 1988-1989), this possibility was foreclosed. See Chapter 2 by Acuña and Chapter 3 by Canitrot in this volume.

11. In spite of the diminishing role of congress and the increasing weight of executive decrees in the decision-making process, the legitimacy of the *decretazos*, as well as their effectiveness, tends to rest on signals (public opinion polls, elections, statements by opinion makers and/or influential actors that in some cases include the U.S. ambassador) of majoritarian preferences for measures that are presented as urgent and difficult to process through negotiations, a property usually related to congressional debates and decisions. On the other hand, there are issues that in some societies cannot avoid congressional review (either due to political conditions or clear unconstitutionality), a circumstance which does not allow the executive to "forget" congress when analyzing the political feasibility of certain measures.

12. Although new identities and solidarities might eventually emerge in a process of *embourgeoisement*, it is also possible that the expulsion of blue- and white-collar workers from the formal labor market could lead to deepening anomie and mass withdrawal of citizen participation from the electoral arena as well as from conventional interest-group politics. See Zermeño (1991) for a provocative discussion of anomie and "disidentity" in the context of economic crisis and reform.

13. For elaboration of these arguments, see Fanelli, Frenkel, and Rozenwurcel (1994) and Bresser Pereira, Maravall, and Przeworski (1994). We speak in terms of probabilities because, as we stated before, such contingency variables as international commodity prices or levels of economic activity in the northern industrial economies, which may fluctuate significantly, drastically alter international capital flows, Latin American growth trajectories, and the attendant macroeconomic equilibria.

14. For the particular properties of business peak associations, see Acuña (1992).

15. See CEPAL (1990 and 1992) for important efforts to explore an alternative strategy of development seeking to combine a stress on equity with structural reform and greater external competitiveness.

16. The thrust of these institutional changes would be to increase the probability that electoral coalitions become governing coalitions assuring majoritarian support for reformist initiatives (e.g., industrial policies and, especially, ameliorative social policies) that advance beyond neoliberal recipes. For the parliamentarism versus presidentialism debate, see Mainwaring (1990) and Stepan and Skach (1993). Also see the suggestive discussion of party systems and governability in Haggard and Kaufman (1992).

17. In the case of the state, those members of the executive promoting institutional change are frequently charged by other members of the governing coalition with squandering the government's democratic mandate by "caving in" to pressures from corporate actors. Similarly, business actors, and especially, union leaders face "internal" pressures from rival factions and must calculate the risk of cooperation with state elites to their own positions of power. Maximalist, even unfeasible, demands are very often the result of political competition within the union or the business leadership.

18. For recent analyses of transformations of the Latin American Left, see Cavarozzi (1992b), Castañeda (1993), and Carr and Ellner (1993).

19. Some of the features identified by O'Donnell (1994) are also present in S_2.

20. Some of the more radical free-marketeers among the supporters of the attempt at S_2 are likely to perceive this scenario mistakenly as inherently unstable because, from their perspective, it carries the reform process only "halfway" to the desired goal.

21. For an earlier effort to analyze alternative scenarios for these countries, see Smith (1993).

22. Our discussion of the Argentine case draws upon a series of studies, such as Acuña (1989 and Chapter 2 in this volume) and Smith (1989, 1990, 1992).

23. For a more detailed analysis, see the essays in McCoy et al. (1994).

24. This process is similar to what occurs at point C in Figure 1, although this figure refers specifically to the dynamics of adjustment under democratic conditions.

25. For more specific analysis of the military's "fiscal enclave," including the defense budget and the privileged status of military industries in Chile, see Acuña and Smith (1994b).

26. See Acuña and Smulovitz (forthcoming) for a detailed reconstruction of this process and an analysis of military conditionality in Chile in a comparative perspective with Argentina and Brazil.

27. At this point in our analysis, inclusion of scenario S_3 refers only to the minimalist variant, since the maximalist version lies beyond the current limits of feasibility for all the countries of the region.

References

Acuña, Carlos H. 1989. "Intereses empresarios, dictadura y democracia en la Argentina (O, sobre por qué la burguesía abandona estrategias autoritarias y opta por la estabilidad democrática)." Paper presented at the XV Congress of the Latin American Studies Association. Miami, Florida. December 4-6. (An updated version is forthcoming in *Business and Democracy in Latin America*. Eds. Ernest Bartell and Leigh Payne. Pittsburgh: University of Pittsburgh Press.)

Acuña, Carlos H. 1992. "Lucha política y organizaciones empresariales de cúpula: Algunos apuntes teóricos con referencias al caso argentino." Paper prepared for the XVII International Congress of the Latin American Studies Association. Los Angeles. September 24-27.

Acuña, Carlos H., and William C. Smith. 1994a. "The Political Economy of Structural Adjustment: The Logic of Support and Opposition to Neoliberal Reform." In *Latin American Political Economy in the Age of Neoliberal Reform: Theoretical and Comparative Perspectives for the 1990s*, eds. William C. Smith, Carlos H. Acuña, and Eduardo A. Gamarra. New Brunswick: North-South Center/ Transaction Books.

Acuña, Carlos H., and William C. Smith. 1994b. "The Politics of `Military Economics' in the Southern Cone: Comparative Perspectives on Democratization and Arms Production in Argentina, Brazil and Chile." In *Security, Democracy, and Development in United States-Latin American Relations*, eds. Lars Schoultz, William C. Smith, and Augusto Varas. New Brunswick: North-South Center/ Transaction.

Acuña, Carlos H., and Catalina Smulovitz. Forthcoming. "Adjusting the Armed Forces to Democracy: Successes, Failures, and Ambiguities of the Southern Cone Experiences." In *Human Rights, Justice, and Society in Latin America*, ed. Elizabeth Jelin.

Bresser Pereira, Luiz, José María Maravall, and Adam Przeworski, eds. 1993. *Economic Reform in New Democracies: A Social-Democratic Approach*. Cambridge: Cambridge University Press.

Bresser Pereira, Luiz, José María Maravall, and Adam Przeworski. 1994. "Economic Reforms in New Democracies: A Social-Democratic Approach." In *Latin American Political Economy in the Age of Neoliberal Reform: Theoretical and Comparative Perspectives for the 1990s*. Eds. William C. Smith, Carlos H. Acuña, and Eduardo A. Gamarra. New Brunswick: North-South Center/ Transaction Books.

Carr, Barry, and Steve Ellner. 1993. *The Latin American Left: From the Fall of Allende to Perestroika*. Boulder: Westview Press.

Castañeda, Jorge. 1993. *Utopia Unarmed: The Latin American Left After the Cold War*. New York: Alfred A. Knopf.

Cavarozzi, Marcelo. 1992a. "Beyond Democratic Transitions in Latin America." *Journal of Latin American Studies* 24 (3).

Cavarozzi, Marcelo. 1992b. "The Left in Latin America: The Decline of Socialism and the Rise of Political Democracy." In *The United States and Latin America in the 1990s: Beyond the Cold War*, eds. Jonathan Hartlyn, Lars Schoultz, and Augusto Varas. Chapel Hill: University of North Carolina Press.

Cavarozzi, Marcelo. 1994. "Politics: A Key for the Long Term in Latin America." In *Latin American Political Economy in the Age of Neoliberal Reform: Theoretical and Comparative Perspectives for the 1990s*. Eds. William C. Smith, Carlos H. Acuña, and Eduardo A. Gamarra. New Brunswick: North-South Center/Transaction Books.

CEPAL (Comisión Económica para América Latina y el Caribe). 1990. *Transformación productiva con equidad: La tarea prioritaria de América Latina y el Caribe en los años noventa.* Santiago, Chile: Naciones Unidas.

CEPAL. (Comisión Económica para América Latina y el Caribe). 1992. *Equidad y transformación productiva: Un enfoque integrado.* Santiago, Chile: Naciones Unidas.

Conaghan, Catherine M., James M. Malloy, and Luis A. Abugattas. 1990. "Business and the 'Boys': The Politics of Neoliberalism in the Andes." *Latin American Research Review* XXV (2):3-29.

Conaghan, Catherine M. 1992. "Capitalists, Technocrats, and Politicians: Economic Policy Making and Democracy in the Central Andes." In *Issues in Democratic Consolidation: The New South American Democracies in Comparative Perspective*, eds. Scott Mainwaring, Guillermo O'Donnell, and J. Samuel Valenzuela. Notre Dame: University of Notre Dame Press.

Crepaz, Markus M.L. 1992. "Corporatism in Decline? The Impact of Corporatism on Macroeconomic Performance and Industrial Output in Eighteen Countries." *Comparative Political Studies* 25 (2).

Díaz Alejandro, Carlos. 1984. "Latin American Debt: I Don't Think We Are in Kansas Anymore." *Brookings Panel on Economic Activities* 2. Washington, D.C.: Brookings Institution.

Dresser, Denise. 1991. "Neopopulist Solutions to Neoliberal Problems." Center for U.S.-Mexican Studies, University of California, San Diego. Current Issue Brief No. 3.

Fanelli, José María, Roberto Frenkel, and Guillermo Rozenwurcel. 1994. "Growth and Structural Reform in Latin America: Where We Stand." In *Latin American Political Economy in the Age of Neoliberal Reform: Theoretical and Comparative Perspectives for the 1990s*, eds. William C. Smith, Carlos H. Acuña, and Eduardo A. Gamarra. New Brunswick: North-South Center/Transaction Books.

Feldman, Eduardo, and Mary Alice McCarthy. 1993. "Rethinking Development Theories in Latin America: A Rapporteur's Report." Chapel Hill: unpublished manuscript.

Haggard, Stephan, and Robert Kaufman. 1992. "Economic Adjustment and the Prospects for Democracy." In *The Politics of Economic Adjustment: International Constraints, Distributive Conflicts, and the State*, eds. Stephan Haggard and Robert Kaufman. Princeton: Princeton University.

Hellinger, Daniel. 1991. "Venezuela: From Populism to Neoliberalism." Paper prepared for the XVI International Congress of the Latin American Studies Association. April 4-6. Washington, D.C.

Karl, Terry. 1987. "Petroleum and Political Pacts: The Transition to Democracy in Venezuela." *Latin American Research Review* XXI (1).

Mainwaring, Scott. 1990. "Presidentialism, Multiparty Systems, and Democracy: The Difficult Equation." Kellogg Institute Working Paper, No. 144.

Marcuse, Herbert. 1968. *Reason and Revolution: Hegel and the Rise of Social Theory.* Boston: Beacon Press.

McCoy, Jennifer. 1989. "Labor and the State in a Party-Mediated Democracy: Institutional Change in Venezuela." *Latin American Research Review* XXIV (2).

McCoy, Jennifer, Andrés Serbín, William C. Smith, and Andrés Stambouli, eds. 1994. *Democracy under Pressure: Politics and Markets in Venezuela.* New Brunswick: North-South Center/Transaction.

Nylen, William. 1992. "Neoliberalismo para Todo Mundo Menos Eu: Brazil and the Cartorial Image." In *The Right and Democracy in Latin America*, eds. Douglas A. Chalmers, Maria do Carmo Campello de Souza, and Atilio Borón. New York: Praeger.

O'Donnell, Guillermo. 1992. "Transitions, Continuities, and Paradoxes." In *Issues in Democratic Consolidation: The New South American Democracies in Comparative Perspective*, eds. Scott Mainwaring, Guillermo O'Donnell, and J. Samuel Valenzuela. Notre Dame: University of Notre Dame Press.

O'Donnell, Guillermo. 1994. "On the State, Democratization and Some Conceptual Problems (A Latin American View with Glances at some Post-Communist Societies). In *Latin American Political Economy in the Age of Neoliberal Reform: Theoretical and Comparative Perspectives for the 1990s*, eds. William C. Smith, Carlos H. Acuña, and Eduardo A. Gamarra. New Brunswick: North-South Center/Transaction Books.

Pastor, Manuel, and Carol Wise. 1992. "Peruvian Economic Policy in the 1990s: From Orthodoxy to Heterodoxy and Back." *Latin American Research Review* XXVII (2).

Przeworski, Adam. 1985a. "Compromiso de clases y estado: Europa occidental y América Latina." In *Estado y política en América Latina*, ed. Norbert Lechner. México, D.F.: Siglo XXI.

Przeworski, Adam. 1985b. *Capitalism and Social Democracy.* Cambridge: Cambridge University Press.

Przeworski, Adam. 1991. *Democracy and the Market: Political and Economic Reforms in Eastern Europe and Latin America.* Cambridge: Cambridge University Press.

Rasmusen, Eric. 1992. *Games and Information: An Introduction to Game Theory.* Cambridge: Cambridge University Press.

Schmitter, Phillipe. 1974. "Still the Century of Corporatism?" *Review of Politics* 36.

Schmitter, Phillipe, and Gerhard Lehmbruch, eds. 1979. *Trends Toward Corporatist Intermediation.* Beverly Hills: Sage.

Silva, Eduardo. 1992. "The Political Economy of Chile's Transition to Democracy: From Radical to Pragmatic Neoliberal Policies." In *The Struggle for Democracy in Chile, 1982-88*, eds. Paul Drake and Iván Jaksic. Lincoln: University of Nebraska Press.

Silva, Eduardo. 1993. "Capitalist Coalitions, the State, and Neoliberal Economic Restructuring: Chile, 1973-88." *World Politics* 45 (4).

Smith, William C. 1989. *Authoritarianism and the Crisis of the Argentine Political Economy.* Stanford: Stanford University Press.

Smith, William C. 1990. "Democracy, Distributive Conflict and Macroeconomic Policy Making in Argentina (1983-1989)." *Journal of Interamerican Studies and World Affairs* 32 (2).

Smith, William C. 1991. "State, Market and Neoliberalism in Post-Transition Argentina: The Menem Experiment." *Journal of Interamerican Studies and World Affairs* 33 (4).

Smith, William C. 1992. "Hyperinflation, Macroeconomic Instability, and Neoliberal Restructuring in Democratic Argentina." In *The New Democracy in Argentina.* Ed. Edward C. Epstein. New York: Praeger.

Smith, William C. 1993. "Neoliberal Restructuring and Scenarios of Democratic Consolidation in Latin America." *Studies in Comparative International Development* 28 (2).

Stepan, Alfred, and Cindy Skach. 1993. "Constitutional Frameworks and Democratic Consolidation: Parliamentarism versus Presidentialism." *World Politics* 46 (1).

Williamson, John, ed. 1990. *Latin American Adjustment: How Much Has Happened?* Washington, D.C.: Institute for International Economics.

Zermeño, Sergio. 1991. "Desidentidad y desorden: México en la economía global y en el libre comercio." *Revista Mexicana de Sociología* LIII (2).

Argentina

Selected Macroeconomic Indicators for Argentina

	1982	1983	1984	1985	1986	1987	1988	1989	1990	1991	1992p
Real Gross Domestic Product	*(Percent Average Annual Growth Rates)*										
Total GDP	-4.9	3.7	1.8	-6.6	7.3	2.6	-1.9	-6.2	0.1	8.9	8.7
Manufacturing	7.0	7.4	2.5	-9.9	11.4	1.8	-7.1	-4.8	2.0	11.9	7.3
Agriculture	7.0	1.3	0.2	-1.7	0.1	-3.0	9.8	-9.2	11.4	3.9	0.1
Construction	-22.9	-1.5	-11.1	-14.9	20.0	14.5	-2.9	-24.4	-15.7	21.3	21.7
Gross Domestic Investment	*(As a Percent of GDP)*										
	16.9	14.7	12.8	10.8	12.0	13.7	12.6	9.2	8.6	10.6	—
Non-Financial Public Sector	*(As a Percent of GDP)*										
Current Revenue	22.9	18.9	19.3	26.9	24.6	23.5	22.1	24.0	21.0	20.8	21.8
Current Expenditures	29.9	24.6	26.0	26.3	25.2	25.0	24.8	25.2	22.0	21.5	22.0
Overall Balance (-Deficit)	-15.1	-9.6	-7.0	-4.0	-3.1	-5.0	-6.0	-3.8	-2.8	-0.9	-0.1
Prices, Salaries and Unemployment	*(Percent Average Annual Growth Rates)*										
Consumer Prices	163.2	345.0	627.5	672.2	90.1	131.3	343.0	3079.2	2314.0	172.8	23.0
Real Wages in Manufacturing	-10.5	17.3	27.4	-9.3	-3.9	-8.3	-1.0	-8.8	-5.1	-5.1	-0.6
Unemployment	4.8	4.2	3.8	5.3	4.4	5.3	3.9	7.3	8.6	6.3	6.6
Real Effective Exchange Rate	*(Index 1980 = 100)*										
	121.6	202.6	174.7	193.5	216.5	238.3	260.4	297.5	200.2	147.2	125.3
Balance of Payments	*(Billions of Dollars)*										
Current Account Balance	-2.4	-2.5	-2.5	-1.0	-2.9	-4.2	-1.6	-1.3	1.9	-2.8	-8.6
Trade Balance	2.8	3.7	4.0	4.9	2.4	1.0	4.2	5.7	8.6	4.6	-1.6
Exports	7.6	7.8	8.1	8.4	6.9	6.4	9.1	9.6	12.4	12.0	11.8
Imports	4.9	4.1	4.1	3.5	4.4	5.3	4.9	3.9	3.7	7.4	13.5
Capital Account Balance	2.1	0.4	2.7	2.5	1.7	2.4	3.6	0.2	0.8	5.8	13.0
Change in Reserves (-Increase)	0.7	2.5	-0.2	-1.0	0.9	1.9	-1.9	1.3	-3.4	-2.6	-4.4
Total External Debt	*(Billions of Dollars)*										
Disbursed Debt	43.6	45.9	48.9	50.9	52.4	58.5	58.7	65.0	61.9	63.7	65.0
	(In Percent)										
Interest Payments Due/Exports	53.6	58.4	57.6	51.1	50.9	50.9	42.0	51.2	38.9	36.3	29.1

p = preliminary

Sources: Inter-American Development Bank, *Economic and Social Progress in Latin America*, 1992 and 1993 Reports, and the International Labor Organization.

Chapter Two

Politics and Economics in the Argentina of the Nineties
(Or, Why the Future No Longer Is What It Used to Be)

Carlos H. Acuña

Introduction

This chapter presents three hypotheses about Argentina's simultaneous process of democratization and economic reform. First, I argue that because of their long-term consequences, the socioeconomic policies implemented by President Carlos Menem, regardless of whether they eventually achieve economic stability and sustained growth, constitute a neoliberal revolution. Second, the completion of a number of political and economic reforms suggests that democracy in Argentina has been consolidated. Finally, I argue that present trends foreshadow the consolidation of a highly exclusionary but stable democratic regime. What accounts for the dramatic economic transformation that took place in Argentina? What political factors explain these changes?

These arguments are developed in four sections. The first and second section review the politico-economic process from Argentina's democratic opening to the present (1983-1993). The third explores the feasibility of the reforms initiated by Menem immediately upon taking office. It examines the logic behind Menem's decision to pursue a neoliberal policy as well as the factors allowing the government to neutralize the behavior of potentially defiant actors such as party opposition, unions, and capitalists. The fourth section explains why Argentina's current democratic regime will probably enjoy long-term stability, regardless of the fate of present government policies, and it comments briefly on the nature and type of democracy that is likely to emerge from current transformations.

Transition under the Radical Government:
Democratic Stability Independent of the Economic Process

The unexpected 1983 electoral victory by the Unión Cívica Radical (UCR) initiated a significant transformation in the meaning of Argentine democracy. First, it overturned the foregone conclusion that democratic elections meant Peronist victories. The "iron law" by which Peronism was synonymous with "majority" no longer held. Second, the "anti-corporatist" discourse employed by the Radicals during the electoral campaign partially forestalled the expected escalation of union demands. After 1983, democracy ceased to ensure Peronist government and the aggrandizement of union power. Nevertheless, at the moment of transition, the role of the state and the economy in the Radical agenda remained unclear: was there still space for implementing Keynesian formulas?

Raúl Alfonsín's government moved swiftly to control the main economic variables — prices, wages, interest and exchange rates — on the grounds that the economic crisis left a narrow margin for maneuver.[1] The Radical formula for overcoming the crisis rested upon the assumption that 1) traditional state instruments for regulating the economy would be sufficient to confront the crisis and 2) the Radical government's style and planned institutional changes would elicit "comprehension" among developed capitalist societies regarding Argentina's external financial obligations. Consequently, the government simultaneously aimed to achieve three objectives: raising real wages, achieving growth, and reducing the service on the external debt substantially below the amount requested by creditor banks and the International Monetary Fund (IMF).

With the objective of reducing the social cost of the adjustment, Bernardo Grinspun, minister of economy, sought to increase both investments and salaries. Locked in an "n-player" Prisoner's Dilemma,[2] made up of multiple domestic actors (unions, capitalists, provincial governments) and external ones (IMF, the World Bank, and private creditor banks), the Alfonsín government made no effort to implement a cooperative strategy with the principal social actors. Instead, it opted for a "Hobbesian" solution to the crisis[3] and tried to channel social and political forces — including the Radical party (Acuña forthcoming; Smith 1990, 33) — in directions supportive of government economic policy. This tactic attempted to place the state over and above the actors in conflict and enforced limits on their actions.[4]

To centralize decision making, the government chose to neutralize potential labor reaction by "reforming" union organizations. These reforms sought to both weaken the capacity of the labor movement to defy government policy and increase the political power of progovernment sectors in the labor movement. Nevertheless, the failed attempt at union reorganization and the meager results of the economic policy provoked significant negative reactions among different socioeconomic actors. Business associations, which had been largely denied access to decision making, opposed the economic team's basic policies such as price controls, tax increases on exports, and increased public spending. Moreover, Congress's failure in early 1984 to pass the labor reform legislation opposed by the unions left the Radical government without a coherent labor policy. The government "postponed" consideration of new labor legislation and resorted to legal mechanisms established by the military government in order to set prices and salaries.

The government's position had important consequences for union leadership. In a context of relative political weakness (because of the Peronist party's electoral defeat, lack of governmental will to negotiate, and the government's threat in the form of its anti-union program), an important part of labor leadership embarked upon a strategy of systematic opposition. Thirteen general strikes occurred between 1984 and 1989.

During 1984 the Alfonsín government became aware that political "sympathy" for the Radical party by the international financial institutions and private banks and the United States would not translate into a reduction of the debt nor any significant easing of interest payments. The creditors congratulated the Radicals for their victory over Peronism, wished them luck, and demanded prompt payment of an unpayable debt. Grinspun's Keynesian strategy soon produced IMF and U.S. distrust. Moreover, despite the government's intentions, economic growth and rising real wages led to increased inflation by the end of the year, reaching monthly rates of over 20 percent. Simultaneously, other indicators began to show signs of recession.

The government's loss of control over key indicators, and the exclusion of union and capitalist representatives from the decision-making process, generated a climate of uncertainty. This contributed to the formation of an unprecedented alliance between union leadership and "free-market" liberal business associations, which reinforced the isolation of the minister of economy and sparked confrontations with important social actors. The Alfonsín government soon lost much of the political capital it had enjoyed just a year earlier. In an effort to neutralize the costs of Grinspun's policies, in January 1985 the government appointed a new minister of economy, Juan V. Sourrouille. In June 1985, after months of silent effort (to avoid pressure from sociopolitical actors, as well as the party in power and sectors of the executive) and behind-the-scenes consultations with international financial authorities (who granted their strategic support despite the "heterodox" nature of the measures), Sourrouille launched his *Plan Austral.*

The fundamental objective of the adjustment plan was to contain price increases by means of an anti-inflationary shock that would both cause socioeconomic actors to redefine their expectations and generate credibility on the part of domestic capital, as well as to instill confidence among external creditors and international financial institutions. The Austral was an attempt to control the principal macroeconomic variables. Monetary reform and measures to reduce the fiscal deficit were also prominent in the package. The Austral was successful in controlling inflation, decreasing the fiscal deficit, and stimulating economic reactivation. It, thus, allowed the Alfonsín government to recover some of the confidence lost during its first year in office.

The successful launching of the plan coincided with the commencement of public proceedings against former members of the military *juntas* responsible for systematic human rights violations. In the second half of 1985, Argentina appeared to break with its past: inflation was under control and military officers were on trial for their crimes. Victories in the September 1985 congressional elections demonstrated the gains that the Radicals had made among the public. Official sectors interpreted the Austral's success and the government's new-found popularity as signaling the end of the crisis. The climate was so deceptive that government officials began to speak of the emergence of a "third historical movement," a movement Alfonsín and his advisors hoped would be as hegemonic and majoritarian as those backing Hipólito Yrigoyen and Juan Domingo Perón in earlier decades.

Given that the *Plan Austral* was successful in controlling inflation by freezing wages and prices, the government confronted a new dilemma: how to liberalize without reproducing the inflationary conditions that had characterized the Argentine economy for decades. A number of forms of "thaw" were attempted during 1986, but all resulted in inflationary surges. Price controls were eased, only to be soon reinstated. Failed attempts to break inertial inflation by imposing "floors" and "ceilings" on salary negotiations (prohibiting increases on the basis of past inflation indexes and establishing maximum limits as a function of expected inflation) forced the government again to set salaries by decree.

Near the end of 1986, the government vacillated in the face of rising inflation and renewed activism by organized labor and different capitalist factions seeking to maintain their relative positions in a situation perceived by the participants to be a zero-sum game.[5] The government's new response involved a modification of the model of accumulation prevalent in Argentina since 1930. According to the economic team, this semi-closed economy had reached a point of exhaustion, in which relative price distortions and distributional struggles resulted in recurrent cycles: nominal wage increases led to higher prices, and higher prices led to demands for higher wages, and so on. The team's proposal was to open the economy in "two directions." They expected that opening the local market to greater international competition would have two beneficial consequences: first, it would drive down the costs of inputs for exportable manufactured products, thus increasing exports and easing the scarcity of foreign exchange; and, second, it would force capitalists and workers to modify their behavior in ways that would attenuate the distributive contest over income shares.[6]

Along with the opening of the economy, the economic team pursued another objective linked to the model of accumulation: state reform. The Radical government tried to bring public spending under control through such measures as reducing the salaries of public employees (relative to the private sector), cutting benefits, and raising public-sector prices and tariffs. However, these policies were not sufficient to "close" fiscal accounts. Payments on the service of the public-sector external debt (including the cost of the military government's nationalization of private-sector debt), the deficit of the most burdensome public firms, and declines in tax collection together had created a fiscal crisis imposing major sacrifices upon consumers, public employees, and the retired. The government concluded that a profound reform of the state was needed to solve the fiscal problem.

In other words, after three years in power, the Radical government's diagnosis of the socioeconomic crisis had changed considerably. Opening the economy and state reform appeared necessary to end the old problem of inflation, scarcity of foreign currency, and growth bottlenecks. This new diagnosis showed that the situation was much more complex than initially thought in 1983. And this "learning" process was not cost-free: by the end of 1986, the government's political resources were more limited than upon entering office in 1983. As a result, the probability of successfully implementing the new goals was grim, to say the least. Although the suppression of inflation and the trials of the military officers during the second half of 1985 gave the impression of a rupture with the past, the continued vitality of the "old" Argentina made itself fully apparent during 1987. Changes in governmental priorities were inevitable in this much more difficult context. In addition to resurgent inflation, the military uprising of the *carapintadas*[7] during Holy Week of 1987[8] left an image of government capitulation. Moreover, the government's electoral ploys contradicted the socioeconomic strategy — the appointment of a union leader from one of the most powerful labor factions (the "Group of 15") as minister of labor and the designation of a representative of the Sociedad Rural Argentina (Argentine Rural Society — SRA) as secretary of agriculture being two examples. The recomposition of a more democratic Peronist leadership defeated the Radicals in the elections to the Chamber of Deputies. The goal of a "third historical movement" gave way to one more humble yet still challenging: to govern while controlling inflation and the military challenge at least until the 1989 presidential election.

In the 1987 elections the government lost its majority in the lower house and its control of a number of provincial governments. Lost also was the political capacity to maintain its "Hobbesian" strategy for managing the economic crisis. Following the Radicals' loss of control of the Chamber of Deputies, Peronism supported tax increases (needed to control the growing fiscal deficit) in exchange for approval of the union and collective-contract labor laws. By allowing the free negotiation of salaries and working conditions between firms and workers, these laws neutralized the government's capacity to set salaries and prices by decree. Since price and salary controls were the central instruments of the *Plan Austral,* 1988 marked the effective demise of the plan. Faced with the fiscal deficit, a declining trade surplus, increases in the external debt, a fall in real wages and employment, and the need to raise taxes, all actors — the state, capitalists, and workers — expected increases in tariffs, price hikes, and intensified wage demands.

After early 1988 the struggle to maintain or recover positions in the distribution of resources intensified, with accompanying effects on the rate of inflation.[9] Having suspended interest payments on the foreign debt in April and faced with time constraints to lower inflation (seconded by official Radical presidential candidate, Eduardo Angeloz), Argentina's economic team launched a last gambit: the *Primavera* (Spring) plan.[10] This plan was based on an agreement with the Unión Industrial Argentina (Argentine Industrial Union — UIA) and the Cámara Argentina de Comercio (Argentine Chamber of Commerce — CAC), two associations particularly concerned that the economic crisis might give the presidency to the Peronist candidate, Carlos Menem.

Primavera's effects were almost immediate: a decline in the rate of inflation (monthly increases in retail prices fell to 11.7 percent in September, 9 percent in October, and 5.7 percent in November) and the approval by the U.S. Treasury Department, the IMF, and the World Bank, of a series of credits to be disbursed in staggered payments. These agreements were key components in the strategy of containing inflation by using the exchange rate as a brake on internal prices. The plan also had immediate effects upon intracapitalist struggles: all of the agriculture and livestock associations (SRA, Confederaciones Rurales Argentinas — CRA, Confederación Intercooperativa Argentina — CONINAGRO, and the Federación Agraria Argentina — FAA) publicly denounced the *Primavera* plan as "a plundering of the countryside and the consumers" (*La Nación,* August 10, 1988).

While intracapitalist conflicts among urban and rural organizations smoldered, in late August 1988 the Unión Obrera Metalúrgica (Metallurgical Workers Union — UOM) won a 47.4 percent wage increase as well as a commitment for future reviews of salary levels through negotiations with the entrepreneurial organization Coordinadora Sidero-Metalúrgica (Iron and Metallurgical Coordinated Action). Inflation surged due to a complex concatenation of factors: expectations of greater pressures on wages, intensified interfirm competition, and the heating up of the presidential campaign (with the Peronist candidate alluding to a possible debt moratorium and a large salary hike or *salariazo*). A 6.8 percent jump in consumer prices in December 1988 brought strong pressure on the exchange rate, and the government's attempt to control price increases by means of a "cheap" dollar led to an increasing sale of foreign exchange reserves by the Central Bank and a sharp hike in interest rates on bank deposits. Betting that the government would be unable to maintain the overvalued domestic currency, large businesses reaped profits from higher returns on the interest rate, while a good portion of their profits "ran" to the dollar as the Central Bank currency reserve rapidly dwindled.

By the end of 1988, both domestic and international actors had lost confidence in the *Primavera* plan. The combination of inflation, high interest rates, declining rates of investment, recession, and the devaluation of the dollar with a growing external debt precipitated a crisis of an enormous magnitude even for Argentina. When the Central Bank was forced to declare a bank holiday in February 1989 and announced the suspension of foreign currency operations, the dollar "took off" in the parallel market. The effects on prices were devastating, with an immediate doubling of the rate of inflation. At the end of February, the UIA and the CAC broke their alliance with the government and declared themselves free of previous price agreements, while exporters refused to sell their foreign exchange earnings at the official rate. The World Bank's suspension of $350 million in disbursements was announced on March 3. A few weeks later, Radical presidential candidate Angeloz publicly called for the resignation of the economic team. There was little the two Radical ministers who succeeded Sourrouille could do to halt the hyperinflationary spiral. With a government so isolated that it lacked even the support of its own party's candidate, retail prices rose 33.4 percent in April and 78.5 percent in May, while wholesale price increases for the same months were 58.0 and 104.5 percent. The value of the dollar in the parallel market nearly tripled during these months.

Radical efforts to convince the electorate that a Peronist government would only do worse had little effect. On May 15 the Peronist candidate, Carlos Menem, won a majority in the electoral college with 47 percent of the popular vote; Angeloz received 32 percent. Although Alfonsín stepped down six months before he was scheduled to leave office, it was nevertheless significant that for the first time in Argentine history a government democratically transferred power to the opposition. But this important achievement did not imply that Argentine democracy was efficient in socioeconomic terms.[11] The final debacle of the *Primavera* plan came in July, when wholesale and retail prices skyrocketed 208.2 and 196.6 percent, respectively. Official data reveal that during the period spanning the plan's initial application in August 1988 through the end of July 1989, retail prices rose 3,610 percent, while wholesale prices increased 5,061 percent.

Why the Future No Longer Is What It Used to Be

Menem is changing everything done by Perón
after the Second World War.

— *Domingo Cavallo,* Minister of Economy

At the time of Argentina's May 1989 presidential election, Peronism was still unpredictable. Menem's campaign proposals had not been very clear. The candidate's statements regarding how he would handle the foreign debt, as well as the relation between salaries and profits, had been contradictory. Ambiguity was reinforced by the presence in Menem's inner circle of those advocating a debt moratorium and traditional neo-Keynesian formulas. Nevertheless, the unexpected appointment of Miguel Roig — a representative of Bunge & Born, one of the most powerful multinational grain oligopolies of Argentine origin — to the key post of minister of economy began to clarify the direction of socioeconomic policy. Other appointments drew upon advisors to business associations, such as the UIA and the CAC, and even leaders from the principal liberal Right party, the Unión de Centro Democrático (Union of the Democratic Center — UCeDé). The UCeDé accepted this unusual move and gave its support to the socioeconomic program. The Peronists' new course appeared to maintain the Radicals' policies reforming the model of accumulation, but now with an even more orthodox character.[12]

This strategy pursued was not the result of a coherent plan or a clear division of labor among the different areas of government. Thus, a trial-and-error style of policy making and implementation developed and was layered over the already existing tension between long-term objectives and conjunctural imperatives. Up until the 1991 designation of Domingo Cavallo as minister of economy, government policies systematically ratified and deepened the initial neoliberal direction adopted at the outset. Nevertheless, the implementation of these policies was often erratic, inefficient, contradictory, and plagued by power struggles within the executive branch (Palermo 1991). As we will see, in this context the government assigned particular importance to certain measures — such as privatization, opening the economy, and foreign policy changes — which, despite contradictions in their implementation, sent a strong signal to international organizations, the United States, and domestic capitalists.

Confronted with Roig's death on July 14, 1989, only six days after the new government had taken office, Menem took pains to publicize his consultations with Jorge Born, the head of the Bunge & Born group, in the search for a successor to Roig. Thus, the legitimacy of the incoming minister of economy, Néstor Rapanelli, like that of Roig, rested on his representing the policies that Bunge & Born considered appropriate for Argentina. Some authors have correctly noted that this reflected a traditional Peronist conception of the exercise of power: in an effort to avoid the political isolation suffered by Alfonsín, Menem formed "a cabinet expressive of all that exists in social and political life and that can only be ignored at a high cost."[13] But this implied a break with important aspects of the Peronist conception of constructing and administering political power. Peronism historically involved participation by businessmen in the economics ministry (and workers in the labor ministry). These individuals were closely tied to third- and fourth-level national business associations — such as the Confederación General Económica (General Economic Confederation — CGE) and Confederación General de Industria (General Confederation of Industry — CGI). A confrontational stance was maintained vis-à-vis the most powerful firms and economic groups (such as, precisely, the Bunge & Born conglomerate), as well as their representative associations, for example, the UIA or the SRA (Acuña 1992a, 1992b).

Under traditional Peronism, the CGE or the CGI redefined economic power by focusing on small- and medium-size firms, whose organizations were useful for coordinated action among the state, workers, and business. The neo-corporatist and Keynesian strategies of Peronism typically involved a tripartite equilibrium, in which business leaders did not directly express the interests of the most powerful domestic economic groups. Thus, the appointment of the Bunge & Born representative implied abandonment of the balance between the state and social actors previously sustained and mediated by national labor and business confederations. This represented an important redefinition in the Peronist conception of how political power is shaped and administered in government. Thus, Menem's government strategy involved both continuities and striking ruptures with "Peronist politics."

Immediately upon taking office, the new minister of economy reached agreements with 350 leading firms to stabilize prices in exchange for maintaining stable public-sector prices and tariffs, as well as interest and exchange rates. These agreements bypassed entrepreneurial representatives. The measures were briefly successful: increases in the consumer price index fell from 196.6 percent in July to 38 percent in August, 9.4 percent in September, and 5.6 percent in October.[14] The government knew its margin of maneuver was limited: its short-term success with inflation implied considerable lags in the real income of both salaried workers and firms whose earnings were tied to the frozen exchange rate. The government could exploit a variety of factors: its capacity to pressure Peronist members of Congress, the Radical opposition's commitment not to obstruct the economic policy (given the gravity of the crisis), and capitalist support for the policy about-face. The government presented and gained approval for the "Reform of the State" (August 17, 1989) and "Economic Emergency" (September 1, 1989) legislation, in a bid to broaden its margin of action.[15] By the end of August, the bourgeoisie had exchanged initial shock for broad majority support. At the inauguration of the Sociedad Rural's annual exhibition, Menem was given a strong ovation, and during the annual celebration of "Industry Day," the president received support not only for reforming the state and fighting the fiscal deficit, but also for more specific measures such as his promise gradually to reduce export rights (from 20 percent to 0 in two months), reform the tariff system, provide incentives to increase industrial production, and reintroduce export prefinancing (*La Nación*, September 2, 1989, 1, 14, 16, 17).[16]

Menem's new economic course, which he called the "popular market economy" and an *aggiornamento* of Peronist doctrine, now enjoyed greater support among capitalist circles and right-wing parties than within the governing party and the union movement. As a result, the government systematically sought to neutralize the more militant unions, in anticipation of labor's reaction. Favored by a conjunction of factors that mutually strengthened the government's hand vis-à-vis the unions (as shown below), from the outset of his government Menem prepared the "assault" on the most combative unions by appointing union leaders from the "Group of 15" to the ministry of labor. With the ministry in the hands of pro-Menem unionists and an intransigent Confederación General del Trabajo (General Labor Confederation — CGT) led by Saúl Ubaldini (who was under strong pressure from public-sector unions), the government succeeded in October 1989 in splitting the CGT into two: the pro-Menem CGT "San Martín," officially recognized by the state, and the confrontational CGT "Azopardo," which embarked upon a path of increasing political rigidity and isolation, with both factions claiming the right exclusively to represent workers. State strategy toward labor became a consistent and powerful sign to the bourgeoisie that the government was determined to pursue its new policy direction.

Although state-reform legislation and economic emergency, coupled with the division of the CGT, created important conditions for effecting the controversial medium-term reforms, hyperinflationary pressures remained latent in the short run. Unexpected tensions emerged toward the end of 1989, such as the conflict between Rapanelli and the Bunge & Born group over extending the value-added tax. Rapanelli was more concerned with macroeconomic indicators and the fiscal balance than the interests of the group that had placed him in office. In negotiations with the IMF, he argued for extending the value-added tax, thereby eliciting the wrath of Jorge Born, who publicly accused his former executive of failing duly to consider business interests.

November 1989 was a month in which exporters' opposition to the stable exchange rate — in a context still beset by inflation —translated into a fall in the supply of dollars. Toward the end of the year exporters retained an estimated $2 billion. With inflation rising (the November increase in the consumer price index was 6.5 percent), disputes within the economic team over the lag in official exchange and interest rates culminated in a series of resignations, including that of the president of the Central Bank. The crisis renewed expectations of economic ungovernability and rekindled bids by the state and business firms to defend their resources. In early December, the state finally gave in. The Austral was devalued by 54 percent, the foreign exchange market was split into official and free markets, and import tariffs were lowered by 10 percent. On the other hand, the government sought to reduce the fiscal deficit by raising fuel prices, rates on public services (by 20 to 80 percent) and export taxes (by 11 percent), as well as granting two-year "extensions" on the maturity of state bonds, which had accumulated into an unmanageable short-term internal public debt. In an increasingly difficult context,[17] Minister Rapanelli was replaced in mid-December by Antonio Erman González, a Christian Democrat who had served as minister of economy in the province of La Rioja during Menem's term as governor there.[18] Menem presented the new measures as an "all or nothing" gamble, in which "we all embark, absolutely everyone, on this aircraft in which — for Heaven's sake! — there are no parachutes" (*La Nación*, December 19, 1989, 1, 16).

In an attempt to reconcile long-term objectives with short-term measures, the new economic package included decontrolling prices, unifying the foreign exchange market and freeing the rate of exchange, deregulating foreign exchange transactions, nullifying the increase on export taxes, and — in anticipation of a surge in inflation — a 20 thousand Austral wage increase. As was to be expected, the business associations publicly supported the new minister's plan.[19] And, as was also to be expected, firms raised their prices.

The combination of government measures and capitalist reaction resulted in a 40 percent increase in consumer prices and a jump in the dollar from A960 to A2,000 in December, as well as expectations that inflation would go hyperinflationary by the beginning of 1990. Expectations came true: consumer prices rose 79.2, 61.6, and 95.5 percent in January, February, and March, respectively. Once again, Argentina had the dubious honor of breaking records: consumer prices rose 20,594 percent between April 1989 and March 1990. In 1989 the consumer price index rose 4,923 percent, gross domestic product fell 5.1 percent, and the external debt ballooned from $58 to $64 billion.

Facing the prospect of renewed socioeconomic collapse, the government initiated a course of action based upon the progressive imposition of tougher liberalization packages each time confronted with new signs of instability.[20] Thus, on January 1, 1990, the government converted the majority of bank deposits (some $1.5 billion with short-term maturities) into long-term dollar debt,[21] suspended the prefinancing of exports as well as all bidding for state contracts (for four months), and legalized bank deposits in dollars. The government's priority was to stop the rise in the dollar as a condition for controlling inflation. The meshing of hyperinflation with the cessation of monetary emissions and the nonpayment of bank deposits produced a fall in the money supply. This had three consequences: first, the monthly interest rate rose from 38.5 percent in December to 74 percent in January; second, the recession deepened with falls during the first trimester of 1990 of 2.7 percent in GDP, 14 percent in industrial output, and 34 percent in construction; and, third, business firms were forced to sell their dollar reserves to obtain Australes, causing the dollar to fall sharply.[22]

The high rates of inflation in December 1989 and January 1990 caused a lag in public service rates, while the low liquidity and recession led to a decline in taxes collected. Faced with the resulting fiscal deficit, the government increased utility rates by an average of 90 percent and extended the value-added tax to previously exempt activities. While peak business organizations were silent, other business groups expressed "concern" about new taxes and the troubling economic outlook. Thus, business agreement with the general economic strategy did not necessarily translate into support for short-term measures. In early March, Minister of Economy Erman González announced a new "package" of measures to reduce the fiscal deficit.[23] With these fiscal adjustments, the rate of inflation remained between 11 and 16 percent from April through September 1990. With inflation on the rise, Minister Erman González once again announced an acceleration of the adjustment, this time involving more cuts in state and public firm spending, layoffs and forced retirements of public employees, an elimination of tax exemptions and the indexing of tax payments, as well as a hastening of privatization of state firms (*La Nación*, September 1, 1990, 1).

The results were a success: retail inflation fell to 4.7 percent in December 1990. During this period the government accelerated its program of privatization by completing the sale of the state telephone company and Aerolíneas Argentinas, the national airline;[24] resumed payments on the external debt (suspended since April 1988), with $5.8 billion in arrears; signed integration agreements with Brazil that laid the basis for MERCOSUR; and concentrated political power even more to neutralize any potential obstacles to the economic plan.

Right-to-strike restrictions were among such measures. Finding little support in Congress, these new anti-labor policies were implemented by administrative decree. Paradoxically, the decree curtailing the right to strike, Decree 16.936/90, was signed on October 17, a momentous date in the annals of Peronism. To sidestep potential constitutional objections to procedures used to privatize firms or convert savings deposits, Menem gained congressional approval for Law 23.764, which increased from five to nine the number of Supreme Court justices. This maneuver allowed the pro-Menem majority in the senate to name judges sympathetic to his policies. Blurring of the lines separating the executive and the judiciary further concentrated power in the executive branch.

The economic results of 1990 revealed an unstable equilibrium. Although inflation had declined to 1989 levels, stagflation persisted. During the year the CPI increased 1,343 percent, wholesale prices rose 798 percent, while the GDP declined 3.5 percent, industrial output fell 4 percent, and real wages dropped 3.5 percent. On the other hand, recession led to a simultaneous increase in exports (21 percent) and a fall in imports (4.5 percent). As a result, there was a US$8.2 billion balance-of-payments surplus. Thus, toward the end of the year, reserve levels stood around US$3 billion, even though the dollar's relative value in comparison to its level at the beginning of 1990 had fallen by 54 percent. Business, industry, and construction suffered under the impact of the recession and the tax increases, while agricultural and livestock interests were adversely affected by the taxes and the devaluation of the dollar. Consequently, business increasingly turned critical of the economic policy. Uncertainty regarding the state's capacity to control the fiscal deficit and the customary year-end increase in demand for the dollar combined to cause the value of the dollar to increase from 5,820 Australes at the end of December to 9,450 Australes at the end of January. Despite this trend, inflation remained steady at 7.7 percent.

During the first quarter of 1991, a number of factors altered this precarious balance, eventually culminating in another ministerial change. These were 1) the unexpected rise of the dollar, 2) charges by the U.S. ambassador that officials close to Menem had engaged in corruption and discriminatory practices against U.S. firms, and 3) an expected fiscal deficit of US$200 million in February, which — when tallied with the deficits of the preceding two months — implied a systematic failure to comply with the IMF accord demanding a US$300 million fiscal surplus during the quarter. As a result, Economics Minister Erman González resigned and was replaced by Domingo Cavallo.

The Menem government began 1991 with economic problems, but politically strengthened by its resolution of the military problem. Since his electoral campaign, Menem had embarked upon an ambiguous dialogue with the rebellious *carapintadas*. In the process, he generated expectations that he would grant pardons to the few military officials still imprisoned for human rights violations (those not covered by the "Due Obedience Law" approved during the Alfonsín government, including the former members of the *juntas*, as well as former heads of the police and army corps) and to military personnel imprisoned for their responsibility in the military rebellions during Alfonsín's term. Menem sought an implicit exchange: he would grant pardons to those convicted and accused of either human rights violations or the uprisings, in exchange for a commitment of military obedience to civilian authority.

Free from Alfonsín's electoral promise to punish military crimes, Menem tried to solve the military problem by propping up the general staff while he negotiated with the *carapintadas*. His success was only partial. The rebels tired of listening and, despite a first pardon in 1990 which led to the release of two hundred people, the *carapintadas* staged a bloody uprising on December 3, 1990. In contrast to what occurred under Alfonsín, however, forces loyal to the general staff obeyed orders to repress the insurgents ruthlessly and effectively, thus asserting the chain of command. This was a major achievement for Menem. The severe punishments imposed by military and civilian courts on participants in the rebellion put the finishing touch on Menem's new rules governing relations with the military. Crimes committed in the past would be pardoned, but any present or future disobedience would be rigorously punished.

Despite extensive opposition (over 60 percent of public opinion), massive demonstrations, and the costs that such a strategy implied for justice and human rights in Argentina, in January 1991 Menem granted a second pardon, this time liberating the former members of the military *juntas* as well as a former leader of the Montoneros, Mario Firmenich. Having demonstrated the capacity to resolve the military problem that had haunted Alfonsín during the second half of his presidency, Menem began 1991 on a triumphant note. In this context, Cavallo's strategies rounded out a new moment in which the government recomposed and broadened its control of the politico-economic process.

The "Cavallazo"

Cavallo encountered a more "manageable" situation than had his predecessors. Short-term demands were pressing (such as the foreseeable rise in inflation during February and March), but he enjoyed substantial foreign exchange reserves. To meet short-term challenges, Cavallo announced a new and severe adjustment policy.[25] Nevertheless, difficulties in gaining congressional approval revealed the persistence of tensions between Menem and the Peronists. The first stumbling blocks were placed by Peronist deputies. After strong presidential pressure, in mid-February Congress approved a new tax structure. Cavallo then faced a railroad workers' strike, which paralyzed services during February. During the months of February and March, the government followed its initial strategy toward strikes — it used a law limiting the right to strike against a public utility immediately to declare the strike illegal; proceed with massive layoffs; intervene in La Fraternidad, the railroad union; close down locals and branches; and accelerate the privatization of the branch railroad lines. The strike was lifted following negotiations in which the union retracted its demands.

The government's difficulties were not limited to the unions. Problems also emerged with the agriculture and livestock producer groups after the government failed to respond to a proposed "fiscal pact." Faced with imminent tax strikes by these producers, Cavallo threatened to respond "as firmly as during the railway strike." This set the stage for a two-day strike by three of the principal rural associations (CONINAGRO, CRA, and FAA; Sociedad Rural did not participate). This third trial was overcome when the strike was suspended upon the announcement of a series of government concessions: elimination of export taxes on agricultural and livestock goods, refinancing of liabilities, and granting of specific lines of credit for rural production (*La Nación*, March 17, 1991).

Having surmounted these problems and finding himself in a calmer political climate, Cavallo announced another "all or nothing" gamble in late March. This plan, known as the "Convertibility Plan," was put into effect in April. It included measures to end the crawling peg exchange system and return to the peso (with a parity fixed by law at $1 = 1 peso), requirements that the Central Bank maintain the existing ratio between reserves and the monetary base, and the suspension of all contract clauses providing for wage indexing in wage agreements. Minister Cavallo promised that the fiscal deficit would disappear immediately. If it did not, deficits would be covered with internal credits only, not with monetary emissions (*La Nación*, March 21, 1991). The Convertibility Plan was approved with the support of a majority of the Peronist deputies and right-wing deputies.

Given existing reserve levels, the announced exchange rate seemed credible, and the effects on the market were immediate. On April 1 annual interest rates fell from 44 to 22 percent, while the value of the dollar remained stable. Inflation also began to drop (from 27 percent in February to 3.1 percent in June). The second quarter thus presented a favorable context for economic activity. Tariffs on imported inputs had already been cut to an average of 11 percent; there was greater stability and cheaper credit. Negotiations with organizations representing branches of industry, such as automotive, iron, and food, led to reductions in taxes in exchange for price reductions. The stock market was buoyant, and demand for consumer goods increased. In comparison with the first quarter, industrial reactivation during the second quarter was significant: 221 percent in electronics, 108 percent in automobiles, 97 percent in metallurgy, 45 percent in chemicals, 40 percent in glass, 28 percent in tractors, and 22.7 percent in auto parts (*La Nación*, August 15, 1991, 1).

The Convertibility Plan called for the implementation of eleven measures. The first five measures aimed at the redefinition of the state and improvement of fiscal accounts:

1. Cutting the public deficit by speeding up the privatization of deficit-ridden public-sector firms and reducing the foreign debt through the creation of external debt bonds that could be used for the purchase of public enterprises.[26]

2. Deregulating the economy, by means of Decree 2284/92, which ended the state's involvement in a number of control functions and markets (production regulatory commissions, the National Sugar Directorate, the Meat Board, and the National Grain Board were dissolved).

3. Proceeding with administrative reform, which between 1989 and 1991 had reduced the number of jobs in the central administration from 347 thousand to 200 thousand.

4. Setting as a goal the reduction of the foreign debt by at least 30 percent during 1992. This was accomplished by means of a stand-by agreement with the IMF. Careful fulfillment of the agreement would provide access to IMF credits and free up loans already approved by the Inter-American Development Bank (IDB) and the World Bank. Similarly, it would allow a renegotiation of the debt with foreign banks and entry into the "Brady Plan" (the final accords to enter the "Brady" were signed in December 1992). In the medium term, such a remission would increase available fiscal resources by reducing the debt burden and by allowing access to lower interest rates denied to the Argentine state.

5. Improving tax collection by increasing the value-added and the income tax. By eliminating deductions for past losses from the tax on profits, firms were forced to pay according to fiscal-year results and to exchange past losses for long-term public bonds in dollars. These reforms were approved in February and March 1992.[27] Measures were also announced to prevent tax evasion, such as a simplification of the tax structure, the introduction of a single bill of sale for services, industry, and commerce (beginning in January 1992), as well as a simultaneous reduction in labor costs (see below), and conspicuous publicity for offenders, which made it less risky to "clean up" activities than to remain illicit (implemented during 1991 and 1992).[28]

The second part of the Convertibility Plan focused on prices and costs of production:

6. Continued deepening of trade liberalization and the opening to the world economy, which acted as a "ceiling" on price increases and lowered the cost of inputs.[29]

7. Lowered labor costs via a number of measures, including new legislation approved in November 1991 on occupational accidents

and employment. This legislation was intended to lower labor costs by imposing limits and lower levels of compensation for accidents, by easing requirements for the temporary hiring of personnel, and by lowering the ceilings on compensation for unjustified layoffs.[30]

8. Salary increases linked to productivity to avoid transfer onto prices via Decree 1334 issued in July 1991. During 1992 the government also introduced legislation to weaken union clout.

9. Modified legislation regarding professional associations and collective bargaining, removing obstacles to the existence of more than one national labor confederation, lowering barriers to forming unions at the level of the trade or firm, reducing the role of the union leadership in negotiations, and strengthening the firm level in collective bargaining over wages and work conditions.

10. State centralization of collection and administration of workers' contributions, including the end of compulsory contribution by workers to the unions' *obra social* funds. Although labor representation on the board appointed to oversee these funds was maintained, the new law, nevertheless, struck a significant blow to organized labor's traditional base of economic power.[31]

11. Reform of the retirement system (approved by Congress in September 1993) for the purpose of reducing business contributions, privatizing the pension system to eliminate the public deficit occasioned by the bankruptcy of the majority of pension funds, reducing the cost of credit by expanding the capital market with an injection of pension funds controlled by the banking system and privately-controlled retirement plans, and increasing the minimum retirement age.

As can be seen, these measures and the speed of their implementation formed the basis of a veritable neoliberal revolution in the model of accumulation and the structure of social relations in Argentina. As Minister Cavallo himself stated, virtually with the innocence of the child proclaiming the emperor's nakedness while others hypocritically praise the new clothes, "Menem is changing everything that Perón did after the Second World War" (*La Nación*, February 11, 1992, 13).

The public seemed to agree with the changes. The electorate ignored blatant signs of corruption in the Menem administration and voted for stability, granting an important victory to Peronism in the congressional elections of September and October 1991. The image of stability that this political context conferred to the economic strategy was intensified by signs of economic reactivation, including price stability (consumer prices rose 1.4 percent in October, 0.4 percent in November, and 0.6 percent in December). For the twelve months ending in September 1991, automobile production increased

64.9 percent and automobile sales rose by 74.2 percent, while sales of cement (despite the standstill in public works) during the first three-quarters of the year increased 26.6 percent over the same period a year earlier. Deposits in dollars in local banks (totaling $7.3 billion in February 1992) were another sign of market confidence in the government's policies. The impressive 8.5 percent growth rate achieved in 1991 further burnished the government's image of economic success.

In 1992, Cavallo's strategy continued to rack up successes. According to official estimates, GDP grew 9 percent in 1992. Consumer prices rose only 17.5 percent (the lowest since 1970), and wholesale prices grew 3.1 percent (with actual wholesale price deflation in November and December 1992). From the beginning of the plan in April 1991 to the end of 1992, consumer prices increased 42.4 percent, and the wholesale prices increased only 6.6 percent. However, clouds began to appear on the horizon. First, the differential impact of the economic opening on tradable and non-tradable goods caused increasing distortions in relative prices (due to the greater weight of non-tradable goods — such as services or apartment rents — in the composition of the CPI). As a result, retail prices increased six times as rapidly as wholesale prices. Second, the maintenance of a fixed exchange rate ($1 = 1 peso) despite the 42.4 percent increase in consumer prices resulted in a serious overvaluation of the peso.[32] Third, exchange-rate parity became increasingly precarious since it was sustained by high levels of foreign currency reserves and large foreign capital inflows. When, with the completion of the first phase of privatizations, capital inflows fell from a monthly average of $1 billion in late 1992 to $300 million during the third quarter in 1992, the entire scheme suddenly became more fragile.[33] Fourth, the undervalued dollar, combined with low import tariffs and growth in economic activity, resulted in rising imports and stagnating exports, causing a balance-of-trade deficit of approximately $3 billion, the first deficit since 1989. And, fifth, statistics for 1992 and 1993 demonstrated that the type of growth generated by the Convertibility Plan was insufficient to reduce the high level of unemployment.[34]

Paradoxically, political stability and economic growth complicated the sociopolitical climate. Perception that a certain degree of economic success and of democratic stability had been achieved implied lower risks for those engaged in collective action. Many social actors began to demand increases in their share of resources.[35] The government found it difficult to convince foreign investors that success had been achieved while, simultaneously, telling domestic actors that Argentina was still in a precarious transition period and that it was too soon to reverse regressive tendencies in income distribution.[36]

During 1992 the government launched an attempt to reform the constitution — so that Menem could be reelected in 1995 — and to increase its influence in Congress and at the provincial level. The government suffered a series of political embarrassments when the official senatorial candidate for the Federal Capital was defeated, and opposition victories in senate races in San Juan and Chaco "forced" the government to nullify the election results. Even more damaging was the government's decision to intervene in the province of Corrientes to redress an institutional stalemate. And the government paid very high political cost when the *menemista* candidate failed to win the provincial elections for the governorship of Corrientes.

Approaching the 1993 congressional elections, the Menem government faced recurrent allegations of high-level corruption, rising tensions in the provinces, increased labor conflicts, and a deterioration of the government's public image. The executive shifted from defiance to a defensive stance and vice versa several times. These shifts were reflected in cabinet changes in December 1992 (involving the ministries of interior, labor, and education) and August 1993 (involving the outgoing interior minister's criticism of the way the government was attempting to force constitutional reform to permit Menem's reelection), as well as in public conflicts among Peronist senators and deepening tensions with the opposition parties. Nevertheless, in the October 1993 congressional elections, as in 1991, the electorate was apparently willing to overlook the *menemista* image of corruption, political intolerance, and concentration of power in the executive, placing greater emphasis on economic stability and continuity of economic policies: Peronism won 42.3 percent of the national vote (and nine additional seats in the Chamber of Deputies), while the Radicals received 30 percent of the vote (losing one seat).

The outlook for 1994 and beyond is problematic, although expectations are that inflation, which was 17.5 percent in 1992, will decline further to slightly less than 10 percent in 1993 and remain low. Moreover, growth is projected to slow to around 5 percent in 1993 and even less in 1994. Slower growth will imply the continuation of high unemployment (9.9 percent in May 1993 in the Federal Capital and greater Buenos Aires), lower tax revenues, and a fragile fiscal equilibrium. This tendency toward slower economic growth will exacerbate the problem of an overvalued exchange rate, while making it even more difficult to attain the large surpluses in public finances required to bail out the bankrupt pension system and meet Argentina's commitments with its creditor banks and the international financial agencies. The next several years, therefore, will probably witness a continuation of social demands on the part of the political opposition and those groups that have been hurt the most by the Convertibility plan. Similarly, these policies may lead to increasingly vocal protests from entrepreneurial critics, along with capitalist demands to participate in the decision-making process.

In the long term, the potential for higher sociopolitical tensions in 1994 and 1995 is clear given the slowdown in economic growth and difficulties with the exchange rate and meeting of external debt agreements. Choosing between recession or the enactment of a risky stimulus package combined with a currency devaluation (with the implied threat to monetary stabilization) will be a tough dilemma for the government to confront at the same time that the official party prepares the presidential election to be held in late 1994 or early 1995.

This electoral contest itself presents the government with a difficult conundrum. On the one hand, relative economic stability should strengthen the Peronist candidate. But this may be true only if the electorate perceives stability as being still fragile. In such a case, voters might reason that a "maximizing" strategy to punish the incumbents by casting ballots for the opposition could endanger stability, something that after several hyperinflationary episodes most Argentines wish to avoid at almost any cost. On the other hand, if the public views economic stability as achieved, the result could be electorally devastating for the incumbents. Why? Because if stability is thought to be definitive and irreversible, then voters would be more likely to abandon a risk-adverse strategy and to cast a "cost-free" ballot for the opposition party. In short, there is no direct correlation between political support and economic stability. A decline in the incumbent party's popularity and electoral support cannot be inferred directly from an erosion of economic stability. This relationship behaves quite differently depending upon the context.[37] This was clear, for example, in 1992, when government success in stabilizing macroeconomic conditions was accompanied by rising dissatisfaction and popular contestation. The key seems to be how actors perceive the costs and benefits involved in supporting the status quo or, alternatively, pursuing a maximizing strategy. The other key factor is whether actors perceive the opposition as a feasible alternative, and Peronism in this respect is emerging as dominant in the 1995 presidential elections. Radicalism, as the main opposition party, has not managed to articulate a unified, credible posture. The Radicals' internal squabbles and the rivalries among its likely presidential candidates, plus its impotence in the face of successful structural reforms, all make the Peronist candidate (whether or not Menem is able to reform the constitution and stand for reelection) the probable next president of Argentina.

Despite political and economic problems confronted by the Argentine government, the current context of political and economic stability — reinforced by the failure of opposition actors to present credible alternatives — suggests future continuity in the socioeconomic strategy. Regardless of their success or failure, the revolutionary character of these policies also suggests that the long-term future of Argentina will have little in common with the dominant political and economic patterns that prevailed from 1930 until recently.[38]

The Political Conditions for the Feasibility of Neoliberal Reform

Why did Menem's government opt for a such an orthodox neoliberal scheme and why has it been able successfully to overcome political obstacles to its implementation? The answers are not obvious. The following discussion analyzes a number of hypotheses regarding the elements that made it possible to pursue this socioeconomic strategy and the factors that allowed the government to neutralize unions, capitalists, and the opposition parties.

Menem's Option for Bunge & Born

The speed of the liberal shift and the decision to put the ministry of economy in the hands of the Bunge & Born group represent the "foundation" of Menemism. Four fundamental causes lay behind this decision. First was the presence within Menem's entourage of influential advisors with little background in Peronist militancy, but with close ties to business groups. These people constituted a pole of influence unconstrained by the ideological rigidity characteristic of the party and union militants. A second factor resided in the solid relations that old Peronist militants had established with the Bunge & Born group, as well as the presence within Menem's inner circle of unionists with close ties to business. These Peronist union leaders had already revealed their willingness to abandon traditional Peronist positions when they opposed CGT leader Saúl Ubaldini and supported union participation in the Radical government. Their presence eliminated any possibility of a confrontation along Peronist and non-Peronist lines. Third, after the experience of the Alfonsín administration and the subsequent economic and social crisis, Menem's most influential advisors rejected confrontation with international creditors and local capitalists, since the state lacked both the resources and the political power successfully to sustain such a strategy.[39] Fourth, Roig's appointment overcame opposition because this decision implied the commitment of the Bunge and Born group to the design and implementation of the Menem government's economic policies. This powerful multinational group, which produces and exports grain and other food products, was in a strong position because of its international governmental, financial, and business contacts, as well as its lack of important contracts with the state, which implied a greater possibility of implementing fiscal reforms without hurting the specific interests of the group's holdings.

The Neutralization of Union Reaction

Several factors explain how the government managed to impose its policies on the unions. First, in 1989, Peronist presidential candidate Menem, in an effort to avoid threatening the middle class vote, reached agreements with unions to curtail strikes and mobilizations. Second, outbursts of looting, hyperinflation, and economic stagnation brought increased unemployment, creating a situation of extreme uncertainty. This forced the unions to avoid mobilizations, despite real wage losses incurred during the period between the 1989 election and Menem's inauguration. Third, union demobilization, combined with stagflation and workers' support for Menem as the Peronist candidate, weakened an already hard-pressed union apparatus with little capacity to react against the economic measures that were swiftly introduced once Menem was in power. The leadership split among those few who supported neoliberalism either as "the only way out" or because their union gained with the changes, those who supported it out of solidarity with their candidate (and only until economic conditions improved), and those who opposed it on the grounds that the workers had neither voted for Bunge & Born nor for a liberal solution to the economic crisis. Fourth, the government exploited this division in leadership and skillfully implemented a "carrot-and-stick" strategy of punishing those responsible for labor conflicts and rewarding those in compliant unions. Such benefits included appointments to state agencies administering social work funds. Unions could oppose the government and risk layoffs, political isolation, and reduced benefits for their members. Or they could support the government while attempting to attenuate the negative impact of the new policies by obtaining concessions, such as credits or the state's absorption of debts incurred by union social benefit programs during the military government. Union leaders who either supported the project or clearly opposed it dominated the public spotlight, but "tolerant" leaders — those critical of the direction taken by the government but not willing to confront it "until conditions improve" — have been a key to the government's success in union conflicts. Their repeated lack of participation in anti-government movements on short-term tactical grounds systematically avoided the creation of a majoritarian union opposition front.

The Neutralization of Capitalist Opposition

Argentina's profound reform of capitalism implies a clear transfer of resources from workers and the public sector to capitalists. As a result, the majority of business, both at the level of the firms and of interest organizations, supports the government. Together they support measures to weaken unions, roll back the state, and privatize.

Nevertheless, not all capitalists can exploit the lower costs being created by the new policies. Those sectors with difficulty facing increased foreign competition — textiles, electronics, car parts — do not have much capacity to respond at the level of their associations. With the CGE extremely weakened, these sectors are dependent on the willingness of the UIA to take up their demands against a government that is intransigent regarding opening of the economy, the exchange rate, taxes, and tariff levels. The president of the UIA, Israel Mahler, clearly described the limited room for maneuver: "The extent of decline in the productive sector, which is reflected in the fact that the per capita production in industry is today 40 percent less than what it was in 1970, decidedly influenced the decision to reject combative attitudes leading nowhere" (*La Nación*, September 1, 1991, sec. 3, 1).

As a result, those industrial sectors in crisis sought channels of dialogue with the government. The government's response depended on the capacity of these firms to defend their interests at the micro level, while eschewing the costs of collective action in conjunction with other firms or sectors. For example, the pharmaceutical laboratories, which had raised their prices at the beginning of 1992, were forced to roll back prices in the face of government-induced foreign competition. This strategy demonstrated the government's determination to accelerate and deepen the opening of the economy, regardless of opposition.

Groups that strengthened during the dictatorship were politically and economically important in the capitalist sector, but their interests were subsequently harmed by the shrinking of the state. Though often horizontally diversified and capable of exporting, profits for these groups largely stemmed from supplying the state — usually, as contractors for large works. Furthermore, some firms depended on "over-billing" the state to be able to offer the same products at internationally competitive prices. These firms might have sought an alliance with unions in pursuit of "nationalism" and "defense" of the state. The government prevented this politically potent reaction by allowing these firms to appropriate, through privatization, public sector firms that have ended up as monopolies or oligopolies. This helped to mitigate the loss of profits from retraction of state contracts. Although not every firm received such benefits from privatization, the losers in the competition to acquire public firms are not sufficiently powerful — as a group — to thwart the government's policies.

The Neutralization of Party Opposition

In many ways, 1990 represents a turning point. First, the government's resolute implementation of neoliberal policies has implied redefinitions within the political party system. The convergence of the Peronists with the rightist UCeDé has led to an important shift in the UCeDé electorate toward support for Menem's politics. Peronists and the UCeDé have reached formal alliances in some districts, such as the Federal Capital. And UCeDé specialists and professionals hold government positions including secretariats in the ministry of the interior, provincial offices, and management of firms being privatized.

Support for the UCeDé has been double-edged, however. Internally, the UCeDé has been torn by the tension between its support for pro-liberal government policies and the cost paid by the UCeDé in terms of loss of party identity and electoral strength. This strain has created schisms between the party and its congressional bloc, and it is the central issue defining the party's internal discussions.

Tensions also emerged between the Menem government and Peronism itself. Pro-government deputies took part in arduous discussion prior to approving legislation regarding reform of the state. Furthermore, when Cavallo explained his first adjustment plan to the Peronist bloc of deputies, in February 1991, the Peronist deputies harshly criticized him and charged that there were insufficient grounds for the plan's severity and that it failed to take into account the hardships experienced in the provinces. Cavallo's response was, "If you don't like the economic plan, then tell Carlos [Menem] to appoint another minister of economy." The meeting ended with the minister leaving amidst threats that Peronist deputies would withhold support for the plan (*La Nación*, February 7, 1991).

Eventually, under pressure from the executive, the package was approved. Nevertheless, a dissident faction of Peronist deputies was formed, the so-called "Group of Eight." Menem was also forced to engage in public arguments with Antonio Cafiero, at that time president of the Partido Justicialista (the Peronist party — PJ) and governor of Buenos Aires province. Cafiero advised Menem to "return to the sources of Peronist doctrine" (*La Nación*, March 17, 1990, 1). Menem counteracted the reaction within party ranks in several ways. He exploited the extreme crisis that prevailed when he entered office by deflecting criticism, which usually centered on the social costs of the policies adopted. He argued that alternatives didn't exist — the room for maneuver was limited. Finally, he filled party leadership positions with individuals close to the executive.

Menem also displayed considerable pragmatism in choosing candidates for elections. Whenever non-Peronists were likely to win an election or support the government's economic course, the executive did not hesitate to incorporate them. Even those Peronists with little party experience were nominated as candidates. This occurred in Tucumán, Santa Fé, and the Federal Capital. Of course, the success of the economic policy strengthened this strategy.

However, the conjunction of stagflation and Menem's policies had the effect of rapidly "emptying" Peronist ideology and doctrine of its Keynesian thrust in economic policy and its neocorporatist organization and participation of social actors. Regardless of the outcome of this process, Peronism will never again be what it once was. Neoliberal policies, the weakening of the labor movement, the forging of political alliances with liberal parties, the inclusion of nonparty candidates on Peronist lists, the lack of a social policy, close ties with the United States (referred to by the Foreign Minister himself as "carnal relations"), together represent transgressions that strike at the heart of the social and political alliance responsible for Peronism's emergence and surprising resiliency.

A clarification should be made regarding the relationship between progovernment sectors and the Radical party, beginning with the Alfonsín government. Although a "Hobbesian" style of decision making marked the design and implementation of socioeconomic policies under both Alfonsín and Menem, the degree of harmony and collaboration between the government and the opposition on some important issues was much greater under Alfonsín than was perceived by public opinion or portrayed in analyses of the period. These issues go beyond socioeconomic policy to encompass such key matters as legislation on military matters, judicial appointments, divorce (a particularly conflictive issue with the Catholic Church), and the Beagle Channel border agreement with Chile.

As the first minority in the Senate during Alfonsín's government, the Peronist party was in a position to precipitate an institutional crisis or to block passage of the budget. All that was required was making alliances and hence becoming the majority, or else simply not attending sessions, thereby denying the Senate the quorum required to make decisions. One careful study of the decision-making process in congress during the Alfonsín period revealed not only "the high percentage of laws unanimously approved, but also that this was achieved through broad majorities, invariably composed of the UCR and the PJ (Mustapic and Goretti 1991, 30). Issues on which accords could not be reached, or were highly unlikely (such as the economy), were precisely those matters that the executive tended to resolve by decree. Negotiation and agreement were important, however; and in Congress there always "existed at least a minimal compromise to guarantee institutional continuity" (Mustapic and Goretti 1991, 32).

Notwithstanding their partial success since 1991 in reasserting their opposition role, the Radicals were neutralized by two governmental strategies. First, the government effectively controlled Congress through its majority in the Senate and its ability to forge alliances with center-right and provincial parties in the Chamber of Deputies, alliances which were occasionally necessary in the face of weak party discipline among Peronist deputies. Second, when other measures were to no avail, the government resorted to a more "Hobbesian" approach through the activist use of executive decree powers (Ferreira Rubio and Goretti 1993), a course of action that exacerbated tensions with Radicalism.

Menem's policies also had repercussions within the ranks of the Radical party. A schism emerged between Alfonsín, who maintained a critical posture toward the Menem government on the one hand, and Angeloz, the former presidential candidate and governor of Córdoba, who supported the government. The convergence of Angeloz with the Menem administration was such that Angeloz was offered a cabinet position, which he eventually declined. At the UCR party convention, these internal differences erupted, with delegates backing Angeloz walking out after a sharp confrontation over the content of the party's platform (*La Nación*, October 15, 1990, 1).

To date, the Radical party remains divided over how to confront the Menem government. One faction questions the economic policies but offers no viable alternative. Linked to former President Alfonsín, this faction is still paying the political costs of leaving a legacy of hyperinflation and the decision to accelerate the transfer of power to Peronism. Other groups attempt to compete with Peronism for power at the regional level, but they do not question the logic of the overall economic policy. In any event, criticisms of government corruption, inefficiency in privatization, or reform of the constitution to allow reelection of the president are not issues around which a unified Radicalism can coalesce and present itself as an alternative to Menem.

Finally, the political tone of Menem's policies carried the debate on structural reforms into a terrain beyond organized social and political actors. In early April 1990, an estimated eighty thousand people filled the Plaza de Mayo in support of privatization and the shrinking of the state apparatus. The meeting, held under the slogan "Yes to Menem," was convoked by journalists. In attendance were a mix of party leaders — both Peronists and from right-wing parties — representatives of business, pro-Menem union leaders, and many unaffiliated people. Even Cafiero, then Peronist party president, was pressured into attending. According to *La Nación*, he "received some lukewarm applause...and some warnings...'Support the President, because if you don't, you will be left behind'" (April 7, 1990, 1,4).

The rapid and profound redefinition of the inter- and intraparty lines of opposition and alliance indicate not only the high degree of political power attained by the government but also the fact that Menem's strategies amount to a political revolution.

Why Democracy Is Consolidated

Any discussion of alternative scenarios must focus on whether future sociopolitical disputes will take place within a democratic context or not. This requires paying particular attention to two actors who, since 1930, have repeatedly placed Argentine democracy in check: the armed forces and the bourgeoisie. In this section I argue that both the armed forces and the bourgeoisie expect and support long-term democratic stability.

Armed Forces and Political Regime[40]

Although Menem was able successfully to repress the last *carapintada* uprising in 1990, the question remains: what prevents the generals, in the absence of an internal threat to the military, from slowly reasserting power and returning to their traditional role as coup makers?

The present situation of the armed forces in Argentina cannot be attributed solely to circumstantial factors. The military's administration of government during the years 1976 to 1983 considerably eroded military institutions. Conflicts between the general staff and the *carapintadas* are only one symptom. Systematic violation of human rights by the armed forces during the repression of guerrilla movements and popular sectors gave rise to widespread indignation. Consequently, the judicial investigations and trial of *junta* members compounded already existing sentiments within Argentine society. In fact, the judicial proceedings themselves were a consequence of demands for justice that marked the electoral process in which the armed forces abandoned power.

The deep socioeconomic crisis precipitated by the military's policies also created hostility among the popular sectors and antagonized capitalist groups — traditionally, a principal base of the political and economic alliance supporting military rule. Between 1976 and 1983 the military's policies became a source of uncertainty for the interests of capitalists. Then the Malvinas disaster, in addition to creating another source of civilian discontent, illustrated just how unpredictable and risky military behavior could be for the bourgeoisie and for such long-standing international allies as the United States and Europe. The Malvinas defeat gave rise to two profound internal cleavages within the armed forces. First, a breakdown in interforce relations occurred during the last phase of the dictatorship when the navy and the air force withdrew from the military *junta* and refused to participate in the election of General Reynaldo Bignone as president. Second, a "horizontal" cleavage separated generals — who held responsibility for the army's policies and actions — from subordinate officers — who had been on the front lines during the repression as well as the war in the Malvinas. Officers in the latter group blamed the general staff for its poor planning and execution of the fighting on the islands. Accusations of corruption during the dictatorship were also launched.

The intramilitary conflict that broke out during Holy Week 1987 took place within a context shaped by the following factors: 1) the defamation and isolation of the armed forces, not only by popular sectors, but also by the armed forces' traditional pillars of support; 2) budget cuts that were introduced at the outset of the democratic government; and 3) internal confrontation that accompanied the settling of accounts following the defeat in the Malvinas. The breakdown of the chain of command both accelerated the military crisis and was a consequence of it.

Solidarity initially given the *carapintadas*, coupled with "internal" discrediting of the general staff, presented a new scenario for intramilitary conflicts. The confrontation no longer turned on the traditional conflicts of *azules* (blues) against *colorados* (reds) or "nationalists" against "liberals." In these clashes of the 1950s and 1960s, the military divided vertically, and, regardless of which faction emerged victorious, the institution remained intact. This was a showdown between junior officers, supported by NCOs, and the generals. In such a context, the strength of *carapintada* influence created a de facto nightmare for the army. This "class struggle" could only destroy the institution as such. A *carapintada* victory implied the dismissal of the majority of the higher level officers, while a victory by the general staff was likely to lead to massive discharges among junior officers and the NCO cadre.

Although the most conflictive points of the internal struggle have been resolved, the armed forces' performance during its last stint in power continues to be seen as the principal cause of its social and political isolation and the severe internal conflicts of recent years. The victors in the defeat of the *carapintadas* have been clear on this point. If institutional considerations are the priority, then the armed forces are in no condition to risk an intervention in politics.

As with other social actors, subordination of the military to the constitutional order is not necessarily a result of nascent democratic values. Rather, it reflects the recognition that the survival of the military institution as such will be in danger if certain limits are transgressed. Thus, it is possible to foresee that in the long term the military, as a result of the internal crises that have racked it, will not have the capacity to question the constitutional order and, thus, will be obliged to accept a subordinate role. In short, evaporation of "threats" arising from the "communist bloc," waning external tensions as a result of economic integration with Brazil and the border agreements with Chile, as well as the dismantling of the military-industrial apparatus and the cuts in military personnel, promise a future in which the armed forces no longer loom as a threatening political actor.[41]

The Bourgeoisie and the Political Regime[42]

Political activity by business associations is no novelty in Argentina. Even prior to the 1940s, business organizations participated in the formulation of national policies and influenced the breakdown and change of political regimes, as was the case with the coup that overthrew Hipólito Yrigoyen in 1930. With the rise of Peronism, democracy became a high-risk game for the bourgeoisie. Thus, from the 1950s onward, capitalist organization and political strategy have been consistent in stance toward authoritarianism and democracy. During periods of democratization they have pursued defensive and frequently conspiratorial actions. They have consistently supported the installation and maintenance of military regimes, since such regimes were traditionally the only ones that offered them loyalty and guarantees for their interests. Nevertheless, in 1976 the political significance of military authoritarianism for the bourgeoisie began to change. In 1983, a similar process began regarding democracy.

The experience of military dictatorship between 1976 and 1983 led many capitalists to modify their perception of the costs and benefits of authoritarian rule. During this period, capitalists were systematically excluded from the design and implementation of policies. The negative impact of the military's economic policies on bourgeois interests was often greater than the costs suffered during democratic periods. With total political power in its hands, the military ceased to be predictable. The implementation of technocratic policies adversely affecting important economic groups and the Malvinas misadventure were two examples. In the eyes of capitalists, the armed forces became a risky actor. Insurgent military groups that burst forth during Holy Week 1987 were even less attractive to capitalist interests. Though the *carapintadas* disparaged the military's "liberal" experiment, which had been so costly to the bourgeoisie, their modes of action, populist slogans, and occasional references to U.S. and British "imperialism" were clearly unattractive to the middle classes. Consequently, the array of business organizations — SRA, UIA, CAC — which usually supported military demands or, at least, remained "neutral" in clashes between democratic governments and seditious military units, came out in strong support of democracy during the Holy Week, Monte Caseros, and Villa Martelli military crises.[43]

Concomitantly, the relationship between the bourgeoisie and democracy was also shaped to a great extent by the experience of Peronism. From the 1940s until 1983, democratic elections meant Peronist victories, advances for the labor movement and business organizations such as the CGE — representing small- and medium-size firms — and the implementation of policies strengthening the socioeconomic role of the state. Furthermore, at times Peronist governments pursued policies that clashed with the interests of the landowning bourgeoisie of the pampas (through taxes and the nationalization of foreign trade), of multinational capital (through the nationalization of firms controlling public services), of finance capital (through the nationalization of bank deposits and the handling of credits), and of the capitalist class (through the enactment of a long list of labor rights and consistent efforts to increase real and absolute wages). To make matters worse, Peronism's proscription led to governments headed by the Radicals and the Movimiento de Integración y Desarrollo party headed by Arturo Frondizi that implemented policies to strengthen the state and displace multinational capital (as occurred under the Radicals) or to negotiate the integration of organizations linked with Peronism rather than produce their disorganization. In 1958, for example, the *desarrollista* government struck a bargain to exchange the legalization of the CGT and the CGE for Peronist electoral support.

In synthesis, democracy traditionally posed a threat for the economically most important capitalist sectors, which were organized in free market-oriented business associations. Democracy meant advantages for labor and the CGE and, consequently, a decline in the influence of Argentina's most powerful economic groups. Democracy also was seen by the dominant entrepreneurial groups as signifying a reduction in the importance of the market in allocating resources, while threatening the influence of some national business umbrella groupings (third- and fourth-level business organizations, such as the UIA and the Acción Coordinadora de Instituciones Empresarias Libres [Coordinated Action of Free-Enterprise Business Organizations — ACIEL]) and the possible implementation of policies that challenged immediate bourgeois interests.

In contrast to this traditional interpretation of democracy by capitalist actors, the 1983 Radical electoral victory promised to inaugurate a change in the meaning of democracy for business groups and organizations. The "iron law" of Argentine politics, whereby elections invariably meant Peronist victories, had been broken. Furthermore, the Radical's anticorporatist discourse also attempted to block any explosion of union demands, thereby ending the long-standing identification of democracy with progress for the labor movement. From the 1983 elections to the June 1985 launching of the *Plan Austral,* the UCR democratic alternative offered business interests four major advantages: 1) the electoral defeat of Peronism; 2) assurances that business organizations would not be displaced or dismantled; 3) government recognition of the political hegemony of the UIA over its long-standing adversary, the CGE-CGI; and 4) legislative challenges to foundations of union power, such as industry-wide collective bargaining and union administration of workers' social benefits.

Leaving aside the chaotic aftermath of the *Austral* and *Primavera* plans, the Radicals demonstrated their willingness to accept capitalist participation in decision making,[44] as well as to implement modifications to the model of accumulation that would be useful to big-business interests, such as opening the economy, privatization, undermining union power, and reducing the role of the state in production and in the allocation of resources. In short, the Radicals demonstrated that these probusiness goals were no longer the exclusive monopoly of the Right and the armed forces.

Even more surprisingly, the Peronists, once in power, not only maintained this course but also deepened the neoliberal reorganization of the economy and society. Astonishingly, Peronist policies have been more successful than those of their Radical and military predecessors in creating economic stability and undermining potentially defiant actors opposed to the model, particularly the labor movement.

Given this framework, the bourgeoisie now find political options offered by democracy in Argentina to be better suited and less risky for their interests than any authoritarian alternative. Furthermore, in view of the fact that previous attempts to install de facto regimes have only been successful with the support of the most important bourgeois economic organizations and groups, this suggests that a deterioration in the economic situation will not necessarily threaten democratic stability. The bourgeoisie's preference for democratic stability is a long-term option and will have long-term effects.

The Future of Democracy

Since the 1950s economic and political conflicts in Argentina cycled through recurrent crises, with each increasing in intensity and violence. Despite this unfavorable environment, organized labor managed for decades to maintain its capacity to defend workers' rights and interests. Up until the mid-1970s, the outcome of repeated conflicts over the distribution of political and material goods resulted in a stalemate. Even today some observers complain that workers and the popular sectors enjoy excessive purchasing power, which they claim strengthens union power and represents a latent inflationary risk.

Nevertheless, the situation today is radically different from the Argentina of the 1940s through the early 1970s. From 1983 to 1990, real wages of salaried workers fell by more than 50 percent; unemployment and underemployment in the Federal Capital and Greater Buenos Aires have nearly doubled, and the number of people unable to satisfy their basic needs is estimated between nine and ten million (Smith 1992). These statistics refer to the situation prior to the two most recent hyperinflationary crises. Therefore, despite improvements in some markets, open unemployment approached 10 percent. Nor did income distribution improve: the poorest 40 percent of the families living in Greater Buenos Aires received 16.9 percent of the total income in 1977, 15.7 percent in 1983, and 11.7 percent in 1989. The wealthiest 10 percent of the families, on the other hand, received 31.6 percent in 1977, 32.5 percent in 1983, and 41.6 percent in 1989 (Barbeito 1991, table 4). Trends in income distribution are even more regressive when provincial levels are considered.

Despite a generalized perception that redistribution is "relative" and nearly everyone bears "absolute" losses — and receives smaller slices of a shrinking pie — not all suffered losses since the beginning of the economic crisis in 1980. For some business groups, the crisis was an opportunity for not only relative but also absolute gains.[45] Unions have lost considerable power; their membership has declined, and they currently struggle to retain control over their insolvent social welfare programs. Thus, during the last fifteen years, the distributional stalemate has tilted strongly toward capital and the Argentine minority receiving the highest share of income.

Finally, the different logics underlying political stability in different variants of democracy should be emphasized, because they are of relevance to the skewed distribution of wealth. The 1983 democratic opening involved a gradual displacement of the focus of political struggle from a "democracy versus authoritarianism" axis toward a dimension focused on defining the type of democracy that would best assure governability and stability. In this sense, the "economic" crisis that marked the Argentine transition was symptomatic of an intense struggle to redefine — within a democratic framework — who would govern whom, under what rules, and respecting which rights.[46]

Two opposite ideal types of organization and articulation of social interests are related to conditions found in consolidated democracies. At one extreme lies the "neocorporatist" model, in which regime governability is based on densely organized and highly aggregated social actors. The basis of "neocorporatist" democracy involves negotiations among organized labor, business, and the state. Labor foregoes militancy in exchange for participation in decisions aimed at increasing investment, jobs, and salaries while pressing for more generous welfare policies (education, health, equal justice, and so on). Thus, this type of democracy achieves stability and social welfare by incorporating subordinate social groups into the political and institutional order, which, in turn, is sustained by the extension and deepening of the process of distributing economic and political goods within society.[47]

At the other extreme are those democratic regimes whose governability and stability are founded on the disorganization of the capacity for mobilization of the popular sectors. Such regimes are characterized by highly skewed distributions of material resources (defined in terms of salary, employment, and social welfare levels) and less equal distribution of political resources. There is limitation of the scope of social rights and the existence of rules and organizational resources that encourage collective action by subordinate social groups. Weak social actors, highly skewed distributions of wealth, and highly concentrated decision-making processes characterize this type of "neoliberal" or "fragmentary" democracy. Here, governability is based on the political and economic exclusion of important social groups.

Most societies — indeed, even the northern democracies — tend to be "hybrids" that mix institutional arrangements based on different logics of interest, organization, and representation. As William Smith and I show (1994a), this does not imply that different political and economic systems are located on a continuum between neoliberal and neocorporatist equilibria. Nevertheless, most societies also tend to rely more on one logic than another. The United States and Sweden, for example, exhibit different logics of political domination. It is clear that the trend in Argentina is toward the consolidation of a democracy that reinforces the neoliberal features of political domination, namely fragmentation of sociopolitical actors and economic exclusion. Whether the outcome of this process results in a neoliberal scenario or in a *dual democracy* (Acuña and Smith 1994a) will depend on the outcome of political struggles in the next few years.

Conclusion

Still, there are many loose ends to consider. Nevertheless, this analysis permits us to maintain that the democratic regime in Argentina has been consolidated and that this democracy tends to be exclusionary and fragmentary, both politically and economically. Without a doubt, the depth of Menem's reforms and the speed with which they are being implemented amount to a revolution, though a revolution very different from that expected by the political movement that brought Menem into power. The present model points to an equilibrium point with high levels of distributive injustice and monopoly power. Nevertheless, it is understandable why Menem, unlike either the military dictatorship or the Radicals, is able to fulfill his objectives with the support of capitalists and obtain electoral majorities, despite his policy's costs for the popular sectors. The two major "stalemates" characterizing economic and political conflicts in Argentina since the rise of Perón resolved in favor of the large bourgeoisie. The small- and medium-bourgeoisie, represented by the CGE, no longer threaten such organizations of the *haute bourgeoisie* as the UIA, SRA, and CAC. Moreover, the weakened working class now values stability, even if it is only a stable poverty, over the risks of social change — risks which, in Argentina, are associated with state terrorism and the anxiety of stagnation and hyperinflation.

Albert Hirschman, in a classic work (1970), has defined the options available to actors evaluating their welfare and preferences. Either they are loyal to the game that maintains the status quo, or else, if they are dissatisfied, they can continue to play while exercising dissent — by protesting and seeking change or else abandon the game. In Argentina a good part of the present stability results from a fourth option, opted for by actors dissatisfied with the status quo: resignation to their lot.

Resignation, nevertheless, cannot by itself guarantee the long-run stability of neoliberal policies. In Argentina, as we have seen, the more remote the risks of political violence and economic crisis appear to be, the more inclined members of society will be to demand an equitable distribution of resources. A more just redistribution would require fundamental changes that would strike at the core of the neoliberal economic program. The continuity of neoliberal policies, therefore, will depend on the ability of the state and dominant sectors of the bourgeoisie to constrain the popular sectors' capacity for contestation. In conclusion, the long-term stability of neoliberal policies depends on a particularly perverse combination of discontented acquiescence with the active disarticulation as collective actors of the majority of the working class and other popular sectors.

Notes

1. This economic crisis was characterized by fiscal and external indebtedness, a fall in the rate of investment, salary lags, and stagflation. The magnitude of the crisis can be seen in the following indicators: the ratio of total gross internal investment relative to the GDP fell from about 20 percent during the 1970-1981 period to 15.0, 13.5, and 11.6 percent in the three subsequent years, while real wages fell sharply during the 1981-1982 period of adjustment. Wages underwent a partial recovery during the final semester of 1983, since the weakened military government chose to ease labor tensions by accepting wage demands. Finally, GDP grew by 1.6 percent in 1980, and then fell by 6.7 percent in 1981 and 4.5 percent in 1982, before growing again by 2.8 percent in 1983. During the same years the annual consumer price index increases rose from approximately 70 to 200 percent.

2. In a Prisoner's Dilemma, the players choose between (C) collaboration in a common enterprise or (D) defection in an attempt to free-ride at the other players' expense. The particular structure of the payoff matrix in this game makes defection the dominant strategy for both players. This game's paradox is that while the second best option to collaborate is collectively optimal, the payoff matrix makes defection the rational course of action, and the resolution of the game implies individual gains that are lower, and hence Pareto suboptimal, than if the players had collaborated. "N-players" simply means that more than two players are involved in making choices.

3. In a "Hobbesian" solution to the Prisoner's Dilemma, a hegemonic actor operating above and beyond the game acts authoritatively to redefine the payoff structure so as to neutralize the costs of cooperation and reduce the benefits of defection.

4. The expectations surrounding the return to democracy left little room for publicly justifying the "need" to concentrate power. Such justifications emerged only in outbursts by angry functionaries in response to charges of authoritarianism. For example, on one such occasion, Minister Grinspun, in response to a query seeking his position on and definition of concerted economic policy, expressed his support for the process and defined concertation as the coming together of social actors *to approve* the economic plan presented by the government. This would be the case with the "Concertation Roundtable" in 1984, the "Economic-Social Conference" from 1985 on, and the "Emergency Agriculture and Livestock Council" in 1986 and 1987. Nevertheless, significant aspects of economic policy were never discussed in these state, business, and union forums. Furthermore, until 1988 on those occasions that the government did negotiate relevant points with unions or business, the exchanges occurred with a faction of these sectors, were informal, and took place alongside institutional forms of representation. These factions were the "15" in the case of unions and the "captains of industry" for business. On the relation between government and the unions, see Ricardo Gaudio and Andrés Thompson (1990); for the relationship with the "captains," see Pierre Osteguy (1990). Juan Carlos Torre in two essays (1990, 1991) discusses how the respective logics of the government and the unions diminished possibilities for cooperation. The relation between the absence of concertation and the nature of the emergent political regime is analyzed in Acuña, et al. (1988) and the

historical impact of politico-institutional instability and concentration of power is treated in Acuña (1991, 1992a).

5. As Smith (1992, 25) points out, "every policy directed toward [...] a problem in one area has the unanticipated consequence of creating additional problems elsewhere."

6. In this scheme, opening the economy to international competition creates a "ceiling" that reduces business capacity to transfer price increases to consumers. Union demands, on the other hand, are limited by business resistance and the threat of unemployment if firms fail to compete with international prices.

7. Literally, "painted faces," the name coined for the insurgent military movement, whose members darkened their faces with camouflage paint in "commando" fashion.

8. Despite massive and unconditional support from all social and political actors, the government's handling of the events of Holy Week 1987 created an image of capitulation before the rebels.

9. From January to August retail prices climbed incessantly, with increases of 9.1, 10.4, 14.7, 17.2, 15.7, 18.0, 25.6, and 27.6 percent each month. According to the Instituto Nacional de Estadísticas y Censo (INDEC), the annual variation in prices from September 1987 to August 1988 reached 440 percent, while wholesale prices rose 606.5 percent.

10. The Primavera Plan included the following measures: price accords for 180 days with the UIA; the formation by the Secretary of Internal Trade, the UIA, and the CAC of a commission to track compliance with the agreement; an 11.4 percent devaluation of the *Austral*; 30 percent increases in public utility rates; a dual foreign exchange market; a commitment to reduce the fiscal deficit to 4 percent of GDP; a 3 percent reduction in the value-added tax (VAT); the suspension of public investments in works such as the Yacyretá and Atucha II energy generating projects; the reduction of tariff barriers; reductions in export tariffs; a 25 percent increase for public employees; and free negotiation of salaries in the private sector.

11. The postelection period was particularly tense for society as a whole. As the dollar reached A540 in the parallel market and retail price inflation hit 114.5 percent, important regions of the country began to suffer food shortages. Deep in one of the worst economic crises in Argentine history, the transfer of office took place amidst spontaneous looting of supermarkets in Córdoba, Rosario, Tucumán, and Greater Buenos Aires. The context of the transition was completed by the imposition of a state of siege, declarations by the Minister of the Interior Juan C. Pugliese attributing the massive acts of violence to a plan orchestrated by "leftist subversives," arrests of the former presidential candidates of a Trotskyist party (which had garnered only 0.3 percent of the vote in the election), a failed presidential bid to design a joint transition policy with the incoming authorities, as well as President Alfonsín's unexpected announcement to the president-elect, via an official broadcast over national radio and television, of his decision to hand over the government on June 30 rather than December 10, 1989 — almost six months early.

12. In the hyperinflationary context, the first measures announced on July 9 were a 300 percent devaluation of the *Austral*, price hikes for fuel and public services (of between 200 and 600 percent), a suspension of export subsidies while maintaining export taxes (30 percent on agriculture and livestock products and 20 percent on manufactured goods), a halt on monetizing the fiscal deficit, salary and pension

increases, followed by freezes until October, price freezes for ninety days (retroactive to July 3), a suspension of restrictions on foreign investment, a reduction of public expenditures, and the announcement of the privatization of public services, as well as tax reform that included extending the value-added tax to the majority of activities. Business associations supported this, although they criticized the price freezes and the export taxes.

13. I draw on comments on an earlier draft of this chapter by Juan C. Torre for this phrase. A similar argument is also developed by Vicente Palermo (1991, 3).

14. The decline in inflation that began in August was also a success since it followed immediately upon a round of salary negotiations without any "ceiling." The government expressed its conformity with these results. In short, workers bettered their earnings, but without returning to the real wage levels prevailing prior to the onset of hyperinflation. See *La Nación,* July 28 and 29, 1989.

15. These laws authorized the state to privatize all state firms totally or partially (regardless of whether they engaged in service, extractive, or productive activities) and to suspend the following: industrial and mining promotion subsidies, preferential state purchases of locally produced goods, hiring of additional personnel by the state, and job security for public employees. These measures basically threatened the interests of regional economies, firms supplying the state, and public employees.

16. The support of the industrialists, however, was more nuanced than the backing of the SRA. These qualifications were expressed by Israel Mahler, who would later be elected president of UIA (in May 1991). Mahler clarified his support for the modernization of the state, deregulation, breaking up of monopolies, and privatization: "The severe contraction of the internal market, the paralysis of public investment, the suspension of contracts, and the blunt changes in variables associated with exports, in their present form constitute a situation that for some sectors of metallurgical activity is approaching the limit." He concluded that industry should be "convoked" by the government; thus, he implicitly criticized industry's exclusion from the decision-making process." See *Clarín* (1989).

17. This context was shaped by meetings among prominent businessmen, the presidents of the UIA, SRA, and CGE, and the leadership of the two CGTs concerning an improbable "social pact"; comments by Menem affirming that the new measures were not "a retreat, but a step forward"; tensions between the minister and the Bunge & Born group; and renewed shortages as a result of uncertainty regarding price stabilization.

18. An example of the distribution of power in Argentina is the page-wide headline of *Ambito Financiero,* "Let's Make It Clear: The Country Has Entered The Era Of Market Coups Rather Than The Old Coup D'Etat Made By The Military." In an editorial, this important financial daily explained that it was the market, not the military, as in earlier epochs, that had reduced Alfonsín's mandate. It also claimed that the same thing had happened to Rapanelli in his dispute with Bunge & Born over the devaluation of the currency and the unilateral refinancing of the internal debt. In an original twist on why the market is the best safeguard for democracy, the financial newspaper affirmed that "The unionists and the majority of the politicians do not believe in freedom. At most, they can believe — since it also benefits them — in 'political freedom' and the 'vote at the polls,' but not in 'economic freedom' and the 'vote in the market.' This democratic Argentina doesn't want any more military coups,

but it has adopted a strategy to guard itself against political demagogues" (*Ambito Financiero* 1989).

19. The "revolutionary character" of the measures was sufficient ground for the "Group of Eight" (UIA, SRA, ADEBA, ABRA, the Commodity Exchange, UAC, CAC, Chamber of Construction) — which had suffered an internal crisis during the *Primavera* plan — to close ranks and issue a common endorsement. The SRA was the only business association to express doubts: while approving of the measures, it questioned "the manner in which the internal debt will be handled" (*La Nación*, December 19, 1989, 19).

20. See William C. Smith (1992) for a detailed analysis and reconstruction of the progression of liberalizing measures under Erman González.

21. The package authorized the banks to redeem deposits of less than five hundred dollars, while individuals with larger deposits were given *BONEX* (external bonds in dollars), redeemable in ten years and earning 6 percent annual interest.

22. Given the lukewarm, when not silent, entrepreneurial support for these measures, which affected a large number of firms, the government attempted to justify the plan by drawing upon rather novel "authorities" for the Peronist tradition: presidential advisor (and leader of the right-wing UCeDé) Alvaro Alsogaray expressed his support in a speech broadcast on the national television and radio network. He claimed that the December 18 plan "will mark a milestone between two different epochs" (*La Nación*, January 3, 1990, 1). Terence Todman, the U.S. ambassador to Argentina, praised Menem's courage and suggested that support would lead to economic improvements (*La Nación*, January 10, 1990, 1); while President Bush, in a letter to Menem, pledged to continue to bolster economic reform and to champion the program's success (*La Nación*, January 11, 1990, 1). This support, however, could not stop the reaction of private banks against the Bonex plan, and in this confrontation, the president of the Central Bank was forced to resign.

23. The *Banco Hipotecario* was closed; the posts of 136 secretaries and subsecretaries in the Executive branch were eliminated (to reduce state bureaucratic operating expenses by 25 percent); taxes were increased by 5 percent on exports and 1.5 percent on capital (expected to lead to a $600 million increase in tax receipts); payments to state contractors were suspended for 60 days; public firms were obliged to save the equivalent of 5 percent of their total earnings; and emissions by the Central Bank of new currency to alleviate the fiscal deficit were prohibited. See *La Nación*, March 5, 1990, 1.

24. These privatizations were plagued by inefficiency and charges of corruption. Nevertheless, they allowed the government to achieve the important political objective of sending another strong signal to business that the government was determined to carry through the structural reforms.

25. The plan proposed raising the value-added tax rate to 16 percent for registered tax payers and to 25 percent for those non-registered; to double the tax rate on assets (from 1 to 2 percent) and fix the rate at 4 percent for assets in the service sectors; to raise by 33 percent the tax component in fuel prices; to adjust public service rates in accordance with the new value of the dollar (railroads, mail, and water rates rose 25 percent, gas by 50 percent, and electricity an average 40 percent); to increase the tax on foreign exchange transactions, eliminate specific import rights and replace them with a 22 percent tariff (11 percent for inputs); to privatize the *Caja de Ahorro y Seguro*,

and, in compensation for a probable fall in wages, a 250 thousand *Austral* raise was granted to public-sector workers and a 200 thousand raise to retirees (see *La Nación*, February 4, 1991, 1).

26. Total revenues from privatization from 1990 to the end of 1992 were nearly $18 billion, including $5.9 billion in cash and $12.1 in external debt bonds. See CEDES (1993, 17), based on data from the subsecretariat for privatizations of the ministry of economy.

27. In Argentina this was a significant change. As a result of the ability of large businesses to deduct the updated value of past losses, not one of the hundred largest firms in the country appears in the list of the top one hundred tax payers (see López 1990).

28. Since the beginning of the *cavallazo* (April 1991) to December 1992, monthly tax revenues in constant pesos increased 107 percent. The VAT increased its contribution to total tax revenues from 37.7 percent in 1991 to 55.3 percent in 1992; the share corresponding to income taxes increased from 6.2 percent to 10.7 percent in the same period. Total tax revenues received by the *Dirección General Impositiva* (DGI) fell by 1.1 percent in 1990 before increasing by 42.9 percent and 26.0 percent in 1991 and 1992, respectively. Measured as a percentage of GDP, income taxes represented only 0.7 percent of total revenues in 1990 and 1991 and 1.7 percent in 1992. The VAT represented 3.1 percent of GDP in 1990, 3.2 percent in 1991, and 9.0 percent in the last trimester of 1992. Total fiscal revenues increased from 18.6 percent of GDP in 1990, and 22.2 percent in 1991, to 24 percent in 1992. See IADB (1992) and statements by Carlos Tacchi, secretary of public revenue, in *La Nación*, February 4, 1993.

29. The average tariff had been 37 percent from 1982 to 1988, 17 percent for 1989-90, and 10 percent in 1991. When Cavallo entered office, the maximum tariff of 22 percent applied to 80 percent of the customs items; the remaining items had tariff levels of zero. Cavallo reduced the average tariff to 10 percent with a three-level tariff structure: 5,000 items were set at zero, 2,700 at 11 percent, and 3,800 at 22 percent (*La Nación*, November 9, 1991, 6). In the second half of 1992, owing to the combination of an overvalued exchange rate and lower tariffs on imported goods that competed with local production, the government resorted to the imposition of a "statistical tax" on imports. This artifice allowed the government to maintain the new tariff structure on imports while raising the effective levy on imported goods by 2 to 3 percent.

30. Surprisingly, union representatives in Congress supported these laws — in exchange for the government's absorption of the US$400 million in debt incurred by the union's social welfare services. This clearly indicated the weakening of union power. This debt had been accumulated during the military government.

31. It should be noted that a few, powerful unions, whose social services have been restructured, will be positioned to take advantage of their members' freedom to choose among different alternatives. In these cases, the more powerful unions will not only maintain their affiliates but probably will also absorb some of the members previously belonging to other union's *obras sociales*. Even if this does occur, the application of market-driven criteria to the management of union social services should reduce political manipulation of union funds (Victoria Murillo called to my attention the importance of the relative handful of powerful unions that stand to gain with the current reforms).

32. Manuel Herrera, a high official of the most important entrepreneurial association, the Argentine Industrial Union (UIA), stated recently that the Argentine

economy has only one problem: the fact that "the effective exchange rate for imports and exports does not correspond with the burdens the country imposes upon the productive sector" (*La Nación*, January 25, 1993).

33. The combination of an exchange rate perceived as below its real value with this decline in foreign capital inflow caused a short financial crisis in October. As a first warning about a potentially explosive situation, there was a rush for the dollar that the government solved by selling, for the first time since the inauguration of the plan, approximately US$300 million in a three-day period. Nevertheless, although the government beat the market, it is only rational to expect that once the privatization of state enterprises is completed and most of the related capital inflows stop (toward the end of 1993) the government will face an important dilemma: either to devalue (jeopardizing relative price stability) or try to improve the effective exchange rate (see CEDES 1993, 1).

34. Although the total number employed increased somewhat during this period, the number of persons wanting to work increased even more. Consequently, in May 1993 INDEC's figure for open unemployment in the greater Buenos Aires metropolitan area (the Federal Capital plus the surrounding industrial belt) reached an astonishing (for Argentina) 9.9 percent.

35. The CGT with closer ties to the government organized the first general strike against the Peronist administration's policies in October and organized weekly rallies — many of which turned violent — to pressure the executive and Congress to increase pensions. Similarly, the "educational community" — teachers' and professors' unions, high school and university students, and parents — staged a major rally in defense of public education.

36. On the reasons why economic improvement triggers increasing sociopolitical tensions, see Acuña and Smith (1994a).

37. A direct relationship between economic stability and electoral support seems to hold at the extreme margins: if the situation is extremely chaotic, the electorate probably will not perceive that giving someone else "a shot at it" may increase uncertainty and personal costs; on the other hand, if the situation is extremely satisfactory, why risk a change? Nevertheless, the relationship doesn't behave in this fashion in contexts of "intermediate" levels of either stability or instability, a situation all too common in processes of economic reform and political transition.

38. One could also pay attention to continuities within these changes. An example is the strong oligopolistic ring of firms that "surround" the state as a consequence of the process of privatization of public services. As Adolfo Canitrot argues in his chapter (this volume), the weight that these firms will have in terms of investment and GDP might reproduce a central feature of the old semi-closed, state-centered model of accumulation — namely, a privileged position for a small number of firms whose profits are based on a monopolistic ability to sell nontradeable services to the internal market. Nevertheless, this is coupled with 1) changes from public to private property and in decision making within these firms (which may or may not affect the logic of pricing and investment of a monopoly, depending on the state's ability to impose conditions to firms' behavior); 2) changes in the socioeconomic functions of the state; 3) changes in the system of capital-labor organization and relations; 4) changes in the relationship between the domestic and the international market for the national economy, which amounts to a radical change in the ISI model; and 5) in the set of political changes that have

concomitantly taken place along this process (something we shall pay attention to in the following section). Therefore, I am convinced that despite continuities, the overall result of the ongoing process is a set of swift and radical changes in the global politico-economic structure of Argentina — in other words, a revolution.

39. Once the inner circle began to refer to this latter strategy as the "Nicaraguan" solution — since it was expected to generate high levels of conflict — the impasse between these advisors and the proponents of a debt moratorium and Keynesian policies began to resolve itself. The eventual policy was based on the supposition that international creditors and the local bourgeoisie so distrusted Peronism that no alternatives existed between a "Nicaraguan" strategy and a "capitalist" strategy, which had to be implemented by capitalists capable of eliciting the confidence of their peers.

40. This section is a synthesis of the arguments and conclusions advanced in Acuña and Smulovitz (1991).

41. For a detailed analysis of the emergence and subsequent dismantling of the arms industry and budget cuts, as well as of their consequences, see Acuña and Smith (1994b).

42. This section is based on Acuña (1993 and forthcoming).

43. This support took a number of forms. Business associations, as well as the political parties, repeatedly issued public statements expressing unqualified support for the constitutional government. Association leaders also accompanied legislators in efforts to pressure insurgent units into abdicating. During the December 1988 carapintada uprising in Villa Martelli, business leaders and the CGT decided to paralyze production until the rebellion ceased. Nevertheless, this joint strike by business and labor never went into effect, as the crisis was resolved the day before the strike was to begin.

44. In spite of the Hobbesian character of the Austral Plan, the influence of the "captains of industry" was very significant, and the Primavera Plan was based on an agreement with the UIA and the CAC.

45. Mario Damill and José María Fanelli (1988), for example, concluded in their study of 122 large firms: "the average cumulative annual rate of growth was around 8 percent. This is impressive, given that 90 percent of the firms belong to the industrial sector. During the same period (1979-1985) industrial output declined at an annual rate of 4 percent....In a context of instability and adjustment, the largest economic units were able to avoid paying the costs of the adjustment and to improve their relative positions." Daniel Azpiazu, Eduardo Basualdo, and Miguel Khavisse (1986) demonstrate that 85 percent of the external private debt nationalized during 1982-1983 corresponded to the debt of only 5 percent of all debtors. Those favored represent a highly concentrated group of industrial firms, virtually equivalent to the set of firms studied by Damill and Fanelli. Given their supremacy in a number of industries and the treatment they received under Alfonsín, these firms were cast as "the captains of industry" and are presently playing a central role in the privatization process.

46. Of course, this does not imply a denial of the impact of "external" determinants, such as the debt and price fluctuations of major export commodities, on the context in which economic and political conflicts are played out.

47. This "ideal type" corresponds to Phillpe Schmitter's definition of "neocorporatism" and Adam Przeworski's notion of class compromise as the foundation of democracy (see, among other works, Przeworski 1985 and Schmitter 1974).

References

Acuña, Carlos H. 1991. "La relativa ausencia de exportaciones industriales en la Argentina." *Realidad Económica* 100.

Acuña, Carlos H. 1992a. "Lucha política y organizaciones empresariales de cúpula: Algunos apuntes teóricos con referencias al caso argentino." Paper prepared for the XVII International Congress of the Latin American Studies Association. Los Angeles. September 24-27.

Acuña, Carlos H. 1992b. "Organizaciones empresariales y políticas públicas en la Argentina." In *Organizaciones empresariales y políticas públicas*, ed. Ciesu/Fesur/ICP. Montevideo: FESUR/Ediciones Trilce.

Acuña, Carlos H. 1993. "Política democrática y cambio de modelo de acumulación en la Argentina: Su impacto sobre la organización y comportamiento de los empresarios." Paper prepared for a seminar on "The New Matrix of Argentine Politics," CEDES, Buenos Aires, November 26-27.

Acuña, Carlos H. Forthcoming. "Entrepreneurial Interests, Dictatorship, and Democracy in Argentina: (Or Why the Bourgeoisie Abandons Authoritarian Strategies and Opts for Democratic Stability)." In *Business and Democracy in Latin America,* eds. Ernest Bartell and Leigh Payne. Pittsburgh: University of Pittsburgh Press. (An earlier version of this chapter was presented at the XV Congress of the Latin American Studies Association. Miami, Florida. December 4-6, 1989.)

Acuña, Carlos H., and Laura Golbert. 1990. "Los empresarios y sus organizaciones. Actitudes y reacciones en relación con el plan austral y su interacción con el mercado de trabajo." In *Estabilización y respuesta social*, eds. PREALC-OIT. Santiago: PREALC-OIT.

Acuña, Carlos H., and William C. Smith. 1994a. "The Political Economy of Structural Adjustment: The Logic of Support and Opposition to Neoliberal Reform." In *Latin American Political Economy in the Age of Neoliberal Reform: Theoretical and Comparative Perspectives for the 1990s*, eds. William C. Smith, Carlos H. Acuña, and Eduardo A. Gamarra. New Brunswick: North-South Center/Transaction.

Acuña, Carlos H., and William C. Smith. 1994b. "The Politics of 'Military Economics' in the Southern Cone: Comparative Perspectives on Democratization and Arms Production in Argentina, Brazil and Chile." In *Security, Democracy and Development in United States-Latin American Relations*, eds. Lars Schoultz, William C. Smith, and Augusto Varas. New Brunswick: North-South Center/Transaction.

Acuña, Carlos H., and Catalina Smulovitz. 1991. "¿Ni olvido, Ni perdón? Derechos humanos y tensiones cívico-militares en la transición argentina." *Documento de Trabajo CEDES* 69. Buenos Aires: CEDES.

Acuña, Carlos H., et al. 1988. "La relación estado-empresarios con referencia a políticas concertadas de ingresos. El caso argentino." In *Política económica y actores sociales*, eds. PREALC-OIT. Santiago: PREALC-OIT.

Ambito Financiero. 1989. "Entendamos: El país entró en la era de los golpes de mercado en lugar de los antiguos golpes que hacían los militares." (December 15).

Azpiazu, Daniel, Eduardo Basualdo, and Miguel Khavisse. 1986. *El nuevo poder económico*. Buenos Aires: Legasa.

BCRA (Banco Central de la República Argentina). Various years and quarters. *Estimaciones trimestrales sobre oferta y demanda global*. Buenos Aires: Banco Central de la República Argentina.

Barbeito, Alberto. 1991. "Distribuición de ingresos, pobreza y Estado de bienestar." Documento de Trabajo No. 3, CIEPP. Buenos Aires.

CEDES (Centro de Estudios de Estado y Sociedad). 1993. *Argentina: Informe anual 1992*. Mimeo.

Clarín. 1989. *Suplemento Especial por la muestra "Metalurgia '89* (October 3), 3.

Damill, Mario, and José M. Fanelli. 1988. "Decisiones de cartera y transferencias de riqueza en un período de inestabilidad macroeconómica." *Documento CEDES* No. 12. Buenos Aires: CEDES.

Ferreira Rubio, Delia, and Mateo Goretti. 1993. "The Emergency and the Relationship between the Executive and the Congress during President Menem's Administration in Argentina: Use and Misuse of Prerogative Powers." Working Papers on Comparative Legislative Studies, IPSA, Lawrence University, Appleton, Wisconsin.

Gaudio, Ricardo, and Andrés Thompson. 1990. *Sindicalismo peronista/gobierno radical: Los años de Alfonsín*. Buenos Aires: Fundación Friedrich Ebert/Folios Ediciones.

Hirschman, Albert C. 1970. *Exit, Voice, and Loyalty: Responses to Decline in Firms, Organizations and States*. Cambridge, Mass.: Harvard University Press.

IADB (Inter-American Development Bank). 1992. *Economic and Social Progress in Latin America: 1992 Report*. Baltimore: IADB and Johns Hopkins University Press.

López, Juan. 1990. "Political Determinants of Private Investment in Argentina: Field Work Impressions." Manuscript. University of Chicago.

Mustapic, Ana M., and Mateo Goretti. 1991. "Gobierno y oposición en el congreso: La práctica de la cohabitación durante la presidencia de Alfonsín (1983-1989)." *Serie documentos de trabajo, centro de investigaciones sociales* No. 117. Buenos Aires: Instituto Torcuato Di Tella.

Nación (La). Various dates.

Osteguy, Pierre. 1990. *Los capitanes de la industria*. Buenos Aires: Legasa.

Palermo, Vicente. 1991. "Condicionamientos políticos e institucionales de procesos de reforma económica y estatal: Privatizaciones, reforma tributaria y apertura económica en la Argentina." Mimeo.

Przeworski, Adam. 1985. *Capitalism and Social Democracy*. Cambridge: Cambridge University Press.

Schmitter, Phillipe. 1974. "Still the Century of Corporatism?" *Review of Politics* 36:85-131.

Smith, William C. 1990. "Democracy, Distributional Conflicts, and Macroeconomic Policymaking in Argentina." *Journal of Interamerican Studies and World Affairs* 32, 2 (Summer): 1-42.

Smith, William C. 1992. "Hyperinflation, Macroeconomic Instability and Neoliberal Restructuring in Democratic Argentina." In *The New Democracy in Argentina: The Search for a Successful Formula*, ed. Edward C. Epstein. New York: Praeger.

Torre, Juan C. 1990. "El gobierno de la emergencia económica en la transición democrática argentina." Unpublished manuscript.

Torre, Juan C. 1991. "En torno de los condicionantes políticos e institucionales de los programas de reforma económica." Paper presented at the Workshop on Methods of Comparative Analysis of Public Policy Reforms. Santiago, Chile. May.

Chapter Three

Crisis and Transformation of the Argentine State (1978-1992)

Adolfo Canitrot

Introduction: The Nature of the Crisis

The basic thesis of this chapter is that the Argentine state itself is a root cause of the crisis of the 1980s. Ideologically conceived as the leader in the process of social and economic transformation, the state, in fact, rarely gained enough autonomy from political forces to be perceived as more than an instrument of power or a prize for the winners of recurrent political struggles. This perception was closely related to traditional authoritarian practices and to the scant legitimacy given to the law and to constitutional rights.

The main contestants in the political struggle were Peronism and the armed forces. Peronists governed Argentina from 1945 to 1955 and from 1973 to 1976. The military carried out five *coups d'état* between 1943 and 1976 and were in power 23 years out of 40. The rivals shared a nationalistic and Catholic ideology and declared themselves strongly anti-Marxist. When in power, the military typically allied itself with liberals espousing right-wing economics and usually was backed by the entrepreneurial sector. Peronism received the support of the working and lower-middle classes and won all electoral contests between 1946 and 1983. Given their success in the electoral arena, the Peronists favored democratic elections, though they never made particularly fair use of them within their own party.

Economic policy was largely subordinated to political struggle. The best example of such subordination was the end in 1969 of the successful economic experiment of Adalberto Krieger Vasena, a liberal minister of the economy in the administration of General Juan Carlos Onganía. Krieger Vasena implemented an economic program that lowered the inflation rate to levels of the developed world, balanced fiscal accounts, boosted investment to unprecedented heights, while also moderately increasing real wages. Notwithstanding these results, Krieger Vasena was ousted by a popular uprising known as the *cordobazo*, whose root cause was the mounting reaction against the exclusion of Peronism from electoral contests since 1955.

The crisis may be presented also in fiscal terms as the result of increasing demands on the state, coupled with a reduction in financial resources to meet them. The consequence of that imbalance was overall instability, extended uncertainty, and the loss of efficiency of public services.[1]

The Outbreak of the Crisis

In April 1981, the first president of Argentina's military regime, General Jorge Rafael Videla, ended his term and transferred the government to General Roberto Viola. This transfer was not mere formality. Also retiring from the government was Minister of the Economy José A. Martínez de Hoz, responsible for a program of economic stabilization and liberalization initiated at the end of 1978. That program had failed in its main objective of lowering inflation and had left behind a huge external debt.

The first decision of the new minister, Lorenzo Sigaut, was to devalue the domestic currency in order to correct an overvaluation. This was followed by a series of further devaluations that continued until the third quarter of 1982. The outcome was a depreciation of the Argentine peso by more than 100 percent in real terms.[2] It was achieved at the price of complete economic disorder: monthly inflation rose to 20 percent; the fiscal deficit climbed to 16 percent of the GNP, and real wages fell, the level of activity receded, investment faded, and savings fled Argentina. This was later named "the wild adjustment" process.

General Viola was forced to resign in December 1981. Four months later in April 1982, the new president, General Leopoldo Galtieri, invaded Las Malvinas (the Falkland Islands) and started an armed conflict from which Argentina would emerge defeated in June. That defeat prompted Galtieri's resignation, and the new head of the government, General Reynaldo Bignone, was faced with no other political solution than to call general elections with the declared purpose of returning the country to civilian rule. Thus, it was the complete failure of the military regime that brought democracy back to Argentina.

The Mexican debt crisis in August 1982 prompted American and European creditor banks to halt lending to all Latin American countries. Short on foreign reserves, the Argentine government nationalized the private external debt and began to negotiate its refinancing. As an immediate answer to that crisis, money holdings in the domestic financial market fell by half.

This series of events, lasting a year and a half, marks what is known as the "explosion of the crisis." From late 1982 on, the Argentine economy experienced high instability, huge fiscal deficits, reduction of the money supply to a bare minimum, and the general deterioration of government capacities. Less recognized are the effects on the military itself: the armed forces lost the political prominence they had enjoyed since the early days of the independence wars at the beginning of the nineteenth century.

From Isolation to Crisis
The Autonomous Development Project

In response to fear of further international trade protectionism following the end of World War II, the military formulated Argentina's first strategy of autonomous industrial development. Development was conceived initially as a means to overcome the difficulties undergone during the war from lack of equipment and military technology. This inspirational model — like the military's authoritarian ideology — was derived from the industrialization experience of nineteenth-century Germany, based on large industrial hold-ings closely allied to the state. At the instigation of Colonel Manuel Savio, the director of *Fabricaciones Militares*, the iron and steel industry was placed under military jurisdiction. In the ensuing years, this creative impulse generated a significant number of nascent state enterprises encompassing a wide spectrum of activities.

The armed forces, following a tradition that began with independence from Spain, considered themselves the final arbiters of the nation's future. Industrial development planning in that perspective was simply patriotic duty. They never thought of themselves as encroaching upon civilian territory; theirs was the task of opening up new markets and new activities and of not intruding where these had already been established.[3] The main reason for failure of the military's project was a weakness in the hierarchical political framework needed to accelerate the pace of capital accumulation. The presence of Peronism as a successful channel of popular demands made this impossible.

What remained of the military's original project was a mix of contradic-tory orientations. On the one hand, big state enterprises multiplied; on the other, macroeconomic policy followed a populist pattern: higher wages and fiscal deficit fostered domestic demand, with protection necessary to keep wages high and to limit the negative effects on external accounts of peso appreciation and overheating of economic activity. The rate of inflation fluctuated around 30 percent a year, thus making possible a negative interest rate in real terms that was highly conducive to investment in housing and small enterprises. The negative interest rate financed the huge urban expansion of the 1960s (Díaz Alejandro 1970; Mallon and Sourrouille 1973).

The result was an ensemble of big state enterprises providing public services and basic industrial inputs like steel, oil, chemicals, paper, along with an extensive sector of light industry with limited capacities for capital accumulation. In the 1960s, Arturo Frondizi's government launched a program of industrial integration, with active intervention by multinationals and the state, which deepened the density of the private sector, most notably in the automobile industry. However, none of these sectors, public or private, was able to expand beyond national borders until the middle of the 1970s.[4]

Confined within the limits of the state and isolated from dynamic impulses emanating from the private sector, public enterprises shrunk over time like the rest of the public sector. With initial impetus lost and subjected to fiscal restrictions and regulations, state companies became bureaucratized. By the end of the 1970s, they were colonized by their labor unions and private contractors.

Dollarization of Private Savings

Up to the 1960s, the rate of interest in real terms was usually negative. The annual rate of inflation fluctuated around 30 percent, but the nominal rate of interest, regulated by the monetary authority, rarely climbed as high. The Central Bank provided a regular flow of funds to commercial banks that kept their accounts in equilibrium. Householders and small firms usually performed as lenders and borrowers on both sides of the financial market. What they lost in depositors, the banks recovered in borrowers.

Things began to change in the early 1970s, with the escalation of violence in the political struggle. Growing uncertainty coincided with the emergence of the dollar as an alternative financial asset available to common people. People chose the dollar as a guarantee against the uncertainty of future inflation because of the dollar's advantages for securing the real value of savings, for its liquidity, and for the simplicity of its use in relation to other financial assets.

The consequence of dollarization was the reduction of the quantity of money relative to the GNP. Maturity terms shortened and credit to the private and public sectors tightened considerably. Deprived of its source of subsidized financing, the entire postwar economic model began to crumble. The immediate effect of dollarization was to increase private demand for subsidized credit to the public sector. Tax exemptions, designed for large projects at the end of the 1950s, were generalized through extended systems of sectoral and regional promotion. Most of the subsidies, however, went to a small number of firms closely related to government activities. State contractors became the new bourgeoisie that displaced multinationals from the top-rank positions they held in the 1960s.

With reduced tax collections and limited financing, fiscal expenditures became increasingly unbearable. Awareness of a fiscal crisis, underlined by the brief hyperinflationary explosion of 1975-1976, led to a policy of fiscal austerity during the first three years of military government (1976-1978). But as of 1978, foreign credit was resurrected in unlimited supply, and all barriers restricting fiscal spending broke down. The military resumed its perennial fantasies of nation-building by the state and launched a series of grand projects — nuclear plants, production of heavy water, construction of submarines and missiles, new heavy-industry factories, large dams and highways — whose completion would require at least a decade. As it turned out, economic crisis intervened. When external credit was abruptly cut off in 1982, the state collapsed.

The Foreign Debt

At the end of 1978, Economy Minister Martínez de Hoz adopted a stabilization program that replaced the existing program based on monetary and fiscal restrictions. The alleged reason for that change was that the ready availability of cheap foreign credit made it impossible to control the money supply: any restriction of domestic credit was bound to attract capital from abroad and, thus, to stimulate demand. Behind that reason there was a less confessable one: fiscal expenditures by the military could not be controlled. The new approach sought to set aside the fiscal question as long as foreign credit was forthcoming. Open-economy macrotheory taught that, under conditions of certainty, fiscal expenditures will always attract the money to finance them.[5]

The key variable was the exchange rate. By fixing this rate in nominal terms, tradable goods prices were fixed as well. The strategy was less clear in relation to non-tradable goods, but a common-sense assumption was that their price could not increase beyond an upper limit as long as the prices of tradable goods remained fixed. Regardless, the spectrum of tradable goods was extended by liberalizing imports of foreign goods to the domestic market and reducing tariffs.[6]

Once in practice, and in contrast to earlier policies, the new stabilization program induced the expansion of domestic demand. Activity levels, real wages, and fiscal revenues grew, and the inflow of foreign credit accelerated. Greatly contrary to expectations, prices of non-tradable goods continued to rise without any sign of convergence at an upper limit. Inflation declined somewhat, although at such a slow pace that growing appreciation of the domestic currency could not be avoided.

By mid-1980, public confidence in the program began to erode. Anticipation of a future currency devaluation gave strength to the demand for dollars. Reserves of foreign money at the Central Bank decreased. In a effort to sustain the program, and without any policy alternative capable of avoiding catastrophe, the military government took on additional foreign debt in order to satisfy growing demand. The final explosion came in the first quarter of

1981, when the government headed by General Viola announced its intention to abandon the program and to carry out a devaluation.[7]

The 1980s: From Adjustment to Hyperinflation
"Statization" of the Foreign Debt

The chain of devaluations that began in April 1981 was intended to achieve an external trade surplus high enough to supply the financial resources needed to service the foreign debt. In practice, exports did not respond to price incentives at the required speed, and it was necessary to resort to import prohibitions in July 1982.[8]

Devaluations were decided formally by the government, but, in fact, they could not be avoided if fiscal accounts, overloaded with debt interest, were cut off from foreign financing. Printing money was the only means available to finance the fiscal deficit, but this policy, compounded by the fall in demand for pesos due to heightened uncertainty, resulted in excessive expansion of the money supply. This generated excessive demand for dollars and growing pressure for an exchange-rate devaluation. In short, devaluations were by-products of capital outflows, but the external current-account surplus did not help to service the debt. This surplus went to private accounts abroad, while the government, unable to raise resources by means of taxation or domestic borrowing, saw its foreign currency reserves decline precipitously, finally forcing a suspension in interest payments on the external debt.

Exchange depreciation also had the effect of increasing the value of the foreign debt as measured in domestic currency. For a year and a half, the government, in desperate need of foreign reserves, induced private debtors to refinance their debt by granting them subsidies and by guaranteeing external loans against the risk of future currency devaluations. When foreign credit was cut, in August 1982, the private debt was nationalized: the Central Bank assumed the private dollar debt and became the creditor of local debtor firms in domestic currency. The next step was to extend the maturity terms of that debt and to deal with the resulting imbalance of the financial system by means of loans from the Central Bank. In the third quarter of 1982, the flow of rediscounts given to commercial banks mounted to 450 percent of the monetary base. A leap in inflation followed, wiping out much of the private sector's debt. In real terms, the monetary stock was cut in half.

This huge transfer of wealth rescued many enterprises from bankruptcy. But it was a gift to others, who, by having foreign liabilities backed by foreign assets, got rid of the former while keeping the latter. The effect was to place the private sector in a net creditor position, leaving the government as the sole debtor without means of domestic financing.

The Economic Policy of the New Civilian Government[9]

As the only alternative to a popular insurrection following defeat in the Malvinas, the military called for elections to reinstate a constitutional regime. The extreme cruelty of the "dirty war," the subsequent failure of the stabilization program, the surging foreign debt, and the defeat in the Falklands removed any possibility for negotiated transition between the military and political parties.

In this polarized context, politicians, following public opinion and the mass media, rejected everything done by the military regime. The illegitimacy of repression was extended to the illegitimacy of the external debt. The failure of the stabilization program was seen as a proof of its intrinsic perversity at the service of the powerful. Peronists and Radicals, the two majority parties, took up their old "national and popular" banners and the practices of popular mobilization.

The Radical party, led by Raúl Alfonsín, emphasized democracy, human rights, and the return to the Constitution. Alfonsín coined the magic phrase "with democracy you eat, you get educated, and you get cured." Two related theses were implied in this discourse: first, that the economic crisis stemmed from the moral perversity of the authoritarian regime; and, second, that democracy would be sufficient to overcome the economic crisis. In other words, the crisis was recognized but its economic content denied. Economic policy had no firm underpinning and was conceived of only as a set of rules and technologies serving political decisions.

This view of economic policy was reflected in the initial economic program of Alfonsín's government. Bernardo Grinspun, the new minister of the economy, applied a program designed to balance fiscal accounts. It was based on austerity, honesty, and the reduction of military expenditures. Inflation was to be controlled by means of a general agreement on wages and prices. Economic expansion and income distribution were to be the result of a joint policy of higher wages and lower interest rates. The foreign debt was declared illegitimate. Alfonsín tried to implement an imminently political solution to the debt crisis by promoting a unified political response by all indebted Latin American countries via the "Cartagena Consensus" and by seeking the support of friendly European governments.

These policy approaches failed. The fiscal deficit declined, but the agreement on prices and wages did not materialize. For several months, economic activity expanded and real wages grew, but inflation accelerated month after month and finally ran out of control. Grinspun resigned in February 1985. Simultaneously, the strong negative reaction by the U.S. government to the proposed political solution based upon Latin American solidarity, and its reiteration that the debt was strictly an economic problem to be solved case by case, left Alfonsín without alternatives. With his position weakened by growing inflation, Alfonsín was forced to accept U.S. terms after September 1984.

The Austral Plan: "Democracy plus Stability"

This initial experience taught the Alfonsín government that price stability was an absolute priority and that no promise of growth or income distribution would be taken seriously as long as inflation continued at high monthly rates. That experience also showed the government that economic reality had to be taken into account and that a stabilization program required a more solid base than a simple appeal for an agreement on prices and wages. A further lesson was that money holders, fearing uncertainty, would continue to send their capital abroad unless some kind of understanding was reached with the International Monetary Fund (IMF) and the creditor banks. Since a first condition for carrying out a stabilization program was to staunch capital flight, the government was forced to give up its initial pretensions of implementing an independent economic policy.

The Austral Plan was designed as an urgent response to an inflationary phenomenon whose pace was gathering steam month after month. Because that acceleration was perceived as the main threat to recently established democratic institutions, the new minister of the economy, Juan V. Sourrouille, focused his attention on inflationary inertia and adopted a price freeze as the core of his stabilization policy. A new currency, the *austral*, substituted the old peso and gave the program its name.[10]

During its successful phase, the Austral Plan achieved stability and established, without recession or other major costs, a stable structure of relative prices that seemed to extend the democratic creed to the sphere of economic relations. By guaranteeing the legitimate economic interest of each citizen, price stability crowned the constitutional architecture of individual rights. The magic formula was now "Democracy plus Stability."

One can readily comprehend why the government, and the middle classes supporting it, thought that the "essential has been done" and that economic growth and social justice was assured as long as the leadership of the president and the confidence in the technical capacities of the economic team were preserved.

The Agreement with the United States

The first reaction of the U.S. government was to see the debt crisis as a private affair between creditor banks and debtor governments. It was assumed that debtor economies could correct, almost automatically, their foreign current account deficit by means of a devaluation of their currencies. The resulting change in relative prices was assumed to continue until reaching an equilibrium point where the trade account surplus would match the interest payment due on the foreign debt. The implicit condition was that fiscal accounts were to be balanced along the entire movement of relative prices.

But devaluation was not neutral with respect to fiscal accounts. Relative price changes had inflationary effects that damaged fiscal revenues in real terms. Real depreciation exacerbated the debt burden in dollars and, consequently, increased fiscal expenditures. The large imbalances that resulted had the effect of destabilizing most debtor economies and, in addition, of lessening debtor government capacity to service the debt. It then became clear to creditor banks that restoring debtor countries' capacity to service the debt was essential to securing future interest payments. As usually happens, creditors were forced to help debtors, by becoming involved in the debtor's domestic affairs.

The Argentine military in its final hour was not to be counted on for any lasting agreement, compelling the United States to wait for the transfer to civilian government. Once in place, and after a delay of several months due to the Alfonsín government's unsuccessful insistence on a political solution for the debt problem, a first debt agreement was signed in September 1984. That agreement opened the door for a second agreement in June 1985, signed at the launching of the Austral Plan. The Austral Plan benefitted from the support given to Alfonsín's economic team by highly ranked officials in the U.S. government. The new plan was bolstered by the refinancing of the current external debt in exchange for the payment of debt arrears. Implicit in those agreements was the U.S. government's commitment to give full political support to Argentina's new democracy.

Peronists reacted negatively to this substantial change of policy on the foreign debt, while many Radicals also remained dubious. Opposition was initially subdued by the enthusiastic public reception of the Austral Plan. But resistance to the new plan was later manifested in the public enterprises and state banks, which — though controlled by members of the government party — carried out policies of wage hikes and increased expenditures in opposition to the stabilization program. Some members of the Radical party even joined the Peronists in demanding the end of the stabilization program and its substitution by a growth policy.

The U.S. government upheld its commitment to the defense of democracy by dissuading the military and its potential allies from taking action against the Alfonsín government. U.S. authorities also gave good-faith support to the stabilization program. But in 1986, due to its own budgetary problems, the U.S. government released part of its grain stock, which thereby provoked a fall in international prices that severely damaged Argentina's exports and fiscal accounts.

Relative Prices and Exchange Appreciation

Inflation fell immediately after the Austral Plan's price freeze: monthly inflation of retail prices in the three quarters that followed was less than 1 percent, while wholesale prices rose at 3 percent a month in the same period. This result, plus economic reactivation, gave the Austral Plan wide popularity. But the gap between retail and wholesale prices over the medium term soon yielded a significant change in the structure of relative prices. Wholesale prices represented mainly tradable-goods prices that were pegged to the exchange rate, while retail prices represented a larger share of prices of non-tradable goods and services. The gap between wholesale and retail prices resulted from a process of appreciation of domestic goods relative to foreign ones or, in other words, of overvaluation of the domestic currency.

Indexation practices linked to the Consumer Price Index (CPI) provoked wage increases in tandem with rising retail prices. Wage increases were initially absorbed by firms through the productivity gains brought about by price stability and expansion of production and sales, but eventually wage increases encroached on profit margins. Firms selling tradable goods were especially affected. By the end of March 1986, the real exchange rate, measured against a combination of the wholesale and the consumer price indexes, had appreciated by 17 percent since June 1985.

Given the fate of the prior stabilization program in the early 1980s, overvaluation of the currency was considered the worst evil. The government knew that a further move in that direction would erode public confidence and lead to the Austral Plan's failure. Moreover, the IMF maintained that appreciation of the exchange rate contradicted the agreed-upon objective of increasing the trade surplus. Consequently, the price freeze was called off in April 1986, to be replaced by a system of price guidelines, including the exchange rate, loosely adjusted to current inflation. This new price regime checked the trend toward overvaluation (although it did not reverse it) and generally kept relative prices constant, although this had an inflationary cost (above 5 percent a month) that could not be ignored. The first consequence of this higher plateau of inflation was to reduce fiscal revenues by 2 percentage points of the GNP (Olivera-Tanzi effect on lagged fiscal revenues).

Fiscal Disequilibrium and the Reform of the State

The criticism most frequently leveled at the Alfonsín administration in political, business, and academic circles was that it did not take advantage of the opportunity offered by the success of the Austral Plan to undertake a thorough-going reform of the state. That criticism usually came from the liberal-conservative right wing of the political spectrum and pointed to the apparent lack of a strong will on the part of the government to privatize public enterprises and reduce the fiscal deficit.

A clear definition of what is meant by state reform is essential. Alfonsín's ideas on state reform were directly related to his democratic creed. Alfonsín saw himself as a reformer when he restored the Supreme Court to its former dignity and independence, or when he made it a point of principle not to intervene in the affairs of provincial governments. His initiatives — such as the settlement of the long-standing border conflict with Chile and the proposed reform of the Constitution to introduce a parliamentary system and the plans for a new site for the federal capital — all demonstrate that Alfonsín's reformist intentions were limited to political and institutional arenas.

Alfonsín, his political entourage, and most of the Radical party lacked the ideology needed for the economic reform of the state. They rejected the Thatcherian model without having an alternative to it. Even at the end of his government, when Alfonsín sent Congress a proposal for privatization of the airline and telephone state companies and favored other public-sector reforms, he seemed to act more out of political necessity than true conviction. Apparently uncommitted, Alfonsín relied on the technical capacities of his economic team to administer the state crisis without solving it.

But reform was necessary. The lack of any reliable domestic financing after the statization of the foreign debt in 1982 forced the public sector to observe a strict rule of fiscal equilibrium. When Alfonsín assumed the presidency in late 1983, the fiscal deficit had reached 16 percent of the GNP. Grinspun brought the deficit down to 9 percent of GNP, and Sourrouille further reduced it to almost 1 percent in 1986. But this achievement proved transient because it had only been achieved by means of emergency measures enacted at the beginning of the Austral Plan that could not be sustained over time.

Aware of the fleeting nature of this achievement, the government persuaded Congress to approve a project of tax reform designed to institutionalize the emergency measures. But this reform failed to produce the required fiscal revenues, thus dealing a fatal blow to the Austral Plan.[11] After that failure, and in spite of the administrative efforts made, fiscal revenues declined and continued to fall until the end of 1990. Though fiscal expenditures were reduced year after year, the fiscal deficit climbed back up to 8 percent of GNP in 1988, while the monthly inflation rate averaged more than 10 percent (with a tendency toward gradual acceleration) from the second quarter of 1987 through the first half of 1988.

Unable to maintain the level of fiscal revenues achieved at the beginning of the Austral Plan, policy makers wavered between fulfilling the government's current obligations, which required increased spending, and attempting to reduce the fiscal deficit further. They fell short on both counts. Public discontent with rising inflation and poor government services led to the Radical party's defeat in the September 1987 congressional elections. Lack of foreign reserves, partly due to the fall of world export prices in 1987 and partly to growing uncertainty, forced the suspension of foreign debt payments in April 1988.[12]

Hyperinflation

Launched in August 1988 was the *Plan Primavera* (Spring Plan), the last of the stabilization programs of the Radical government. Recognizing its political weakness, the government's objective with this plan was quite modest; it was basically limited to avoiding hyperinflation before the presidential elections scheduled for May 1989. As usual, the program enjoyed an initial phase of declining inflation until December 1988. But to the surprise of Central Bank authorities, assets in the financial system accumulated to a level never witnessed since the Austral Plan's initial success. The trouble, however, was that the average maturity of these assets was less than seven days.

The Peronist candidate for the presidency, Carlos Menem, held a strong lead in public opinion polls based upon shrewd manipulation of a nationalist-populist discourse, including promises of a moratorium on the foreign debt, recovering the Malvinas by "blood and fire," a maxi-devaluation and a big wage increase. Menem's platform made it was obvious that, unless his lead in the polls could be reversed, there would soon come a point at which money holders would convert their assets into dollars, probably more in a stampede than in an orderly retreat from the peso. That moment came when the U.S. government decided to discontinue its support for the Alfonsín government's economic policies until after elections were held.

Facing a demand for dollars that would have rapidly exhausted its reserves, the Central Bank suspended sales on February 6, 1989. The price of the dollar exploded, and inflation soon followed. The exchange-rate price of the dollar rose from 14.7 australes in February to 650 australes in July; monthly inflation between February and August 1989 averaged 87 percent. This leap into hyperinflation lasted until July 1989, when Alfonsín resigned and Menem assumed the presidency. The Central Bank's exhausted foreign currency reserves were replenished in just a few days. Some referred to this hyperinflationary episode and its denouement as a "market coup d'état."

Menem, Cavallo, and the Convertibility Plan
The Reform of the State as a Political Program

The May 1989 presidential elections, occurring at the peak of hyperinflation, gave an easy victory to the Peronist candidate Carlos Menem. The hyperinflationary process that destroyed Alfonsín's government led Menem to conclude that runaway inflation could not be halted unless the government obtained the support of the local "establishment" and the approval of the U.S. government. Peronism secured Menem's popular base, but Peronism's nationalistic and populist traditions were clearly unsuited to the task at hand.

Aware of this, Menem emphasized his conversion to economic liberalism. Once elected, he made known his intention to initiate a program of market deregulation and privatization of state enterprises. To this announcement Menem added two political gestures: he named Alvaro Alsogaray, historically a political advocate of economic liberalism, as his personal adviser, and he appointed the president of Bunge & Born, a huge conglomerate enterprise with origins in traditional cereal exports, as minister of the economy.[13] To demonstrate his reformist zeal, Menem also moved immediately to secure approval of a so-called Law of Economic Emergency giving the executive branch full powers to modify legislation without the intervention of Congress.

This initial conversion to neoliberalism made some people suspect Menem of political opportunism. But the president remained faithful to making state reform and the liberalization of markets the centerpieces of his government. In fact, Menem's policy objectives could not have contrasted more with Alfonsín's, who six years before had made the strengthening of civil liberties and republican institutions his highest priorities. By 1989 democracy seemed consolidated, but the erosion of governmental capacities, dramatically underlined by hyperinflation, had become the main source of public discontent. The shift from concern with institutional questions under Alfonsín, to Menem's focus on economic issues reversed policy priorities. Economic policy was no longer perceived as the potential source of trouble to the political program, as it was in Alfonsín years; rather, economics moved to center stage and became the best argument available to defend the Menem administration against the objections leveled against it on ethical and institutional grounds.

Stabilization Programs and the Convertibility Plan

Menem learned from the Austral Plan and the ensuing hyperinflation that stability was absolutely required for the successful implementation of any economic policy. When his initial stabilization program, the so-called "B.B. Plan," failed and led to a second hyperinflationary outbreak in the first quarter of 1990, Menem also learned that even the most powerful political alliances were insufficient guarantees against the evils of inflation. The B.B. team resigned in December 1990.

Behind the B.B. Plan's failure were the same problems that subverted the Spring Plan in early 1989: the accumulation of short-term assets in the banks financing the current fiscal deficit and growing overvaluation of the domestic currency. This second round of hyperinflation was less acute than the first; it lasted three-and-a-half months with monthly price hikes averaging 67 percent. In the first hyperinflationary round of 1989, domestic prices and wages lagged behind the exchange rate to yield a real depreciation of the domestic currency and a fall in real wages. But in this second round of hyperinflation, prices and wages kept pace with the dollar; there was no change in relative prices and no appreciation of the real exchange rate.

By January 1990, cornered in a situation requiring extreme decisions, the government extended the maturity of the public debt to nine years, with dollar-denominated, long-term bonds (BONEX) being substituted for current-time deposits (a rediscount provided by the Central Bank to allow banks to restore their balances) in the banking system. This policy enabled the new minister of the economy, Antonio Erman González, to initiate a highly restrictive monetary policy in March 1990 that ended hyperinflation that very month. Monetary restriction was made possible because a free-floating exchange regime had been adopted previously and government payments were strictly reduced to the level of fiscal revenues.

While the emergency policy lowered inflation to less than 10 percent a month after October 1991 and greatly increased foreign reserves, it was maintained too long. Monetary restriction led to excess demand for money, which led to a large overvaluation of the domestic currency. When fiscal payments could no longer be postponed and the fiscal deficit climbed again, the explosion was inevitable. This third round of hyperinflation was less severe than the preceding ones: it lasted two months, with monthly inflation reaching 28 percent and the dollar rising 75 percent in nominal terms. Strong recession helped to translate most of this nominal devaluation into real terms. Erman González resigned and was moved to the ministry of defense.

Erman's resignation, however, was but one aspect of a larger political crisis touched off by the U.S. embassy's denunciation of requests for bribes made to an American company by high-level government officials. Domingo Cavallo, minister of foreign relations at the time, considered fully reliable by the U.S. government, was very active in finding a solution. Menem gave new proof of his political reflexes by offering Cavallo the position of economy minister.

Given the precarious political position of the Argentine government, Cavallo had very limited options when he took charge of the ministry. He worried that a new devaluation would lead to a general price increase. Thus, he had to accept the existing exchange rate and postpone policies to hasten economic recovery. Cavallo imposed a nominally fixed exchange rate of one peso to the dollar and had this parity made into law by congressional approval.

The so-called "Law of Convertibility" requires the monetary base to be backed fully by an equivalent amount of foreign reserves in the Central Bank. This requirement prohibits the use of reserves for any other uses, foreign debt payments included. If the treasury needs dollars, it must buy them with its own supply of local currency, just like a private citizen. As in the past, the nominally fixed exchange rate acts as an anchor for domestic prices. In order to expand the number of goods whose price is pegged to the exchange rate, imports were liberalized with tariffs set at 22 percent, 13 percent, and 5 percent.

Results were highly positive. Inflation fell, economic activity picked up, and external capital flowed in. Redressing initial pessimistic expectations, the government won midterm elections in the third quarter of 1991. Average monthly inflation fell from 5.2 percent in 1991 to 1.3 percent in 1992. When measured by the consumer price index (CPI), whole prices fell from 3.8 percent to 0.2 percent over the same period.

The CPI, however, was still too high, given that the exchange rate was fixed in nominal terms. The result was an increasingly overvalued domestic currency (by more than 30 percent in the first year of the new plan). Argentina became an expensive country. Wages and the prices of non-tradable goods and services rose compared to foreign goods and services, and local firms lost competitiveness in domestic and foreign markets. The expansion of domestic demand and the opening of the economy to foreign supply encouraged imports (which increased by more than 100 percent) and led to a $2.5 billion deficit in the trade account, the first such deficit recorded since 1981.

The trade deficit, added to foreign debt payments in the service account, compounded a current external deficit that previously had been compensated for by capital inflows. Foreign reserves increased. Convertibility insured a positive relationship between the current account deficit and capital flows: the larger the inflow of foreign capital, the higher the deficit in the current account and vice versa. Reversing the sequence would mean that outflows of capital would erode foreign currency reserves and cause the money supply to contract. Contraction would then lower the level of economic activity until the current account became positive once again.

Still, capital flows move faster than commercial flows. This poses no problems when the economy is expanding: differences in the velocity and amount of capital flows and commercial flows will be reflected in the accumulation of foreign reserves and growth of the money supply. But when recession hits, the financial system may react too slowly to accommodate outstanding loans to declining deposits. Since the rules of convertibility do not allow the Central Bank to intervene, every initial disequilibrium may potentially become a financial crisis and a source of acceleration of capital outflows. The still unanswered question is whether or not an orderly recession is feasible.

Cavallo believes that the risk of a reversal of capital flows is minor as long as the economic policy remains faithful to the original design. Consequently, Cavallo and his economic team repeatedly assure that the exchange rate will remain unchanged. Cavallo's bet is that he will be able to bring down inflation to First World levels during 1993 and then be able to reverse the process of currency overvaluation. In order to achieve this goal, he needs to slow the pace of economic expansion. Since use of monetary instruments is not an option (the convertibility scheme makes the money supply an endogenous variable), the only policy left to Cavallo is a restrictive fiscal policy.

Tax Policy

By matching the monetary base with the stock of foreign reserves at the Central Bank, the Convertibility Plan strictly excludes the possibility of domestic credit creation, although a limited issuance of long-term bonds is possible. This constraint compels the treasury to keep fiscal accounts in permanent short-term equilibrium, a condition which has been satisfied by supplementing current revenues with the proceeds of the privatization of public enterprises. This process cannot continue, however, because the bulk of privatizations has already been completed.

The government has achieved a substantial increase in tax revenues by means of tax reform with an important reduction in tax evasion.[14] Notwithstanding these efforts, the two main sources of higher revenues following the launching of the Convertibility Plan have been lower inflation and expanded economic activity. During the first stage of the stabilization plan, lower inflation was positively associated with the expansion of domestic demand. Subsequently, however, any further reduction in the inflation rate requires a brake on economic expansion, which raises the question of the feasibility of maintaining government revenues at their current high levels.

The correct textbook answer is to cut fiscal expenditures, which is what the IMF recommends. Yet the growing demand for improvements in public education and public health, the increasing deficit of the retirement system, the scheduled increase in foreign debt payments in coming years, and the resistance on the part of provincial governments to reducing their budgets, all represent serious political and economic obstacles militating against fiscal restraint.

Privatization

The political benefits of the privatization program have been mentioned already. Other advantages are the following: 1) by promoting a threefold increase in the market value of Argentine debt bonds, privatization helped earn the good will of creditor banks and helped achieve a transitory reduction of interest payments until the admissions requirements for the Brady Plan could be met; 2) the sale of public assets contributes to fiscal equilibrium in the transition period of two or three years (according to official calculations) before fiscal revenues rise to match expenditures; and 3) complaints from the business community regarding exchange-rate policy have been muffled by the prospective bargains offered in the sale of public assets.

Long-run benefits are more substantial. First, privatization may be conducive to reinvigorating investment in basic infrastructure and to improving the quality of public services. This argument acknowledges the experience of the last ten years: public enterprises shrank in part because of their own shortcomings, but this has primarily been due to fiscal constraints resulting from the heavy burden of external debt payments and to the lack of financing. That will not change in the next few years, but investment and improvement of public services cannot wait. This is the negative side of the argument. On the positive side, the argument for privatization assumes, or rather hopes, that the newly created private enterprises will commit themselves as investors in major projects with long maturities, projects that usually are related to public works. Whether this will happen remains to be seen. (It has not happened in Argentina since the British built the railways in the nineteenth century.)

Privatization is more than economics and politics, however. The Argentine program is an all-out effort targeted to eradicate public enterprises completely. Privatization is driven by an ideological credo bent on the destruction of the core of the corporatist system that was built gradually in Argentina since the end of the First World War. In this context, it is important to note that a central feature of the privatization process has been the extent to which ownership and control have been concentrated in the hands of not more than ten large domestic conglomerates. These economic groups have been able to carve out a dominant position in the newly privatized enterprises. Among foreigners, Italians, Spaniards, and Chileans garnered the largest share of the privatized firms.

Toward a Market Economy?

The 1982 debt crisis triggered a process of transformation of the Argentine economic system that would not have taken place otherwise. This transformation has followed its own dynamic but has been closely monitored from Washington, D.C., by the joint action of the IMF, the World Bank, and the U.S. treasury. From 1983 to 1989, economic policy was conditioned by the new civilian government's commitment to the reconstruction of the institutions of representative democracy. No significant attempt was made by the Alfonsín government to introduce reforms in the economic structure of the state.

Hyperinflation in 1989 was a crucial event on the road to transformation. Analyzed as a purely economic phenomenon, hyperinflation was the consequence of the persistence of a fiscal deficit that could not be financed except on the basis of speculative time deposits in the banking system. That problem had a technical solution: to balance fiscal accounts. But the answer came in political terms: hyperinflation was presented as the evidence of the irreparable failure of the state-centered economy — a failure that could only be overcome by freeing private initiative from state intervention and by reducing the size of the government sector to its bare minimum. Privatization of public enterprises was seen as the immediate answer. Conscious of the strength of this claim, the government headed by Carlos Menem adopted the neoliberal credo and espoused the "Washington Consensus" as its fundamental policy principle. The Menem government advanced in this new direction to the point of defining as its objective the complete disappearance of state enterprises.

But the fiscal deficit persisted and was the source of two new spurts of hyperinflation at the beginning of 1990 and 1991. Cavallo's Convertibility Plan, launched in March 1991, saw stability as an economic necessity, but it also recognized that stability was a political requirement for securing public acceptance for the proposed project of state reform. Conversely, privatization facilitated the convertibility program by supplying the revenues needed to balance fiscal accounts from the sale of public assets.

Two current developments will be highly relevant to the Argentine economy over the next twenty years. One is the future of the stabilization program. The structure of such programs, relying on the exchange rate as the anchor of prices, will lead inevitably to overvaluation of the domestic currency. The consequence will be to maintain the tradable-goods sectors (most of agriculture and industry) in a highly constrained condition of low profits and low investment. The second development is privatization, a process that is now in its final stage. A large share of privatized public services and public monopolies have come to be controlled by a small, closed group of private, local holding companies. In most cases, foreign partners providing technical and financial services have a minor property share. This creates a highly profitable monopoly nucleus at the center of the new model of capital accumulation.

The transformation of the Argentine economy in accordance with this dichotomous pattern of a strong center and weak peripheral sectors scarcely fits the image of a outward-oriented market economy, as was promised by advocates of neoliberal reform in Buenos Aires and in Washington, D.C. Rather this emergent model more closely resembles a modernized version of the old authoritarian project envisioned by the military in the post-war years. Whether this project can be compatible with uncorrupted democracy is still unknown.

Notes

1. The definition of the crisis as a "crisis of the state" has conceptual consequences. It gives relevance to political factors as much as economic ones. This notion denies that the crisis may be explained by the essential inefficiency of markets interfered with by government action or by high levels of protection kept within the narrow limits of the domestic market. Both excessive government intervention and protection may have had perverse effects on economic behavior, but not to the extent of imputing full responsibility for the crisis to them.

2. For these and other data, see the tables included at the end of this chapter.

3. Recognition of this is important because some interpretations of the origins of the interventionist state in Argentina assume the preeminence of socialist leanings in postwar ideology. This is not the case — the interventionist state was a military invention.

4. In 1987, 70 percent of exports were rural staples traditionally produced in the pampas. The initial expansion of nontraditional manufactured exports was curtailed, first by the appreciation of the domestic currency that came with the stabilization program at the end of the 1970s, and later by the collapse of Latin American markets in the wake of the 1982 debt crisis.

5. Under the assumption of perfect certainty, capital is a universal substance that moves, like air, across frontiers, and the idea of "foreign debt" is void of significance. Only when uncertainty is introduced, institutional divisions, like countries, come to life, and the distinction between domestic and foreign capital becomes meaningful. The theoretical approach underpinning the stabilization program assumed certainty; this assumption may explain why the growth of foreign indebtedness was not a cause for concern.

6. The exchange rate was not fixed at the start of the program; rather, it was to be determined by a preannounced schedule of declining mini-devaluations converging to zero (the famous *tablita*). It was hoped that this mechanism would provide the program with the degree of certainty required to bring inflation under control.

7. The analysis of the stabilization and liberalization programs at the end of the 1970s in the Southern Cone gave rise to extensive discussion. Calvo (1986), Canitrot (1981), and Cavallo and Cottani (1988) provide different views on the Argentine experience.

8. Import prohibitions, though attenuated, were maintained up to 1991.

9 Between July 1982 and December 1983, there was an interval of populist policies carried out by the military government, in alliance with labor union leaders, as part of a defensive strategy toward the future civil government: nominal wages were raised above the rate of current inflation. The outcome was a real wage increase of 57 percent and a 10 percent expansion in the level of economic activity. The fiscal deficit

reached 15 percent of the GNP. Despite these measures, inflation remained stable at a rate of 20 percent a month.

10. The birth of the new currency obeyed a legal rationale. The government could not interfere in current private contracts by trying to modify the usual provision that future payments should be indexed by the rate of inflation of the preceding months. If such provisions were maintained, the sudden fall of the inflation rate that was to follow the price freeze would have produced a real, one-time increase in the amount of all payments due. Such a transfer of real income was declared unfair, so the government found the solution in a new currency to which future payments were to be converted over time according to a declining scale between the old peso and the new money.

11. The destruction of the emergency tax structure that accompanied the Austral Plan occurred in rapid sequence. The "voluntary savings" tax ended by December 1986 and was not renewed; higher inflation revived the negative Olivera-Tanzi effect. A few months later, in 1987, the fall in world prices of Argentina's traditional exports obliged the government to remove export taxes. On fiscal matters, and their relation to macroeconomic performance in the 1970s and 1980s, see Carciofi (1990).

12. The trial of the military juntas for their crimes in the "dirty war" was probably the most relevant event of the Alfonsín administration. The trial and its verdicts gave a strong signal supporting law and human rights and contributed to strengthening the public's commitment to democracy after so many years of authoritarian practices. However, the trials set in motion a growing number of judicial proceedings involving a large number of officers of the armed forces. That created a political problem whose intensity was reinforced by budgetary restrictions and the fall of officers' salaries. A first military mutiny erupted during Easter Week of 1987, prompting an active popular reaction in defense of democracy. The mutiny was called off after Alfonsín talked to its leaders. A few days later, the government ordered and the Congress approved the "Law of Due Obedience" absolving subordinate army officials of any criminal responsibility. Though always denied by Alfonsín, the public perception was that he had compromised with the mutineers. Alfonsín's public image was seriously damaged. Two further military mutinies occurred the following year, with the latest one in December 1989 during Menem's administration.

13. The initial stabilization program was called the "BB Plan" after the name of the cereal giant. Bunge & Born was the main Argentine trader of cereals since the nineteenth century. It also has extensive interests in the industrial sector linked to the domestic market. The company had a controversial relationship with Perón when he nationalized foreign trade in the 1940s.

14. The tax strategy relies heavily on the expansion of the VAT (Value Added Tax) that has been set at 18 percent and generalized to all transactions. Revenues from that tax rose more than 100 percent since March 1991. The next step was to raise the level of direct taxes with the help of the information provided by the VAT. Taxes applied to exports and bank loans are scheduled to be phased out in the future. In global terms, current fiscal revenues of the federal government rose 5 percentage points of GNP between 1990 and 1992, to reach a level of taxation slightly above that obtained in 1986 during the Austral Plan (though two of those five percentage points correspond to the sale of public enterprises).

References

Calvo, Guillermo. 1986. "Fractured Liberalism: Argentina under Martínez de Hoz." *Economic Development and Cultural Change* 34, 3.

Canitrot, Adolfo. 1981. "Teoría y práctica del liberalismo. Política antiinflacionaria y apertura económica en la Argentina (1976-1981)." *Desarrollo Económico* 82: 131-189.

Carciofi, Ricardo. 1990. "La desarticulación del pacto fiscal. Una interpretación sobre la evolución del sector público argentino en las últimas dos décadas." Documento de la CEPAL Nº 36. Buenos Aires.

Cavallo, Domingo, and Juan Cottani. 1988. "The Timing and Sequencing of a Trade Liberalization Policy: The Case of Argentina." Washington, D.C.: World Bank.

Díaz Alejandro, Carlos. 1970. *Essays on the Economic History of the Argentine Republic.* New Haven, Conn.: Yale University Press.

Mallon, Richard, and Juan V. Sourrouille. 1973. *La política económica en una sociedad conflictiva. El caso argentino.* Buenos Aires: Amorrortu Editores.

Table 1
Aggregate Supply and Demand
(1980 = 100)

Year	GNP	Imports	Consump.	Invest.	Exports
1980	100.0	100.0	100.0	100.0	100.0
1981	93.5	90.7	95.8	77.3	103.6
1982	88.8	52.1	85.5	61.8	108.5
1983	91.5	49.8	88.9	55.2	116.9
1984	93.9	52.8	94.5	48.7	115.3
1985	89.9	45.1	88.6	39.9	128.8
1986	95.0	53.1	96.0	46.6	120.2
1987	97.1	56.2	97.3	53.8	118.1
1988	94.6	49.8	91.4	48.1	139.9
1989	90.2	41.0	86.7	33.9	150.0
1990	90.6	41.0	84.2	30.0	178.2
1991		81.4			172.7

Source: Economic Commission for Latin America, Buenos Aires Office. *Macroeconomic Indicators.* Buenos Aires Office (BAO).

Table 2
National Income, Savings, and Investment
(Percent of GNP)

Year	GNP	Y	C	DS	FS	X-M	I
1980	100.0	100.0	83.2	16.8	6.9	-6.9	23.7
1981	100.0	97.7	85.4	12.3	7.1	-4.8	19.4
1982	100.0	92.6	80.3	12.3	4.1	3.3	16.4
1983	100.0	90.9	81.0	9.9	4.3	4.8	14.2
1984	100.0	91.6	83.7	7.9	4.4	4.0	12.3
1985	100.0	90.5	82.1	8.4	2.0	7.6	10.3
1986	100.0	90.9	84.0	6.8	4.6	4.5	11.5
1987	100.0	90.7	83.4	7.3	5.8	3.5	13.1
1988	100.0	90.6	80.5	10.1	2.0	7.5	12.0
1989	100.0	-89.0	80.3	8.7	0.0	10.9	8.7
1990	100.0	87.4	77.5	9.9	-1.7	14.4	8.1

Source: See Table 1.

GNP — Gross National Product
Y — National Income
C — Aggregate Consumption
DS — Domestic Savings
FS — Foreign Savings
X-M — Trade Balance
I — Total Investment

Table 3
Average Monthly Inflation Rates
(Percent)
Yearly Data

Year	Consumer Price Index (CPI)	Wholesale Price Index (WPI)
1980	5.4	3.9
1981	7.2	8.8
1982	9.9	12.7
1983	15.0	14.9
1984	18.8	17.4
1985	14.1	13.6
1986	5.1	3.9
1987	8.8	9.0
1988	14.1	14.9
1989	38.6	39.6
1990	24.9	20.1
1991	5.2	3.8
1992	1.4	0.8

Quarterly Data

	Quarter	CPI	WPI		Quarter	CPI	WPI
1985	I	24.1	22.2	1989	I	11.8	11.3
	II	24.8	34.9		II	72.2	96.1
	III	3.7	0.4		III	64.8	50.9
	IV	2.5	0.8		IV	16.4	15.4
1986	I	3.1	0.7	1990	I	78.2	73.2
	II	4.4	3.4		II	13.0	7.8
	III	7.6	7.1		III	13.9	9.9
	IV	5.4	4.4		IV	6.2	1.3
1987	I	7.4	6.7	1991	I	14.9	15.1
	II	5.2	4.5		II	3.8	1.1
	III	11.8	13.5		III	1.9	0.1
	IV	10.9	11.7		IV	0.8	-0.4
1988	I	11.4	13.9	1992	I	2.4	0.8
	II	17.0	21.3		II	0.9	0.3
	III	21.4	20.6		III	1.4	0.7
	IV	7.2	4.7		IV		

Source: See Table 1.

Table 4
Real Exchange Rate Index
(Pesos x CPI USA / dollar x CPI Arg; 1983 = 100)
Yearly Data

Year	Exchange Rate
1980	37.3
1981	46.0
1982	83.3
1983	100.0
1984	90.3
1985	103.6
1986	91.3
1987	94.8
1988	103.1
1989	127.3
1990	82.6
1991	56.3
1992	50.1

Quarterly Data

Year	Qtr	Rate	Year	Qtr	Rate
1985	I	97.1	1989	I	89.3
	II	105.1		II	176.7
	III	108.1		III	128.9
	IV	104.1		IV	114.3
1986	I	96.9	1990	I	122.7
	II	91.6		II	87.0
	III	87.7		III	69.7
	IV	89.0		IV	50.9
1987	I	92.2	1991	I	59.2
	II	91.6		II	57.4
	III	92.7		III	54.4
	IV	102.7		IV	51.7
1988	I	104.2	1992	I	50.1
	II	107.0		II	48.5
	III	106.2		III	
	IV	94.9			

Source: See Table 1

Table 5
Real Wage Index
(Average Urban Private-Sector Wage/CPI; 1983 = 100)

Year	Real Wage
1980	101.2
1981	97.5
1982	85.2
1983	100.0
1984	127.4
1985	115.6
1986	111.2
1987	101.9
1988	101.0
1989	92.1
1990	87.5
1991	83.0
1992	82.5

Source: Instituto Nacional de Estadística y Censos (INDEC).

Table 6
Employment and Unemployment

Year	Industrial Employment Index (1970 = 100)	Unemployment Rate	Underemployment Rate
1980	88.2	2.6	5.2
1981	77.1	4.8	5.5
1982	73.0	5.3	6.6
1983	75.4	4.7	5.9
1984	77.6	4.6	5.7
1985	74.8	6.1	7.3
1986	71.7	5.6	7.6
1987	71.0	5.9	8.4
1988	71.7	6.3	8.5
1989	65.7	7.8	8.9
1990	62.6	7.4	9.3
1991	——	6.5	8.6
1992	——	6.0	8.3

Source: See Table 5.

Table 7
Foreign Trade
(Millions of US Dollars)

Year	Exports	Imports	Trade Balance	Terms of Exchange
1980	8,021.4	10,540.6	-2,519.2	117.7
1981	9,143.6	9,430.2	-286.6	124.6
1982	7,624.5	5,336.9	2,287.6	105.2
1983	7,836.2	4,504.3	3,331.9	101.9
1984	8,107.4	4,584.9	3,522.5	110.3
1985	8,396.1	3,814.2	4,581.9	95.0
1986	6,851.9	4,724.2	2,127.7	80.7
1987	6,360.2	5,818.8	541.4	72.3
1988	9,134.8	5,322.0	3,812.8	78.1
1989	9,573.0	4,200.1	5,372.9	75.7
1990	12,352.6	4,077.4	8,275.2	73.2
1991	11,965.0	8,093.0	3,872.0	67.8

Source: See Table 5.

Table 8
Balance of Payments
(Millions of US Dollars)

Year	Trade Balance	Real Services	Financial Services (+ or -)	Current Balance	Foreign Reserves
1980	-2,159	-740	-1,531	-4,767	-2,677
1981	-286	-705	-3,700	-4,714	-3,457
1982	2,287	43	-4,719	-2,358	-755
1983	3,331	-400	-5,408	-2,461	-76
1984	3,523	-205	-5,712	-2,391	74
1985	4,582	-230	-5,303	-953	2,017
1986	2,128	-573	-4,416	-2,859	-563
1987	541	-285	-4,485	-4,238	-1,106
1988	3,810	-255	-5,127	-1,572	1784
1989	5,373	-255	-6,422	-1,294	-1700
1990	8,276	-321	-6,122	1,903	2,338
1991	3,872	-975	-5,634	-2,668	2,520

Source: Banco Central de la República Argentina.

Table 9
Foreign Debt
(Billions of US Dollars)

Year	Total Debt	Public Debt	Private Debt
1975	7.9	4.0	3.9
1976	8.3	5.2	3.1
1977	9.7	6.0	3.7
1978	12.5	8.4	4.1
1979	19.0	10.0	9.0
1980	27.2	14.5	12.7
1981	35.7	20.0	15.6
1982	43.6	28.6	15.0
1983	45.1	31.7	13.4
1984	46.2	35.5	10.6
1985	49.3	40.9	8.5
1986	51.4	44.7	6.7
1987	58.3	51.8	6.5
1988	58.5	53.5	5.0
1989	63.3	58.4	4.9
1990	61.0	——	——
1991	60.0	——	——

Source: See Table 8.

Table 10
Total Public Sector*
(Percent of GNP)

Year	Current Revenues	(1) Current Expenditures	Current Savings	Capital Expenditures	Financing Gap
1980	27.48	24.51	1.73	9.20	7.47
1981	25.25	27.21	-3.86	9.40	13.26
1982	22.86	26.03	-7.04	8.07	15.11
1983	23.33	26.46	-5.70	9.45	15.15
1984	22.69	25.59	-4.34	7.58	11.92
1985	27.70	25.39	0.80	6.81	6.01
1986	26.50	24.99	1.96	7.27	4.73
1987	24.84	24.63	0.40	7.53	7.02

*Consolidated Accounts include Central Administration, Provinces and Federal Capital, Social Retirement System, Public Enterprises, and State Banks.
(1) Includes profits of public enterprises.
Source: Secretaría de Hacienda.

Table 11
National Government[*]
(Percent of GNP)

Year	(1) Current Revenues	Current Expenditures	Current Savings	Capital Expenditures	Financing Gap
1985	21.95	22.68	-2.24	4.05	5.42
1986	21.05	22.03	-.053	4.28	4.10
1987	20.06	21.82	-1.56	5.28	6.73
1988	18.72	21.46	-3.34	5.99	8.56
1989	17.52	17.68	-1.54	3.91	4.81
1990	17.72	20.56	-2.85	2.56	5.11
1991	20.50	21.79	-1.56	2.25	2.17

[*]Consolidated Accounts for the national government only. Includes Central Administration and Social Retirement System. Excludes Provinces, Federal Capital, Public Enterprises, and State Banks.
(1) Revenues from taxes shared by Provinces and the Federal Government included.
Source: Secretaría de Hacienda.

Table 12
Domestic Money Supply
(Liquidity Coefficients as percentage of GNP)

Year	M1/GNP	M2/GNP
1980	7.5	28.4
1981	6.3	28.2
1982	4.9	20.0
1983	3.8	13.6
1984	3.8	12.8
1985	3.6	12.4
1986	5.7	17.2
1987	5.2	18.2
1988	3.3	15.4
1989	2.8	13.2
1990	2.5	5.5
1991	4.4	8.5
1992	7.4	13.7

Source: See Table 8.

Bolivia

Selected Macroeconomic Indicators for Bolivia

	1982	1983	1984	1985	1986	1987	1988	1989	1990	1991	1992p
Real Gross Domestic Product	*(Percent Average Annual Growth Rates)*										
Total GDP	-4.4	-4.5	-0.6	-1.0	-2.5	2.6	3.0	2.8	4.1	4.6	3.4
Manufacturing	-12.4	0.2	1.0	-8.3	1.9	2.5	5.4	2.6	6.4	7.1	4.3
Agriculture	6.9	-17.2	19.0	7.7	-3.5	3.5	2.4	-2.4	1.2	10.5	-4.3
Construction	-8.9	0.4	-5.3	-3.7	-21.5	-0.9	14.5	10.7	4.1	2.6	15.3
Gross Domestic Investment	*(As as Percent of GDP)*										
	8.9	8.9	12.3	15.9	14.2	15.3	11.2	9.9	9.0	12.7	—
Non-Financial Public Sector	*(As a Percent of GDP)*										
Current Revenue	31.7	24.0	19.0	22.4	26.4	23.9	24.2	24.6	25.9	27.5	28.9
Current Expenditures	32.6	31.1	29.7	25.6	25.1	25.6	23.4	23.5	23.5	24.9	25.9
Overall Balance (-Deficit)	-14.2	-18.4	-22.9	-8.8	-2.5	-7.3	-5.9	-5.3	-4.2	-4.1	-4.9
Prices, Salaries and Unemployment	*(Percent Average Annual Growth Rates)*										
Consumer Prices	185.7	200.0	1300.0	11804.8	276.4	14.6	16.0	15.2	17.1	21.4	12.1
Real Wages	-7.9	2.8	-1.6	-20.1	-23.1	5.4	19.6	2.4	6.4	6.9	7.0
Unemployment	10.5	14.2	15.1	18.0	20.0	20.5	18.0	20.0	19.0	—	—
Real Effective Exchange Rate	*(Index 1980 = 100)*										
	69.0	75.0	57.8	33.7	114.4	118.6	125.0	130.2	154.4	149.5	153.0
Balance of Payments	*(Millions of Dollars)*										
Current Account	-179.2	-138.1	-174.2	-281.9	-384.0	-422.7	-255.4	-263.7	-191.5	-262.1	-586.9
Trade Balance	331.7	259.1	312.2	160.6	-51.0	-127.6	-48.4	-6.0	55.2	-43.9	-432.3
Exports	827.7	755.1	724.5	623.4	545.5	518.7	542.5	723.5	830.8	760.3	608.4
Imports	496.0	496.0	412.3	462.8	596.5	646.3	590.9	729.5	775.6	804.2	1040.7
Capital Account Balance	166.6	107.6	305.2	57.4	362.4	199.7	165.4	191.0	221.0	231.2	550.6
Change in Reserves (- Increase)	-27.8	-41.0	-118.9	34.5	-114.7	48.4	43.3	104.8	-18.1	-22.4	-57.1
Total External Debt	*(Billions of Dollars)*										
Disbursed Debt	3.3	4.1	4.3	4.8	5.6	5.8	4.9	4.1	4.3	4.1	4.3
	(In Percent)										
Interest Payments Due/Exports	43.4	39.8	49.8	46.8	42.1	38.4	41.0	30.2	25.0	26.9	25.0

p = preliminary

Sources: Inter-American Development Bank, *Economic and Social Progress in Latin America*, 1992 and 1993 Reports, and the International Labor Organization.

Chapter Four

Crafting Political Support for Stabilization: Political Pacts and the New Economic Policy in Bolivia

Eduardo A. Gamarra

Introduction

On August 29, 1985, via Decree 21060 Bolivian President Víctor Paz Estenssoro introduced the *Nueva Política Económica* (New Economic Policy — NPE). In a move that surprised the Left and other groups that had supported his election, Paz Estenssoro announced a program that restructured the state capitalist development strategy established thirty-three years earlier by the then-populist *Movimiento Nacionalista Revolucionario* (Nationalist Revolutionary Movement — MNR).

The NPE sought three basic objectives: liberalization of the economy, ascendance of the private sector as the central actor in economic development, and recoupment of control over key state enterprises which had been captured by factional cliques and labor groups. The NPE shock therapy included reducing fiscal deficits, freezing wages and salaries, devaluing the currency, and drastically cutting public-sector employment. The government also announced the privatization of certain state enterprises and other measures.

Within one year, the NPE was credited with reducing inflation from the record-breaking level of 26,000 percent in 1984-1985 to a mere 10 percent in 1986.[1] Government officials claimed that the foundations for economic recovery had been established. Bolivia's NPE became a showcase as international financial institutions and foreign governments praised it extensively. Bolivia's economic recovery, however, did not proceed rapidly. The collapse of the tin market in October 1985 and the decline in the price of natural gas — the country's only legal sources of hard currency — threatened to derail the NPE. In 1987 the economy finally showed signs of growth for the first time in the 1980s.

Dubbed the "Bolivian miracle," the NPE produced impressive long-term results in controlling inflation and resuming growth over the four years in which the country was governed by Victor Paz Estenssoro and the MNR. Stabilization suffered a minor crisis during the period of uncertainty generated by the 1989 election when a return of capital flight threatened the financial system.

The coming to power of Jaime Paz Zamora and his party the *Movimiento de Izquierda Revolucionaria* (Revolutionary Left Movement — MIR) also contributed to uncertainty following the national elections. In fact, the MIR/ADN (*Acción Democrática Nacionalista*) government stubbornly continued with the policies of the NPE despite incurring considerable political costs.

While Paz Zamora pledged continuity with NPE reforms, he attempted to establish a new and distinct economic identity. By introducing Decree 22407 in January 1990 to replace Decree 21060, which had launched the NPE, the Bolivian government claimed that these new measures definitively opened the nation's economy. Under the terms of the decree, foreign investment in mining and hydrocarbons was permitted and the government moved ahead with plans to privatize key state enterprises.

My intention in this chapter is not to tell yet another story of the so-called "Bolivian miracle" but to analyze the political dynamics that have accompanied the imposition of neoliberal market reforms. Using the government's own measures of success — namely, resumed economic growth and consolidation of democracy — I explore how two successive governments crafted political support for stabilization.

In the first part of this chapter, I argue that the imposition of austerity measures by the Paz Estenssoro government was possible only because of the crafting of the *Pacto por la Democracia*, a pact between the ruling MNR and the *Acción Democrática Nacionalista* (ADN), the principal opposition party. The pact enabled the government to control threats from the National Congress and from organized labor. In the second part, I explore attempts by the MIR and ADN to renew the governing pact, under the rubric of the *Acuerdo Patriótico*. Both pacts illustrate the importance of crafting political support for stabilization programs. And, finally, I draw some concluding comparative observations about the Bolivian experience with democratization and market reforms.

Crafting Support for the NPE: The *Pacto por la Democracia*

The key to the *Nueva Política Económica*'s success entailed filling a power vacuum at the center of the Bolivian political system. Because Congress was dominated by the opposition and the *Central Obrera Boliviana* (Bolivian Labor Central — COB) was poised to prevent the imposition of harsh austerity measures, this was a difficult task. Nevertheless, Víctor Paz Estenssoro set in motion a pattern of governance which allowed his government both to impose economic stabilization and to control opposition from Congress and labor. The relative success of Paz Estenssoro and the MNR suggests that the crafting of political support is essential for the imposition of austerity measures.

Considering the extreme crisis faced by the Paz Estenssoro government in 1985 and the structural weaknesses of Bolivian presidentialism, the political mechanisms of the NPE must be explained in more detail (Palermo 1990). To neutralize labor, the MNR government launched a state-of-siege, banishing hundreds of labor leaders, including COB leader Juan Lechín Oquendo. It is worth recalling that the COB sabotaged every attempt by the Hernán Siles Zuazo government (1982-1985) to impose austerity (Malloy and Gamarra 1988). In the process, however, organized labor also eroded the effectiveness and legitimacy of strikes. Thus, when 22,000 mineworkers were fired, the COB barely mustered enough support to call a general strike.

As in most presidential systems, in Bolivia continuation of the state-of-siege depended on congressional approval.[2] Almost immediately, opposition groups in Congress set in motion interpellation maneuvers to counter the launching of the NPE and the state-of-siege. Owing to its association with Siles and the *Unidad Democrática y Popular* (Popular and Democratic Union — UDP) and its humiliating defeat in the general elections, the left received little popular support for their congressional maneuvers. The only left-of-center party of significance was Jaime Paz Zamora's MIR, which had shrewdly abandoned the UDP and recast the party in a more acceptable social-democratic guise. In short, left-of-center groups in Congress lacked the votes to overturn the state-of-siege.

The only real threat in Congress came from General Banzer's *Acción Democrática Nacionalista* (Nationalist and Democratic Action — ADN). Shortly after launching the NPE, Paz Estenssoro moved to form a so-called *Pacto por la Democracia* (Pact for Democracy), aimed mainly at securing congressional ratification for the state-of-siege. Beyond patriotic gestures and democratic rhetoric, the pact provided legislative support for the NPE in exchange for an ADN share of state patronage.[3] A secret addendum, signed in May 1988, provided for alternability as the MNR pledged to support Banzer's candidacy in the 1989 general elections. On a smaller scale, the *Pacto por la Democracia* introduced elements similar to those present in Colombia's governing pact between Liberales and Conservadores: a share in state patronage and a mechanism to insure the rotation of the presidency between the MNR and ADN. In short, the *Pacto* was one of the most significant attempts at institutionalizing a working arrangement between the government and the principal opposition party. In my view, this was key to ensuring the continuity of the NPE.

The *Pacto por la Democracia* revealed a basic reality about the imposition of austerity measures in democratizing nations. To govern, presidents must be able to form and sustain coalitions in Congress to support their policy initiatives. Because the pact allowed decision-making authority to be concentrated in the executive branch, the National Congress was reduced to legitimating a policy-making process conceived by a few technocrats in the executive branch (Conaghan, Malloy, and Abugattas 1990).

The pact allowed the president to overcome the severe conflict between a weak executive and an opposition-controlled legislature. As was evident during the Siles Zuazo period, this tension had made more salient the parliamentary characteristics of the system. This conflict was temporarily resolved by the *Pacto por la Democracia*; however, unless this contradiction is resolved through constitutional amendments or electoral reforms, in the future, every president will be forced to replicate a version of the pact in order to govern. Paradoxically, this is both the principal strength and the main weakness of the system.

One of the most significant aspects of the pact was that it allowed Paz Estenssoro to overcome a problem of "dual legitimacy," which had plagued Siles Zuazo.[4] Defenders of the arrangement argued that because the first- and second-place finishers in the 1985 elections entered into the pact, approximately 55 percent of the electorate was duly represented. That the MNR placed second was an important consideration in Paz Estenssoro's decision to enter into a governing pact with the winner of the elections. In Bolivia in 1985, the key to forming and sustaining the pact rested mainly on the ability of Paz Estenssoro and General Hugo Banzer Suárez to control their respective parties and maintain discipline in the coalition.[5] Owing largely to their stature, no faction could significantly challenge the grip of these two men over their respective parties. Thus, a crucial factor in the formation and maintenance of this pact was the role of statesmanship and old-fashioned *caudillismo*.

The pact resolved many of the institutional dilemmas facing Bolivia's political system but ratified the significance of patronage. Paradoxically, the pact increased party patronage pressures on public employment despite the high-flown neoliberal rhetoric of reducing the size of the state. This logic also undermined the president's ability to assert authority over the state bureaucracy.[6] In short, Paz Estenssoro's government faced Bolivia's most pressing problem: the need to provide employment to the dependent middle classes. As in other Latin American nations, in Bolivia "*empleomanía*" or job factionalism drives the logic of political party competition and is crucial to the survival of presidents. Under the context of stabilization, however, patronage demands have the potential of undermining the coherence of neoliberal reforms.

By emulating certain parliamentary features, President Paz Estenssoro was also able to transcend the problems associated with job factionalism. To implement the NPE, he established an economic cabinet team headed by Gonzalo Sánchez de Lozada, the "super" minister of planning, who became a de facto prime minister for economic affairs. Paz also established a political cabinet, headed by Foreign Affairs Minister Guillermo Bedregal, to control party discipline. In setting up two quasi-prime ministerial posts, Paz Estenssoro insulated himself from the day-to-day party squabbles and the battles constantly faced by the economic team. While this style proved successful for Paz Estenssoro, it would be difficult to replicate (Malloy 1989).

To institutionalize this governing style, the key was to reform the electoral mechanisms that had given birth to Bolivia's complex multiparty system. ADN and MNR strategists envisioned a two-party dominant system. The opposition, headed by Jaime Paz Zamora's MIR, charged the two allies with attempting to establish a new "hegemonic" party; instead, the MIR proposed a new electoral court staffed by members of the top three vote getters in 1985.

In a round of political bartering, the MIR's electoral reform proposals were accepted in exchange for its support for a far-reaching tax code which effectively institutionalized the NPE. As some have noted (Mayorga 1989), the principal objective of the 1986 Electoral Law was to concentrate parliamentary representation in a few parties (ADN, MNR, MIR) through the revision of a proportional coefficient that had favored minority parties. The authors of the new law believed the reforms could prevent the atomization of political parties and would make the Congress into a more efficient legislative body. In short, these electoral reforms aimed to reestablish presidential supremacy. Time would reveal that the electoral reforms, especially the makeup of the National and Departmental Electoral Courts, only added to the problems of electing presidents. Paradoxically, the new law positioned the ADN and the MIR for a joint assault on the MNR during the 1989 general elections.

The May 1986 approval of the electoral reforms marked an important turning point for Bolivia's political system. The MIR announced it would carry out "constructive" opposition in Congress. This announcement could be interpreted as the MIR's official endorsement of the 1985 neoliberal reforms. For the next three years, the *Pacto por la Democracia* and the MIR's mild opposition allowed the Paz Estenssoro presidency to impose two more congressionally sanctioned states-of-siege, delivering punishing blows from which organized labor has yet to recover.[7] The pact also allowed the imposition of NPE-related legislation, including the new tax code and three successive national budgets.

Although the *Pacto por la Democracia* demonstrated that stable congressional coalitions are essential to stability and to effective government under presidential systems, it also revealed that governing pacts seldom are flexible enough to become viable electoral coalitions. Despite the pact's success in forcing through the NPE and related legislation and the fact that popular support for the policy initiatives of the MNR government was quite high, it could not survive the 1989 election campaign. At issue was the refusal of the MNR to live up to the terms of the secret agreement of May 1988 which had assured support for General Banzer's candidacy. Once again the patronage logic of the political parties destabilized the Bolivian political process. Despite the "modern" tone between 1985 and 1989, old ways of doing politics, specifically the determinant role of patronage and clientelism, survived as political parties revealed that they were interested more in controlling state patronage than in ruling effectively.

Based on the belief that popular support for the NPE could lead the MNR to an outright victory in the elections, the MNR named as its candidate Gonzalo Sánchez de Lozada, the "super" minister of planning and one of the principal architects of the 1985 stabilization measures. Sánchez de Lozada promptly broke the pact with ADN and conducted a bitter, negative campaign, which mimicked the worst of American presidential campaigns.[8]

The decision to break the pact and the MNR's campaign style proved fateful. Although Sánchez de Lozada won a slight plurality of 23.07 percent to Banzer's 22.7 percent and Jaime Paz Zamora's 19.6 percent, neither the ADN nor the MIR would contemplate supporting the MNR's claim to the presidency. The insult of breaking the pact, compounded by the tone of the campaign, contributed to the MNR's isolation.[9] As a result, between May and August 1989, Bolivia lurched through three months of intense negotiations between the ADN and MIR and futile attempts by the MNR to strike a deal. On the eve of the convening of Congress to elect the next president, as Banzer ordered his party to support Paz Zamora's bid for the presidency, he revealed that the least likely outcome had prevailed: a coalition between ADN and MIR.

Recrafting Support for Stabilization: The *Acuerdo Patriótico*

Latin American nations attempting to impose stabilization measures could well afford to review the Paz Estenssoro period. It became clear in Bolivia that the fundamental instrument required to govern and impose stabilization was a ruling political pact between the dominant party and the principal opposition force in Congress. Apart from coordinating legislative actions with presidential initiatives, pacts provide decision-making capacity and efficiency for the executive branch. Pacts, such as the *Pacto por la Democracia*, also allow presidents to breach claims to legitimacy from Congress, thus providing the mechanisms to overcome crisis situations.

The ability to make and hold together coalitions that enabled (in the constitutional-legal sense) Paz Estenssoro to act decisively depended upon the institutional feature by which the Congress determines who occupies the top executive post. This parliamentary feature strengthened congressional control over the executive as compared to what it would be with a president formally answerable only to the electorate. Thus, Paz Estenssoro was capable of overcoming the problem of dual legitimacies which had plagued the Siles Zuazo government. While parties in Congress complained about the executive (and thereby gave an appearance of dual legitimacy), it was a congressional majority that supported every piece of legislation, especially those related to the NPE. The Paz Estenssoro period also demonstrated how critical the congressional election of the president is for the balance of power between branches and for interparty relations. Congressional selection of the executive in a multiparty system suggested to every party that another two-party or multiparty coalition would be needed next term. Thus, collaboration among parties was extremely important. In 1989, Bolivian politicians appeared to have achieved an *equilibrium* that could not have existed were the system purely presidential and especially if the president were elected by a majority runoff (Shugart and Carey 1992). This is not the case, for example, in Peru or Ecuador, where presidents are legitimated only via popular votes in a second-round runoff. In both cases, dual legitimacy constitutes a serious issue. Moreover, a second round has exacerbated tensions between the executive and legislative branches.

These lessons were learned partially by Jaime Paz Zamora, Bolivia's new president elected on August 6, 1989, with the support of General Banzer's ADN. Before assuming office, Paz Zamora entered into a so-called *Acuerdo Patriótico* (Patriotic Accord) with General Banzer, claiming they would not sign a document formalizing the arrangement because both leaders had pledged their word of honor.[10]

On August 24, 1989, Paz Zamora and Banzer established the *Consejo Político del Acuerdo Patriótico* (Political Council of the Patriotic Accord — COPAP). Intended to serve as a link between the cabinet and the two parties that made up the *Acuerdo Patriótico*, it was lauded as the instrument necessary for the consolidation of Bolivian democracy and the modernization of the Bolivian state. Opposition parties accused the government of establishing a "super state" that would exercise authority beyond constitutional limitations. Still others argued that the council divided the governing domestic and foreign policy responsibilities between the ADN and MIR, respectively. In other words, General Banzer and ADN would be charged with running Bolivia, while Jaime Paz Zamora concentrated on becoming a part of the "Latin American political jet set."[11]

Despite all the controversy, COPAP became a relatively important institution. Above all it served to coordinate relations between ADN and MIR. Because it is essentially a political instrument, however, it has proven ineffective in providing guidance to the cabinet on economic policy. Moreover, owing to recurrent charges that Banzer was overshadowing

President Paz Zamora, the old general moved out of La Paz to his native Santa Cruz and showed up only on special occasions. Members of COPAP argued privately that, beyond purely political roles, it was completely ineffective.[12]

The new pact attempted to emulate many of the dimensions of the *Pacto por la Democracia*. First and foremost, its role was to push through Congress legislation designed to deepen NPE economic reforms. But the major problem of the *Acuerdo Patriótico* was to find an "economic personality" of its own. Because it pushed through NPE-related legislation, the new government was unable to create for itself a distinctive flavor to distinguish it from its predecessor. In January 1990, to overcome this situation, Paz Zamora announced Decree 22407 intended to replace Decree 21060 which had introduced the NPE in 1985. Under careful examination, however, the new decree revealed that it was simply a ratification of the main premises of the political economy of the Paz Estenssoro government.

Taking a page from the Paz Estenssoro government, the new government also declared a state-of-siege to control organized labor's opposition to economic policy. In November 1989, the *Acuerdo Patriótico* arrested hundreds of union leaders and banished them to remote jungle towns. Unlike his predecessor, however, Paz Zamora could not seek congressional approval for his government's actions. Although the *Acuerdo Patriótico* controlled a majority in both houses of Congress, it did not command a two-thirds majority required to approve states-of-siege.[13]

Utilizing similar mechanisms, the *Acuerdo Patriótico* also crushed the opposition in the legislature for approval of controversial policies, such as investment laws, which call for joint ventures in the hydrocarbon and mining industries, as well as privatization law. In the case of these particular laws, the government resorted to extra-constitutional measures to win passage. Indeed, the Paz Zamora government's principal concern has been with pursuing privatization programs and encouraging foreign investment. Privatization advocates, such as Harvard's Richard Mallon and Argentina's María Julia Alsogaray, have been tapped by the government to aid Bolivian efforts in this direction. Government technocrats have also traveled extensively to learn from the Argentine, British, and U.S. privatization experiments. But the problems the Bolivian government has faced exemplify the difficulties that Latin American nations must overcome to follow through with neoliberal reforms such as privatization. In Bolivia, as elsewhere in the region, privatization theory has found little practical and political support. Moreover, Bolivia's problems confirmed that governments must develop a political base before embarking on controversial privatization schemes.

Bolivia's drive toward the free market has met several obstacles which could well undo the successes achieved in the past five years. Opposition from political parties, regional civic committees, and the COB to foreign investment and announced privatization measures has weakened the resolve of the Paz Zamora government. Critics in the private sector argued that the government caved in to popular pressure to demonstrate it had not lost its concern for social issues.

Several events illustrate the troubled path faced by Bolivia's government. In May 1990, owing to growing opposition from civic committees and other social groups, Paz Zamora rescinded a contract with LITHCO, a U.S.-based company that negotiated monopoly rights to exploit lithium deposits in Bolivia. U.S. Embassy officials and members of the Bolivian private sector complained privately that Paz Zamora's action revealed a lack of political will to deepen free market reforms. Then, in September 1990, when hundreds of indigenous people staged a march to La Paz to protest the deforestation of their Amazon basin homes by private companies, Paz Zamora signed a decree forbidding further logging activity. This action generated a bitter confrontation with logging companies who complained about the anti-free market tone of the presidential decree.

Nevertheless, the government claimed success in carrying out economic reforms. According to government reports, public confidence in the Bolivian economy was such that record levels of U.S. dollar deposits in the banking system had been achieved. Proudly, the government pointed to the elimination of all non-tariff barriers to trade, the reduction of import tariffs on all goods to an across-the-board maximum of 10 percent, and legislation guaranteeing free flows of capital, including the repatriation of profits by foreign companies, as examples of its commitment to profound economic reforms.

If government projections were correct, the general health of the Bolivian economy appeared quite promising in the early 1990s. For example, hydrocarbon and mineral exports rose from $815 million in 1989 to $918 million in 1990, while nontraditional exports increased by nearly 40 percent reaching $276 million. Moreover, the gross domestic product (GDP) rose for the fourth consecutive year reaching 2.6 percent growth in 1990 and 4.0 percent for 1991. Government officials also point out that while inflation reached 17 percent in 1990, and bottomed at 15 percent in 1991, it was still one of the lowest in Latin America. They pointed to the repatriation of capital, measured by a significant increase in dollar and dollar-linked time deposits in the banking sector, as a sign of confidence in the Bolivian economy.

The Paz Zamora government also pursued initiatives to resolve its debt problems with its neighbors, international financial institutions, and the United States. For example, in a controversial accord signed in December 1989, Bolivia and Argentina eliminated their mutual bilateral debts. In early 1990, Bolivia signed another agreement which established the basis for the refinancing and the repurchasing of its debt to Brazil (Barrios Morón 1991).

Government officials claimed that these actions reduced the country's foreign debt by $900 million.

Paz Zamora's policies were rewarded by international financial institutions, which monitored the country's economic policies. The Interamerican Development Bank (IDB) agreed to lend Bolivia $900 million until 1993, while the International Monetary Fund (IMF) approved $30 million in structural adjustment loans. Officials of the World Bank have also lavished praise on Bolivia's initiatives.

While searching for debt reduction mechanisms, Paz Zamora's government also aimed to strike a few politically correct chords in the international arena. By declaring a five-year "Ecological Pause on the Environment" in the totality of Bolivian territory, the government hoped to determine the degree of ecological damage the country has suffered and to design projects aimed at conservation and environmental protection. Building on the debt-for-nature schemes orchestrated by the previous government and Conservation International in September 1990, the Paz Zamora government presented the United States with a proposal for debt reduction and environmental protection. Under the terms of the Bolivian government's proposal, a National Fund for the Environment (FONAMA) was established to design, evaluate, finance, implement, and coordinate all conservation efforts. Through this debt-reduction arrangement, Bolivia intended to clear its bilateral debt to the United States while becoming eligible for greater Enterprise for the Americas advantages.

The Bolivian government also took seriously the George Bush administration's promises about the Enterprise for the Americas. In fact, in May 1990, two months before Bush's speech announcing the Enterprise, Bolivia and the United States had already signed a so-called framework agreement, which established a Bilateral Council for Trade and Investment designed to encourage private-sector investment and the promotion of exports from Bolivia. The Paz Zamora government noted that Bolivia was the first Latin American nation to sign a framework agreement "even before such agreements were espoused by Bush." Under the terms of the framework agreement, in September 1990, representatives of the U.S. Department of Commerce and the U.S. Trade Representative met with Bolivia's Minister of Foreign Relations and the Minister of Industry and Trade in the first consultative meeting of its kind.

The Paz Zamora government has been incapable of addressing, much less resolving, several post-stabilization problems that remain. Clear signs of growth remain absent; with the exception of 1991 figures, growth rates have been below the average population growth rate. Except for a noteworthy jump in mining, production figures in every sphere have also raised concerns regarding the future of the Bolivian economy. Foreign investment and investment by the private sector also have been minimal.

Moreover, social indicators in Bolivia have not improved and, according to the World Bank, they are comparable to those of Sub-Saharan Africa, India, and Bangladesh. Bolivia's infant mortality rate, for example, is the highest in South America — comparable only to those found in India and Tanzania. The same situation is found across the board for health indicators. With the deepening of NPE reforms, including initiatives for the privatization of education, social security, and the health care system, several groups have voiced their concern that the situation could deteriorate.

But more pragmatic problems have been the focus of the government's efforts. To deal with revenue shortfalls, the Paz Zamora government has periodically raised the price of gasoline (the so-called "*tarifazos*") to balance public accounts and to create savings. A few economists argue that, as a result, private-sector investment has been negatively affected. In fact, the *tarifazos* are somewhat contradictory to the goals of the NPE. Private-sector investment must now compete with the Paz Zamora government's decision to increase public investment (Morales 1991).

Similar contradictions are evident in the size of public-sector employment. Following the initial cutbacks between 1986 and 1988, public employment has increased dramatically. According to one estimate, in the first two years of the *Acuerdo Patriótico* as many as twenty thousand new employees have been hired (*Informe R* 1991). This trend clearly contradicts the NPE objective of shrinking the size of the state and reducing public spending. The patronage logic that drives the process of governance in Bolivia prevents any government from seriously engaging in employment reductions, however.

Finally, under the guise of modernization of the state, the government of the *Acuerdo Patriótico* has embarked on a campaign aimed at combatting political corruption. In July 1990, for example, a law for the Administration and Control of Government, known as the SAFCO law, was signed by President Paz Zamora. In theory, the SAFCO law regulates government administrative mechanisms and public-service accountability. SAFCO designed a system of penalties for transgressions ranging from professional irresponsibility to dishonesty. It also provides for the full independence of the Central Bank (Morales 1991, 15). The SAFCO law has become the government's response to rampant corruption; however, its effectiveness has been put into question by continuous charges of political corruption within the ranks of the two ruling political parties.

Any analysis of the Bolivian economy must note that the successes of the NPE are only partially the product of the implementation of the "correct" structural adjustment policies. Most economists and government officials now admit that cocaine revenue is still Bolivia's principal source of income. Few deny that revenue from coca and cocaine has been a great source of stability and that if the country were to stop producing coca leaves, overnight the

116 Democracy, Markets, and Structural Reform in Latin America

national economy would face a catastrophe.[14] The Bolivian government estimates that the economy receives an annual boost of about $600 million from the coca-cocaine industry. For obvious reasons, the government has been unwilling to risk economic stability to satisfy external demands for greater control over the production of coca leaves.

The key to overcoming post-stabilization problems has been to strengthen the *Acuerdo Patriótico*. In this sense, the government has attempted to follow the "executive prerogative" decision-making style which proved successful for Paz Estenssoro. The *Acuerdo*, however, has not had an easy time with the opposition. With no clout in the National Congress to challenge the government, members of the opposition resorted to the Supreme Court, whose entire membership was named by the previous MNR government. This further weakened and undermined the effectiveness of the *Acuerdo Patriótico*. The judiciary became the focus of political conflict as individuals and political groups pressed the Supreme Court to review not only all recent economic policy but also political decisions of President Paz Zamora.[15] The conflict stems from a Supreme Court ruling declaring unconstitutional a tax on beer. Claiming that the ruling was the product of corruption, namely the bribing of the justices by the two largest beer factories in Bolivia, the executive refused to accept the Court's decision. Instead, the *Acuerdo Patriótico* initiated a malfeasance trial in the National Congress against eight Supreme Court justices. The MNR escalated the conflict by resubmitting a lawsuit demanding that the Court declare the 1989 elections null and void.

An impasse emerged between Congress and the executive, controlled by the *Acuerdo Patriótico*, and the judiciary, controlled by the opposition. As in the past, the preferred outcome was a short-term unconstitutional "*salida*." On February 5, 1991, a tentative agreement was reached with the opposition whereby the justices would be forced to step down in return for a new electoral law. When the government appeared to renege on its promises to reform the electoral law, the arrangement broke down.[16] In mid-May 1991, faced with declining popular support and accusations of deep-seated corruption, the government allowed the eight suspended Supreme Court justices to return to their posts.

Many of the problems facing the *Acuerdo Patriótico* have to do with the nature of this governing pact. In contrast to the *Pacto por la Democracia*, the *Acuerdo* is a pact between two parties exercising control over the executive branch. It does not constitute an arrangement between a ruling party and the principal opposition force but an arrangement between two ruling parties to share power. The opposition has been shut out of virtually all major decisions and posts, including membership in congressional committees or leadership posts. This is a key dimension which has rendered President Paz Zamora's government ineffective vis-à-vis the opposition.

Unlike the *Pacto por la Democracia*, the new pact gave the presidency to the third-place finisher, thereby excluding the MNR, which won a plurality in May 1989. Although Banzer won the 1985 elections, the pact with the MNR and the resulting distribution of patronage resolved contending claims to legitimacy from the legislature. Moreover, the subsequent informal entry of the MIR as a "loyal" opposition had much to do with the duration and stability of the three-year agreement. In contrast, and to reiterate a point made above, the *Acuerdo Patriótico* excluded the MNR and most opposition parties from any patronage spoils.[17] The MNR, in turn, challenged the legitimacy of the ADN-MIR government, arguing that by electoral fraud they had been deprived of the presidency. Moreover, the principal dispute has been over the "paternity" of the NPE. While the MNR implemented the policy, the ADN claimed to have designed it.

Moreover, the distribution of patronage among members of the *Acuerdo Patriótico* runs deeper than was the case under the *Pacto por la Democracia*. While the government has issued several plans to reduce state employment, such as dismissals in the state mining corporation and in other state agencies, the patronage requirements of Bolivia's political class have resulted in the establishment of several new ministries and vice-ministerial posts.[18] Again, the political needs of the pact run counter to the neoliberal logic of reducing the size of the state. But the main political conflict has little to do with the economic logic of stabilization and everything to do with the exclusion of the MNR and other opposition parties from patronage spoils.

Along these lines, the critical conflict in 1991 was the *Acuerdo Patriótico*'s refusal to live up to its promises to reform the electoral law. Blocking the MNR's attempts to reform the law in the legislature, the ADN-MIR coalition crafted an alliance formula which would carry General Banzer to the presidency in 1993. As proposed by the leadership of both ruling parties, the presidency would rotate back and forth between the ADN and MIR for the remainder of the 1990s. These maneuvers can be interpreted as attempts by the *Acuerdo Patriótico* to establish the façade of a two-party system that disguises a de facto single-party structure.

As others have noted, locking the opposition out of the rotation of patronage does not bode well for the continuity of the democratic process (Linz 1990; Mainwaring 1990b). In Bolivia, these maneuvers by the ruling alliance have already led to the discussion of scenarios where the opposition resorts to anti-democratic mechanisms to inject itself back into the power-and-patronage game. Whatever scenario plays itself out in the 1990s, unless Bolivian rulers can address the issue of patronage rotation among all sectors of the dependent middle class, democratic stability will be in question.

As of the early 1990s, the principal political institutions in Bolivia have little or no public support. Because political parties, Congress, and the judiciary have extremely low confidence ratings, a likely scenario in the 1993 elections may be the coming to power of nontraditional quasi-populist parties and leaders. Max Fernández (*Unión Cívica Solidaridad* — UCS) and Carlos Palenque (*Conciencia de Patria* — CONDEPA) — a controversial beer factory owner and a radio-television station owner, respectively — have become the front runners in most public opinion polls.[19] Much of their support is based on appeals to race and class, but their strategy is essentially patrimonial.

The greatest threat to the electoral ambitions of traditional parties comes from Max Fernández. In a short period, Fernández has translated the UCS into a mechanism to deliver promises to vast and remote sectors of Bolivia. The slogan "Max obras" ("Max works") has become more than simple political statement. Throughout the country, Fernandez has built hospitals and schools, paved roads, and handed out sporting equipment and generators.[20]

Fernández made his appearance in 1986 when he managed to purchase enough stock to control the Cervecería Boliviana Nacional (CBN), Bolivia's largest brewery. Fernández, a Cochabamba native of humble background, claims that his business skills enabled him to establish a monopoly over the commercialization and distribution of beer in Santa Cruz, which he then used to control the entire company.[21] It is worth noting that control over the commercialization and distribution of beer in Bolivia of the mid-1980s was a very profitable venture. During the hyperinflationary period of 1984-1985, for example, rumor had it that the government could pay its salaries only when the CBN paid its taxes. Much speculation has surrounded the origins of Fernández's fortune. Until recently, the U.S. Embassy was obsessed with indicting him for alleged ties to the narcotics industry. Little evidence is available; however, unsubstantiated charges are often made linking Fernández to the *"Cartel de los Techos,"* Bolivia's prominent drug cartel based in Santa Ana de Yacuma. U.S. Embassy officials now consider it imprudent to go after Fernández primarily because of the increase in his popular support.[22] In short, he will no longer face the obstacles placed in his path during the 1989 elections. Because Fernández's UCS was not allowed to run in the 1989 elections, it holds no seats in the National Congress. The government and the opposition parties have used this as an excuse to exclude him and his party from all major and minor negotiations. The UCS was conspicuously absent, for example, from any of the negotiations which led to electoral law reform. Thanks to arrangements worked out with the MNR during the December 1989 municipal elections, however, the UCS was able to occupy prominent positions in the mayoralties of Cochabamba, Oruro, Trinidad, and several other provinces.

Fernández runs the UCS in an authoritarian manner and, in classic populist style, control over his political party is determined by his capacity to deliver perquisites. His wealth has enabled him to establish a wide network based on old-style vertical and hierarchical patron-clientelism. Fernández names the party leadership; in fact, no assemblies or elections have been held to elect the governing body of the UCS. Most striking, however, is Fernández's rather unappealing personality. He lacks charisma, speaks lower-class Spanish, and is unable to articulate a party platform. To overcome this, Fernández has hired prominent members of the political class to present UCS campaign promises.

As Jorge Lazarte argues, Fernández resembles the MNR's Gonzalo Sánchez de Lozada in many ways. Both are entrepreneurial, pragmatic men of action rather than words (Lazarte 1991). Because both appeal to the same social sectors, the lower-middle classes and the urban proletariat, Fernández's humble social origins may give him an electoral advantage. Lupe Andrade, a prominent Bolivian journalist, has aptly described Fernández's appeal:

> His humble origins coupled with blatant wealth convey the idea that his success story could be replicated. He has become a combination Donald Trump and Santa Claus (Andrade 1991).

Most appealing to the working classes is Max's innovative employer-worker relations at the CBN. Workers in the brewery enjoy high wages and other benefits not available to blue-collar employees elsewhere in the private or public sector. On one occasion when the government decreed a wage increase, Fernández doubled the salaries of his workers. Periodically, newspapers carry declarations from grateful workers who defend him from his political opponents.[23]

Fernández has attracted a number of experienced political hacks who have become his advisers and candidates for office. Over the course of the past two years, dozens of dissidents from major and minor parties have flocked to UCS. The expectation is that the trend will continue.[24] The likelihood of a UCS electoral victory has already forced strategists from every political party to ponder an alliance with Max Fernández.

Carlos Palenque, the other rising political star, has also been the source of much discontent in Bolivia's political class. In 1989 Palenque parlayed his electoral victory in La Paz into a patronage concession from the ruling *Acuerdo Patriótico* which handed control of the La Paz Development Corporation (*Corporación de Desarrollo de La Paz* — CORDEPAZ) to CONDEPA. In the December 1989 municipal elections, CONDEPA also captured the city of La Paz, but Palenque was shut out of the mayor's office by virtue of the ruling *Acuerdo Patriótico*'s control over the municipal council. In December 1991, however, CONDEPA's victory in La Paz was ratified by the municipal council when the defeated ADN candidate pledged to support the winner even if the victory was only by one vote.[25]

In the two years since, CONDEPA's fortunes have been mixed. Its support continues to be drawn from marginal and displaced sectors, especially El Alto and the slums surrounding La Paz. Charges of corruption in the administration of CORDEPAZ confirmed the worst suspicions of members of the upper and middle classes but did little to dissuade the marginal sectors who support CONDEPA unconditionally. Palenque's hobnobbing with the *Acuerdo Patriótico* did raise some concern among his supporters who feared their leader's cooptation.

In late 1990, however, CONDEPA's split with the government thrust CONDEPA firmly into the opposition camp. Although Palenque had previously expressed major reservations about joining forces with the MNR, in February 1991 Palenque had no other alternative but to join Sánchez de Lozada as one of the leaders of the opposition.

Palenque and CONDEPA may play a crucial role in the stability of Bolivian democracy and may be a mitigating force that prevented the emergence of radical groups among the marginal sectors of El Alto and La Paz. As is the case with Max Fernández's UCS, CONDEPA is primarily a populist movement which employs patrimonial rewards to attract and keep followers. Unlike Max Fernández, however, the *Compadre* Palenque has developed ties to marginal sectors through the use of his radio and television stations. For these displaced groups and for recent arrivals to the capital city, Palenque's stations provide not only a vehicle for integration into city life but also an alternative to a discriminatory justice system. Broadcasting in Aymara, Palenque often inflames racial tensions that are of concern to the "white" population of La Paz. Because Palenque's CONDEPA channels these tensions, they have also remained somewhat subdued and controlled. In this sense, CONDEPA may be a uniquely Bolivian way of dealing with racial tension, which has prevented (or delayed) the emergence of radical groups in the urban centers of the country (Gamarra 1991). In short, Fernández and Palenque have positioned themselves to become the two most powerful political contenders; a Fujimori-style phenomenon in Bolivia is not beyond possibility.

Were this to be the case, the problems facing the continued implementation of economic stabilization would remain and perhaps be aggravated. Rumors of coalitions between Fernández's UCS and the MNR, MIR, ADN, CONDEPA, and others are already circulating. As these outsiders enter the system in full force, the system will undergo its most severe test.

Conclusion

The imposition of neoliberal reforms in Bolivia was possible because of political mechanisms that enabled civilian presidents to overcome severe institutional tensions. In 1985 the establishment of the *Pacto por la Democracia* provided President Paz Estenssoro with the political capacity to impose and sustain a draconian neoliberal austerity program. The pact translated into a significant vehicle for transcending executive-legislative impasses which, in turn, gave way to a three-year process of stable and effective governance. A strong executive monopolized all policy initiatives, while the legislature functioned as a "rubber stamp" to legitimize presidential initiatives.

The "Bolivian miracle" and the formation of the pact had much to do with factors specific to the situation in that country in 1985. Consequently, any attempt at replication is unlikely elsewhere in Latin America, or even in Bolivia. Moreover, a key dimension of stabilization, pact formation, and the process of governance rested upon the leadership skills of Victor Paz Estenssoro and General Hugo Banzer Suárez, the leader of the principal opposition party. By controlling factional disputes, both men were able to provide legislative discipline to support policy initiatives related to stabilization.

The political pact was also possible because of a convergence around the basic premises of the *Nueva Política Económica* by the three principal political parties. The emerging "modern and pragmatic" style of Bolivian politics eliminated ideological confrontations between parties while establishing a political center contested by the ADN, MIR, and MNR. From the perspective of members of all three parties, the decline of ideologies and the acceptance of neoliberalism form part of a new Bolivian political system. In this system, ideological conflicts have given way to competition focusing on issues related mainly to institutionalizing the NPE reforms. In my view, however, this "consensus" is largely a product of the lack of policy alternatives available to Bolivian policy makers.

The emergence of a political center and a strong ruling coalition have not been enough, however, to overcome constitutional and electoral mechanisms, which give the Bolivian National Congress the power to elect the president when no candidate wins a majority. As a result, in Bolivia three distinct types of coalitions have to be formed: electoral coalitions, which allow parties to establish a broad platform to appeal to wider segments of the electorate; congressional coalitions, which enable the election of a president; and a ruling coalition to govern the country. These principal characteristics anchor the entire system in the role and functioning of political parties and Congress.

One of the ways to overcome the dilemma of reconstituting alliances is to convert a ruling coalition into a viable electoral vehicle. As the breakdown of the *Pacto por la Democracia* reveals, ruling coalitions lack the flexibility to become viable electoral alliances because the practice of alternating control of the executive branch between the members of the coalition entails recomposing and redistributing patronage. Moreover, to win elections, political parties must form broad conjunctural alliances and propose populist platforms. By the same token, converting an electoral or congressional coalition into a viable governing coalition has proven extremely difficult.

One of the keys to institutionalizing the present system and to imposing stabilization effectively will be to form governing alliances that can fare well during electoral battles. Alliances must be able to transcend postelectoral bargaining. These objectives must take into consideration that, in Bolivia, the principal function of elections has been to allow competing leaders periodically to restructure patronage networks. In short, the recomposition and redistribution of political patronage is the Achilles' heel of Bolivia's political system.

Most of the structural and institutional problems in Bolivia revolve around the dynamics of political parties and their demands for state patronage. Paradoxically, while parties are the main problem of governance in Bolivia, they are also the only source for a solution. Because hard sources of wealth have been limited in number and are not readily transferable, wealth and status have been dispersed primarily from state resources. Political office, the only means to access such resources, has been converted into one of the few conveyable "commodities." As noted elsewhere, in Bolivia, whatever the formal organizational facade, a central dynamic of politics has always been to circulate the commodity of government positions (*cargos, puestos, y pegas*) among the dependent middle class which does not control hard sources of wealth on its own (Malloy and Gamarra 1988, Gamarra 1991; Malloy 1970).

This dynamic explains the steady expansion of the size and extractive demands of Bolivia's state and the prevalence of "*empleomanía*" or job factionalism as a driving force among the political class and the political party system. In Bolivia, political parties depend more on the state for resources than on class formations or interest associations. Their dependence on the state is so great that it would not be an exaggeration to argue that political parties have been extensions of the state, a quasi "political class" rooted as much in the state as sectoral or class formations are rooted in "civil society."

Stabilization and neoliberal reforms, of course, run counter to this basic dynamic. In this context, generating economic growth is politically crucial because it is the key to providing resources to maintain the Bolivian state. In other words, economic development is crucial to any hope of generating alternative sources of wealth and status which may diminish the stakes in the political-class game of *cargos, puestos, y pegas*.

These are the challenges facing the current *Acuerdo Patriótico*, which attempted to emulate the principal dimensions of the defunct *Pacto por la Democracia*. Recent ADN and MIR attempts to establish a governing arrangement that would allow for the rotation of power while preserving a grip over the legislature build on the previous pact's projects to institutionalize a three-party political system. Such a system would not only allow for the concentration of power in the executive but would also provide an effective mechanism for the rotation of patronage among members of the political center, defined along the "pragmatic" lines of the NPE.

The *Acuerdo Patriótico* has survived a conflict-riddled three years. Because of institutional crises it has had to face, the alliance has been forced not only to ensure satisfaction within the governing pact but also to address the demands for access to patronage by the principal opposition parties. This entailed coming to terms with key demands for reform from the MNR and other opposition groups, including reforming the current electoral laws and even Article 90 of the constitution, which provides for the congressional election of presidents.

The critical issue raised by the Bolivian experience is the impact on policy outcomes of the method of selecting the executive. Owing to this fact, a recurrent need to form coalitions has paradoxically become both the strength and the weakness of the system. Coalitions, such as the *Pacto por la Democracia* and the current *Acuerdo Patriótico*, have enabled executives to overcome recalcitrant congressional opposition in order to impose economic stabilization measures. By demonstrating a capacity to enter into long-term pacts, these coalitions have also revealed a degree of political maturation in Bolivia's political class. Less than five years ago, it would have been improbable and even absurd to suggest the possibility of a coalition between ADN and MIR; the ability to form coalitions has given the system stability. It is noteworthy, therefore, that recent Bolivian governments have possessed the capacity to carry forth a democratization process while simultaneously implementing draconian austerity measures.

Coalitions, however, have also served to shut out the opposition from patronage spoils and from the decision-making process. In domestic policy, the opposition has been excluded from participation in (or discussion of) the enactment of key legislation such as mining codes, investment laws, privatization laws, and the like. This situation has also revealed itself rather dramatically in the manner in which the government has negotiated foreign policy, especially counter-narcotics agreements with the United States. Owing to this exclusionary style, Congress has demonstrated a lack of knowledge regarding the details of international agreements it must approve as well as technicalities of economic policy. This exclusionary pattern does not bode well for the future as opposition groups consider extra-systemic ways to influence policy making.

Notes

1. Jeffrey Sachs (1986) claimed that between May and August 1985 Bolivian inflation surged to an annual rate of 60,000 percent.

2. See Article 111 of the Bolivian Constitution. This is the main reason why Siles Zuazo was unable to launch a state-of-siege to control unrest between 1982 and 1985.

3. Because the MNR had adopted many of the elements of ADN's economic stabilization program, Banzer was put into an untenable situation. He could either oppose the NPE for purely political reasons or support a program designed by members of his own economic team. For an extension of this analysis, consult Conaghan, Malloy, and Abugattas (1990).

4. Juan Linz (1990) defines "dual legitimacy" as competing claims to plebiscitarian legitimacy on the part of legislatures and executives. This situation results from zero-sum elections which produce fixed-term minority governments, in which losing contenders are locked out from executive power and patronage.

5. Throughout the three-year duration of the pact, members of ADN and the MNR complained about the alliance. MNR militants were upset by the loss of sources of patronage and the perceived loss of the party's traditional populist electorate. ADN members, in turn, did not trust the MNR's promises of support for Banzer's presidential bid in 1989. Weekly meetings of representatives from each party resolved many of these issues. On the whole, the role and presence of both Banzer and Paz Estenssoro prevented party discipline from breaking down earlier.

6. The situation was made worse by the fact that the MNR had surrendered government posts to the MIR in return for its vote in Congress for Paz Estenssoro. After the signing of the pact, the government was forced to generate patronage to meet the demands of three party organizations.

7. The MIR's votes were not necessary to impose a state-of-siege; however, it is important to note that the MIR did not join any interpellation maneuvers that could have threatened the government's attempt to defeat organized labor's strikes.

8. The role of Sawyer and Miller, a New York-based consulting firm, was crucial in the decision to break the pact. It was also responsible for the tone of the campaign. For an extension of this analysis, consult Gamarra and Malloy (forthcoming).

9. The fact that together the MIR and ADN controlled the electoral court proved to be the key to the MNR's exclusion. Charges and countercharges of fraud were rampant. In the end the three parties pledged before the Catholic Church that the first priority of the new government would be to reform the electoral law again.

10. This was a statement aimed at the MNR in response to its violation of the alternability addendum to the *Pacto por la Democracia*.

11. Gonzalo Sánchez de Lozada interview, August 9, 1989.

12. Interviews with ADN members of COPAP, La Paz, May 1991.

13. Instead the congressional leadership, dominated by the ADN-MIR coalition, declared a recess which lasted for most of the ninety-day state-of-siege. Because the recess was approved without a quorum, it correctly gave rise to charges of unconstitutionality.

14. Interview with Javier Lupo, president of CONALID, La Paz, Bolivia, July 9, 1991. Lupo also pointed out the importance of the coca-cocaine industry to national employment figures. Nearly 200,000 people depend on the production of coca leaves for their livelihood.

15. Tensions with the Supreme Court began when, despite the absence of an extradition treaty, Paz Zamora turned over to the Drug Enforcement Administration (DEA) Colonel Luis Arce Gómez and Herlan Echevarría, two former officials of the Alan García Meza government, who were accused of drug trafficking. For an analysis of this conflict, consult Gamarra (1991).

16. The government's bargaining leverage was undermined by the naming of retired Colonel Faustino Rico Toro, whom the DEA suspected of ties to the narcotics industry, to head the *Fuerzas Especiales de Lucha Contra el Narcotráfico*, Bolivia's principal counternarcotics force. In the scandal which followed, the MNR spearheaded efforts to reduce Paz Zamora's term by calling for early elections.

17. The only party which has shared in the patronage distribution is *Conciencia de Patria* (CONDEPA), led by the populist radio and television station owner Carlos Palenque. CONDEPA's share came because it carried the department of La Paz in the 1989 elections.

18. According to one report, contrary to promises of austerity and cut-backs in the size of the state, the AP members have distributed 20,000 new jobs among themselves since taking power. Consult *Informe R*, May 15-30, 1991.

19. For an excellent discussion of Carlos Palenque's rise to power and prominence, consult Joaquín Saravia and Godofredo Sandóval (1991).

20. In one specific instance, Max Fernández offered to build a *matadero frigorífico* in Santa Cruz at a cost of $800,000. For a good analysis of the Fernández phenomenon, consult Fernando Mayorga (1991).

21. Interview with Max Fernández, La Paz, March 3, 1989.

22. Interviews with several U.S. embassy officials, La Paz, Bolivia, July 1991.

23. For example, workers defended "Don Max" against charges of ties to the drug industry from Guillermo Lora, Bolivia's oldest Trotskyite leader. Lora was subsequently jailed following a lawsuit for defamation and libel brought against him by Max's lawyers.

24. Reports of defections to UCS from ADN have been revealed since as early as February 1991.

25. As is true in the national elections, if a candidate fails to win 50 percent plus one vote, it is up to the municipal council to elect the mayor from the top two finishers.

References

Andrade, Lupe. 1991. "The Road from Beer Barrels to Pork Barrels." *Hemisfile* 2 (5).

Barrios Morón, Raúl. 1991. "Bolivia: Retórica y realidad de la diplomacia en línea directa." Documento de Trabajo No. 37. La Paz: Facultad Latinoamericano de Ciencias Sociales (FLACSO).

Conaghan, Catherine M., James M. Malloy, and Luis Abugattas. 1990. "Business and the Boys: The Origins of Neoliberalism in the Central Andes." *Latin American Research Review* XXV (2):3-29.

Gamarra, Eduardo, and James M. Malloy. Forthcoming. "Mass Politics and Elite Arrangements: Elections and Democracy in Bolivia." In *Bolivia After Hyperinflation*, eds. Jerry Ladman and Juan Antonio Morales. Tempe: Arizona State University, Center for Latin American Studies.

Gamarra, Eduardo A. 1990. "The Privatization Debate in Bolivia." In *Privatization and Deregulation in Global Perspective,* eds. Dennis Gayle and Jonathan Goodrich. New York: Quorum Books.

Gamarra, Eduardo A. 1991. *The System of Justice in Bolivia: An Institutional Analysis.* Miami, Center for the Administration of Justice, Florida International University, Monograph Series.

Informe R. May 15-30, 1991.

Lazarte, Jorge. 1991 "Partidos, democracia, problemas de representación e informalización de la política: el caso de Bolivia." Unpublished manuscript.

Linz, Juan. 1990. "The Perils of Presidentialism." *Journal of Democracy* 1 (1):51-69.

Mainwaring, Scott. 1990a. "Presidentialism in Latin America." *Latin American Research Review* XXV (1):157-179.

Mainwaring, Scott. 1990b. "Presidentialism, Multiparty Systems, and Democracy: The Difficult Equation." Paper presented at Annual Meeting of the Midwest Political Science Association, April 5-7, Chicago, Illinois.

Mainwaring, Scott, and Matthew Shugart. Forthcoming. *Presidentialism and Democracy in Latin America.* Cambridge: Cambridge University Press.

Malloy, James M. 1970. *The Uncompleted Revolution.* Pittsburgh: Pittsburgh University Press.

Malloy, James M. 1989. "Democracy, Economic Crisis and the Problem of Governance: The Case of Bolivia." Paper presented at the XV Annual Congress of the Latin American Studies Association, Miami, Florida, December 4-6.

Malloy, James M., and Eduardo Gamarra. 1988. *Revolution and Reaction: Bolivia 1964-1985.* New Brunswick: Transaction Books.

Malloy, James M., and Eduardo Gamarra. Forthcoming. "The Patrimonial Dynamics of Party Politics in Bolivia." In *Building Democratic Institutions: Parties and Party Systems in Latin America*, eds. Scott Mainwaring and Timothy Scuddly. Stanford: Stanford University Press.

Mayorga, Fernando. 1991. *Max Fernández: La política del silencio.* La Paz: ILDIS.

Mayorga, René A. 1989. "Tendencias y problemas de la consolidación de la democracia en Bolivia." Paper presented at the XV Annual Congress of the Latin American Studies Association, Miami, Florida, December 4-6.

Morales, Juan Antonio. 1991. "La nueva política económica y la modernización del estado." Paper presented at the conference on "Democracia y gobernabilidad en Bolivia y América Latina." La Paz, Bolivia, May 16-17.

Muller, Herbert, and Flavio Machicado, eds. 1987. *El diálogo para la democracia.* La Paz: Quipus.

Palermo, Vicente. 1990. "Programas de ajuste y estrategias políticas: las experiencias recientes de la Argentina y Bolivia." *Desarrollo Económico* 30 (119).

Sachs, Jeffrey, and Juan Antonio Morales. 1986. "The Bolivian Hyperinflation and Stabilization." Working Paper No. 2073. Cambridge: NBER.

Saravia, Joaquín, and Godofredo Sandóval. 1991. *Jach'a Uru: ¿La esperanza de un pueblo?* La Paz: Instituto Latino Americano de Investigaciones Sociales (ILDIS-CEP).

Shugart, Matthew, and John M. Carey. 1992. *Presidents and Assemblies: Institutional Design and Electoral Dynamics.* Cambridge: Cambridge University Press.

Chapter 5

Democracy, Economic Liberalism, and Structural Reform in Bolivia

---

Juan Antonio Morales

Introduction

S hortly after being proclaimed president of Bolivia in August 1985, Víctor Paz Estenssoro launched an ambitious program of inflation containment and structural reforms, which he called the New Economic Policy (NEP). The NEP signaled a well-defined break with the development model that Bolivia had been following since the 1950s.[1] NEP reforms are not only the most important since the 1952 Revolution, but they are also among the boldest in Latin America's movement toward liberalism. The adoption of this liberal economic policy did not take place at the same time as the restoration of democracy in Bolivia; instead, it occurred several years later, following a very serious deterioration of the national economy.

After some hesitation, the government of Jaime Paz Zamora, who succeeded Paz Estenssoro in 1989, continued the NEP and proposed additional structural reforms in order to deepen it. The most important theme in Paz Zamora's reform agenda is privatization.

The original set of NEP reforms consisted of 1) liberalization of internal markets and suppression of price controls, 2) opening of the national economy to foreign trade and international capital flows, and 3) opening of the labor market. These reforms, along with fiscal "cleansing" measures that achieved the immediate reduction of inflation, restored significant margins of action to the private sector while eliminating the most serious distortions in prices, which had been the sources of considerable economic inefficiencies.

These liberalizations were executed simultaneously and quickly, often out of the sequence suggested by economic experts and by the experiences of other countries. They achieved significant reduction in the size of the central government, which reserved for its direct administration only the national petroleum company (Yacimientos Petrolíferos Fiscales Bolivianos —

129

YPFB) and the profitable mines, or those with confirmed potential, of the Bolivian Mining Corporation (Corporación Minera de Bolivia — COMIBOL). All other enterprises were ceded to Regional Development Corporations (RDCs) and to municipal control. The NEP also imposed important reductions on the scope of the central bank and, later in the Paz Zamora administration, closed the state development banks.

With the advent of the NEP, the Bolivian government abandoned the directive (*dirigista*) model of development. This model had been heavily dependent on public investment, was essentially financed with foreign debt, and was based on a system of reciprocities between the public and private sectors that were unmediated by the market.[2] Although government programs that protect the most vulnerable social groups have not entirely disappeared, they have been greatly reduced.

During the first few years, the NEP and the liberal model confronted only moderate political opposition, largely because the demand for price stability prevailed over all other considerations. Only recently have the new "populist" parties, along with some internal factions in traditional parties, urged modifications to the liberal model. Nevertheless, these proposals are not yet very specific. Beyond the parties, however, there are clear signs that the population is becoming impatient with the difference between the promises and the results of the model. This impatience presents the most significant challenge to the continuity and deepening of the liberal model.

This chapter deals, above all, with the political economy of the structural reforms, emphasizing the reduction of state control over the economy. The first section identifies the principal political actors that have been relevant to the economic reforms. The second consists of a discussion of the ideology of the Bolivian liberal model and the controversies that it continues to generate, even among some of its advocates. The third section analyzes the role of the public sector since the implementation of the NEP and includes an analysis of the various attempts at privatization. The fourth and final section examines the new incentive structure for private and national investment and the factors that explain its less than impressive record.

Political Actors of the Liberal Model
The Paz Estenssoro Government

Víctor Paz Estenssoro began his administration in 1985 under extremely difficult conditions. The country was in the midst of a grave economic crisis chiefly manifested by hyperinflation. Bolivia was also mired in a serious political crisis that had forced President Hernán Siles Zuazo to shorten his presidential mandate by one year. In addition, Paz Estenssoro's party, the Movimiento Nacionalista Revolucionario (MNR), no longer had the vitality it had exhibited in the years after the 1952 Revolution and over the years suffered internal fragmentations; by the elections of 1985 MNR had a rather poor showing in Bolivia's urban centers. However, the severity of the crisis conferred a broad mandate to the new government, which obtained the necessary consensus to stop inflation and to carry out the NEP. The Democratic Pact, a strategic alliance of the MNR and its 1985 rival, the Acción Democrática Nacionalista (ADN) of former President Hugo Banzer, assured congressional and media support for the NEP.

The Paz Estenssoro government followed a pattern that soon would become typical of other Andean economies — the combination of economic liberalism with political democracy (Conaghan, Malloy, and Abugattas 1990). Liberal policies were not new in the region; they had been applied, with mixed results, by the Southern Cone military dictatorships of the 1970s. The innovation of the 1980s, however, was their adoption by democratic regimes.

The reestablishment of order and the principle of authority was an important *leitmotif* of the Paz Estenssoro government. To this end, it took energetic measures against labor organizations and the more radical leftist parties. This exaggerated emphasis on establishing order hurt the democratic process.[3]

MNR weaknesses forced Paz Estenssoro to call on independents, entrepreneurs, and technocrats to take part in his government. The presence of the business sector was important to the reestablishment of internal confidence. In addition, experts from the International Monetary Fund (IMF) and the World Bank were provided unprecedented access to the governmental decision-making process. The close collaboration between Bolivian technocrats and functionaries of international credit agencies established external credibility, which was at least as important as internal credibility.

The dominance of technocrats in the government underscored aspects of a procedural democracy tinged with substantive authoritarian attributes. As noted by Conaghan, Malloy, and Abugattas, "The boys [*técnicos*] looked upon the decisions as being of a technical nature. As such, they believed that these decisions should not be subjected to negotiations or political discussions" (Conaghan, Malloy, and Abugattas 1990, 19). Thus, technocratic rationalism, coupled with a good measure of arrogance, clearly prevailed over the demands of social, entrepreneurial, and labor interests.

Another manifestation of the influence of authoritarianism in the application of the NEP was the practice of regulating the economy via presidential decrees that circumvented Congress. In the few cases in which the executive opened discussions in the national legislature (often with considerable misgivings that were only outweighed by the possibility of committing flagrant constitutional violations), the MNR-ADN congressional majority was quickly utilized to approve the measures before emergence of widespread public debate. This practice has been carried to extremes by Paz Zamora.

The Paz Zamora Government

Despite its rigors, by 1989 the NEP was widely accepted by the electorate and public opinion. The three parties that supported the NEP — the MNR, ADN, and the Leftist Revolutionary Movement (Movimiento de Izquierda Revolucionaria — MIR) — obtained 65 percent of the popular vote in the May elections. Jaime Paz Zamora, who had placed third, was chosen president as a result of an unexpected congressional alliance between the MIR and Banzer's ADN. These parties formed a coalition government that they termed the Patriotic Accord.[4]

The transition between the two governments was not as smooth as might have been expected. Paz Zamora's election created an unstable situation in the financial market and people "stampeded" to the banks shortly after they found out in early August 1989 that Paz Zamora would be the new president.[5] The composition of the cabinet, however, calmed many fears. The private sector felt reassured by appointments of the president of the National Association of Banks and Financial Institutions and of an experienced official of the Inter-American Development Bank, who were placed in the top positions in the finance and planning ministries, respectively. The entrepreneurs expected that the forceful personalities of these two key ministers would prevent members of the cabinet from moving away from the NEP.

Paz Zamora's election, as a result of the uneasiness it created, probably delayed the recovery of Bolivia's economy following the drastic anti-inflationary program. Only by 1991 was the private sector's uncertainty substantially reduced. During his presidential campaign, Paz Zamora had vaguely promised to change the NEP. Only a few months after taking office, however, he announced via decree 22407 (January 1, 1990) that he would continue to accelerate the NEP's liberal reforms. Since then his government has adhered to the NEP and the liberal model. Indeed, Paz Zamora in some cases has adopted more orthodox liberal policies than those implemented by Paz Estenssoro, and the IMF and the World Bank's influence in internal decision making has also increased.

Paz Zamora confronted the dilemma faced by virtually all social democratic governments of the region: he first had to see that the economy achieve vigorous growth before carrying out his redistributional policies. He also faced pressure from his ally, the ADN, and from international organizations.

As could be expected, Paz Zamora's embrace of liberal economic policies created conflicts within the MIR. These were controlled through political clientelism and the practice of co-opting intraparty dissenters with public appointments. A similar process occurred with regard to the other, smaller leftist parties in alliance with the MIR. Nevertheless, due to these conflicts many liberal policies were implemented without enthusiasm. Clearly, many cabinet ministers felt compelled to accept measures that they did not really support.

Opposition to the Liberal Model

Leftist political parties and labor unions suffered an almost complete erosion of power during the 1982-1985 hyperinflationary period, making possible, in great measure, the advent of the liberal revolution. Parties of the left and unions could offer only weak resistance to the measures that affected them. In addition, the political and economic collapse of socialist countries in central and eastern Europe deprived them of an alternative model to follow. This factor cannot be underestimated, given the strong level of politicization of the labor unions and the traditional influence of Marxist intellectuals on their leadership. Support for the NEP appears to have changed since 1989. The strongest opposition to the neoliberal model now comes from populist parties, which enjoy significant electoral support but lack well-defined economic programs. Indeed, these parties convey a mood of popular discontent with the NEP but fail to articulate specific proposals for reforming the model. The results of the December 1991 municipal elections, in which the populist parties Unión Cívica Solidaridad (UCS) and Conciencia de Patria (CONDEPA), obtained favorable results — to the detriment of the MIR-ADN alliance — confirmed the political weakening of support for the model. The national uproar over the public sector budget, presented early in 1992 and dramatized by large and violent street demonstrations, offered more evidence of this loss of momentum.

New political parties constitute an enigma to analysts. In particular, neither the ideology nor economic program of the UCS are known, and it is not clear if the populist label often ascribed to it is even appropriate. CONDEPA, in contrast, exhibits many of the ultranationalist positions that have been presented by some leftist factions and the so-called "nationalist revolutionary" movement throughout Bolivia's twentieth-century history.

It is true that municipal election results are not good predictors of national trends, partly because elections center on local personalities rather than national platforms. However, the results of local elections, coupled with other indicators, seem to signal popular demand for a different political discourse.

Much of the opposition to the model centers on privatization, which originally garnered considerable public support due to the perception that it would combat corruption, but in a surprising twist it is now seen in the opposite way. The political opposition and the media express fears that the sale of public companies will benefit only government functionaries rather than private entrepreneurs.

Renewal of Political Parties

An important point — not sufficiently emphasized in most analyses — is the profound change induced by the NEP on political parties, which have almost unwittingly abandoned the pursuit of short-term political advantage in order to attain long-term political viability. This is true even for parties that do not participate directly in the administration of the state. Those that do are not preoccupied with the possibility that their successors will reap the benefits of their administration. This attitude has less to do with the vision of party elites than with the need to improve chances for reelection.

The NEP has reinvigorated the MNR. The party now has a young membership, and its critical capabilities and policy proposals have improved substantially. As a result of its support for democracy since 1982, the other liberal party, ADN, has succeeded in making people forget the years of de facto government headed by its leader, Hugo Banzer. The MIR, in turn, has shown its ability to manage the economy, dispelling doubts that once existed about its representatives' fiscal responsibility. It should be underscored that the MNR has reformed its statutes to allow a greater measure of internal democracy; ADN and MIR have not yet done so, but quite possibly will follow suit. This is a very important change given the essentially *caudillista* structure of Bolivian political parties in the past, when each party's boss (*caudillo*) traditionally acted as a dictator within the party structure. Now, parties are operating more democratically.

The Ideology of the Bolivian Liberal Model
Liberals and Neoliberals

The adoption of the liberal model has not been devoid of contradictions. President Paz Estenssoro and Planning Minister Gonzalo Sánchez de Lozada, architect of the NEP, envisioned the plan more as a tool for the reconstitution of the state and the reestablishment of the principle of authority than as a vehicle leading toward a libertarian objective. The following declaration, made by Sánchez de Lozada, illustrates this point:

> Rather than a strictly economic program the NEP is a political plan that aims at reestablishing principles that are fundamental to the functioning of the Republic and without which we run a grave risk of following a path of national state disintegration (ILDIS 1985, 5).

Neither Paz Estenssoro nor Sánchez de Lozada subscribed to the classic liberal argument that a market economy produces a better distribution of resources and, thus, an optimal economic outcome. Instead, they embraced the political-economy axiom that market liberalization is the only way to avoid "klepto-patrimonialism." In their vision, a reduced state would diminish influence peddling and the role of pressure groups that regard government as the best vehicle to obtain a larger share in the distribution of national income. In addition, governability was seen as being closely linked to a reduction of the role of the state. This perspective can be described more accurately as neoliberal rather than liberal.[6]

The concepts underlying the NEP reforms should be seen within the context of important changes that had taken place since the early 1970s in political and economic thought emanating from North American and European academic circles and from the influential international financial organizations. With the adoption of the NEP in 1985, the government aligned itself with the "minimalist" perspective of the role of the state. Traditionally, the MIR was not in the least receptive to liberal economic thought. In fact, it had combated it for years. For many MIR activists, especially at the local level, acceptance of this perspective was simply a matter of pragmatism and opportunity. The ADN, on the other hand, had liberalism as its ideological patrimony, but even within the ADN there was resistance to the model by ECLA-oriented economists,[7] some of whom hold important positions in the party hierarchy.

The privatization positions adopted by the Paz Estenssoro and Paz Zamora administrations underscore the ambiguities of Bolivian liberal policies. Privatization, as we have seen, was not included in the nucleus of essential NEP reforms advocated by Paz Estenssoro, whose vision emphasized liberalization as a means to restore state authority. During his administration, some national public enterprises were transferred, as opposed to privatized, to regional development corporations (RDCs) and municipal governments. For its part, the Paz Zamora administration has only belatedly proposed a privatization program to Congress.

Conjuncturalists and Structuralists

Between late 1985 and late 1986, some MNR leaders presented the NEP to the public as a package of emergency measures designed to combat hyperinflation and to restore relations with the international financial community. According to these leaders, the measures were taken in order to curtail runaway inflation and to control the strains that it placed on the external debt. They made it clear that once the crisis was weathered, the "flags of April" — a historic reference to the strongly redistributionist policies of the 1952 revolution — would once more be flown. Since about 1987, the MNR has abandoned this short-term, conjunctural vision and has attempted to tie future governments to the enforcement of the NEP. Legislation was prepared to this end, but the MNR failed to get it approved before a congressional deadline.

Stability of rules and norms has now become one of the principles of economic policy. The goal is to extend to the private sector the necessary guarantees against problems of temporary inconsistency, which are frequent in economics. The dominant forces of the MNR and the Patriotic Accord are trying to present liberal policy as a permanent change in the rules and incentives available to the private sector.

With the exception of the tax code, the Paz Estenssoro reforms were launched via presidential decrees, which are administrative instruments that require legislative approval in order to gain legitimacy and stability. The Paz Zamora government has approved many measures prepared and left behind by its predecessor, although obviously with modifications. In particular, the Paz Zamora administration has insisted on legally clarifying the contractual obligations between the government and the private sector, and among private agents. The legislative reforms center on property rights, their associated guarantees, taxes, and the right to remit profits and repatriate capital.

As important as the legal enshrinement of the NEP are the agreements reached with international financial institutions by both the Paz Estenssoro and Paz Zamora administrations. There has been an important strategic attempt by the two governments and international financial institutions to restrict spending and maneuvering capabilities of future nonliberal governments.[8]

The search for continuity and deepening of liberal policy has prompted the MNR, ADN, and MIR to propose constitutional reforms, both to electoral/representative aspects and to what can be called the "economic constitution" (Urioste 1991). The aim is to return to a constitutional framework that emphasizes individual rights as opposed to the social rights prevalent in most constitutions since World War II. Another goal is the elimination of constitutional limitations to the sale of COMIBOL and YPFB (state-owned mining and petroleum companies), as well as to agricultural land transactions.

Social Market Economy as a New Paradigm

Harder-line liberal positions present in the Paz Estenssoro and Paz Zamora governments appear to be losing ground to more flexible visions. Lately, there has been renewed interest in the so-called "social market economy," which has had a significant impact in postwar West Germany and constitutes one of the ideological foundations of Christian Democracy. The main tenets are 1) the maintenance of broad market freedom, 2) institutional development conducive to the establishment of a measure of consensus among the principal social actors, and 3) social welfare mechanisms designed to protect those who are excessively burdened by competition and a lack of sufficient physical and human capital. State intervention in the economy is not ruled out, although principally only in its role as a referee of last resort in conflict situations.

In addition, the MNR's cornerstone of social policy is based upon the lessons of the Social Emergency Fund, the Paz Estenssoro administration's star project in the attempt to ameliorate extreme suffering caused by the 1985 stabilization program. The parties of the Patriotic Accord have also insisted on what they term social policy, recognizing the importance of raising the standard of living in the poorer sectors. Their focus is not on income distribution but rather on combating poverty.

Changes in the Public Sector
The Administration of the Budget

The crucial role of the public sector in investment and employment was probably the most salient characteristic of the pre-NEP Bolivian economy. The NEP aimed at changing this role. Almost simultaneous with the adoption of the NEP, Bolivia suffered major drops in the prices of its two main export products, tin and natural gas. Due to the combined effects of the NEP and the depreciation of international prices, there has been a substantial reduction of the size of the public sector, at least as measured through the proportion of public spending to GNP. The latter decreased to 27.6 percent in 1990 from an average of 44.9 percent in 1980-1981 (see Table 1). The full implications of this public sector reduction, which was forced in part by external circumstances, will take time to be revealed. It is important to note that the reduction of public spending as a percentage of GNP has been accompanied quite unexpectedly by an increase in public investment since 1988. Despite a substantial spending adjustment, the global fiscal deficit was very high between 1987 and 1989. It is striking that other macroeconomic equilibria were maintained in spite of these deficits.

Table 1
Consolidated Non-Financial Public Sector Operations, 1980-1990
(Percent of GNP)

	average 1980-81	average 1982-85	1986	1987	1988	1989	1990
Current Income	37.4	23.0	24.4	22.1	22.4	22.1	23.0
Current Expenditures	38.2	28.1	23.2	23.6	21.3	20.9	20.7
Current Net Transfers	0.0	0.0	0.0	0.0	0.0	0.5	0.6
Current Surplus/Deficit	-0.8	-5.1	1.2	-1.6	1.0	1.8	3.0
Capital Income	0.5	0.1	1.0	0.2	0.7	1.2	1.3
Capital Expenditures	6.7	4.3	4.6	5.3	6.8	6.6	6.9
Net Capital Transfer	0.0	0.0	0.0	0.0	0.0	-0.6	0.0
Capital Deficit	-6.2	-4.2	-3.6	-5.2	-6.1	-5.9	-5.6
Other Expenditures	0.6	5.8	0.0	0.0	0.4	0.0	0.0
Total Deficit	-7.7	-15.1	-2.3	-6.7	-5.5	-4.2	-2.7
Net Financing	7.7	15.1	2.3	6.7	5.5	4.2	2.7
External	4.6	1.3	5.5	2.2	4.0	1.7	1.9
Domestic	3.1	13.8	-3.2	4.5	1.5	2.4	0.8

Sources: Fiscal data of the Unidad de Análisis de Políticas Económicas (UDAPE), 1991, Estadísticas Económicas 2, La Paz. UDAPE's data reflected the Central Bank's calculation for nominal GNP, with corrections for 1988-1990.

The 1986 tax reform is one of the controlling components of the NEP. A major structural change has taken place as a result of its implementation: there has been a substantial reduction of the role of import taxes, which were most important prior to the reforms, when they accounted for a significant portion of government revenue. The contribution of internal taxes has now increased. The principal tax of the reform is the aggregate value tax, with a uniform value of 10 percent. Although they have not disappeared, corporate taxes now have different characteristics and a lower rate than in the past. As of yet there are no studies on the specific effects of personal income taxes. What is known is that neither equity nor, surprisingly, efficiency was a dominant aspect in their design: the chief goal was the quick resumption of fiscal revenue, although longer-term implications later became evident.

Initially, the results of the tax reform appeared to be quite good, especially when compared with the collections (in real terms) obtained during the hyperinflationary period, when revenues were abnormally low as a result of the Olivera-Tanzi effect.[9] After an initial increase, however, tax collection has stagnated at around 8 percent of GNP (excluding dividends from state corporations), a percentage lower than the Latin American average.

Public Sector Employment

Except for Cuba, pre-NEP Bolivia was probably the Latin American country with the highest percentage of its economically active urban population employed in the public sector. Public employment was reduced by a little over 10 percent during the first year of the NEP (Table 2). Following the public employment cuts of 1986, however, it again started to grow in 1989.

Employment reduction occurred as a result of layoffs (euphemistically called "relocations") and abandonment of employment due to extremely low wages. The most dramatic case was that of the Bolivian Mining Corporation layoffs. This event has been widely documented in excellent works (for example, see Jetté 1989).

What is now needed is more detailed research on the remaining public employment structure. It appears that there has been 1) a negative self-selection process, which resulted in the abandonment of public sector careers by the most competent and competitive functionaries; 2) a significant loss of efficiency, with clear signs of unenthusiastic work by those who remain; and 3) a growing reliance on the temporary hiring of skilled Bolivian workers, whose salaries are paid increasingly by international financial and technical aid. The important point is that, despite higher than average salaries, these bureaucrats are not career public sector functionaries and thus are not eligible for advancement or promotions.

Table 2
Public Sector Employment, 1980-1989

	# of Employees			Indexes (1985=100)		
	Companies (1)	Government (2)	Total (3)	Companies (4)	Government (5)	Total (6)
1980	55,193	137,925	193,188	90	75	79
1981	56,643	143,319	199,962	92	78	81
1982	55,888	148,128	204,016	91	80	83
1983	59,718	164,717	224,435	97	89	91
1984	60,851	175,071	235,922	99	95	96
1985	61,514	184,065	245,579	100	100	100
1986	54,827	166,156	220,983	89	90	90
1987	41,327	171,115	212,442	67	93	87
1988	35,846	168,889	204,735	58	92	83
1989	34,731	174,351	209,082	56	95	85

Source: Unidad de Análisis de Políticas Económicas (UDAPE), 1991, Estadísticas Económicas de Bolivia 2, La Paz.
Note: Column (1) consists of public and mixed companies. Column (2) includes employees of the central, decentralized not included in companies, deconcentrated, local, and university administrations. Column (3) is column (1) plus column (2).

Without disregarding political and social difficulties engendered by massive public sector layoffs and frequent abuse of public prices as a fiscal instrument, it nonetheless may be claimed that this was the easy phase of public sector reform. The reconstitution of administrative structures is taking more time and will require more comfortable fiscal account margins than those now in place. Has the reduction of state employment diminished corruption? Judging by frequent press allegations, the answer appears to be negative. There might even be an increase of corruption, possibly as a result of 1) public sector wage policy, which forces functionaries to supplement their meager income with bribes taken from the public, especially where government employees are in routine contact with it; 2) the excessive use of temporary employees, who may not be interested in investing in a "reputation" precisely because they are not eligible for promotions; 3) the high incidence of excessively large public investment projects financed by providers who often extend illegal commissions to their operatives; and 4) the influence of narcotrafficking.

Social Spending

Social public spending in proportion to GNP suffered sizeable cuts during the first two years of the NEP (see Table 3). The largest reductions were related to education. Health services reductions were less important because foreign aid compensated for the lack of domestic resources. Although as yet there is no confirming data, it appears that since 1988 there has been a sustained increase in the health and education budgets. Recent government statements have emphasized the need to increase social services expenditures.

The Paz Zamora administration has been trying, rather timidly until now, to reduce the military and public university budgets in order to finance social services expenditures without increasing overall spending. At the insistence of the World Bank, the Bolivian government has attempted to implement a social spending policy that focuses on care for the very poor and avoids the diversion of spending to the middle sectors. It is too early to evaluate the results of this basic needs approach, which has been amply criticized elsewhere.

Table 3

Evolution of Social Public Spending, 1980-1989
(Percent of GNP)

	Education(1)	Ministry of Health(2)	Social Security(3)	Total(4)
1980	4.1	0.8	1.4	2.2
1981	2.9	0.5	1.2	1.7
1982	3.2	0.4	1.1	1.5
1983	3.4	0.4	0.8	1.2
1984	3.2	0.4	2.0	2.4
1985	3.3	0.4	1.0	1.4
1986	2.3	0.3	0.7	1.0
1987	2.6	0.5	N/A	N/A
1988	2.6	N/A	N/A	N/A

Sources: World Bank, 1989, "Public Sector Expenditure Review with a Special Emphasis on the Social Sectors."

Note: Column (1) includes transfers from the central government to universities. Column (2), national treasury funding of the Ministry of Social Welfare and Public Health, does not include either regional development corporation or municipal spending. Column (3) is the contribution of employees, employers, and government to social security system health plans.

Privatization

Privatization is a central issue of political and economic debate in Bolivia. It has a very high priority on the Paz Zamora administration's agenda.[10] The arguments employed by the government in favor of privatization are the same as those found in the international debate.[11] It is important to highlight some of its elements. First, privatization would send an unambiguous message regarding the government's will to reduce its own size and scope in the economy and hence induce more private investment. Second, privatization would provide more resources for public sector social spending and thus have an important effect on long-term growth (at least according to the "new" economic-growth theories). Finally, privatization is a condition stipulated by foreign lenders and is required for the continued inflow of external aid.

Many of the arguments *against* all-encompassing privatization are also present in the international debate. The domestic opposition is centered in the large, state-operated natural resource exploitation and utilities companies, which are natural monopolies. Clearly, there is no economic rationale to oppose the privatization of small firms that operate in competitive markets.

The implications of privatization on public sector solvency, including the possibility of incurring loss of revenue, are a crucial consideration. It must also be borne in mind that many of the difficulties related to transactions between private actors, used to justify privatization, will persist due to the imperfections of the market (Vickers and Yarrow 1991).

Another obstacle to privatization is the difficulty in obtaining adequate valuation of public property to be sold. This problem also creates potential conflicts between the government, which does not wish to fail politically in its effort to transfer property to the private sector, and its operatives, who fear subjection to future lawsuits for misuse of state patrimony. Valuation is also behind the corruption charges being voiced against the process. Undoubtedly, the most delicate aspect of privatization lies in its redistributive implications, which will depend on 1) the present profitability of each public enterprise, 2) the prices at which they will be sold, 3) the post-privatization price regime that will determine the value of its products, and 4) the use of the resources generated by the privatizations. Regarding this final point, it is important to ensure that this revenue constitute an *additional* resource to the social sector and not simply a substitute for funds that would have flowed to it anyway.

Since privatization did not explicitly form part of the Paz Estenssoro reform program, some important utility companies remained in the public sector, as did a large number of small companies, despite the general rule aiming at state disinvestment in the 1985 reform package.[12] Nevertheless, it is clear that the transfer of the Bolivian Development Corporation to the RDCs and municipalities was indeed visualized as an intermediate step toward privatization.

The Paz Zamora administration has only recently presented its privatization plan to the national legislature and has managed to have it approved by the Chamber of Deputies (lower house). However, this has been achieved amidst the greatest of controversies, and there is a danger that it will be annulled by the Supreme Court due to procedural violations. The Paz Zamora program will principally affect the RDCs.

Private Investment and Development Laws
Private Investment

The main long-term objective of the NEP is GNP growth propelled by private investment. The Paz Zamora administration has correctly insisted on legal guarantees and the need to clarify contractual relationships to promote investment. Toward this goal the Mining Actualization Law, the Hydrocarbons Law, and the Investment Code were approved between 1990 and 1991. The first two laws contain provisions to facilitate joint ventures between state and private companies, and they also include tax modifications. As a result, the opening of nonrenewable national resources to foreign capital has been substantial — indeed, possibly greater than in other Latin American countries. The Investment Code simply reiterates what was already law, but it served to announce the government's pledge to respect the property rights of investors.

The medium-term test of the success of this legislation consists not only of the measure of the volume of investment it attracted but also of the tax revenues generated. It should not be forgotten that in the not-too-distant past one of the principal arguments for the expansion of the "entrepreneurial state" was precisely the belief that private investment in natural resources did not contribute sufficient taxes to finance a growing social spending agenda.

Deqpite the reestablishment of important macroeconomic equilibria and favorable legislation, private investment has taken a long time to make an impact. Between 1986 and 1990, private investment levels, measured as a percentage of GNP, were unusually low and similar to those of the crisis years of 1982 and 1985 (see Table 4). Preliminary 1991 figures (not included in Table 4) point to a vigorous growth of both private investment and GNP, although their sustainability remains in question.

Table 4
Public and Private Gross Fixed Capital Formation, 1980-1990
(Percent of GNP)

	Public (1)	Private (2)	Total (3)	GNP growth (%)(4)
1980	7.0	7.3	14.3	-1.4
1981	7.2	3.8	11.0	0.9
1982	6.9	6.9	13.8	-4.4
1983	5.0	3.6	8.6	-4.5
1984	4.5	4.0	8.5	-0.6
1985	3.5	3.7	7.2	-1.0
1986	4.8	4.7	9.5	-2.5
1987	6.2	4.1	10.3	2.6
1988	8.1	4.1	12.2	3.0
1989	8.7	4.1	12.8	2.7
1990	8.0	5.2	13.2	2.6

Sources: For 1980-1989, "Bolivia: From Stabilization to Sustained Growth," World Bank, August 1991. For 1990, author estimates.

Domestic and foreign investors do not seem willing to relinquish their right to "wait and see." Meanwhile, the influential Bolivian Private Entrepreneurs' Federation (Confederación de Empresarios Privados de Bolivia — CEPB) has increased the list of conditions it deems necessary for the awakening of the investors' "animal spirits." It has demanded that the government deregulate and privatize the utilities companies as well as the social security contribution agencies. This last measure is considered essential in order to develop a capital market.[13]

"Sociological" interpretations could be offered as counterarguments to the perspective of business organizations. Gonzalo Chávez (1991) has argued that the successful transfer of responsibility from the public to the private sector depends on the degree of entrepreneurial and capital-market development, the sociological profile of the private entrepreneurs themselves, and the evaluation of country risk, including political factors, by foreign investors.

Private Sector Beneficiaries

Redistributive arguments are not altogether absent in the liberal reforms. To begin with, the struggle against corruption, which is a perverse form of redistribution, is a central issue in Bolivian liberalism. More conventionally, it has been argued that although the NEP could temporarily hurt union workers and middle-class bureaucrats, it would favor the poorer sectors — the peasantry and informal urban workers. Statistics, however, do not support this premise, at least as far as the peasantry is concerned (Morales 1991).

Unfortunately, there are no recent studies on income redistribution. The existing information, although nonsystematic, seems to indicate that those who have benefited from the NEP are, above all, the export and commercial elites, those with financial means, and the upper- and middle-class sectors able to channel the flow of international aid resources to their benefit.

Conclusion

Current Bolivian economic policy presents a clear break with the *dirigista* development model that prevailed after 1952. The changes that have taken place in Bolivia's economy and society after the 1985 liberal revolution are profound. The principal characteristics of the present model include an opening of the national economy to foreign commerce and international capital flows, a government reduced in its functions and participation in the economy — although with the capacity to maintain price stability — and a structure of incentives favorable to private economic activity. All of this is important. However, is it enough? The answer is no. The agenda of unfinished tasks is large: in particular, 1) institutional development is lacking, 2) democratic participation mechanisms are insufficient, 3) there is a lack of coordination among private economic entities (and between them and the government), 4) there are no effective channels of expression for the most extreme social conflicts, and 5) there is inadequate preparation for sustained, long-term growth. A structural public administration reform, which may be even more important than privatization, remains to be carried out. The state has indeed reduced its role; however, increased efficiency has not resulted. Performance in areas such as health and basic education, activities conceded to the state by even the most liberal observers, is the same or worse than six years ago. Nor does it appear that the political-economy hypothesis that the shrinking of the state diminishes corruption has been realized, although this may be attributable to the insufficient nature of the self-reduction schemes.

Despite the difficulties, it is expected that the model will continue to be utilized, albeit with some changes from the last six years. The MNR, MIR, and ADN appear to concur in giving the model a very social overtone, especially as it refers to public spending on the poor. In a change of position, the three parties now maintain that the shrinking of the state does not imply that the government will cease to intervene in the economy. They do insist, however, that public investment must complement private investment rather than be a substitute for it.

It is still early to pass judgment on the full impact of the Bolivian liberal revolution, which will doubtless confront many more obstacles in upcoming years. If there are no concrete changes for the better in economic output, employment, real wages, and increased access to public services, the largest challenge may come relatively soon from electoral populism via the ballot box. Within this context, the need for political and economic democratization will become increasingly urgent.

Notes

---

1. The hyperinflationary period and the anti-inflationary measures are documented in Sachs (1987) and Morales (1988).

2. For a critical account of pre-NEP Bolivian development from a neoclassical perspective, see Morales and Sachs (1990).

3. Paz Estenssoro declared two states of siege in his first year in office and continuously applied political pressure to the labor unions, harassing them while acting within the law. This style of governing has been continued by Paz Zamora. To demonstrate his authority, for example, Paz Zamora declared a state of siege only a few weeks after coming to power, ostensibly in order to suppress a teachers' strike. This measure was clearly unnecessary in view of the existence of less extreme legal means that would have accomplished the same goal.

4. In addition to the MIR and ADN, the Patriotic Accord also included two minor parties, the Partido Demócrata Cristiano (PDC) and the Frente Revolucionario de Izquierda (FRI).

5. It should be noted that a significant number of large bank withdrawals had already taken place in the period between the May popular elections and the August congressional election.

6. There is an abundance of neoliberal research that is strongly critical of the state. Among others, see the theoretical elaborations of economists such as Bhagwati (1982) and Krueger (1990). This position is also close to that of Olson (1982) and, even more so, to Buchanan's "public choice" school (1987).

7. ECLA is the United Nations' Economic Commission for Latin America, whose analysts generally subscribe to dependency-oriented views of Latin American underdevelopment and advocate a major role for the state in the economy.

8. An analogy can be made with the U.S. fiscal situation in the recent past, in which former President Ronald Reagan, by significantly increasing the public debt, succeeded in reducing the spending capacity of future Democratic presidents (Alessina and Carliner 1991).

9. The Olivera-Tanzi effect occurs when inflation and real interest rates are high. Taxpayers have the incentive to delay paying taxes as long as possible, thereby reducing the value of tax collections when ultimately received by the government.

10. Here we will use the term privatization in the narrowest sense, referring to the transfer of property from the public to the private sector. Elimination of public enterprises will not be considered as privatization but rather as a public sector reorganization measure.

11. See Vickers and Yarrow's (1991) excellent revision of the economist's perspective on privatization. Remarkable political approaches on this appear in

Suleiman and Waterbury (1990) and Starr (1990). For specific aspects related to Bolivia, see Chávez (1991).

12. State participation in the provision of public services such as electricity, railroad and air transport, and communications remains substantial.

13. The demands of private entrepreneurs are not limited to services and social security companies; they include all state-owned companies. Surprisingly, the CEPB has in the last two years assumed a position as militant as that exhibited during the Siles Zuazo administration. It considers itself the standard-bearer of the liberal reforms, which it aggressively advocates. As a result of this stance, public opinion has been less receptive than the CEPB had hoped.

References

Alessina, Alberto, and Geoffrey Carliner. 1991. "Introduction." In *Politics and Economics in the Eighties*, eds. Alberto Alessina and Geoffrey Carliner. Chicago: The University of Chicago Press.

Bhagwati, Jagdish N. 1982. "Directly Unproductive Profit-Seeking (DUP) Activities." *Journal of Political Economy* 90 (October).

Buchanan, James M. 1987. "The Constitution of Economic Policy." *American Economic Review* 77.

Buiter, Willem H. 1990. *Principles of Budgetary and Financial Policy*. Cambridge: MIT Press.

Conaghan, Catherine M., James M. Malloy, and Luis A. Abugattas. 1990. "Business and the 'Boys': The Politics of Neoliberalism in the Central Andes." *Latin American Research Review* 25 (Spring).

Confederación de Empresarios Privados de Bolivia (CEPB). 1991. "¿Porqué no hay más inversión en Bolivia?" Mimeograph. La Paz: CEPB (July).

Chávez, Gonzalo. 1991. "La macroeconomía de la privatización en Bolivia." La Paz: Instituto de Investigaciones Socioeconómicas, Universidad Católica Boliviana. Unpublished paper.

Instituto Latinoamericano de Investigaciones Sociales (ILDIS). 1985. "La nueva política económica (primera parte)." *Foro Económico* 5. La Paz: ILDIS.

Jetté, Christian. 1989. *De la toma del cielo por asalto a la relocalización*. La Paz: HISBOL.

Krueger, Anne O. 1990. "Government Failures in Development." *Journal of Economic Perspectives* 4 (Summer): 3.

Morales, Juan Antonio. 1988. "La inflación y la estabilización en Bolivia." In *Inflación y estabilización: La experiencia de Argentina, Brasil, Bolivia y México*, eds. M. Bruno, Guido di Tella, Rudiger Dornbusch, and Stanley Fischer. Mexico: El Trimestre Económico.

Morales, Juan Antonio. 1991. "Structural Adjustment and Peasant Agriculture in Bolivia." *Food Policy* 16 (February): 1.

Morales, Juan Antonio, and Jeffrey Sachs. 1990. "Bolivia's Economic Crisis." In *Developing Country Debt and Economic Performance*, Volume 2, ed. Jeffrey Sachs. Chicago: The University of Chicago Press.

Olson, Mancur. 1982. *The Rise and Decline of Nations*. New Haven, Conn.: Yale University Press.

Sachs, Jeffrey. 1987. "The Bolivian Hyperinflation and Stabilization." *American Economic Review* 77 (May): 2.

Starr, Paul. 1990. "The New Life of the Liberal State: Privatization and the Restructuring of State-Society Relations." In *The Political Economy of Public Sector Reform and Privatization*, eds. Ezra N. Suleiman and John Waterbury. Boulder, Colo.: Westview Press.

Suleiman, Ezra N., and John Waterbury. 1990. "Introduction: Analyzing Privatization in Industrial and Developing Countries." In *The Political Economy of Public Sector Reform and Privatization*, eds. Ezra N. Suleiman and John Waterbury. Boulder, Colo.: Westview Press.

Unidad de Análisis de Política Económica (UDAPE). 1991. *Estadísticas Económicas de Bolivia* (June). La Paz: UDAPE.

Urioste, Juan Cristóbal. 1991. "Constitución, economía y política económica." In *Bolivia: Ajuste Estructural, Equidad y Crecimiento*, ed. Juan Cristóbal Urioste. La Paz: Fundación Milenio y Baremo.

Vickers, John, and George Yarrow. 1991. "Economic Perspectives on Privatization." *The Journal of Economic Perspectives* 5:2 (Spring).

World Bank. 1989. "Bolivia: Public Sector Expenditure Review With a Special Emphasis on the Social Sectors." Mimeograph.

World Bank. 1991. "Bolivia: From Stabilization to Sustained Growth." Mimeograph.

Brazil

Selected Macroeconomic Indicators for Brazil

	1982	1983	1984	1985	1986	1987	1988	1989	1990	1991	1992p
Real Gross Domestic Product					*(Percent Average Annual Growth Rates)*						
Total GDP	0.6	-3.5	5.2	7.9	7.6	3.6	-0.1	3.3	-4.4	0.9	10.9
Manufacturing	-0.2	-5.8	6.2	8.3	11.3	0.9	-3.4	2.9	-9.5	-0.5	-0.3
Agriculture	-0.5	-0.6	3.3	10.0	-8.0	15.0	0.8	2.9	-3.7	2.5	6.0
Construction	-1.3	-13.9	0.8	6.0	18.5	1.0	-2.8	3.2	-8.4	-4.0	-4.4
Gross Domestic Investment					*(As as Percent of GDP)*						
	25.6	20.6	20.3	22.0	25.0	24.0	22.8	22.3	21.4	20.6	—
Non-Financial Public Sector					*(As a Percent of GDP)*						
Operational Balance (-Deficit)	-7.3	-4.4	-2.7	-4.4	-3.6	-5.7	-4.8	-6.8	1.3	-1.3	—
Prices, Salaries and Unemployment					*(Percent Average Annual Growth Rates)*						
Consumer Prices	98.1	142.0	196.7	226.9	145.3	229.7	682.3	1287.0	2938.0	440.8	1000.0
Minimum Wages	1.1	-9.8	-8.3	3.5	-0.3	-23.4	-1.6	30.6	-42.7	14.9	5.3
Unemployment	—	4.9	4.3	3.4	2.4	3.7	3.9	—	—	—	—
Real Exchange Rate					*(Index 1980 = 100)*						
	109.1	130.1	134.6	138.6	147.8	147.7	136.9	109.7	93.5	116.5	129.8
Balance of Payments					*(Billions of Dollars)*						
Current Account Balance	-16.3	-6.8	0.0	-0.3	-5.3	-1.5	4.2	1.0	-3.8	-1.4	6.3
Trade Balance	0.8	6.5	13.1	12.5	8.3	11.2	19.2	16.1	10.7	10.6	15.7
Exports	20.2	21.9	27.0	25.6	22.3	26.2	33.8	34.4	31.4	31.6	36.2
Imports	19.4	15.4	13.9	13.2	14.0	15.1	14.6	18.3	20.7	21.0	20.5
Capital Account Balance	11.5	5.5	4.9	0.3	2.0	4.4	-1.6	1.5	5.3	0.8	8.8
Change in Reserves (- Increase)	5.2	1.9	-5.4	0.5	3.2	-2.2	-1.7	-1.7	-1.2	-0.2	-15.1
Total External Debt					*(Billions of Dollars)*						
Disbursed Debt	92.9	98.4	105.4	106.1	113.7	123.9	115.7	111.4	116.4	116.5	120.7
(In Percent)											
Interest Payments Due/Exports	57.1	43.5	39.6	40.0	42.4	33.1	29.4	29.2	31.4	27.6	—

p = preliminary
Sources: Inter-American Development Bank, *Economic and Social Progress in Latin America*, 1992 and 1993 Reports, and the International Labor Organization.

Chapter Six

The State, Structural Reform, and Democratization in Brazil

Lourdes Sola

Introduction

The complex relationship among macroeconomic disequilibria, extremely slow-paced economic reforms, and ongoing political instability make Brazil a case apart, for which the outcome of structural adjustment remains indeterminate. The civilian governments since 1964, headed by presidents José Sarney (1985-1990) and Fernando Collor de Mello (1990-1992), perfectly illustrate the hybrid democracies that have emerged in the wake of adjustment crises. While formally democratic, these governments were, nonetheless, characterized by elitist and highly exclusionary decision-making mechanisms and a pattern of economic "decisionism" marked by the extraordinary ability of the governing elites to surprise society repeatedly with a never-ending escalation of emergency economic packages and sudden shifts in strategy and policy (Malloy 1990; O'Donnell 1990; Weffort 1992; Torre 1993; Sola 1987 and 1991).

The most acute manifestation of the explosive path followed by the Brazilian economy under civilian rule was the megainflation accompanying the 1989 presidential elections and the transition interregnum.[1] Following Collor's inauguration in March 1990, the reduction in the monthly rate of inflation (from 82 percent in 1990 to 23 percent in 1992), plus the lifting of price controls and the strong increase in international reserves to almost US$ 22 billion, decidedly reduced the likelihood of a hyperinflationary crisis.

Nevertheless, economic recovery with low inflation and stable growth remains as elusive as ever. This uncertainty became acute with the polarized context of the 1989 presidential election, an election which further aggravated the tendency of heterogeneous interests to form short-lived coalitions. More than any real impetus for specific reform, these coalitions were formed primarily to prevent the election of the leftist candidate, Luis Inácio Lula da Silva.

The reform coalition was fragile because the victorious party, the National Renovation Party (Partido de Renovação Nacional — PRN), held only 5 percent of the deputies and senators in Congress, reflecting the ad hoc nature of its creation at the margin of the dominant party system.[2]

Similarly, President Collor's impeachment on charges of corruption left ambiguous results. The process, conducted by Congress under strong public and media pressure, may eventually result in new institutional controls on public expenditures, particularly those of the executive. In contrast, the general thrust of the reforms and policies of the Collor administration is now being revised (with some progress and setbacks) by Itamar Franco, who assumed the presidency in October 1992. The fact that Franco — who, as Collor's vice-president, should have supported the same economic program in principle — questioned his predecessor's policies is indicative of the fragile nature of electoral coalitions supporting liberalization and market-oriented reforms in contemporary Brazil.

Seen from a broader perspective, Brazil is Latin America's "latecomer" in the completion of structural adjustment. Of the sequence of changes effectively carried out in other Latin American countries — external adjustment, stabilization, and economic liberalization — only external adjustment has been substantially achieved in Brazil, and this occurred primarily during the last years of the military regime (1981-1984). The characteristics of the Brazilian structural adjustment experience stand out. On the one hand, Brazil managed to close the external gap quite early due to the generation of large trade surpluses (Barros de Castro and de Souza 1985; Damil, Fanelli, and Frenkel 1992). On the other hand, Brazil typifies to an extreme degree the high price to be paid for postponing the fiscal and administrative reforms necessary for successful adjustment.

The absence of a clear strategy, coupled with the erosion of trust and the growing inefficacy of economic policy under both Sarney and Collor, has exacerbated the fiscal crisis of the Brazilian state, thereby further undermining the capacity of the executive-dominated political system to carry out the reform of state financing and public expenditures.

The repetition of this vicious cycle raises interconnected questions. Successful cases of liberalization have taken place when the state acted as a main agent in the initiation (although not necessarily the consolidation) of liberalizing reforms (Haggard and Kaufman 1992; Evans 1992). How do general insights such as this one unfold in Brazil? More specifically, what are the mechanisms linking the state's fiscal crisis, governability, and the role of the state as a political actor in the initiation and consolidation of liberalizing reforms? These questions, combined with the simultaneous occurrence in Brazil of democratization and changes in the economic regime, require us to explore the dynamic mechanisms linking democratic governance and the protracted difficulty in closing the fiscal gap.

Perspectives on the Brazilian crisis have changed since 1990. Today, the previously secondary question of governability occupies a central role in the diagnoses of economists and other political actors. There is growing consensus among specialists on the need for far-reaching reforms but not on the subject of the political capability to implement those reforms. What are the conditions for governability in the specific circumstances that combine economic liberalization and democratization? To what extent are these processes contradictory? Do economic liberalization and democratization tend, over time, to reinforce one another mutually, as proposed by neoliberal doctrine and as assumed by the "Washington Consensus"? How can we determine the threshold at which democratization and economic liberalization become mutually reinforcing processes generating a "virtuous cycle"? In the event that these two processes are governed by contradictory principles, what are the country's prospects for the near future?

Brazil's economic reform is a case of "muddling through," rather than what Adam Przeworski (1992) refers to as the "bitter pill" of a rapid, coherent, and tightly linked sequence of market-oriented structural adjustment. One explanation of the Brazilian experience focuses on the evolution and subsequent crisis of the "developmentalist state" and has been advocated by the more coherent critics of neoliberalism in Brazil (Fiori 1990 and 1992).[3] A second explanatory framework is espoused by the "Washington Consensus," which concentrates its criticism on a form of specific *dirigismo* that emerged as an inherent aspect of the import substitution model.

Paradoxically, these interpretations share a common denominator: both view the state as the principal protagonist. The crisis of the 1980s and its persistence into the 1990s is explained by both interpretations by highlighting the domestic context rather than external shocks. Moreover, both perspectives are macrohistorical in that they postulate a basic continuity of the post-World War II accumulation model and attendant patterns of state-market relations. As Brazil constitutes the most complete example of this deepening process through several successive cycles of import substitution, it provides a unique opportunity to examine these alternative perspectives. A convenient point of departure is to sketch the reforms already under way as well as the conditions that explain their inception.

Political Limitations on Economic Restructuring

Many of the economic reforms in postauthoritarian Brazil took place during the short-lived Collor government. However, movement toward market-oriented reform began in the late 1980s, when proposals for new regulatory policies for commerce and industry were first advanced by the

Sarney administration. Not surprisingly, these initiatives came from within technobureaucratic agencies traditionally protected from competitive politics. The formation of a new sensibility among segments of the political and economic elites, making the criteria for allocation of public resources more stringent and critical, also dates from this period (Sola 1993).

This shift toward market-oriented reform resulted from the confluence of several factors. Economists became aware of the scale and duration of the macroeconomic restrictions generated by external shocks first in 1987 after the failure of the first two heterodox stabilization plans (Plano Cruzado and Plano Bresser).[4] The unfolding of the democratization process also conferred a sense of urgency by unleashing fierce competition for public resources among social and regional interests. Recognition of new international paradigms of technological innovation, new educational and labor training requirements, and the need for higher efficiency and competitiveness all played a crucial role (Franco and Fritsch 1992). Democratization, under conditions of economic emergency, also revealed large-scale corruption in the state's distribution of privileges and penalties, while undermining conservative norms regulating clientelistic and corporatist practices. As a result, most educated Brazilians no longer gave credence to their previous conceptual framework, whether neoliberal or social democratic, although no new and coherent alternatives emerged to take their place (Sola 1993).

The 1980s were a "lost decade" in terms of economic stagnation, income concentration, and a perverse transition from high to very high inflation, bordering on hyperinflation. However, considering the conceptual, organizational, and politico-institutional resources existing prior to the crisis and ensuing liberalizing reforms, Brazil's learning curve was really quite impressive. Adjustments were made in the cognitive and ideological "maps" of traditional and emerging actors, whose political identities and expectations had been formed in the context of *dirigismo* when the state acted both as an entrepreneur and a source of patronage (Sola 1991 and 1993).

Political learning was particularly intense among the technocrats in the governing elite responsible for defining the regulatory framework for each specific reform. These technocratic sectors, whose origins date back to the so-called "pockets of efficiency" created under Getúlio Vargas, formulated and implemented state initiatives during decades of rapid economic development. In the 1980s, they were quick to adapt to the new forms of democratic control, especially in relation to the expansion of judicial and congressional power and the restrictions imposed by the 1988 Constitution.[5]

In this context, Collor's economic reforms catalyzed a series of partial intellectual adjustments on the part of sectors extending well beyond the president's electoral coalition to encompass broader segments of the political and economic elites, including organized interest groups and members of

Congress. Moreover, these changes forced the restructuring of organizational resources within a broad ensemble of technocratic agencies. Legal knowledge, in particular, became increasingly relevant in the political game; each new ordinance advancing commercial liberalization, deregulation of the economy, and privatization had to be made consistent with the new parameters dictated by the 1988 Constitution.

The destabilizing effects of the new constitution extended far beyond the redistribution of power from the executive to the Congress and state and local governments within Brazil's federal system. Concomitantly, the significant measure of judicial initiative granted to ordinary citizens after 1988 also rendered executive decision-making prerogatives more vulnerable to obstruction and delay.

The uncertainty introduced by the 1988 Constitution stemmed, in part, from excessive detail as well as from the constitutional process's own dynamic, disconnected from the economic emergency. The constitution was a reflection of the competing ideological and programmatic currents comprising Brazilian political culture (Lamounier and de Souza 1990). Despite its length and excessive detail, the new constitution was incomplete because its framers let many important provisions stand alone, without the usual legislation required to translate general precepts into practical rules and regulations. The deleterious consequences of this "unfinished business" became far too obvious as the Collor government attempted to introduce trade and commercial reforms into the system of public property.[6]

The Collor Administration Reforms, 1990-1992[7]

As noted by Franco and Fritsch (1992), one of the leitmotifs underpinning trade reform was the need to increase productivity in order to reconcile the objective of increasing real salaries with the partly contradictory objective of bolstering savings and investment capabilities. A gradual approach to liberalizing imports distinguished this strategy. Another feature was the selective application of new regulations. Protectionist barriers were eliminated much more rapidly among sectors producing consumer goods than in the capital goods and intermediary goods sectors, which maintained high levels of non-tariff barriers in compliance with the "similarity" and "local integration" regulations. However, these exceptions and limitations should not obscure the broad extent of the transformation that took place in commercial and industrial regulations.

Many factors converged to produce this strategy. Import liberalization under the Collor administration used the reduction of tariffs on consumer goods as an anti-inflationary tool and a restraint on the power of local oligopolies. Simultaneously, reforms were introduced to allow the technocrats to ascertain each reform's impact on industrial structures and employment. This was significant, since many of these effects were difficult to anticipate. Tariff reduction included a new classification scheme, with seven main criteria covering some 13,500 items. The goal was to reach an average tariff level of 20 percent by 1994, within a range extending from zero to a maximum of 40 percent (Franco and Fritsch 1992).

On another reform front, industrial deregulation and the adoption of new measures to stimulate internal competition also illustrate the short- and long-term political difficulties of economic reform. The efficacy of the antimonopoly policies announced in August 1990 depended on new institutions designed to control monopolistic practices. These new institutions would replace ineffective agencies and would be given enough authority to apply sanctions and to avoid long bureaucratic delays. The efficacy of these policies depended on severing long-established ties between the state and the private sector, both national and foreign, in order to reverse the pattern of monopoly and oligopoly competition, which had intensified significantly under the authoritarian regime.[8]

A first step in this direction was the creation of the National Secretariat of Economic Legislation (Secretaria Nacional de Direito Econômico—SNDE), thereby partially displacing the Ministry of Justice, a traditional locus of pressure for the maintenance of the status quo. But these efforts to break the ties between business and the state rapidly failed. Failure can be attributed in part to the government's own stabilization efforts, which exacerbated the economic team's inclination to transform its rhetoric against the evils of monopoly into what many in the business sector perceived as an anti-entrepreneurial crusade. Members of Collor's economic team apparently held the naive belief that antimonopolistic measures could rapidly overcome the deeply entrenched symbiosis between regulators and the regulated.

Notwithstanding these failures and the fact that antimonopolistic initiatives were basically limited to price control efforts, the medium-term impact of these policies was significant, particularly because they promoted a process of microeconomic restructuring that began to lower costs by an average of 20 percent to 40 percent.[9] Media and public opinion were also sensitized to the pathologies and inequities of an extremely concentrated, oligopolistic model of industrialization, thereby changing the focus of public debate from an emphasis on ideological differences to a concern with determining this who benefitted from this newly found emphasis on allocative efficiency and free market forces.

Public-sector property reforms and privatization had surprisingly similar results, despite their limited scale.[10] In contrast to the international trade liberalization scenario, conflicts in the privatization process took place openly in the political arena, involving Congress as well as various regional constellations of local interests that had benefitted from the decentralization of economic expansion in the late 1970s. Privatization was hampered by limited public understanding[11] and because exposure of widespread corruption in other areas of the government tended to negate the privatization team's efforts at transparency and a modicum of equity in the transfer of public assets to private ownership. Constitutional constraints on the level of foreign capital participation (40 percent) and the exclusion from the privatization program of monopolistic sectors of strategic importance also posed serious difficulties.

Initial resistance proved to be broader and more heterogeneous than expected. Some opposition was ideological, and others sought to protect interests among nationalist segments of the political, military, and economic elites. Labor unions belonging to the Central Union Confederation (Central Única dos Trabalhadores—CUT) and cartels of suppliers, shippers, and consumers of products of the affected enterprises were also vocal in their opposition. Many top-level managers of the state enterprises in question, along with part of their respective technocracies, engaged in systematic obstruction. And fierce competition took place within the executive branch for the succulent political and economic privileges the privatization process would produce.

These circumstances account for the plodding and conflictive character of the first round of privatizations. Furthermore, the return of high inflation toward the end of 1990 increased uncertainty and made the evaluation of the assets of state enterprises more problematic. Two years elapsed between the decision to initiate the program, in mid-1990, and its final formulation, which made it legally possible to carry out the first sale (of the Usiminas steel complex in Minas Gerais) in October 1992. By the end of 1992, however, twenty-two of the twenty-six steel, petrochemical, fertilizer, machinery, and airline and shipping enterprises originally slated for privatization had been sold in public auctions.

This record of partial reform highlights one of the distinctive characteristics of the Brazilian experience — the absence of active social forces advocating trade liberalization, industrial deregulation, and privatization. The hypothesis that these questions emerge on the political agenda in response to a new correlation of internal forces favorable to neoliberalism is not substantiated. Instead, the evidence points to an adaptive process on the part of segments of the entrepreneurial class and other organized interests. The neoliberal reforms also result from decisions by the governing elites, who had themselves undergone an intellectual *aggiornamento* unprecedented in Brazil's policy-making tradition.

Bearing this in mind, how and under what conditions did the reforms enter the broader political agenda? Because the institutions initiating these reforms are relatively protected from pressures of political competition, few details of the decision-making process are known. Nevertheless, it seems that the governing elites acted in response to four interrelated stimuli.

First, the multilateral financial institutions and advanced industrial countries imposed new and more stringent forms of conditionality on debtor countries. Second, the exhaustion of the previous model of industrialization hastened recognition that economic recovery would require major innovations in economic strategy: after the failure of three heterodox attempts to contain inflation, many actors became convinced that there was no viable alternative for reversing the explosive inflationary spiral other than by deepening orthodox reforms. Third, given Brazil's extreme income concentration, political and economic elites feared that a hyperinflationary episode could spark uncontrollable social and political upheavals, as had occurred in 1989 in Argentina. This fear engendered widespread political acquiescence when Collor announced "last resort" initiatives. Finally, the legitimacy conferred on Collor by the first direct presidential elections since the return to civilian rule, and the effects of the political polarization that preceded his ascension to power, dissipated political resistance to economic reform.

These circumstances explain the surprising responses of public opinion to the reforms, such as the responses of workers and employees in state-owned enterprises, many of whom became supporters of privatization. This support, combined with that of local private capital, contributed greatly to the neutralization of some of the principal sources of resistance, such as Leonel Brizola, the governor of Rio de Janeiro, and the leaders of CUT, who exerted considerable power in the state-owned banks and enterprises.

The impact of these changes in ownership on the country's politico-institutional and ideological makeup remains to be explored. It seems irrefutable, however, that the expected "winners" and "losers" of privatization have been reversed, since the employees who were entitled to the purchase of shares in the privatized firms have become beneficiaries, albeit indirectly, to the enormous investment potential of the pension funds of public-sector enterprises. Similarly, the participation of national capital in these changes of ownership may have led to a revision of expectations among military officers of nationalist orientation, who comprise a large part of the managerial elite in state-owned enterprises and who continue to play a decisive role in national politics.

Public opinion also warmed to privatization as the distributive dimensions of the deepening economic crisis became apparent to broader sectors of the population. Collor's impeachment contributed to this realization by exposing the corruption endemic in the operation of clandestine, and frequently illicit, relations between those able to influence key sectors of the state bureaucracy and private interests. Corruption was deeply rooted in both national and foreign entrepreneurial segments of the economy and was attacked under the banner of "ethics in politics," as demands for enhanced democratic control of the decision-making process became part of public discourse.

On a more theoretical plane, the fact that the market-oriented reforms initiated under Collor could be advanced, however sluggishly, by agencies insulated from the tug-of-war of competitive political pressures seems to confirm some hypotheses concerning structural adjustment. For example, the Brazilian case supports the notion that political autonomy of the technocratic sectors is required to initiate — but not necessarily consolidate — economic reforms (Haggard and Kaufman 1993). One of the most relevant aspects of the economic reforms was that they were initiated by the same "pockets of efficiency" (in the heterogeneous institutions comprising the Brazilian state) that had guided rapid growth in the 1950s and again in the 1970s. Concentration of power and knowledge in a few institutions, therefore, may be indispensable for the inception of economic reforms. Along with Evans (1992), one may thus conclude that (as demonstrated by the "Asian tigers" and Japan) the political and administrative capabilities necessary for the success of "market-friendly" policy initiatives can be forged without negating the interventionist bent of the "developmentalist" state.

The Brazilian experience also confirms the importance of sequence and timing in the reform process. In contrast to trade liberalization and privatization, for example, fiscal reform appeared very late on the Collor administration's policy agenda. Proposals for significant fiscal reforms had been formulated within the state bureaucracy but were not presented to Congress and were subsequently buried in the political crisis that culminated in Collor's impeachment. Addressing this question, along with the underlying chronic difficulties associated with the management of the state's fiscal crisis, will help explain the vicissitudes and shortcomings of Brazil's executive-driven reform process.

Between Hyperinflation and a New Fiscal Pact

The intractability of the fiscal gap exemplifies the complex relationship between economic and political factors in the Brazilian crisis and offers a privileged perspective for probing the dynamic interaction between structural adjustment and democratization. As used here, the concept of "fiscal crisis of the state" refers to the paralysis of the state stemming from the erosion of its capacity to save and to finance the public sector of the economy (Bresser Pereira 1993). Endemic fiscal crisis hinders the financing of current expenditures and the servicing of the growing public debt (domestic and foreign) and undermines the state's capacity to invest and provide incentives for long-term growth. Finally, the fiscal crisis affects the performance of distributive functions in the form of severe limitations on social investment in education, water, public health, housing, and so on.

This section argues that the fiscal crisis can be best understood by looking at certain specific characteristics of the Brazilian adjustment-with-democratization experience. In particular, it is necessary to distinguish between the perverse dynamics that act to reproduce fiscal paralysis and the original conditions that are at the root of the distributive impasse; the latter conditions preceded the external shock of 1982, the ensuing structural adjustment, and the democratic transition of the last decade. We also argue that analyses focusing on long historical periods have little explanatory power. Although correct, "developmentalist state" perspectives — as well as analyses that emphasize the legacy of the postwar period (Kaufman 1990) or the pathologies of import substitution ("Washington Consensus") — are too broad for our purposes.

Two hypotheses form the basis of our analysis. First, the origin of the current fiscal crisis can be traced to a fairly recent, specific characteristic of the activist state — the dramatic shift in industrialization and regional development strategy by the Ernesto Geisel administration in the early 1970s. The shift was combined with the initiation of political liberalization guided "from above."

The second hypothesis refers to the reproduction of fiscal paralysis on a larger scale. The concept of governability in reference to "economic liberalization with democratization" is useful for analyzing constraints on the "capacity of governments to create political resources from a given set of institutions" (Malloy 1990). From this perspective, different regimes will have different governance problems. This fundamental distinction will help differentiate between conditions inherited from the authoritarian regime and specific questions of governability faced by the current democratic regime.

The key theoretical assumption that differentiates this approach from that of the "Washington Consensus" is that growth is not automatically guaranteed by a successful stabilization program complemented by liberalizing reforms (Bresser Pereira 1993; Fanelli, Frenkel, and Rozenwurcel 1994). In the Brazilian case, the state lost its capacity to invest and to propel any strategy of transformation and growth, including strategies consistent with the proclaimed commitment to state reform and the promotion of a market-driven economy.

The literature on the so-called "neoliberal paradox" similarly indicates that all successful cases of economic liberalization had, as a precondition, a government capable of assuming the role of initiator and underwriter of intense reform activity. The consolidation of reform is dependent on an additional prerequisite: the degree of "social embeddedness" of the state, as shaped by its networks linking with strategic economic and political actors (Evans 1992).

Under a scenario of fiscal crisis and paralysis of the state, the state becomes "the problem," since it cannot assert itself as the main agent for economic transformation. In neglecting this aspect, neoliberals erroneously define the main problem as a precondition for transformation. It is precisely the fiscal crisis that makes imperative the restructuring of the state's financing and expenditures and its politico-administrative capacities.

State restructuring in new democracies requires, first of all, the formulation of an agreed-upon strategy, whose political viability partly depends on the country's institutional framework, especially its system of representation. Successful state reform also requires the generation or allocation of organizational resources and concentration of technical expertise, which, in turn, hinges on the ability of competent, specialized, and accountable bureaucracies with a degree of autonomy and insulation from societal pressures. Finally, the ability of elected officials in democratic governments to exert effective control over the "state machine" is also crucial (Malloy 1993).

As we shall see, none of these requirements has been fulfilled in Brazil due to the vicissitudes of the dynamic interaction between structural adjustment and democratization. This failure confers on the present fiscal paralysis an indeterminate character commensurate with three possible outcomes: 1) hyperinflation, 2) a preventive strategy based on a new fiscal pact, or 3) continuation of the status quo in a context of a gradual deterioration of cultural, institutional, and economic foundations necessary for the maintenance of social order.

Origin of the Fiscal Crisis: A Hyperactive State in Search of a Coalition

The roots of the fiscal crisis are grounded in political decisions associated with a new project of economic transformation implemented by the Geisel government in the mid-1970s. In analyzing these factors, it is crucial to understand that the economic policies of the post-1964 authoritarian regime were not a simple expression of neoliberal tenets. To the contrary, post-1964 policies were profoundly hybrid in character, calibrated by multiple objectives pursued in a context of partnership among the state, domestic entrepreneurs, and multinational corporations.[12] This partnership was not based originally on the deepening of import-substitution policies, which only became a strategic objective in 1974 under the Geisel government (Serra 1979; Dias and Aguirre 1993). The authoritarian regime's intrinsic instability and preoccupation with assuring its legitimacy through the maintenance of the representative system (no matter how emasculated) resulted in the executive's direct intervention in the party system, not through simple political repression but through the implementation of a new party system and the manipulation of the electoral process (Lamounier 1990; Kinzo 1990).

Intervention in the politico-institutional arena was particularly manifest in the "hyperactivism" of the Geisel government's attempt to reconcile two conflicting objectives: the process of guided political liberalization (opposed by the regime's hard-liners) and the completion of a new cycle of import substitution industrialization that paved the way for the transition to a new pattern of capital accumulation (Dias and Aguirre 1993).

Difficulties with external financing and with the traditional partner, industrialists in the southeast, who were loathe to share in the risks involved in launching the new cycle of import substitution, led to growing regional diversification in the location of heavy industry and capital goods sectors (petrochemical, metal, chemical, and nuclear energy). Emergence of new industrial sectors and regions implied a partial break with the historical pattern of industrial development concentrated in the southeast. In the new industrial "poles" (Bahia, Rio Grande do Sul, Minas Gerais, Amazonas, Pernambuco, and Maranhão), a profound rearticulation of social forces took place with the integration of new partners into the emerging development strategy.

Rearticulation meant the state's traditional industrial partners in the southeast saw their dominant position challenged by a new cycle of import substitution initiated by state enterprises and their new allies among the regional oligarchies. With the support of the financial sector (both private and state-owned), which became the main instrument for channeling public funds and external resources, and with the participation of large public works contractors, entire regions and sectors of the economy were opened to new patterns of capitalist production.

Fueled by growth induced by the expansion of domestic and external debt, the state transformed itself "from an entrepreneurial state into a self-sufficient entrepreneurial state" (Dias and Aguirre 1993). This strategy frustrated the expectations of the bourgeoisie of São Paulo and the center-south, who feared losing their "exclusive right" to institutional protection. Moreover, the strategy did not have the support of the working class. The military regime's difficulties in imposing the burden of capital-intensive projects on workers and their unions became increasingly formidable. Consequently, accelerated growth and structural transformation eroded one of the regime's possible sources of legitimation and undermined the social cohesion on which its hegemonic project rested, while at the same time broadening the scope of regional alliances. The broadening secured both a comfortable majority in Congress and the support of the relevant state governors.

These difficulties were exacerbated by the unintended consequences of the military regime's efforts to facilitate the over-representation of pro-regime forces in the electoral arena. Culminating in the 1977 "electoral package," these efforts consolidated a new alignment of social forces designed to guarantee the permanence and relative stability of the political coalition supporting the new development model. At the same time though, the project of guided political liberalization reduced the political space for difficult reforms, including fiscal and administrative ones that might have prevented the exacerbation of the public-sector deficit. As a consequence, the technocracy's efforts to shift resources (and the penalties and privileges associated with mechanisms of institutional protection) from the producers of durable goods to the new producers of capital and intermediate goods and their suppliers and local consumers proved highly conflictive.

The Geisel administration's decision to "say 'no' to the recession" (Reis Velloso 1986) reaffirmed the state's activist role as the arbiter for resource transfers and the dispensation of privileges and penalties, in accordance with the plan for accelerated growth. Concomitantly, the postponement of stabilization and controversial fiscal and administrative reforms in the face of deepening financial crisis led to a *fuite en avant* in which the state once again resorted to excessive reliance on the same financial mechanisms that had previously proven effective in promoting capital accumulation, namely inflation and foreign capital (Sola 1985 and 1987).

The political decisions described above capture part of the origins of the fiscal crisis. The external shock of 1982 and the interruption of external financing constitute its second central component. These developments took place under conditions of uncertainty arising from earlier economic policy decisions (both strategic and short-term) that had proven exceptionally risky. The domestic need for financing had increased as more socioeconomic sectors became capable of making demands. The large number of opposition governors elected in 1982 also weakened the regime and multiplied rival power sources capable of contesting the federal executive.

Finally, the industrial projects launched in the previous decade had not yet matured and continued to require large injections of new capital. Consequently, the already large (and growing) fiscal deficit had to be financed with domestic savings, primarily through inflationary measures. Simultaneously, the symbiotic relationship between regional entrepreneurs and local and federal technocracies deepened, supported by the state's financial network, which had also been enlarged through the proliferation of regional banks.

In this context, *novo sindicalismo* became a force to be reckoned with. The new, more militant labor movement was characterized by greater participation of workers from state enterprises and banks and by a cohesive strategy of opposition to the government. Moreover, reinforced by the 1982 and 1986 elections, the process of political liberalization and democratization had reaffirmed the principles of federalism and had given rise to a well-organized and aggressive municipal movement. Simultaneously, equally powerful centrifugal forces promoting the proliferation of new political parties asserted themselves. Finally, the entrepreneurial class of the center-south opposed the redistribution of privileges (previously guaranteed through institutional protection), taking full advantage of the fact that the government's policy of external adjustment granted these traditional, export-oriented manufacturing and agribusiness sectors considerably greater bargaining power.

This array of factors weakened the authoritarian regime as well as the first civilian governments.[13] The redistributive struggle over economic and political resources intensified, involving not only changed relations with regional oligarchical elites but also between the executive and legislative branches and between the national government and the states and municipalities. Organized interests and sectors of the opposition also challenged the dominant authoritarian political culture, which continued to legitimate their exclusion from national politics even under conditions of restored democracy.

Fiscal Paralysis and the New Functions of the State

The *coup de grace* to the public sector's capacity to save and invest was the decision to nationalize the private sector's external debt. From that moment on, the state acquired an active role in the acceleration of price increases. This same phenomenon can also be observed in other Latin American countries that followed the so-called "explosive path" of external adjustment (Fanelli, Frenkel, and Rozenwurcel 1994). As occurred elsewhere, the foreign debt crisis led to radical changes in the restructuring of relations between state and market.

The chief mechanism driving the redefinition of the state's role was the reduction in the public sector's capacity to borrow (Gambiasi 1992; Bresser Pereira 1993; Fanelli, Frenkel, and Rozenwurcel 1994). The financial sector, reflecting the state's low level of credibility and public support, can absorb only short-term bonds with high interest rates. In the absence of a drastic change in government financing and spending patterns, the only remaining alternative for reducing the gap between financing needs and available resources was the so-called "inflation tax." As Table 1 reveals, this mechanism resulted in a dramatic acceleration of inflation, with a 1990 level surpassing 2,000 percent.

One of the few instruments of economic policy available to attract private savings was to roll over internal debt at extremely high real rates of interest. It was only a temporary palliative and had serious counterproductive effects. Daily indexation caused public bonds to exert an expansive effect on demand, and the rollover of the public debt at rising interest rates increased the deficit. Additionally, state governments regularly called upon state and regional development banks to issue national government bonds as a way of filling the empty coffers of their treasuries. This political dynamic meant that the level of deficit financing engaged in by state governments became a function of the electoral needs of their governors, thereby causing difficulties for any national government in seeking to impose fiscal and monetary discipline. The state governments' only hope was that the central bank and the federal treasury could carry out constant "emergency rescue" operations to stave off the threat of default.

Table 1

Year	Monetarization Coefficient	Seignorage /GNP (%)	Inflation (%)
1970	8.1	1.3	16
1971	7.9	2.4	19
1972	7.3	1.3	20
1973	6.6	2.7	30
1974	6.3	1.9	35
1975	6.0	2.0	34
1976	5.5	2.3	41
1977	5.4	2.3	46
1978	5.6	2.0	38
1979	5.5	3.2	54
1980	4.5	1.9	90
1981	2.7	1.7	107
1982	2.9	1.9	105
1983	2.3	1.3	141
1984	1.7	2.3	213
1985	1.6	2.3	233
1986	3.1	3.6	146
1987	2.0	2.8	204
1988	1.4	3.5	648
1989	1.2	5.0	1322
1990	2.2	5.0	2562
1991-2	—	1.64	—

Source: Instituto de Economia Industrial, *Boletim de Conjuntura*, various issues, as cited in Gambiasi (1992).

Attempts by national monetary authorities to discipline state banks acquired the character of a regional political dispute involving the corresponding members of Congress and respective governors. As a result, the federal executive could choose either to adopt a permissive attitude, further draining the Brazilian federal government's scarce resources (while reinforcing inflationary pressures), or it could impose discipline, but at the clear risk of further eroding its credibility and political support. This dilemma was temporarily eased after Collor's inauguration, but all solutions continued to depend on the repeated rollover of the states' debt (currently about $57 billion or two-thirds of total public sector debt) in exchange for their congressional delegations' support for a fiscal adjustment to be enacted at some undefined future date.

This perverse pattern of relations between the different spheres of government is also at the root of recurrent episodes of taxpayer rebellion. Rather than turning for additional revenues to debtors and tax evaders or implementing more profound systemic reforms, the federal government repeatedly raised burdens on taxpayers. Not surprisingly, public hostility increases with each tax hike, while growing demands for budgetary restraint are aimed almost exclusively at the federal government.

Following the temporary amelioration of the fiscal situation during the first years of the Collor administration, the conflict worsened. First, the recession that began in 1991 strengthened resistance to tax increases and also reduced revenues for all levels of government. Second, the corruption that led to Collor's resignation was viewed as a rampant and intrinsic byproduct of federal policies. The public did not perceive the underlying, systemic causes behind the government's fiscal crisis and thus resisted the painful reforms needed to correct them.

These factors make it evident that Brazilian political decentralization associated with democratization is partially responsible for the difficulties in closing the fiscal gap. The problem's identification, however, is only one step toward fixing it, because legal restrictions stemming from the reaffirmation of federalist principles during constitutional revision prevent the adoption of appropriate policies. The 1988 Constitution mandates transfers of federal revenues to states and municipalities without a corresponding transfer of obligations for financing their respective social programs. A legal constraint inhibits the implementation of solutions based on negotiated agreements: the executive branch may propose constitutional amendments to correct this distortion through the redistribution of social responsibilities to other spheres of government, but such amendments require the approval of a three-fifths majority of Congress. This impasse effectively guarantees the perpetuation of the tug-of-war between the federal executive's economic team and the finance secretaries of states and municipalities.

Ramifications of these constitutionally mandated fiscal transfers were evident from 1989 forward. As Table 2 shows, federal revenues from taxes on industrial products (Impostos sobre a Produção de Bens Industrializados—IPI) and the federal income tax (Impostos sobre a Renda—IR) declined by 24.2 percent in 1989, with further reductions of over 40 percent in both 1990 and 1991. These transfers absorbed 17.5 percent of total tax revenues in 1989 and 24.6 percent in 1991.

For analytical purposes, however, it is more relevant to look at the magnitude of these transfers in connection with the principal tax collected by the states, the value-added tax (Imposto sobre a Circulação de Mercadorias e Serviços—ICMS), since this tax varies in relation to economic activity. It turns out that the increase in constitutional transfers from the national government to the states was much greater than was necessary to compensate for the negative impact of the recession on the states' finances. Equally clear is the devastating impact of these transfers on the fiscal crisis in the public sector as a whole.

Table 2
Constitutional Transfers to States and Municipalities

	Transfers as % of IPI + Income Tax	Transfers from Gross Revenues as % of Total Tax Revenues	Transfers as % of VAT
1989	24.2	17.5	25.0
1990	41.0	23.0	40.3
1991	44.0	24.6	36.9

Note: IPI = tax on industrial products; VAT = value added tax.

Source: Instituto de Estudos do Setor Público, Indicadores, No. 7 (August 1991), based on data provided in Execução Financiera do Tesouro.

The creation of a broad parliamentary coalition, as well as a federal pact capable of reconciling the policies of governors and other representatives of the most politically and economically powerful states, is essential to forging stable political coalitions for systemic reform. The question becomes more complex when we consider restrictions imposed by the democratization process. One of the factors weakening the federal government's capacity to generate financial resources is the continued affirmation of the autonomy of states and municipalities. This democratic achievement conflicts with the need to redistribute the adjustment burden more equitably and to finance renewed economic expansion. Current economic practices, particularly economic populism vis-à-vis expenditures, as well as systematic delays in paying debts to the federal government and to the national social security system, are deeply antithetical to successful austerity measures.

These governability problems are intertwined with the distortions in Brazil's current system of political representation. Brazil differs from Argentina, Bolivia, Mexico, and other Latin American countries that embarked upon the "explosive path" of adjustment after 1982. In Mexico, a new fiscal pact was forged, while in Argentina (Smith 1992; Torre and Palermo 1992) and Bolivia, the trauma of hyperinflation made the implementation of orthodox policies possible. Notwithstanding the tremendous costs involved, both alternatives generated the political acquiescence necessary to proceed with the state's reorganization (Mexico) or reconstruction (Argentina and Bolivia).

Mexico, Argentina, and Bolivia possess a common trait differentiating them from Brazil. In all three countries, the sequence that led from stabilization to implementation of structural reforms (and particularly to fiscal adjustment) had a political prerequisite absent in Brazil: the capacity of the national political leadership to generate new political resources based on a previously consolidated system of representation. Despite high political costs to the traditional political parties associated with structural adjustment (as in Argentina and Bolivia), or with challenges to the hegemonic party (in Mexico), the previously consolidated system of representation in these countries played a crucial role in the successful initiation of neoliberal reforms.

Viewed from the perspective of the institutional conditions of governance, Brazil presents more radical uncertainties stemming from the fact that its unstable and extremely fragmented party system prevents the establishment of a broad coalition indispensable to the initiation of market-oriented reforms. Brazil's break from the populist democratic system of representation was made irreversible by the recurrent interventions in the party system practiced by the post-1964 military regime.[14] The break with the past challenges the hypothesis that Latin American countries will revert to that stage of institutional development which existed prior to their respective experiences of authoritarian rule (Torre 1993).

Today there are thirty-five parties in Brazil, twenty of which are fully recognized by the Electoral Court (Tribunal Eleitoral). This fragmentation complicates the formation of a stable governing coalition, a problem further magnified by the permissiveness of the pertinent legislation, which does not punish those representatives who systematically deviate from the "party line." Consequently, there is no effective majority. As past president of the Chamber of Deputies Ibsen Pinheiro has noted, the government has to "make deals with seventeen minorities." In fact, no single party controlled as much as 25 percent of the lower house following the 1989 congressional elections. As Table 3 shows, the parties that originally formed the basis of the Collor government accounted for only 33 percent of the deputies. Moreover, at least formally, the majority party, the Partido do Movimento Democrático Brasileiro (Party of the Brazilian Democratic Movement—PMDB), which accounted for 21.7 percent of the vote, was part of the opposition.

The existence of multiparty blocs operating above party loyalty is also a factor preventing the formation of stable congressional and federal coalitions. Some blocs aggregate regional interests, while others represent the corporate interests of unions, public enterprises, or bank directorates and employees. Still others represent rural groups that oppose the elimination of special privileges and fiscal incentives as well as any kind of agrarian reform. A few even represent rapidly expanding evangelical groups. All defend — and if possible, expand — their own privileges, frequently at the cost of blocking projects of general societal concern or proposals pursued by other interest groups.

Table 3

Brazil - Composition of Congress Elected in 1990

Parties	# in Congress	%
PMDB	109	21.7
PFL	82	16.3
PDT	46	9.1
PDS	42	8.3
PRN	41	8.2
PSDB	38	7.6
PTB	35	7.6
PT	35	7.0
Others	72	14.3
Total	503	100.0

Source: Journal do Brasil, July 7, 1991.
PMDB = Partido do Movimento Democrático Brasileiro (Party of the Brazilian Democratic
Movement); PFL = Partido da Frente Liberal (Liberal Front Party); PDT = Partido
Democrático Trabalhista (Democratic Labor Party); PDS = Partido Democrático
Social (Social Democratic Party); PRN = Partido de Renovação Nacional (Party of
National Renovation); PSDB = Partido Social Democrático Brasileiro (Brazilian
Social Democratic Party); PTB = Partido Trabalhista Brasileiro (Brazilian Labor
Party); PT = Partido dos Trabalhadores (Workers' Party).

Like party fragmentation, the constitutional rules defining the composition of the Chamber of Deputies pose major obstacles to a broad-based
strategy to tackle the fiscal crisis. Each state is guaranteed a minimum of eight
representatives, with the rules of proportional representation followed until
a state reaches forty-six representatives, at which point it is necessary to obtain
a disproportionally high number of votes in order to gain additional
representatives. The result is systematic over-representation of the poorer and
less populous states of the north, center-west, and, to a lesser extent, the
northeast. Under a system of across-the-board proportional representation,
twenty of the twenty-seven states would have their representation reduced.
These states hold precisely 50 percent of the votes in Congress.[15]

Electoral over-representation has many implications. The nine under-
represented states have the largest populations (all exceeding three million
inhabitants), generate more than two-thirds of the gross national product, and
have social structures with relatively well-articulated and organized interests.
In contrast, the twenty-one over-represented states have relatively impoverished populations and weakly organized interests. In these states, moreover,
regional oligarchies continue to operate in accordance with patrimonial
patterns of domination. They exercise effective veto power over any future
redistribution of political resources in favor of the underprivileged and over
legislation of concern to the more populous and developed regions of the
country. Not surprisingly, this veto power is frequently wielded against fiscal
adjustment measures.[16]

Table 4
Disproportion in Congressional Regional Representation in Relation to Their Respective Population in 1986 and 1991

REGIONS	Federal Representation 1986		1991		% of Pop.	Ideal #*	Differ- ence
	#	%	#	%			
North	47	9.65	65	12.92	6.55	33	+32
Northeast	149	30.60	151	30.00	28.50	143	+ 8
Southeast	169	34.70	169	33.60	43.63	220	-51
South	82	16.84	77	15.32	15.15	76	+ 1
W-Central	40	8.21	41	8.15	6.17	31	-10
Total	487	100.00	503	100.00	100.00	503	—

Note: Ideal # of representatives assuming "1 person, 1 vote"
North = Rondônia, Roraima, Amapá, Acre, Amazonas, and Pará.
Northeast = Rio Grande do Norte, Bahia, Maranhão, Piauí, Ceará, Pernambuco, Paraíba, Alagoas, and Sergipe.
Southeast = Espírito Santo, Rio de Janeiro, Minas Gerais, São Paulo.
South = Paraná, Santa Catarina, and Rio Grande do Sul.
West Central = Distrito Federal, Tocantins, Goiás, Mato Grosso, and Matto Grosso do Sul.
Source: Fundação Instituto Brasileiro de Geografia e Estadística (IBGE) and Tribunal Superior Eleitoral (TSE), as cited in Lamounier (1985).

The relationship between the national government and other levels of government in the over-represented states is one of extremely asymmetrical interdependence. Under these conditions, self-serving tendencies surface as the federal government attempts to form *ad hoc* majority coalitions serving its immediate interests in exchange for financial resources and federal conces- sions. Television networks and radio stations are powerful levers in the search for votes. In response, congressional leaders and state elites seek to capture key positions in the administrative machinery of the federal executive and in state enterprises and banks. These attitudes are hardly congruent with the image of an "imperial presidency."[17] In short, over-representation creates the conditions for its own perpetuation: amendment of electoral procedures requires a three- fifths majority in Congress, but the majority of votes is in the hands of those interests most desirous of maintaining distorted representation.[18]

We can now better appreciate the impasse at the root of the fiscal crisis and the problem of democratic governance. Both have common origins in the system of "incomplete federalism" and in the macroeconomics of distributive conflict. Extreme fragmentation, structural instability (manifested in the rapid emergence and demise of new parties and in the facility with which representatives switch parties), and the repeated collapse of nascent party identities are the central characteristics of the post-1964 party system (Kinzo

1990) and have made Brazil one of the most extreme cases of ungovernability in the Latin American democracies.

The gulf between the political composition of *electoral* coalitions (that are the origin of a government) and the composition of a *government* coalition required to implement market-oriented reforms has proven untenable. The intrinsic instability of the Brazilian party system (as well as the rules governing it) thus impede the transition from elections to effective government, undercutting both reform and governability. It is not surprising, therefore, that "pockets of efficiency" — traditionally insulated from the pressures of competitive politics —initiated market-oriented reforms.

A related difficulty in contemporary Brazil concerns the weakness of democratic control over the agencies and institutions that make up the state apparatus. Elected governments do not possess sufficient authority and credibility to enforce universal principles of revenue allocation and distribution of appointments to public offices. Nor are elected officials able to carry out the redistribution of privileges and penalties that, in principle, are bestowed on them by virtue of their power to tax. This makes it difficult to achieve the combination of governability and legitimacy needed to create (or recover) the politico-administrative capabilities required for the implementation of reform policies.

Agencies responsible for tax collection and enforcement, specifically the Receita Federal (Federal Revenue Department), have been progressively dismantled. Moreover, the technological resources and relative autonomy of regulatory organs have declined significantly. The democratization process introduced another disruptive factor, namely that the credibility enjoyed by relevant office holders frequently hinges on the goodwill of recently elected and relatively inexperienced policy makers.[19]

The cumulative effect of this process of bureaucratic entropy has been the disarticulation of the state apparatus and the generalization of antidemocratic mechanisms through which taxes are constantly levied on the same small universe of taxpayers, those whose income is easily monitored by the Federal Revenue Department. In contrast, the transfer of tax receipts and payments to the social security system presupposes long-term financing impossible in an economic system in which megainflation is the norm. Economic agents act on the basis of extremely short-term (virtually daily) calculations, providing incentives for pervasive fiscal insubordination. The private sector, states, and municipalities finance their activities by delaying (sometimes up to sixty months) the transfer of collected taxes to federal coffers, thus taking advantage of megainflation to reduce the real value of their payments and to acquire access to financing unavailable through normal financial channels.[20] As a result, the viability of the monetary and fiscal agencies of the federal government is threatened. Without reversing this crumbling of state regulatory agencies, it will be impossible to recoup the necessary level of public savings and the transparency, accountability, and administrative rationality required for the management of public monies.

Advocates of neoliberalism, who delight in attacking the state, have neglected the fundamental importance of state regulatory and extractive capabilities to the reform process. They regard as a precondition for reform precisely those elements that have become problematic in countries in the midst of democratization that embarked on the explosive path of structural adjustment.

This analysis of fiscal paralysis points to a fundamental shift in the relations between state and market that, although typical of many Latin American countries, has been extreme in Brazil. The Brazilian state continues to occupy center stage, but it can no longer play the role of sovereign agent capable of guiding the process of industrial, agricultural, and technological development. Instead, the state has become a central factor in the exacerbation of the fiscal crisis and in the privatization and dismantling of state structures through the proliferation of clandestine networks with predatory ties with civil society.

For these reasons, the 1980s brought radical changes to Brazil and other Latin American countries. The economic regime in the region went from one of chronic but moderate inflation to one of very high inflation, finally reaching hyperinflation in Argentina, Bolivia, and elsewhere. Although hyperinflation was arrested in Brazil, price increases remain at 20 to 30 percent per month.[21] Hence, the norms that regulate contractual arrangements between economic agents operate under conditions of extreme uncertainty. Rather than general norms and criteria regulating monetary correction (fixed by a central monetary authority with adequate enforcement capabilities), the Brazilian economy, as it approaches hyperinflation, functions according to rules that are defined on a quasi-individual basis by economic agents. Under these circumstances, open or disguised forms of indexation prevail, established on a case-by-case basis by the contracting parties.

In light of the analysis of economists concerned with the transition from one inflationary regime to another, it is important to acknowledge the changing role and weight of expectations in price formation, which become progressively more subjective as inflation rises (Cardim de Carvalho 1990). Thus, the transition from an economy regulated through reasonably clear rules of indexation (although lacking homogeneity in terms of criteria and frequency) to a situation in which socioeconomic agents define their own revenue adjustments based on their subjective expectations concerning the future rate of inflation has resulted in the expansion of the indexed and increasingly "negotiated" sphere of the economy vis-à-vis the market-regulated sphere. This process fills the vacuum created by the state's retreat, but it operates on an *ad hoc* basis in accordance with "do it yourself" norms, the very antithesis of any coherent social order and of social practices central to the foundation of political community.

Conclusion

The Brazilian experience forces us to reflect on the question of ideology in processes of democratization combined with structural reform. The democratic adjustment of societal expectations, the impact of economic reforms, and the nature of the interaction between the state and the market economy require a complete redrawing of cognitive "maps" (Sola 1993). The role played by ideological transformations in shaping the conditions of governability that underlie fiscal paralysis is crucial. From this perspective, the Brazilian experience offers a unique opportunity for analysis because of certain features associated with the 1988 Constitution.

We have argued that "incomplete federalism" is one of the main obstacles to a new fiscal pact.[22] Moreover, the truncated federalism created by the new constitution is quite ambiguous and contains several inconsistencies. It froze *in vitro* a key moment in the change of cognitive maps regarding the desired relation between elected representatives, state, and civil society. The 1988 Constitution transformed these still-fluid maps into rigid constitutional precepts that erected legal parameters circumscribing the action of the federal executive and other branches of government. The hope that the constitutional convention was a propitious moment to "clean the slate" and institutionalize profound changes in Brazil's political culture has not been realized (Lamounier and de Souza 1990).

In reality, the problems created by the exaggeration of certain "egalitarian" features of the contemporary version of Brazilian federalism, as well as by other centrifugal forms of political resource redistribution, stem from the difficulty the framers of the new constitution confronted in viewing their deliberations from a more systemic perspective with respect to macroeconomic policy.[23] The absence of such a perspective was only partly due to a lack of understanding of the economic and political issues. Rather, circumstances created by the 1988 Constitution illustrate a more general mechanism regarding distributive conflicts among organized interests, which Juan Carlos Torre (1993) explores in terms of the dynamic impact of organized interests on the democratization process.

Paradoxically, situations of fluid democratic transition tend to restrict, rather than broaden, the opportunities for cooperative interaction. Political identities are still fluid, and the "foundational" character assumed by distributive conflicts in critical conjunctures puts the role of collective actors and political agents in the new order up for grabs. Making the stakes so high can elicit intransigent affirmation of collective identities on the part of protagonists. If social and political pacts are seen as moments of "rest" between confrontations, and if agreement presupposes the existence of an institution-alized contractual space, the prerequisites for a strategy of cooperation were absent in Brazil during the period of constitutional reform. What is surprising may be the fact that a constitutional text was produced at all.

What are Brazil's prospects? All indications point to the emergence of a consensus, both at the societal level and among political actors, regarding the importance of fiscal and administrative reforms. Conventional wisdom has come to understand that the government's capacity to initiate and consolidate these reforms depends on the institutional conditions of governability and on the formulation of an agreed-upon economic strategy.

This unanimity is recent. The diagnosis that confers priority to the fiscal crisis only emerged within government circles during the Sarney government, primarily due to the efforts of Economy Minister Luiz Carlos Bresser Pereira (1986-1987). Within two years, however, acceptance of this diagnosis had become widespread as society was subjected to the threat of hyperinflation, which loomed over the economy from the November 1989 presidential elections until President Collor's inauguration in March 1990. The vicissitudes of Collor's government brought to center stage the minimal requirements for democratic governability by highlighting the enormous gap between the electoral coalition that brought Collor to power and the unstable coalitions his partially liberalizing program (and his personal style) were capable of forging.

The nature of President Collor's removal from power demonstrates that popular expectations, and the learning process that they generated regarding the democratic potential of Brazilian society, should not be underestimated. The impeachment also revealed the economy's capacity to resist a turbulent six-month political crisis without going over the brink into hyperinflation. Most importantly, Collor's ouster illustrated the demand in society for strengthened mechanisms of democratic control over the state.

The combination of a predatory state and intense liberalizing reforms forced this introspective examination of the nature and extent of the crisis. Instead of the hyperinflationary debacle that had been predicted since 1988 by most economists, another type of upheaval, eminently political in nature, was unleashed. The dénouement of the Collor administration and the complexity of the *fenômeno Collor* suggest that processes other than democratization and economic transformation must be considered. The orderly, gradual experiences of economic liberalization produced during the Collor government, such as the first commercial liberalization and privatization packages, were generated from existing state capabilities, organizational resources, and technical expertise accumulated in the surviving "pockets of efficiency."

These reforms were carried out in the shadow of a decomposing semi-developmentalist state, and they were more subject than in the past to the relatively coherent democratic oversight exercised by the judiciary and Congress. Yet, the conditions responsible for the success of the "Asian Tigers" are not present in Brazil, nor elsewhere in Latin America — with the partial exception of Chile, and perhaps Mexico. Consequently, the choice between hyperinflation and the crafting of a preventive fiscal pact remains open. As elsewhere in the region, the eventual outcome in Brazil will depend on the reform of political institutions, notably the electoral and party systems, and the economy's resilience and ability to function while marking time in the hope that key actors in the state and in civil society will eventually carry out structural reforms, including a deepening of democratization, required for a renewal of sustained growth.

Notes

1. The concept of the "explosive path" proposed by Fanelli, Frenkel, and Rozenwurcel (1994) is extremely useful in analyzing the perverse developments affecting a number of Latin American countries in the wake of adjustment crises.

2. The emergence of an electoral coalition that was politically heterogenous and inconsistent in its support for different programs was inevitable, since the PT (Partido dos Trabalhadores — the Worker's Party) represented only 5 percent of Congress as well. Moreover, the PT would have faced even greater difficulties forming coalitions consistent with its electoral platform, based largely on general political directives rather than on an effective plan. From a political party perspective, the 1989 presidential elections represented above all else the defeat of major parties such as the PDS (Partido Democrático Social — Social Democratic Party) and the PMDB (Partido Do Movimento Democrático Brasileiro — Brazilian Democratic Movement Party).

3. Francisco de Oliveira (1990) is an exception among the critics. See Kugelmas and Sallum (1993) for an analysis of the vicissitudes of the developmentalist state in the 1980s.

4. The depth and irreversibility of the fiscal crisis became an issue of convergence (and not controversy) among economists, largely due to the transparency and analytical style that Minister Bresser imposed when dealing with the problem.

5. Among the most affected agencies were the Customs Policy Council (Conselho de Política Aduaneira—CPA), responsible for the far-reaching reforms implemented in commercial and industrial regulatory policies, and the National Bank of Economic and Social Development (Banco Nacional de Desenvolvimento Ecônomico e Social—BNDES). In addition to its traditional function as Brazil's leading development bank, the BNDES assumed the leadership role in the privatization of public enterprises (Werneck 1992).

6. Moreover, instability concerning the rules of the game was part and parcel of the new constitution. This instability initiated a prolonged period of continuous political change including the April 1993 plebiscite over the form of government (presidentialism versus parliamentarism) and a process of constitutional revision to be initiated in October 1993, whose scope and content are now a matter of intense dispute.

7. The information that follows is based on Franco and Fritsch (1992) and on research currently being conducted by the author for the Department of Development of the Economic Commission for Latin America and the Caribbean on the project, *El Estado en América Latina: Propuestas de Políticas para Aumentar la Efetividad del Estado.*

8. As noted by Franco and Fritsch (1992), "Several sectors were born amidst conditions of extreme concentration." Regulations reinforced the market power of national companies as a means to support their competitive status vis-à-vis multinational corporations or to assure the continuation of national and foreign companies' expansion programs negotiated with the government.

9. See Bardella (1993) for the reaction of one of the most important entrepreneurs of the capital goods sector.

10. The following analysis is based on information extracted from Werneck (1992) and various issues of the *Gazeta Mercantil* and *O Estado de São Paulo* during 1992 and 1993.

11. For example, it was difficult for the public to understand the different criteria used to evaluate state enterprises or the basket of different currencies which comprise a large portion of public debt bonds. In contrast, the "rotten currency" (*moedas podres*) denomination was easily accepted, given the levels of corruption suspected in other spheres of government.

12. This observation is valid even for the more economically liberal phase of the military regime (1964-1967), which was dominated by President Carlos Castello Branco's goal of price stabilization. As the subsequent "economic miracle" years of 1968-1974 made clear, activist participation of the state in the economy provided huge incentives to the private sector. The maintenance of this pattern of relations between the national productive sector and the state was made possible by easily accessible external resources (Dias and Aguirre 1993).

13. On the progressive weakening of the military regime and the state as a pact of domination, see Kugelmas and Sallum (1993).

14. The multiparty system of the pre-1964 period was replaced by a two-party system, which lasted until 1977-1978. At that point, the military's strategy of political liberalization led them to attempt to divide the opposition by the imposition of new changes in the electoral system and by forcing a return to a multiparty system. Finally, another intervention followed in 1981-1982, as part of a last-ditch effort to win the first direct elections for state governors. This pattern of disruptive political engineering actively prevented the crystallization of strong party identities and allegiances and thus forestalled the consolidation of any coherent party system.

15. As suggested by Lamounier (1990), the 1988 Constitution was written in accordance with "egalitarian" federative principles that had existed since 1932 and which have been retained despite changes in the political regime. It is not surprising, therefore, that the result was the reproduction, in larger scale, of the distortions consolidated by the political measures of 1977. The same underlying premise was behind the creation of another 1,000 municipalities (currently 5,000) and of an additional four states.

16. This is not to say that over-representation explains the heavy reliance on debt with the federal government practiced by some states. The major debtors, in fact, are São Paulo, Minas Gerais, Rio Grande do Sul, Rio de Janeiro, and Bahia. It is the constant need for "rolling over" the debts incurred by these large, more developed states that contributes so significantly to the virulence of the fiscal crisis.

17. Contrary to this image, the Brazilian presidential system does not grant the elected president autonomy to implement far-reaching structural reforms. In fact, as will be discussed below, the weakening of the executive vis-à-vis the legislative and judicial branches produced by the 1988 Constitution was reinforced by the need to forge ad hoc legislative coalitions at the state and federal levels.

18. This phenomenon does not represent a classical case of clientelism. Instead, its explanation resides in the federal government's manipulative use of the economic and political resources in an effort to extract support for its projects from regional political leaders who emerged during Geisel's regional decentralization program. Examples of this may be seen in the case of cocoa (Bahia) and coffee (Minas), which had subsidies and incentives reduced. This explains congressional support from representatives of these states who voted with Sarney in his struggle to extend his mandate to five years (see Haddad 1992).

19. Before 1979, there were 12,000 federal revenue agents; today there are less than 5,700. The contrast is even greater when compared with the growth of human resources used by the states to collect tax revenues, i.e., 35,000 agents in the states for the collection of the tax on the circulation of merchandise and services (ICMS). See the interview with Fernando Banin, president of the Union of Fiscal Auditors (Sindicato de Auditores Fiscais) and of the National Union of National Treasury Auditors (União Nacional de Auditores do Tesouro Nacional) in Banin (1992).

20. The data available on tax evasion typify the megainflationary conjunctures when this type of behavior assumes the form of rebellion against the state. In August 1992, 51 percent of all companies did not pay their FINSOCIAL taxes used to finance various types of social programs. Alleging unconstitutionality, 260,000 taxpayers have used the courts to protest their tax bills. Thirty-one percent of all companies failed to transfer monies collected for social security contributions from their employees to the federal revenue department. Fifty-six percent of all taxpayers failed to pay personal income tax (see O Estado de São Paulo 1992 and 1993).

21. Such an inflationary regime is an intrinsic component of the "explosive path" of adjustment (see Fanelli, Frenkel, and Rozenwurcel 1994). The comparative literature on structural adjustment neglects this question by failing to establish the conceptual distinction between different inflationary regimes, a distinction crucial to grasping the political dynamics underlying the transition from one regime to another. One of these dynamics concerns the functions of the state trapped in a situation of fiscal crisis. A second involves the expectations and behavior of economic actors in shaping new and highly perverse relations between state and society (Cardim de Carvalho 1990).

22. See Camargo (1992) for an analysis of the institutional aspects of "bounded federalism."

23. One of the exceptions was the Law of Budgetary Directives (Lei de Diretrizes Orçamentarias—LDO). This law was fashioned by the Budget and Finance Commission in a bipartisan agreement, with approval guaranteed by an important emerging political agent in Brazil—the economist-politician (see Serra 1989).

References

Banin, Fernando. 1992. Interview in *O Estado de São Paulo* (*Caderno de Economia*), October 13.

Bardella, Claudio. 1993. "Discutir Neoliberalismo é Bobagem." *O Estado de São Paulo*, January 21: 6 (Caderno Econômia).

Barros de Castro, Antônio, and Fernando Pires de Souza. 1985. *A Economia Brasileira em Marcha Forçada.* Rio de Janeiro: Editora Paz e Terra.

Bresser Pereira, Luiz Carlos. 1993. "Efficiency and Politics of Economic Reform in Latin America." In *Economic Reforms in New Democracies*, eds. Luiz Carlos Bresser Pereira, José Maria Maravall, and Adam Przeworski. Cambridge: Cambridge University Press.

Camargo, Aspásia. 1992. "O Federalismo Acorrentado." Paper presented at the annual ANPOCS meeting.

Cardim de Carvalho, Fernando. 1990. "Alta Inflação e Hiper-Inflação: Uma Visão Pós-Keynesiana." *Revista de Econômia Política* 10 (4).

Damil, Mario, José María Fanelli, and Roberto Frenkel. 1992. "Shock externo y desequilibrio fiscal: La macroeconomía de América Latina en los años 1980. Brasil." Paper presented at "Seminario Regional sobre Reformas de Política Pública," sponsored by CEPAL. Santiago, Chile. August 3-5.

Dias, Guilherme Leite, and Basílio Aguirre. 1993. "Crise Político-Económica: as Raízes do Impasse." In *Estado, Mercado, Democracia: Política e Economia Comparada*, ed. Lourdes Sola. São Paulo: Paz e Terra.

(*O*) *Estado de São Paulo.* 1992-1993, various issues.

Evans, Peter. 1992. "The State as a Problem and Solution: Predation, Embedded Autonomy and Adjustment." In *The Politics of Adjustment: International Constraints, Distributive Conflicts, and the State*, eds. Stephen Haggard and Robert Kaufman. Princeton, N.J.: Princeton University Press.

Fanelli, José María, Roberto Frenkel, and Guillermo Rozenwurcel. 1994. "Growth and Structural Reform in Latin America: Where We Stand." In *Latin American Political Economy in the Age of Neoliberal Reform: Theoretical and Comparative Perspectives for the 1990s,* eds. William C. Smith, Carlos H. Acuña, and Eduardo A. Gamarra. New Brunswick, N.J.: North-South Center/Transaction.

Fiori, José Luis. 1990. "Transição Democrática e a Crise do Estado." *Novos Estudos CEBRAP* 28.

Fiori, José Luis. 1992. "Poder e Credibilidade: O Paradoxo da Reforma Neo-Liberal." *Lua Nova* 25.

Franco, Gustavo, and Winston Fritsch. 1992. "The Political Economy of Trade and Industrial Policy Reform in Brazil." CEPAL. Unpublished paper.

Gazeta Mercantil. 1992-1993, various issues.

Gambiasi, Fabio. 1992. "Impasse Distributivo e Paralisia Fiscal." *Planejamento e Políticas Publicas* 6.

Haddad, Paulo. 1992. Presentation at the National Forum, Rio de Janeiro, August 27.

Haggard, Stephen, and Robert Kaufman. 1992. "The Political Economy of Inflation and Stabilization in Middle-Income Countries." In *The Politics of Adjustment: International Constraints, Distributive Conflicts, and the State*, eds. Stephen Haggard and Robert Kaufman. Princeton, N.J.: Princeton University Press.

Haggard, Stephen, and Robert Kaufman. 1993. "O Estado no Processo de Iniciacão e de Consolidação de Reformas Orientadas Para o Mercado." In *Estado, Mercado, Democracia: Política e Economia Comparada*, ed. Lourdes Sola. São Paulo: Paz e Terra.

Kaufman, Robert R. 1990. "Stabilization and Adjustment in Argentina, Brazil, and Mexico." In *Economic Crisis and Policy Choice: The Politics of Adjustment in the Third World*, ed. Joan M. Nelson. Princeton, N.J.: Princeton University Press.

Kinzo, Maria d'Alva. 1990. "O Quadro Partidário e a Constituinte" In *De Geisel a Collor: O Balanço da Transição*, ed. Bolívar Lamounier. São Paulo: Sumaré.

Kugelmas, Eduardo, and Brasílio Sallum Júnior. 1993. "O Leviatã Acorrentado." In *Estado, Mercado, Democracia: Política e Economia Comparada*, ed. Lourdes Sola. São Paulo: Paz e Terra.

Lamounier, Bolívar. 1985. "Partidos Políticos no Brasil." Unpublished paper.

Lamounier, Bolívar, ed. 1990. *De Geisel a Collor: O Balanço da Transição*. São Paulo: Sumaré.

Lamounier, Bolívar, and Amaury de Souza. 1990. "A Feitura da Nova Constituição Um Re-exame da Cultura Política Brasileira." In *De Geisel a Collor: O Balanço da Transição*, ed. Bolívar Lamounier. São Paulo: Sumaré.

Malloy, James M. 1990. "Statecraft, Social Policy and Governance in Latin America." Unpublished paper.

Malloy, James M. 1993. "Democracia, Crise Econômica e o Problema da Governabilidade na America Latina." In *Estado, Mercado, Democracia: Política e Economia Comparada*, ed. Lourdes Sola. São Paulo: Paz e Terra.

O'Donnell, Guillermo. 1990. "Representação versus Delegação." *Novos Estudos CEPRAP* 31.

Oliveira, Francisco de. 1990. "A Metamorfose da Arribaça: O Papel do Fundo Público na Economia Nordestina." *Novos Estudos CEBRAP* 27.

Przeworski, Adam. 1992. *Democracy and the Market: Politics and Economic Reforms in Eastern Europe and Latin America*. Cambridge: Cambridge University Press.

Reis Velloso, João Paulo dos. 1986. *Um Trem para Paris. De Getúlio a Sarney: "Milagres," Choques e Crises do Brasil Moderno*. Rio de Janeiro: Nova Fronteira.

Serra, José. 1979. "Three Mistaken Theses Regarding the Connection between Industrialization and Authoritarian Regimes." In *The New Authoritarianism in Latin America*, ed. David Collier. Princeton, N.J.: Princeton University Press.

Serra, José. 1989. "A Constituição e o Gasto Público." *Planejamento e Políticas Públicas* 1 (1).

Sola, Lourdes. 1985. "Gestão da Economia e Mudança de Regime." *Ciências Sociais Hoje*. São Paulo: Editora Cortez.

Sola, Lourdes. 1987. "Choque Heterodoxo e Transição Política Sem Ruptura: Uma Abordagem Transdisciplinar." In *O Estado da Transição: Política e Economia na Nova República*, ed. Lourdes Sola. São Paulo: Vértice.

Sola, Lourdes. 1991. "Heterodox Shock in Brazil: Técnicos, Politicians, Democracy." *Journal of Latin American Studies* 23 (February).

Sola, Lourdes. 1993. "Estado, Transformação Econômica e Democratização." In *Estado, Mercado, Democracia: Política e Economia Comparada*, ed. Lourdes Sola. São Paulo: Paz e Terra.

Smith, William C. 1992. "Hyperinflation, Macroeconomic Instability and Neoliberal Restructuring in Democratic Argentina." In *The New Democracy in Argentina*, ed. Edward C. Epstein. New York: Praeger.

Torre, Juan Carlos. 1993. "Democracia em Tempos Difíciis." In *Estado, Mercado, Democracia: Política e Economia Comparada*, ed. Lourdes Sola. São Paulo: Paz e Terra.

Torre, Juan Carlos, and Vicente Palermo. 1992. "A la sombra de la hiperinflación." Paper presented at the "Seminario Regional sobre Reformas de Política Pública" sponsored by CEPAL. August 3-5. Santiago, Chile.

Weffort, Francisco. 1992. *Qual Democracia?* São Paulo: Companhia de Letras.

Werneck, Rogério. 1992. "El primer año del programa de privatización en Brasil." In *Adonde va America Latina? Balance de las reformas económicas*, ed. José Vial. Santiago: CIEPLAN.

Chapter Seven

Renegade Development: Rise and Demise of State-Led Development in Brazil

Antônio Barros de Castro

Introduction

Disagreements arise not so much from different answers to the same question but because different questions are asked. Neoliberals examine an economy through questions appropriate to their framework. Is the economy regulated according to free market principles that permit the price system to reflect the relative scarcity of goods? Or, have the principles of comparative advantage guided decision making by economic agents?

To a typical neoliberal, the Brazilian economy is distinguished by its deviations from free market doctrine: high levels of direct and indirect state intervention in the economy, ostensible protectionism, low import/GNP ratio, and, at least until very recently, an obsession with industrialization unparalleled by any other Latin American country. Given these deviations, the long and profound crisis of the Brazilian economy does not elicit much interest on the part of the neoliberal analyst. In the neoliberal view, the end result of the strategy followed in Brazil could not have been otherwise.

In a critical revision of ideas widely accepted until the beginning of the 1980s (Wade 1990), there is a body of scholarship countering the neoliberal approach. It maintains that development can be fueled and, to a certain extent, orchestrated by the state. Gerschenkron's "latecomers," as well as the recent examples of teleocratic states of East Asia (Johnson 1981, 18), illustrate this possibility. The state's capacity to make and implement decisions to lead the economy toward major objectives is the main trait shared in these experiences. In these cases a considerable degree of autonomy is enjoyed by the state, warranting the use of expressions such as "state-led," "developmental states," and "governing the market." How did these governments acquire their decision-making authority?

In the classic "latecomer" approach, great importance is placed on external challenges (extremely relevant in the Japanese and Russian cases) and on transfers of the latent political energy of previous regimes (the Junkers and Samurai are crucial in this regard). In the case of contemporary teleocratic states, a key factor is the international pressure experienced by these countries. It has even been said that the exceptional performance of the Asian tigers stems from their status as "half nations" whose very survival was under constant threat for an extended period of time. Other factors cited as instrumental in paving the way for state-led strategies are the destruction of dominant classes at the end of the colonial period and under the agrarian and educational reforms immediately following World War II.

Under these criteria, conditions in Brazil have not been particularly favorable for the emergence of an autonomous state. Notwithstanding the brutal shocks of the 1930s depression, Brazilian national sovereignty was never challenged by outside forces (Suzigan 1986). Moreover, no internal political forces, latent in the traditional power structure, were mobilized in support of industrialization. Exemplifying the attitude of the dominant agro-export elites is a remark by Júlio Prestes, their candidate in the 1930 presidential campaign, "Oranges will save coffee" (Prado Júnior 1956, 296). On occasion these elites openly opposed the transfer and concentration of resources required by industrialization (Martins 1976).

Despite the absence of some elements typically associated with the pattern of development centered on an autonomous state and rapid industrialization, the Brazilian government distinguished itself by its success in promoting sustained industrial growth. One of the most significant characteristics in latecomer and teleocratic experiences is remarkable continuity in the drive for industrialization. Brazil reproduced this in a surprising fashion from the early 1930s until 1980. The explanation for the "longevity" of Brazil's growth boom is twofold: not once did the country consider a return to pursuing natural comparative advantages, nor was the paralyzation of the economy ever considered as a "house cleaning" option, even in the face of threats to macroeconomic equilibrium. As a matter of fact, cabinet members who tried to arrest industrial growth in 1955 and 1958, and in less obvious attempts in 1967 and 1979, were ejected from power.[1]

During the long course of state-led development and in vivid contrast with the interruptions and reversals experienced in Argentina (Canitrot 1979 and 1991), national and foreign private capital was persuaded to invest in Brazil. Brazil enlisted the collaboration of private capital in the implementation of plans and programs whose maturation periods sometimes exceeded the terms of governments proposing them. Anxious to take advantage of these opportunities, private capital behaved as if the continuity of development was assured.

As a result of the radical transformations of the postwar period, the Brazilian economy became endowed with a comparatively complete and modern industrial structure. For example, while the export of manufactured goods in 1967 accounted for only 10 percent of total exports, it surpassed 50 percent by 1981 and subsequently sustained this upward trajectory.[2]

Some positive results of this intense transformation can even be found in income distribution, a problematic area for Brazil. Table 1, which ranks the population according to income in ascending deciles, reveals that from 1960 to 1980 the poorest strata made substantial gains in their absolute income. The poorest 10 percent of the population saw their earnings increase by 92 percent in those two decades, while the decile immediately above experienced a 79 percent rise in income. As can be seen in Table 1, the much greater income gains of the richest 10 percent came almost entirely from the sharp concentration observed in the 1960s.

Table 1

Income Distribution in Brazil, 1960-1980
(Percent Change in Earnings of the Economically Active Population)

Decile	1960-70	1970-80	% Change 1960-1980
10th	20	50	92
9th	21	47	79
8th	18	46	72
7th	15	39	60
6th	9	30	42
5th	6	34	42
4th	8	48	60
3rd	21	47	79
2nd	35	51	104
1st	67	53	155

Sources: Data for 1960-1970 from Langoni (1973); data for 1970-1980 from Denslow and Tyler (1983).

Nevertheless, 1980 marked the end of a long cycle of impressive growth, and the Brazilian economy went from being a success story to suffering an interminable succession of crises. As a result, the Brazilian experience is now seen by many analysts as just another failed attempt at import-substitution industrialization. This chapter takes a different view. The broader sweep of Brazilian industrialization should be understood as both a peculiar and successful case of state-led growth which was brutally interrupted in the 1980s.

When compared to authentic cases of successful state-led industrialization, the Brazilian case poses the following questions: How did Brazil achieve high rates of industrial growth until 1980, even though it largely lacked the political resources for the state to design and guide economic development? In light of other Latin American experiences, how did Brazil manage to get beyond the so-called "easy phase" of industrialization? How was it possible to restrain the demands of those interests injured by economic transformations? What historical substitutes have emerged in Brazil for the political power of a full-blown developmentalist state? What are the implications of this peculiar heritage for Brazil's contemporary crisis?

A Synopsis of Rapid Growth

An important aspect of the Brazilian growth experience is the relationship between economic agents and overall economic performance in the cycle of intensive expansion-cum-transformation between the mid-1930s to 1980. As shown in Furtado's classic analysis, the Brazilian government's efforts to protect domestic income after the collapse of exports in 1929 were a first, and largely unintentional, step toward a new pattern of economic growth (Furtado 1975).

In 1934, and especially after 1937-1938, the government began to promote a transformation of the country's productive structure. Institutions were created to accompany — and, to a certain extent, guide — international trade and the growth of modern activities. The main example of this trend was the creation of the Conselho Federal de Comércio Exterior (Federal Council on International Trade—CFCE) (Monteiro and Cunha 1974; Diniz 1978). Also noteworthy was the government's preoccupation with the selection and training of its employees, as indicated by the creation of the Departamento de Administração do Serviço Público (Department of Public Services Administration—DASP) and the Instituto Brasileiro de Geografia e Estatística (Brazilian Institute of Geography and Statistics—IBGE), charged with gathering economic, social, and demographic data. Without doubt, this set of institutions markedly upgraded the state's capacity for the diagnosis and monitoring of the country's development.

Seen in perspective, the state equipped itself with the means to control, and eventually mold, the economic evolution of the country. President Getúlio Vargas' speeches during that period reveal an abiding desire to modernize the country's economy. Vargas declared in 1940, "Brazil will only be able to enter the ranks of developed nations through the restructuring of its organic forces and foundations on the basis of its fundamental industries" (Fonseca 1989, 262). The Brazilian government was largely reacting to acute international conditions, particularly the Great Depression and the coming world war. In an attempt to achieve its goals, the government created new economic policy instruments, and, to some extent, managed to escape the dominance of traditional regional oligarchies.

These institutions and their bureaucratic personnel were transported almost intact to Brazil's post-World War II democratic phase (Campello de Souza 1976). When the Bretton Woods agreement advocated a full return to the free market, certain Brazilian institutions and practices came under growing scrutiny. The conflict over Brazil's growth path clearly expressed itself in the Simonsen-Gudin debate (Simonsen and Gudin 1977) and was also evident in the ambiguity of the presidency of Eurico Gaspar Dutra in the late 1940s, as we shall see next.

With Getúlio Vargas' return to the presidency in 1950, the government's commitment to development regained momentum (Vianna 1987; Fonseca 1989, Chapter 6). The international scenario at the time complemented the president's motivation and the militant determination of his advisers. In this favorable context, the Banco Nacional de Desenvolvimento Econômico (National Bank for Economic Development—BNDE) was created. The manifest intentions of its founders — to rationalize the use of public resources — meant that policies were to be consistent with technically justified criteria. In other words, and according to Finance Minister Horácio Lafer, the BNDE was to "resist the pressures to which public institutions are usually subjected" (Martins 1976).

The Juscelino Kubitschek period (1956-1960) is very important to the hypotheses advanced here. First, long-range goals were conceived in a deliberate effort to advance beyond conjunctural responses to perceived bottlenecks (Malan 1977). The Brazilian automobile industry is an example. To establish an auto industry, markets along the productive chain (from auto parts to final consumption) were shaped and sized, to different degrees, through economic policies such as fiscal and credit incentives. Indeed, backward linkages were deliberately introduced into the automobile industry through regulations created by technocrats of the Kubitschek government in the late 1950s (Hirschman 1968, 237). Since that time, the country's growth horizon has been associated with the constitution of a modern and complete industrial structure, based on the prevailing technological paradigm.

As important, if not more so, was the fact that the commitment to "growth-cum-transformation" ceased to be an objective espoused only by the government. The opinion of two privileged witnesses to economic policy debates of the time illuminates the prevailing climate. Lucas Lopes described the widespread public support for development:

> The shock that Juscelino brought to the country cannot be explained simply by looking at accomplished goals; it can be found in the climate he created in Brazil. Everyone wanted to have their own

business. Even small industries in the countryside would look for ways to advance. Juscelino created in Brazil a climate of generalized economic development (Lopes 1991, 295).

A second witness, Eugênio Gudin, though a ferocious Kubitschek adversary, similarly described the "industrialization that characterized the period." He also noted that the movement was so strong "there was not a person who could resist; there was not an industry that was not built" (Gudin 1965, 202).

Summarizing the country's economic performance in the 1950s, Albert Hirschman affirmed that "there was at least one experience in Latin America — that of Brazil in the 1950s — that closely approached the scenario described by Gerschenkron." In support of this reasoning, Hirschman remarked favorably upon "the rapid and sustained advances in the steel, chemical, and capital goods sectors," the creation of special institutions "aimed at increasing the supply of capital," and the "flourishing of a development-oriented ideology" (Hirschman 1968, 245).

A final point must be added. During this period, the U.S. government, reinforced by international agencies, was actively counseling a slowdown, if not outright abandonment, of Latin American industrialization efforts; pressure was exerted via U.S. enforcement of international rules regarding foreign exchange and trade policies and, in some cases, by patronage of orthodox stabilization plans. Brazil, however, remained steadfast in its promotion of import-substitution industrialization. The government's sole capitulation to these pressures for economic liberalization was the implementation of an active policy to attract foreign investments.

The government's Programa de Ação Econômica de Governo 1964-1966 (Program of Economic Action—PAEG) stressed the need to "accelerate the pace of economic growth," while bringing the inflationary process progressively under control. The ranking of these objectives, as well as the terms used to describe them, is significant. The program was launched at a time of uncontrollable inflation (reaching 140 percent during the first three months of 1964). Yet the government insisted on achieving sustained annual growth rates of 6 percent, while promising to rein in inflation only gradually (Associação Comercial de Minas 1964, 87).

This commitment to "developmentalism" survived the crisis of populist democracy and was one of the hallmarks of the authoritarian regime that came to power through a military coup in 1964. Indeed, the military government's strict adherence to economic growth policies is often explained by its "need" to legitimate its power, which suggests that the commitment to growth was widely embraced in Brazilian society, particularly among the political and economic elites.

The conviction that Brazil could and should achieve sustained economic expansion explains why Roberto Campos, the powerful minister of planning, would defensively proclaim only a few months after the 1964 coup that contrary to public perceptions, he was not taking "precipitated measures that threaten to weaken the country's capacity to invest."[3] The commitment to growth was so strong that the regional interests of the agrarian elite, supposedly triumphant in the coup, found little receptivity (the hardships export interests imposed by Roberto Campos' coffee policy are a case in point). In fact, this elite did not even manage to translate its aspirations into a credible, alternative strategy under the military regime.

The military regime's preoccupation with development was ostensibly reaffirmed by the belligerent *Programa Estratégico de Desenvolvimento* (Strategic Program for Development of 1968-1970) and in a subsequent document entitled *Metas e Bases para Governo* (Goals and Foundations for Government Action). The latter document boldly affirmed that the main objective of the regime's economic policy was "that Brazil become a part of the developed world by the end of the century" (SEPLAN 1970, 15). More important than any plans or programs, however, was the climate prevailing in the country when the economy reached, and then surpassed, an annual growth rate of 10 percent. Perhaps the euphoria is best captured in Minister Antônio Delfim Netto's often-repeated boast that "it is now necessary to run in order to stay in the same place."

During the "Brazilian Miracle," the state seized upon another avenue to rapid growth for Brazil's young industrial structure: local enterprises — backed by government incentives — began to enter into international markets via the export of manufactured goods. This breakthrough meant that the more innovative and agile (but still heavily protected) industries were able to expand internationally (Baumann 1982). Naturally, the means adopted to break into international markets deviated sharply from comparative advantage principles, which were then being rediscovered in Latin America by the post-1973 Augusto Pinochet regime in Chile.

Brazil's commitment to sustained growth, firmly entrenched when the external shocks of 1973 hit, was deeply shaped by belief in rapid and uninterrupted economic growth, which had become incorporated into the worldview of the country's economic agents. This was evident in the Brazilian response to the crisis triggered by the quadrupling of oil prices. High growth rates had to be maintained. According to Planning Minister Reis Velloso, "If in August of 1974 we had set our growth target at 4 to 6 percent, the disappointment would have been widespread" (Barros de Castro and de Souza 1985, 35-40).

Far from adjusting to oil price increases by slowing the pace of economic development, the government of General Ernest Geisel (1974-1979) took an activist role in promoting industrialization. Under Geisel, the restructuring of the economy took precedence over the promotion of growth for the economy as a whole (Barros de Castro and de Souza 1985). According to the authorities, efforts to modernize the economy would depend on taking advantage of opportunities not yet fully revealed by the market. State action was crucial to this effort. Reis Velloso echoed the perceptions that prevailed among the higher ranks of the bureaucracy noting, "government incentives are necessary to set heavy industry in motion, especially in sectors known for their low profitability and long maturation period." He added, "given the current situation of Brazilian industry, if we were to rely on the market economy, the country's private sector would not invest in areas such as iron and steel, fertilizer, petrochemical and non-ferrous metals" (*Visão* 1976).

The Convention of Guaranteed Growth

The preceding analysis suggests that the early commitment of the Brazilian government to economic development had shaped the vision of the country's economic agents. As the government infused the general population and principal economic agents with the idea of continuous rapid growth, an implicit pact or convention was born.[4] This merits a closer look.

If each economic agent believes that all other economic agents will attempt to pursue established goals, then the best alternative for them is to follow suit — despite unforeseen difficulties and obstacles — so as to stay in step. This principle is similar to the one Keynes observed in bankers' behavior: it is preferable to make the mistake that everyone else is making than to be correct in isolation. Consequently, goals and objectives, as well as economic development itself, tend to become self-fulfilling prophecies. The importance of this phenomenon cannot be overstated; the burden of providing decision makers with incentives was lightened, thereby reducing the need for state guidance.

Once the new convention was tacitly adopted, the potential for growth of the economy was no longer restrained by individual short-term expectations. Moreover, receptivity regarding the goals established by government authorities increased, as did the implicit conviction that individual success depended upon synchronization with unfolding global transformations. This phenomenon contributed to altering the way firms looked at the market and interpreted its relevant signals. In other words, each firm would try to occupy a position in a larger structure whose future existence was taken for granted. Furthermore, once economic agents had effectively adjusted their position in accordance with the expected outcome, subsequent experiences justified and reinforced the original decision. In the process, the weeding out of successful and unsuccessful enterprises did not take place according to processes typical of a market economy, but rather through a much more dynamic process driven by "centrifugal forces" whose epicenter was to be found in the state apparatus.

The second pattern, closely intertwined with the first, concerns the maneuverability of the decision-making process. We already know that in Brazil this process was somewhat distanced from the available market signals. Whenever an important decision needed to be taken, state planners would refer to the stable structures operating in the advanced economies.

The process was similar to re-doing a jigsaw puzzle that had already been solved in more advanced contexts (Barros de Castro 1992). For example, if an automobile industry was being established, the economic agent had to gain access to information on the size of the market and the technology that was most likely to prevail within a certain time frame. Quantitative and qualitative adjustments were defined by growth-cum-transformation policies, protectionist measures (domestic content requirements, for instance), credit schemes for financing domestic consumption, and so on. Even though these factors did not nullify the importance of current costs and prices, they certainly limited their relevance in the decision-making process.

New patterns in Brazil's growth strategy illustrate how, as Delfim Netto suggested, a considerable effort was necessary in order not to lag behind transformations taking place in the economy. Obviously, not all actions, even at the individual level, could be understood as reactions to the market. Decisions increasingly (and to a certain extent, consciously) shaped the very environment in which the newly created productive capacity would operate. There was no refuge from the changes that were taking place, but it was possible to evaluate them incorrectly. Given the multifaceted commitment of the public sector to the changes in course and to rapid growth, the tolerance margin for *overestimation* was rather generous. These circumstances propelled economic agents toward what we may call "minimum safety" strategies. In this context, the government aversion to restraining economic growth and the economic agents' obsession with both incentives and guarantees were perfectly understandable.

From a neoliberal perspective, however, state intervention is generally seen as synonymous with rent-seeking behavior and probably corruption. The warnings are incessant: "Private entrepreneurs should learn as fast as possible to obtain profits from their performance in competitive internal and world markets, as opposed to trying to secure their profit-making capability through the political arena" (Ranis and John 1988). These warnings ignore the experiences (some characterized by very favorable growth rates) that do not conform to the neoliberal norm (Evans 1992), focusing instead only on the so-called "development disasters."

The Stability Convention

A nother pertinent question raised by the Brazilian experience is, How was it possible to sustain a compulsion for high growth without incurring uncontrollable inflation? We shall assume that Brazil lacks the political assets of the authentic latecomers. Also, a certain degree of control over the inflationary process (whether real or perceived) is indispensable to the success of the experience because in the absence of relative control, sudden shifts in economic policy are a constant possibility. Under such conditions, economic agents will not undertake the risks that accompany certain investments, especially those that cannot be justified under the economy's *present* situation. In other words, the possibility of shifts in policy introduces doubt as to the viability of expected transformations — in which case the minimum safety strategy would lose its rationale.

Although inflation was identified as a central problem by the military government installed in April 1964, the new regime very soon came to adopt extensive indexing mechanisms. Indexation implicitly ruled out the immediate elimination of inflation. The government simply opted to eliminate the risk that inflation poses for contracts by correcting values over time. The new government's tactic apparently acknowledged the fear that the distributive conflicts (among the different social groups and between the public and private sectors) could not be solved in the short run.

In fact, the authoritarian regime faced another pressing problem: strong public demand for "growth now" (Simonsen and Campos 1974; Resende 1990). That is to say, the demand for growth was so strong and widespread and the inflationary process so complex (characterized by "repressed" inflation in the form of highly subsidized public tariffs) that harsh anti-inflationary policies capable of quickly remedying the situation could not be implemented.

The essence of the new solution was captured by Simonsen, who referred to the policy as "conditioned gradualism":

> ... conditioning factors are that the real GNP must grow at elevated rates in the short run, without being interrupted by any liquidity crisis.... The implementation of such a policy requires high levels of expertise from policy makers: first, it presupposes the continuation of present wage policy, then it requires a fine-tuned monetary policy with open market operations in order to avoid a liquidity crisis, on the one hand, and a reactivation of inflation on the other (Simonsen 1972, 94).

As Simonsen pointed out, this treatment "has the inconvenience of being slow, giving the impression that the government is stabilizing the rate of inflation and not the currency." He recognized, in addition, that this type of policy also required "a certain amount of luck: once in a while, a good harvest is needed to force inflation down a little" (Simonsen 1972, 94).

The post-1964 military regime had, in fact, gradually accepted the criticism — voiced within the bureaucracy itself — that asked for a "qualitative goal" under which a mere decrease in the rate of inflation would be acceptable. However, the fact that stability was *simulated* (meaning the rate of inflation, rather than inflation itself, was being curbed) created a situation where things appeared under control, but the economy seemed somehow vulnerable. And the perception of vulnerability apparently justified an imperviousness to excessive demands by interests with access to the power structure (Hirschman 1984).

While the widespread use of indexation facilitated Brazil's relatively peaceful coexistence with inflation, this did not mean that different groups always accepted the rules of monetary correction and their consequences. On the contrary, many sectors and groups fought to recoup losses (whether real or fictitious) and to alter the rules of indexation. These conflicts produced serious consequences. The rules of indexation in effect in 1966 (when the currency and the exchange rate were not indexed and wages were underindexed) were very different from those in effect at the end of the next decade. Those responsible for the country's economic policy, however, did not seem to realize that the solution they found would necessarily evolve — and lose effectiveness — over time.

By 1979, the exchange rate was being adjusted every three weeks, while wages (no longer underindexed) were adjusted every six months. In both cases, indexation mitigated inflation's damage, but by 1979, the economy's capacity to assimilate adverse shocks without a violent impact on the rate of inflation was all but lost. Counteracting measures had become more agile (Sader 1988), thus making the precarious economic equilibrium even more vulnerable. Some understood the dangers inherent in this situation; President Geisel's year-end address to the nation warned, "the nation cannot coexist peacefully with annual inflation rates higher than 40 percent" (*Conjuntura Econômica* 1978, 4).

Table 2 contrasts the Brazilian inflation experience with that of other countries. It is notable that until 1973, the inflationary process in Brazil was "relatively neutralized" and did not worsen in contrast to the other countries. Furthermore, during the critical period of 1974-1975, the rate of inflation observed in Brazil was comparable to those recorded in Great Britain, Italy, and Japan. It is not surprising, therefore, that at that moment many economists of international stature began to consider the advantages of the "Brazilian solution" to the inflationary problem (Friedman 1991).

Table 2
Inflation Rates in Selected Countries
(Annual Average % Change in Consumer Prices)

	1968	1969	1970	1971	1972	1973	1974	1975	1976	1977	1978
U.K	4.9	5.4	6.4	9.4	7.1	9.1	14.5	28.0	14.8	13.3	11.3
Italy	1.4	2.7	4.9	4.8	5.7	10.8	17.7	17.3	18.3	18.5	13.5
Japan	5.6	5.5	7.2	6.3	4.9	11.7	20.3	7.9	6.5	5.5	4.0
Brazil	21.0	22.0	22.7	20.2	17.0	12.7	25.8	29.2	40.5	44.0	39.1
France	4.6	6.4	5.3	5.5	5.9	7.4	13.7	11.7	9.2	9.5	9.2
USA	4.7	4.7	5.4	4.3	3.3	6.2	9.7	9.6	5.3	5.9	7.5
Argentina	16.0	7.7	13.4	35.0	58.5	61.2	23.4	182.5	443. 2	176.0	175.5

Source: International Monetary Fund and Fundação Getúlio Vargas, as published in Mário
Henrique Simonsen, "A Inflação Brasileira e a Atual Política Anti-Inflacionária."
Brasília: Senado Federal, 1979.

It was the perception of economic agents that the institutions and rules through which the effects of inflation were supposedly neutralized assured a kind of second order or "substitute" stability. Concretely, these institutions and rules were responsible for filtering daily economic information and for reducing the fears of individuals and enterprises that their long-term decisions would be threatened by the general economic situation. Another mechanism of self-fulfillment at work here should be noted: faced with adversities, Brazil's economic agents did not tend to alter their relatively easygoing stance.

While policy makers could take this tolerance, or even passivity, for granted (Carvalho 1992), the parameters within which economic policy could operate were narrowed, because any measure capable of seriously contradicting expectations became virtually unacceptable. This represented, therefore, a permanent veto — occasionally made explicit — of serious attempts to combat inflation.

The two conventions previously examined defined an environment that economic agents perceived as highly safe and conducive to investments of considerable risk. Besides being predisposed to accelerated growth, these conventions gave rise to a "teleocratic culture," in which decisions were guided by the pursuit of goals (Johnson 1981). The emergence of such a purpose-governed culture obviously lightened the burden of government policy makers in their attempts to steer private initiative in the desired direction. Seen from this perspective, the tacit conventions here examined (especially that of guaranteed growth) had the effect of bolstering the political capability of the government.

With these conventions in place, economic agents took their decisions, solidifying the expected growth and (substitute) stability. In order for the process to run smoothly, some provisions had to be in place that regulated the socioeconomic environment and made financial undertakings viable, particularly as far as the state was concerned. The appearance of difficulties, however, did not necessarily endanger these conventions because they were endowed with considerable flexibility and thus allowed for successful management of unforeseen events and challenges. However, the maintenance of these conventions confronted several key questions — state autonomy, implementation of major investment programs, and containment of opposition to the development model — that were resolved in ways unique to the Brazilian experience.

State Autonomy:
Plans, Goals, Bureaucracy, and Other Institutions

In Brazil, as in most of Latin America, the autonomy of the state cannot be taken for granted. By and large, governments lack a solid institutional framework for long-term governance of the economy. Governments also lack a powerful and stable nucleus of bureaucrats capable of assuring the intertemporal coherence of long-range decisions. It may be said, however, that at least some of the conditions required for state-led development (Johnson 1981) were achieved in the case of Brazil through a fluctuating combination of plans, targets, and various institutions created by powerful presidents such as Vargas, Kubitschek, and Geisel.

The implementation of major new investment programs usually called for the formulation of at least one large project which, due to the volume of resources needed, the lengthy maturation period required, the high risks involved, and the technical and organizational advances, necessitated direct government participation in the production of goods and services. For this very reason, we will examine the importance of state-owned enterprises in the vitality and continuity of the industrialization process.

Completing a triangle of difficulties, the maintenance of the growth and stability conventions meant that the development model with industry as its nucleus resulted in the marginalization of traditional activities and secondary geographical regions. An important question emerges: How was it possible to prevent groups from articulating their interests and eventually imposing alternative options on the government, thereby changing its goals in ways that would be detrimental to the industrialization process?

The launching of plans and targets capable of mobilizing Brazil's continental economy required political leaders of great weight and influence. The Vargas, Kubitschek, and Geisel administrations were moments in which these mobilizations occurred, shaping the economy for years to come. The full accomplishment of their programs could not, however, be assured; some projects had expected maturation periods of up to ten years, a period far exceeding each president's term in office. Moreover, despite the prevalence of the growth and stability conventions discussed above, there was a small group of free-marketeers who never embraced the country's state-led industrialization. In the opinion of the tireless Gudin, for instance, "ghostly mechanics were brought to Brazil that were impoverishing, rather than enriching, the Brazilian people" (Gudin 1965, 202).

Plans and targets were, as a rule, the result of studies and proposals by the bureaucracy's leading technocrats. This process, which originated at the CFCE, gained a new dimension with the creation of the Comissão Mixta Brasil-EUA (Brazil-USA Joint Commission) and culminated with the BNDE (Daland 1969; Sola 1982). Incessantly providing successive governments with new ideas and a sense of "frontiers" (basically sectoral), the bureaucracy created for itself a political space and a privileged position that made the traditional politicians appear amateurish (Rudolph and Rudolph 1984, 121). The rapidity with which transformations took place was to the bureaucracy's advantage.

Indeed, fast growth perpetuated bottlenecks, imposed never-ending revisions of the development priorities, and made it necessary to finance long-term investment timetables. The importance of the latter is crucial, since it is through the periodic need for additional financial resources that technocrats exercised "guidance" and reaffirmed the original projects and targets, while resisting many of the pressures and demands of different groups. Here the relevance of the BNDE is unquestionable. Had the resources to be invested by public enterprises been obtained through the annual budgetary process, both the continuity and intertemporal coherence would be impaired.

On the other hand, the so-called "constitutional funds" (the portion of public revenues legally mandated for specific purposes) were also decisive. Through these mechanisms, a country virtually without a capital market and lacking strong planning institutions (like the Japanese Ministry of International Trade and Industry or the Korean Economic Planning Board) was able to sustain a continuous flow of fiscal and parafiscal savings compatible with its compulsive rate of accumulation. Those who focus on the vicissitudes and fragility of Brazil's formal planning mechanisms (and who pay no attention to the unique solutions found along the way) miss completely the relevance of the historical "substitutions" stressed here.

Finally, most large industrial projects backed by public funds corresponded to activities almost nonexistent in the country and which required the integration of new geographical areas into the national economy. Under these conditions, it is not surprising that the resistance to state initiatives was relatively slight. In fact, the very novelty of these projects helped to depoliticize changes which policy makers presented, by conviction or bureaucratic ritual, as *rationally justified.* In other words, the "vacuum-filling" technique — an official doctrine of the Brazilian government — was also an implicit political tactic to explore lines of action that offered the least amount of resistance (for Latin American comparisons, see Mattos 1988 and Torres 1988). Therefore, the constant search for new frontiers — to the detriment perhaps of the consolidation of previous advances — is also a reflection of the state's limited power. On the other hand, and in order to mitigate the frustrations of marginalized regions, institutions like the Instituto Brasileiro do Café (Brazilian Coffee Institute—IBC) and the Instituto de Açúcar e Álcool (Sugar and Alcohol Institute—IAA) were kept alive, thus offering traditional elites some degree of power and economic prosperity.

Public Enterprise Subsystems: Pivots of the Investment Process

Soares Pereira informs us of the difficulties the Brazilian government faced when, in the 1940s and the early 1950s, it attempted to participate in economic activities that required autonomy and flexibility in the decision-making process. According to his analysis, "it was impossible to set a minimum standard of efficiency within the strict regime of public service, due to its dependence on Congress and the need to comply with the Public Accounting Code" (Pereira 1975). The government responded to the inability of the traditional bureaucracy to meet the growing demand for new public initiatives by creating different types of state-owned enterprises. These "hybrid" entities (Abranches 1980) combined a public dimension (to be commented on later) with a "private" capacity to make decisions that, by definition, could neither be controlled nor approved through normal bureaucratic and political channels.

Brazilian state-owned enterprises have been well studied since their creation. Rather than going over old ground, we will look at a select set of these enterprises whose properties and functions are key to understanding the peculiarity of the Brazilian experience. Particular attention is given to the manner in which public enterprises solved, in practical terms, some of the aforementioned problems. The view offered here does not attempt empirical description of the heterogeneous universe of public enterprises, nor will it necessarily coincide with popular interpretations that have emerged after the creation in 1979 of the Secretaria de Controle das Empresas Estatais (Secretariat for the Control of State-Owned Enterprises—SEST) (Wahrlich 1980; Werneck 1991; Dias Leite 1991).

State-owned enterprises pioneering in new activities were given the mission of advancing the country's economic development through the implementation of very large and bold projects. In addition to abundant financial support, this mission usually required a trial-and-error process through which new technologies and organizational arrangements were introduced. Ultimately, dedication to this mission conferred on state enterprise its *res publica* connotation. Rather than public ownership with an alleged "social purpose" guiding their activities, the fundamental role of Brazilian state enterprises was defined with reference to the industrialization process. Luciano Martins (1985, 60) is, therefore, correct in asserting that state enterprises cannot be properly understood as mere reactions to external shocks and sectoral difficulties but must be analyzed as central components of a larger political project.[5]

Based on their broader objective, state enterprises sought to take advantage of opportunities by making alliances with private agents and attempting to increase their capacity to influence government decisions. Petrobrás is a notable example of an enterprise that capitalized on every opportunity by organizing itself into subsidiaries and establishing an extensive network of ties with numerous private enterprises that provided it with equipment, materials, and supplies. Indeed, as a result of its activism, Petrobrás was able to assume virtually exclusive control over Brazil's oil policy (Alveal Contreras 1992).

The branching of state enterprises into subsidiaries led to the formation of "systems" that played a decisive role in the structuring of certain sectors of the economy. The Petrobrás, Vale do Rio Doce, Eletrobrás, Telebrás, and BNDES systems (including not only subsidiaries but also a network of state and regional development banks) are all good illustrations of this evolutionary trajectory. Bear in mind, then, that to evaluate their role as a guiding force in the economy, one should take into account the ramifications of the pioneer enterprise (Justman and Teubal 1991).

The state enterprise was also conditioned by the nature of its sector and by the changing context of the state's role in the economy. These conditioning factors explain the notoriously different experiences in the oil and telecommunications public enterprises (Abranches and Dain 1978). This sectoral determination meant that state enterprises, besides being pushed and pulled in different directions by market signals, possessed distinct behavioral patterns. The counterpoint to this conditioning (which changed over time) was the original mission and the immutable legal principles on which state enterprises were founded. Potential tensions and clashes obviously had their roots here.

Failure to take into account the conditioning factors stressed above has led some observers to misleading conclusions. For instance, the impression that the intensification of investments in oil exploration by Petrobrás in the early 1980s had to do with policy preferences (Fishlow 1988) is erroneous; the oil industry has its own technical constraints and unavoidable decision-making sequences that must be taken into account in evaluating its performance.

State-owned enterprises, once set in motion, had their own resources and rarely had to compete for state monies to fund their *current* expenditures. Indeed, their capacity to generate internal resources and their intense commercial activities gave state enterprises advantages over other state institutions. This privileged situation led Roquete Reis to coin the term "power inversion" to refer to the loss of authority by ministerial institutions over the state-owned enterprises in their jurisdiction (Reis 1980).

Advantages enjoyed by state-owned enterprises vis-à-vis private firms in the period from 1950 to 1980 were of a different nature, including preferential access to the state, greater influence in the formulation of economic policies in their area, and public support for their investment projects. Eagerly exploiting these advantages, some state-owned enterprises became genuine "accumulating machines." While gross domestic product (GDP) was growing at an annual rate of 7 percent, investments of the largest state-owned enterprise escalated from 3.2 percent of the total investment in 1963, to 16 percent in 1970, and finally to 22 percent in 1979 (Trebat 1983, 123). Moreover, investments by state-owned enterprises did not "crowd out" but actually encouraged private investment, which also grew at rates superior to the growth in GDP.

The relationship between large public enterprises and their workers also deserves attention. In some cases, the workers and employees derived their very identity from the missions and challenges faced by the enterprise. This contrasted sharply with the capital-versus-labor relationships common elsewhere in the economy. Consequently, the typical Brazilian state-owned enterprise of the 1950s and 1960s exhibited a high level of motivation — an *esprit de corps* — which might be said to evoke the contemporary Japanese enterprise (Aoki 1984).

State-owned enterprises had a decisive role in molding the sectors to be implanted or modernized, but their leadership was certainly not of a conventional type, centered around price determination. From an economic point of view, the behavior of state enterprises often parallels innovative enterprises positioned in branches of industry at the frontiers of technological change. Consequently, at least in their formative stage, state enterprises in Brazil frequently had little in common with conventional oligopolistic enterprises. By the same token, however, when interacting with other firms, state-owned public enterprises tended to exploit their privileged position and to exercise considerable political power.

A final characteristic of state enterprises was their almost insuperable difficulty in defining their "objective function." In effect, besides its own mission, each enterprise was supposed to pursue different goals that could change over time. Initially, state enterprises were seen as engaged in the equivalent of war. Later on, as routines were progressively established, the sense of mission naturally eroded — as efficiency in the use of resources gained increasing importance. At this stage, state firms tended to approximate the conduct of private enterprises. However, even mature state-owned enterprises had little in common with the typical family-controlled Brazilian firm. In fact, state-owned enterprises, together with multinational firms, introduced into the country the concepts and practices of professional management as well as the utilization of profits for the expansion and diversification of operations.

In addition to promoting growth, profit making also favored growing independence from the state. The government itself strengthened the entrepreneurial aspects of state-owned companies. Decree No. 200 of 1967 explicitly guaranteed state enterprises the same autonomy enjoyed by private enterprises in terms of decision making, financial capacity, and technology. Later, and as an extension of this policy, the government required state-owned enterprises to pay corporate taxes and prohibited them from retaining dividends owed to the government.

The growing professionalism practiced in state enterprises (as the "heroic" phase was surpassed) can be seen as an aspect of the progressive maturation of a modern industrial structure. At the same time, state-owned enterprises performed a decisive role, transforming the government's general goals into attainable entrepreneurial objectives. Through state enterprises, it became possible to attain a certain degree of intertemporal coherence in decisions regarding the long-term transformation of the economy. Administrations came and went; yet, their basic goals were met and surpassed without the presence of a solid planning structure nor the existence of a stable nucleus of technocrats.

Concomitantly, however, social goals, which were left to the auspices of traditional government institutions, remained neglected. As the state-owned productive system expanded and became vigorously autonomous, the government's more traditional social functions were allocated to institutions fully exposed to mounting social pressures and vulnerable to the give-and-take of competitive politics, although politics was highly constrained under authoritarian rule.

As far as the future of state-owned companies was concerned, the complex and sensitive political problem of property ownership made attainment of greater autonomy difficult. This was true not only for genuine state-owned enterprises but also for troubled private companies that the state was forced to acquire in the course of industrialization. There was no a priori reason why a "happy ending" to the autonomy question — in the form of lease agreements, private participation, or even privatization — could not be found (Carneiro 1989, 81-95). However, state-owned enterprises never became effectively autonomous. Furthermore, very few ailing private enterprises were returned to the private sector. Unlike the Japanese and Korean experiences, the country's growth machine never gained a mature entrepreneurial structure.

Instead of promoting their autonomy, the government in 1976 appeared to be utilizing its enterprises as an ad hoc resource to attenuate macroeconomic conflicts and institutionalized them in 1979. These pressures, which emerged with great impetus as soon as it became difficult to obtain foreign funds

(Barros de Castro and de Souza 1985), were followed by growing central governmental interference in pricing policies. The state enterprises' capacity to generate domestic resources was thus doubly hindered, and opportunities previously opened to them began to disappear as a consequence of their declining autonomy and growing financial fragility.

A sequence of events that began with the second oil crisis stampeded the Brazilian economy, which in the late 1970s was poised to become an *industrial* economy. Attention to the country's macroeconomic problems, particularly mounting inflation and the growing trade deficit, took precedence over all else. With the creation of the SEST in the second half of 1979, the government ceased to recognize the long-standing entrepreneurial character of state enterprises. Under the pretext of an elusive austerity and structural adjustment, all state-owned companies (despite their markedly heterogeneous character) began to be used as instruments of macroeconomic regulation. With their autonomy drastically reduced and their financial base eroded by the state's fiscal crisis, they gradually fell prey to traditional politics.

These changes not only interrupted an evolutionary process characterized by considerable creativity but also coincided with the destruction of the previously defined conventions that permeated and informed the behavior of microeconomic agents — and which had imbued them with a special kind of vitality or "animal spirit." Even more unfortunately, these events coincided with the growing international diffusion of new patterns of organization and administration that made it possible for companies to become more efficient, less centralized, and, consequently, more agile in planning and decision making.

Dissolution of Established Conventions

The performance of the Brazilian economy deteriorated profoundly after 1979, especially with regard to stability and growth. The resulting effects clashed with deeply rooted beliefs that had strongly influenced the behavior of both governmental elites and private economic agents for so long. The consequences of this almost systematic frustration of expectations are impossible to gauge precisely.

Orthodox analysts take it for granted that any peculiar set of conventions will in due time be replaced by plain, ordinary economic rationality — once the rules of the game are fully restored. Maybe. The only thing we can be sure of is that a series of economic "earthquakes" during the 1980s effectively destroyed the previous conventions and left the economy in a dismal state. At this point in our argument, it will be useful to comment briefly on three critical junctures at which the conventions were openly defied and the consequences for the economy that followed.

In mid-1979 Brazilians were presented with widely divergent diagnoses of the unfolding crisis. Reacting to the new petroleum shock (which occurred before the government's energy program cut oil imports substantially) and to rapidly intensifying inflationary pressures, Finance Minister Simonsen attempted to persuade the new government, headed by General João Figueiredo, and the public at large of the need to impose a severe austerity and adjustment program.[6] Figueiredo found this advice politically unpalatable, and Simonsen resigned.

Antônio Delfim Netto, in a triumphant return to power as the government's economic czar, rejected his predecessor's somber diagnosis. On the day of his appointment, Delfim Netto proclaimed, "We are going to grow at a rapid pace, and at the same time we will balance our balance of payments and lower the rate of inflation" (*Gazeta Mercantil* 1979). The reasons why Delfim professed such confidence were never understood. In any case, the public repudiated Simonsen and enthusiastically applauded Delfim's optimistic vision, but the ensuing euphoria proved short-lived.

In December 1979, confronted with a rapidly worsening balance of payments combined with skyrocketing inflation, Delfim issued the first of what would be an interminable succession of "packages," promising to regain control of the macroeconomic scenario (Goldenstein 1985). Thus began the most radical shift in Brazilian economic policy in half a century.

We need not dwell on the vicissitudes of policy making that led to the economic downturn in 1981 (Bonomo 1986); a few statistics will suffice. Industrial production, which had expanded steadily by an annual average rate of 8.9 percent during the 1970s, and managed a 9.1 percent growth rate in 1980, shrank dramatically — by 10.4 percent in 1981. The sudden and drastic reversal of industrial performance, together with the inflationary surge amidst severe recession, shook the very foundations of long-standing behavioral patterns throughout the economy. Ultimately, this first economic quake brutally negated the long-enshrined convention of guaranteed growth and the implicit understanding among economic agents that Brazilian-style "administered inflation" was a relatively harmless phenomenon.

In 1981, the government tried to control inflation by announcing *ceilings* for the devaluation of both the exchange rate (40 percent) and the interest paid on public debt bonds (45 percent). The faith in the government which shaped the decisions of so many turned out to be misplaced. It soon became painfully clear that renewed growth was far from guaranteed and that continued high inflation (or, rather, erroneous expectations regarding inflation) would result in tremendous losses. In fact, economic agents began to realize that economic policies could lead down a one-way path in the wrong direction.

The second crucial moment in the dissolution of the past conventions came with the implementation the *Plano Cruzado* (Cruzado Plan). Beginning in 1984, and during three consecutive years, Brazil experienced an exceptional conjuncture as the economy once again began to expand rapidly. The return to growth could, in a certain measure, be attributed to the final maturation of several gigantic projects launched by the *II Plano Nacional de Desenvolvimento* (Second National Development Plan—PND) (Barros de Castro and de Souza 1985). The acceleration of import substitution and the expansion and diversification of exports demonstrated that the daring option chosen by the Brazilian government in 1974 under General Geisel was correct.[7] On the other hand, the considerable progress made in fiscal adjustment from 1981 to 1984 led many analysts to believe that the economy had almost reached macroeconomic equilibrium and that inflation had become an *inertial* phenomenon based upon the formal indexation of the economy (Lopes 1986, Chapter 18).

The events of the period culminated in the launching of the Cruzado Plan in February 1986. The positive aspects of the recent surge of economic growth (including the significant rise in salaries beginning in 1985) were preserved and even strengthened by the Cruzado Plan's "heterodox" policies, while inflation fell almost to zero. In the famous phrase of Economy Minister Dilson Funaro (and the fantasy of many who wanted to believe him), Brazil was poised to achieve "Japanese growth rates with a Swiss inflation rate." It was tempting to believe that the previous conventions concerning growth and stability had, somehow, undergone a glorious revival.

In the heady climate of euphoria that took hold of Brazilian society, the old conventions were now associated with democracy. Indeed, for many, the wage increases, begun in 1985 and vigorously confirmed in 1986 (Camargo and Ramos 1988), marked a fundamental difference between the performance of the economy under the military regime (growth without distribution) and the more equitable growth made possible by the return to democracy.

The downfall of the Cruzado Plan occurred quickly and resoundingly. From late 1986 through mid-1987, inflation exploded, production and employment threatened to collapse, the balance of payments became untenable, and, for the first time in post-1930 Brazilian history, a number of companies teetered on the verge of bankruptcy. The disaster taught economic agents several bitter lessons that harked back to the 1979-1980 experience: 1) growth could not be guaranteed, 2) there was no way to protect against inflationary instability, and 3) perhaps most significantly, government economic "packages" and policy announcements simply could not be trusted.

The remainder of the term of the first postauthoritarian president, José Sarney (1985-1990), transpired in the midst of profound macroeconomic instability and the complete loss of perspective on the part of public and private actors. Inflation now operated in cycles (Leviatan and Kiguel 1992), which began with the introduction of an anti-inflationary shock including price freezes, followed by the decay of the efficacy of government policies, the renewed acceleration of prices, and, finally, the imminent threat of hyperinflation. Following the failure in 1989 of the Sarney administration's so-called *Plano Verão* (Summer Plan), price increases in early 1990 hit hyperinflationary levels, surpassing 50 percent per month for the first time in Brazilian history.

The third earthquake, the *Plano Collor* (Collor Plan) introduced in March 1990, implied an important shift in the diagnosis of Brazil's high and chronic inflation. According to the architects of the Collor Plan, the problem essentially resided in the public-sector domestic debt, which had been transformed into a huge and volatile mass of immediate liquidity. In an "anti-liquidity" offensive, the government temporarily confiscated a considerable proportion of financial assets, including current accounts held by individuals and firms.

Despite its radical character, the experiment proved insufficient to bring inflation under control. In fact, another cycle kicked in soon thereafter, with prices on an ascendant trajectory, thus preparing the way for yet another shock. It came in the form of the so-called Collor Plan II, which proved equally ineffective (De Faro 1991). Monthly price hikes varied between 20 percent and 25 percent during 1992 and edged upward toward 30 percent per month by mid-1993.

The extremely negative impact of the Collor I and Collor II shocks may have negated the positive effects that might have been attained through the opening and privatization of the economy, a step strongly encouraged by the majority of private agents and finally adopted by the Brazilian government. The repeated frustrations to which economic agents were subjected, combined with the acute recession of the early 1990s, led these agents to view Brazil's economic environment as openly hostile. The fate of the Collor Plan, coming on the heels of the previous failures analyzed above, marked the definitive crisis of the conventions of growth and stability in effect from 1950 to 1980.

Final Remarks

The Brazilian economy and the patterns of behavior of its principal economic agents experienced profound transformation during the tortuous decade of the 1980s. A deeply rooted pessimism came to dominate the conduct of individuals and firms. This pessimism was manifest in a precipitous fall in the rate of investment from an average of 25 percent of GDP in the second half of the 1970s to only 14 percent of GDP at the beginning of the 1990s. Made fearful by an endless sequence of shocks, and with their occasional hopes repeatedly frustrated, economic agents adopted survival strategies whose basic elements can be summarized as follows:

- One should avoid exposure to any sort of risk (beyond general risks intrinsic in the Brazilian context). As a consequence, market stimuli should trigger price increases and only rarely, if ever, increases in the quantity of output.

- Individual and group interests should be protected aggressively and tenaciously. The consequences of this posture for others are to be ignored (since economic survival is at stake). As a corollary of this "principle," it is advantageous to eschew cooperation and, instead, act as a "free rider" whenever possible.

- Government decisions should be resisted. This inimical attitude toward the state implies an incessant search for "loopholes" in all laws, decrees, and policy measures. One should employ all legal or (if reasonably safe) illegal means to avoid compliance with governmental policies. This includes contesting governmental decisions in the courts in an attempt to nullify their impact or simply to gain time (an extremely valuable factor under high inflation).

This survival strategy reinforces both instability and stagnation (originally associated with macroeconomic disequilibrium). Previous attitudes of maximum risk taking have been turned upside-down. Old conventions of growth and stability have been repressed and perhaps permanently erased from the memory and behavioral repertoire of state elites and economic agents.

Both the zero-sum culture and the aggressive pursuit of self-interest inherent in such survival strategies make governance an extremely difficult proposition (Barros de Castro 1991; Dos Santos 1993). In these circumstances, economic policy instruments that had long steered the economy in the direction desired by state elites tend to be limited either to avoiding the worst (hyperinflation) or to launching veritable assaults on institutions and private contracts for the alleged purpose of redefining the entire system and initiating a new game.

The first option (avoiding the worst) offers declining returns: as expectations become more volatile and more pessimistic, economic policy makers are forced to intensify the simultaneous use of various "braking" mechanisms (monetary crunch, new taxes, stringent incomes policy) merely to prevent the acceleration of inflation. On the other hand, the damages implied by the second option resulted in growing aversion to shock therapies, obliging policy makers to (re)assure society repeatedly that no significant departures from past policies are contemplated, even when major shifts in strategy and tactics may be called for.

Trapped in this bleak scenario alternating between paralysis and sporadic "magic" solutions to the crisis, the Brazilian state has lost all but one of its previous traits, namely its size. The state remains big, but it is now acephalous and impotent. State enterprises, in particular, have lost their entrepreneurial drive and relative autonomy. Transformed into macroeconomic policy instruments of remarkably low efficiency, many state enterprises barely manage to survive. Gone are the sense of mission and loyalty that (mainly in the 1950s but still in the 1970s) had impelled state enterprises to spearhead economic development.

Even worse, the potential advantages of state enterprises have been converted into handicaps: dispirited by the execration of anything and everything connected with the state (and offended by the squeeze on their salaries), public sector employees have lost their motivation and now struggle merely to extract privileges and concessions from a state prostrated by permanent crisis. In some cases, the appointment of self-serving politicians to the directorships of state enterprises exacerbate this pathological situation. It is hardy surprising, therefore, that many state enterprises, some with exemplary records, have degenerated to the point of confirming the worst indictments of their vituperative opponents.

After twelve years of a destructuring crisis, the Brazilian economy has, in a sense, regressed to a stage of underdevelopment that it was on the verge of surpassing in 1980. The average technological gap between Brazil and the advanced economies has widened across the whole spectrum of industrial and service activities. Domestically, the gap separating those enterprises that tried to accompany the vertiginous rhythm of organizational and technological transformations set in motion internationally during the 1980s and those falling by the wayside has grown enormously, exacerbating the structural heterogeneity of the economy as a whole. Some basic services, such as roads and telecommunications, which had attained European performance levels circa 1980, have now deteriorated dramatically, harming the economy's overall efficiency and jeopardizing its international competitiveness.

Nevertheless, Brazil's heritage of dynamic, modern enterprises, endowed with a trained work force and long accustomed to rapidly changing environments, has not been destroyed. Signs of continuing vitality are evident in the remarkable spurt of growth registered from 1984 to 1986 and in the widespread restructuring movement underway since 1990 (Bielshovsky 1992; Coutinho and Ferraz 1992). Although limited in scope and largely defensive in nature, it is noteworthy that for the first time in modern Brazilian history, a major transformation has been initiated and carried out in decentralized fashion by decision makers in the private sector. On the other hand, this vigorous private-sector response contrasts with the moribund condition of several state enterprises. Suffocated by governmental restrictions and chronically inadequate financing, state enterprises are deprived of the means to keep up in a world economy experiencing radical shifts in decision-making patterns and technologies. The rapid recovery of lost entrepreneurial autonomy —

through privatization or otherwise — is now more than ever the sine qua non of the very survival of these enterprises.

Apparently, the economy's potential for growth has been preserved, but this potential certainly cannot be realized without effective stabilization of the economy. Not an easy task, as the long sequence of failures has eloquently shown. Above all else, a comprehensive program that — at least in its first stages — will be fiercely resisted by many economic agents is imperative. Stabilization presupposes a government with strong political, administrative, and regulatory capabilities as well as considerable autonomy. As this chapter has argued, however, these are features of the Brazilian state that have been severely eroded.

Whatever may happen in the near future, one sad conclusion can already be averred: after more than a decade of conflict, the advocates of neoliberal reform and those resisting the imposition of market-oriented policies have been unable to reconcile their conflicting projects. In the meantime, the old renegade regime of state-led development has been painfully eroded, exhausted, and finally destroyed.

Notes

1. In 1967, Roberto Campos attempted to increase the rigor of monetary and fiscal policies, but this proved impossible for political reasons. As for 1979, the case in point is Mário Henrique Simonsen's attempt to brake growth in order to alleviate the inflationary process and improve the balance of payments in an extremely adverse conjuncture.

2. The momentum surrounding the arrival of Brazilian manufactured goods in the international arena was reflected in a survey of U.S. businessmen conducted in 1987. When asked to name the country posing the most serious competitive challenge to North American industry, two-thirds of the 250 executives surveyed pointed to "emerging nations such as Brazil, South Korea and Taiwan." Only 29 percent selected Japan, while only 5 percent mentioned Europe. See *Business Week* (1987).

3. For Campos' position, see Associação Comercial de Minas (1964, 87). The intense criticism provoked by the new economic program acquired its strongest form of expression in the Confederação Nacional da Indústria (National Confederation of Industry—CNI); see *Revista Desenvolvimento e Conjuntura Econômica* (1965).

4. The notion of convention or shared belief was developed in Lord Keynes' *Tract on Monetary Reform*, published in 1923, in which the author observes that price stability constitutes more a presupposition, and therefore a "convention," than a historically proven experience. See Cardim de Carvalho (1990) and Ferguson (1975).

5. For the traditional view that state enterprises were created to fill "empty spaces," see Baer and Villela (1973), Suzigan (1976), and Rezende (1987).

6. Simonsen's diagnosis and recommendations are contained in his important pronouncement before the Brazilian Senate on May 31, 1979. See Simonsen (1979).

7. See Antônio Barros de Castro and Fernando Pires de Souza (1985) for a quantitative analysis of the extraordinary improvement of the balance of payments as of 1984. This analysis is extended through 1987 in Barros de Castro and Pires de Souza (1988).

References

Abranches, Sérgio. 1980. *A Empresa Pública no Brasil: Uma Abordagem Multidisciplinar.* Brasília: IPEA.

Abranches, Sérgio, and Sula Dain. 1978. "A Empresa Estatal no Brasil: Padrões Estruturais e Estratégias de Ação." Grupo de Estudos sobre o Setor Público. Brasília: FINEP.

Alveal Contreras, Edelmira Del Carmen. 1992. "Elites Empresariais de Estado como Atores Políticos do Brasil Industrial: As Lideranças do Sistema Petrobrás." Instituto Universitário de Pesquisas do Rio de Janeiro. Unpublished manuscript.

Aoki, Masahiko. 1984. *The Co-operative Game Theory of the Firm.* Oxford: Clarendon Press.

Associação Comercial de Minas. 1964. Conference given by Minister Roberto Campos in "Ciclo de Debates sobre a Inflação." *Mensagem Econômica* 139 (September/October).

Bacha, Edmar. 1978. *Política Econômica e Distribuição de Renda.* Rio de Janeiro: Editora Paz e Terra.

Baer, Werner, and Anibal Villela. 1973. "As Modificações no Papel do Estado no Economia Brasileira." *Pesquisa e Planejamento Econômico* 8 (4).

Barros de Castro, Antônio. 1991. "Loucura e Método." *Jornal do Brasil.* Caderno de Ideias: Ensaios, August 29.

Barros de Castro, Antônio. 1992. "O Brasil e as Economias de Crescimento Rápido." In *Estratégia Industrial e Retomada de Desenvolvimento,* ed. João Paulo dos Reis Velloso. São Paulo: Forum Nacional/Editora José Olympio.

Barros de Castro, Antônio, and Francisco Eduardo Pires de Souza. 1985. *A Economia Brasileira em Marcha Forçada.* Rio de Janeiro: Editora Paz e Terra.

Barros de Castro, Antônio, and Francisco Eduardo Pires de Souza. 1988. "O Saldo e a Dívida." *Revista de Economia Política,* April-June.

Baumann, Renato. 1982. "Industrial Exporting and Growth in Brazil." Ph.D. dissertation. Oxford University.

Best, Michael. 1990. *The New Competition: Institutions of Industrial Restructuring.* Cambridge, Mass.: Harvard University Press.

Bielshovsky, Ricardo. 1992. "Transnational Corporations and the Manufacturing Sector in Brazil: Technological Backwardness and Signs of Important Restructuring." Santiago: UN/ECLA.

Bonomo, Marco A. 1986. "Controle de Crédito e Política Monetária em 1981." Master's thesis, Pontifícia Universidade Católica do Rio de Janeiro.

Business Week. 1987. December 1.

Camargo, José Márcio, and Carlos Alberto Ramos. 1988. *A Revolução Indesejada.* Rio de Janeiro: Editora Campus.

Campello de Souza, Maria do Carmo. 1976. *Estado e Partidos Políticos no Brasil.* Rio de Janeiro: Editora Alfa-Omega.

Canitrot, Adolfo. 1979. "La disciplina como objetivo de la política económica. Un ensayo sobre el programa económico del gobierno argentino desde 1976." *Estudios CEDES* No. 6. Buenos Aires: Centro de Estudios de Estado y Sociedad.

Canitrot, Adolfo. 1991. "A Experiência Populista de Redistribuição de Renda." In *Populismo Econômico: Ortodoxia, Desenvolvimento e Populismo na América Latina,* ed. Luiz Carlos Bresser Pereira. São Paulo: Nobel S.A.

Carneiro, João Geraldo Piquet. 1989. "A Revitalização do Setor Público." In *O Leivata Ferido,* ed. João Paulo dos Reis Velloso. Rio de Janeiro: José Olympio Editora.

Carvalho, Fernando Cardim de. 1992. "Elasticidade de Expectativas e Surpresa Potencial: Reflexões sobre a Natureza e a Estabilidade do Equilíbrio sob Incerteza." *Revista Brasileira de Economia.* (June-July).

Carvalho, Fernando Cardim de. 1990. "Alta Inflação e Hiperinflação: Uma Visão Pós-Keynesiana," *Revista de Economia Política,* 10 (4): October-December.

Conjuntura Econômica. 1978. "A Economia Brasileira em 1978." (December).

Coutinho, Luciano G., and João Carlos Ferraz. 1992. "Estudo da Competitividade da Industria Brasileira." Campinas: UNICAMP. Unpublished manuscript.

Cruz, Paulo Davidoff. 1984. *Dívida Externa e Política Econômica.* São Paulo: Editora Brasiliense.

Daland, Robert T. 1969. *Estratégia e Estilo do Planejamento Brasileiro.* Rio de Janeiro: Lidador.

De Faro, Clóvis. 1991. *A Economia Pós Plano Collor.* Rio de Janeiro: Livros Técnicos e Científicos Editora.

Denslow, David, and William G. Tyler. 1983. "Perspective on Poverty and Income Inequality in Brazil: An Analysis of the Change during the 1970s." World Bank, Staff Working Papers No. 67.

Dias Leite, Antônio. 1991. "Revisão do Estado: Uma Avaliação Terra-a-Terra." In *O Leviatã Ferido: A Reforma do Estado Brasileiro,* ed. João Paulo dos Reis Velloso. São Paulo: Forum Nacional/Editora José Olympio.

Diniz, Eli. 1978. *Empresários, Estado e Capitalismo no Brasil, 1930-1945.* Rio de Janeiro: Paz e Terra.

Dos Santos, Wanderley Guilherme. 1993. "Fronteiras do Estado Mínimo — Indicações sobre o Híbrido Institucional Brasileiro." In *Razões da Desordem,* ed. Wanderley Guilherme dos Santos, Rio de Janeiro: Rocco.

Evans, Peter. 1992. "The State as Problem and Solution: Predation, Embedded Autonomy and Structural Change." In *The Politics of Economic Adjustment: International Constraints, Distributive Conflicts and the State,* eds. Stephen Haggard and Robert R. Kaufman. Princeton, N.J.: Princeton University Press.

Ferguson, Adam. 1975. *Cuando muere el dinero.* Madrid: Editorial Alianza Universidad.

Fishlow, Albert. 1988. "Uma História do Dois Presidentes: A Economia Política da Gestão da Crise." In *Democratizando o Brasil,* ed. Alfred Stepan. Rio de Janeiro: Editora Paz e Terra.

Fonseca, Pedro César Dutra. 1989. *Vargas: O Capitalismo em Construção.* São Paulo: Editora Brasiliense.

Friedman, Milton. 1991. "Monetary Correction." In *Monetararist Economics*, ed. Milton Friedman. London: Basil Blackwell.

Furtado, Celso. 1975. *Formação Econômica do Brasil.* Rio de Janeiro: Cia. Editora Nacional.

Gazeta Mercantil. 1979. August 16.

Goldenstein, Lídia. 1985. "Da Heterodoxia ao FMI - A Política Econômica de 79 a 82." Master's thesis. Campinas: UNICAMP.

Gudin, Eugênio. 1965. *Análise de Problemas Brasileiros.* Rio de Janeiro: Editora Agir.

Guimarães, Eduardo. 1982. *Acumulação e Crescimento da Firma. Um Estudo de Organização Industrial.* São Paulo: Editora Zahar.

Hirschman, Albert. 1968. "The Political Economy of Import-Substituting Industrialization in Latin America." *Quarterly Journal of Economics* 82 (1).

Hirschman, Albert. 1984. "The Social and Political Matrix of Inflation: Elaborations on the Latin American Experience." In *Essays in Trespassing, Economics to Politics and Beyond*, ed. Albert Hirschman. Cambridge: Cambridge University Press.

Holland, Stuart. 1972. *The State as Entrepreneur: New Dimensions for Public Enterprises: the IRI State Shareholding Formula.* White Plains, N.Y.: International Arts and Sciences Press.

Johnson, Chalmers. 1981. *MITI and the Japanese Miracle.* Stanford: Stanford University Press.

Justman, Michael, and Miguel Teubal. 1991. "A Structuralist Perspective on the Role of Technology in Economic Growth and Development." *World Development* 19 (9).

Langoni, Carlos Geraldo. 1973. *Distribuição da Renda e Desenvolvimento Econômico do Brasil.* Rio de Janeiro: Editora Expressão e Cultura.

Leviatan, Nathan, and Miguel Kiguel. 1992. "Inflation-Stabilization Cycles in Argentina and Brazil. In *Lessons of Economic Stabilization and its Aftermath*, eds. Michael Bruno, et al. Cambridge, Mass.: MIT Press.

Lopes, Francisco. 1986. *O Choque Heterodoxo.* Rio de Janeiro: Editora Campus.

Lopes, Lucas. 1991. *Memórias de Desenvolvimento.* Centro de Memória da Eletricidade no Brasil.

Malan, Pedro. 1977. *Política Econômica Externa e Industrialização no Brasil (1939-52).* Brasília: IPEA.

Martins, Luciano. 1976. *Pouvoir et Developement Economique. Formation et Evolution des Structures Politiques au Brésil.* Paris: Editions Anthropos.

Martins. Luciano. 1985. *Estado Capitalista e Burocracia no Brasil, Pós 64.* Rio de Janeiro: Editora Paz e Terra.

Mattos, Carlos. 1988. "Estados, Processos Decisórios e Planejamento na América Latina." Brasília: IPEA-CENDEC.

Monteiro, Jorge Vianna, and L.R. Azevedo Cunha. 1974. "Alguns Aspectos da Evolução do Planejamento Econômico no Brasil (1934-1963)." *Pesquisa e Planejamento Econômico* 4 (1).

Pereira, João Soares. 1975. *Petróleo, Energia Elétrica, Siderurgia*. Rio de Janeiro: Editora Paz e Terra.

Prado Júnior, Caio. 1956. *História Econômica do Brasil*. São Paulo: Editora Brasiliense.

Ranis, Gustav, and C. H. John. 1988. "Development Economics: What Next?" In *The State of Development Economics*, eds. Gustav Ranis and C.H. John. London: Basil Blackwell.

Reis, Fernando Roquete. 1980. "A Administração Federal Direta e as Empresas Públicas. Análise de Suas Relações, Recomendações e Alternativas para Seu Aprimoramento." In *A Empresa Pública no Brasil: Uma Abordagem Multidisciplinar*, ed. Sérgio Abranches. Brasília: IPEA.

Resende, André Lara. 1990. "Estabilização e Reforma 1964-1967." In *A Ordem do Progresso*, ed. Marcelo de Paiva Abreu. Rio de Janeiro: Editora Campus.

Rezende, Fernando. 1987. "O Crescimento (Descontrolado) da Intervenção Governamental na Economia Brasileira." In *As Origens da Crise: Estado Autoritário e Planejamento no Brasil*, eds. Olavo de Lima Brasil Jr. and Sérgio Abranches. São Paulo: Vértice.

Rudolph, Lloyd, and Suzanne Rudolph. 1984. "Autoridad y poder en la administración burocrática y patrimonial. Una interpretación revisionista de las ideas de Weber sobre la burocracia." In *Teoria de la burocracia estatal, eds. Lloyd and Suzanne Rudolph*. Buenos Aires: Editorial Paidos.

Sader, Emir. 1988. *Quando Novos Personagens Entraram em Cena*. Rio de Janeiro: Editora Paz de Terra.

SEPLAN. 1970. *Metas e Bases para a Ação do Governo*. Brasília: Secretaria de Planejamento.

Simonsen, Mário H. 1972. *Brasil 2002*. Rio de Janeiro: Editora Bloch.

Simonsen, Mário H. 1979. "A Inflação Brasileira e a Atual Política Anti-Inflacionária." Brasília: Senado Federal.

Simonsen, Mário H., and Eugênio Gudin. 1977. *A Controvérsia de Planejamento na Economia Brasileira*. Rio de Janeiro: IPEA.

Simonsen, Mário H., and Roberto Campos. 1974. "O Modelo Brasileiro de Desenvolvimento." In *A Nova Economia Brasileira*. São Paulo: Editora José Olympio.

Sola, Lourdes. 1982. "The Political and Ideological Constraints on Economic Management in Brazil, 1945-1963." Ph.D. dissertation. Oxford University.

Suzigan, Wilson. 1976. ""As Empresas do Governo e o Papel do Estado na Economia." In *Aspectos da Participação do Governo na Economia*, ed. Fernando Rezende. Brasília: Série Monográfica. IPEA-IPES.

Suzigan, Wilson. 1986. *Indústria Brasileira, Origem e Desenvolvimento*. São Paulo: Editora Brasiliense.

Torres, Juan Carlos. 1988. "A Experiência de Planificação na Argentina." In *Estado e Planejamento — Sonhos e Realidades*. Brasília: IPEA-CENDEC.

Trebat, Thomas J. 1983. *Brazil's State-Owned Enterprises: A Case Study of the State as Entrepreneur*. Cambridge: Cambridge University Press.

Vianna, Sérgio Basserman. 1987. *A Política Econômica no Segundo Governo Vargas (1951-1954)*. Rio de Janeiro: BNDES.

Visão. 1976. Interview with Minister Reis Velloso. April 19.

Wade, Robert. 1990. *Governing the Market: Economic Theory and the Role of Government in East Asian Industrialization*. Princeton, N.J.: Princeton University Press.

Wahrlich, Beatriz. 1980. "Controle Público das Empresas Estatais Federais no Brasil — Uma Contribuição ao Seu Estudo." *Revista de Administração Pública*. (April-June).

Werneck, Rógerio. 1991. *Empresas Estatais e Política Macroeconômica*. Rio de Janeiro: Editora Campus.

Chile

Selected Macroeconomic Indicators for Chile

	1982	1983	1984	1985	1986	1987	1988	1989	1990	1991	1992p
Real Gross Domestic Product	*(Percent Average Annual Growth Rates)*										
Total GDP	-13.6	-2.8	5.9	2.0	5.6	5.8	7.4	10.0	2.1	6.0	10.4
Manufacturing	-20.9	3.1	8.9	2.7	7.9	5.6	8.6	10.0	0.1	5.5	12.2
Agriculture	-0.6	-2.3	8.9	7.3	8.8	3.4	5.3	4.8	3.3	1.8	3.6
Construction	-23.4	-14.4	1.9	17.8	1.6	10.1	6.3	12.7	2.5	5.0	14.2
Gross Domestic Investment	*(As as Percent of GDP)*										
	15.1	12.2	19.8	16.1	17.1	19.8	20.2	23.6	22.5	21.6	—
Central Government	*(As a Percent of GDP)*										
Current Revenue	36.7	30.8	31.4	29.3	30.6	31.4	32.3	30.9	26.5	27.7	27.9
Current Expenditures	34.0	30.9	30.0	26.7	25.9	23.5	21.6	21.6	19.8	21.0	20.3
Deficit or Surplus	-2.6	-3.7	-2.9	-1.8	-0.5	2.4	3.7	5.2	1.4	1.6	2.7
Prices, Salaries and Unemployment	*(Percent Average Annual Growth Rates)*										
Consumer Prices	8.7	28.0	20.3	29.9	19.0	20.2	14.7	17.1	26.0	21.8	15.4
Real Wages	-0.1	-11.0	0.3	-4.5	2.0	-0.2	6.5	1.9	1.8	4.9	4.5
Unemployment	19.6	14.6	13.9	12.1	8.8	7.9	6.3	5.3	5.6	5.3	—
Real Effective Exchange Rate	*(Index 1980 = 100)*										
	91.0	111.8	113.7	141.1	167.0	180.0	192.5	188.1	193.3	187.6	177.5
Balance of Payments	*(Billions of Dollars)*										
Current Account Balance	-2.3	-1.1	-2.1	-1.4	-1.2	-0.8	-0.2	-0.8	-0.6	0.1	-0.6
Trade Balance	0.1	1.0	0.4	0.9	1.1	1.2	2.2	1.6	1.3	1.6	0.7
Exports	3.7	3.8	3.7	3.8	4.2	5.2	7.1	8.1	8.3	8.9	10.0
Imports	3.6	2.8	3.3	2.9	3.1	4.0	4.8	6.5	7.0	7.4	9.2
Capital Account Balance	1.0	0.5	2.0	1.4	0.7	1.0	1.1	1.4	3.4	0.9	2.9
Change in Reserves (- Increase)	1.3	0.5	-0.1	0.1	0.3	-0.1	-0.8	-0.6	-2.3	-1.2	0.2
Total External Debt	*(Billions of Dollars)*										
Disbursed Debt	17.3	17.9	19.7	20.4	21.1	21.5	19.6	18.0	19.1	17.9	18.5
	(In Percent)										
Interest Payments Due/Exports	49.5	38.9	50.1	46.4	37.1	26.4	21.7	18.5	17.8	14.6	11.2

p = preliminary

Sources: Inter-American Development Bank, *Economic and Social Progress in Latin America*, 1992 and 1993 Reports, and the International Labor Organization.

Chapter Eight

The Political Dimension of Processes of Transformation in Chile

Manuel Antonio Garretón

Introduction

This chapter probes the specifically political dimensions of democracy and structural reform in Chile. Economic aspects are not considered. This approach stems from a self-conscious theoretical choice. The process of redemocratization in Chile, along with economic and structural reforms, has frequently been applauded, particularly in contrast with other, less successful transitions. Redemocratization in Chile poses a fundamental question confronting all Latin American societies in the present context of transnationalization: Is there space for the reconstitution of social and political actors, without which societies are unable to reform and transform themselves? From a political economy standpoint, this question cannot be answered, since political economy always refers to structural forces or dynamics that conform to structural logic from which actors are inferred and within which they enjoy little autonomy. Similarly, those theories and practices that do not assign to actors and subjects the historical capacity to create and mold dynamics and structures offer no convincing answers to the problem of societal self-transformation. Perhaps a fundamental characteristic of our time is that we no longer ask how social actors are constituted or what are the determinants of collective or sociohistorical action, but rather we question whether it is even possible for such actors to exist under contemporary conditions.

A second dimension to be considered concerns "structural reform," a concept that in the 1980s became trapped ideologically. During the 1960s, this notion implied change, either in the relationship between social and productive structures (agriculture and industry or city and countryside, for

This chapter stems from a project directed jointly by the author and Marcelo Cavarozzi on "The Restructuring of Latin American Societies: Chile and Argentina," with the support of the John D. and Catherine T. MacArthur Foundation.

example) or when referring to significant institutional changes, such as the overhaul of the educational system. More generally, structural reform often referred to changes in property relations and relations of domination or "power structures." These approaches were colored by broader visions that emphasized social — and even revolutionary — transformation. The military regimes of the 1960s and 1970s were, in part, explained as attempts to reverse this type of structural reform.

This dimension of social transformation is absent in contemporary discussions of structural reform and economic adjustment. Today these concepts are defined in strictly economic terms. They are employed to refer to economic innovations that consolidate adjustment processes and form what, during the 1980s, became the "new economic model." In this widely disseminated view, earlier concerns about redistribution disappear. With the minimization of the state's role as an agent of redistribution and development, conservative ideologies have appropriated the role, seeking to impose new social models. In these conservative models, the market and other economic mechanisms, such as privatization, cease to be instruments and become instead the parameters of a "good society." It is thus necessary specifically to complement economic analyses with an analysis of the political and social underpinnings of such reforms. For Latin America, and especially for Chile, recent structural reforms must be understood as being embedded within the phenomena of authoritarianism and democratization.

This chapter's hypothesis argues that the dominant model of adjustment and structural reform in force in the 1970s and 1980s laid the foundation for political democratization and economic development in the 1990s and is part of a broader and more profound transformation in the relations between state and civil society. This transformation is occurring in the matrix of relations among the state, the system of political representation, and societal actors. While attempting to replace the "classical matrix,"[1] adjustment and structural reforms have led to its disarticulation. In fact, we are witnessing a complex recomposition of the sociopolitical matrix, a phenomenon which thoroughly pervades the current process of democratization and social modernization.

The emphasis in this chapter is on the nature of the Chilean political process, the strategy pursued by the democratic government inaugurated in 1990, and the significance of these factors for social actors. To approach these themes, we first present a schematic characterization of how the democratic regime collapsed in 1973, the nature of the military regime that succeeded it, and the ensuing transition leading to the installation of the current democratic government, headed by Patricio Aylwin.

Democratic Collapse, Military Rule, and Transition[2]

The collapse of the Chilean democratic regime, which had been stable for decades prior to 1973, cannot be attributed to a single structural factor nor to any single purely conspiratorial factor (national or foreign), although such factors were present. Rather, a combination of long-term and more immediate conjunctural factors lay behind democracy's crisis and breakdown. Throughout the 1960s, progressive and centrist political actors proved unable to forge a social and political alliance capable of carrying out the urgent tasks of modernization and democratization. Lacking a project of democratic social change capable of eliciting majority support, the center and the left pursued ideological projects oriented toward radical change, which also lacked sociopolitical and institutional majorities. The effect was to mobilize those actors watching from the sidelines, propelling them toward authoritarian positions. In an increasingly polarized and de-institutionalized climate, the traumatized middle classes and the military put an end to reforms they believed threatened their survival (Garretón and Moulian 1983).

Beyond the causes for democracy's collapse, what factors explain the longevity of the military government and the delay in undertaking the transition, which began only after the opposition defeated the Pinochet dictatorship in the regime's own plebiscite in 1988?

The first factor was the nature of the military regime itself. Headed by General Augusto Pinochet, the regime combined aspects of a personal dictatorship and a military government. It pursued a project of transformation — one backed by enormous repressive power — that dislocated the relations between politics and society. Furthermore, with the creation of the 1980 Constitution, the regime institutionalized itself prior to its own crisis, thus laying the groundwork for passage from a military dictatorship to an authoritarian regime with a significant civilian component. This explains the absence of a "transition from above." Finally, the regime's civil support eroded very slowly and unevenly (Valenzuela and Valenzuela 1987; Drake and Jaksi 1991).

Second, there was the opposition's incapacity to unleash a "transition from below." Social discontent never unified in a political force that could present an institutional solution facilitating termination of the regime. When the 1983 protest movement erupted, problems specific to the political parties took primacy over the political-institutional imperatives of a transition (Garretón 1989). Furthermore, efforts to strengthen ideological identities and organizations, as well as the existence of mutual exclusions expressed as contending ideological blocs within the opposition, undermined the "transition from below."

Third, the institutional and structural transformation of society atomized, fragmented, and circumscribed the spaces in which social actors constitute themselves. Thus, in addition to responding to immediate exigencies, the model of adjustment and structural reform was fundamentally directed at transforming the Chilean sociopolitical matrix. This model achieved its politico-institutional consecration in the 1980 Constitution (Garretón 1987; Garretón and Espinosa 1992). Consequently, beyond the specifically economic dimensions of structural reform (privatization, deregulation, and liberalization of foreign trade), the functions of the state itself were reconstituted. Its coercive dimension increased, while its integrative and redistributive roles were radically diminished. This recasting of the state was accompanied by political, social, and cultural reforms designed to "marketize" all other social spheres. This meant the virtual suppression of political mediation in socioeconomic life apart from state power under military aegis.[3]

The 1988 plebiscite substantially altered the dynamics of the transition. Convoked in accordance with the 1980 Constitution to assure the passage from a military to an authoritarian regime and to maintain Pinochet's power, the plebiscite had very different consequences, creating the conditions for a more significant transition (Garretón 1989). Despite its limits and arbitrary aspects, for the first time a scenario of politico-institutional confrontation emerged between authoritarian leaders and the opposition regarding the question of regime succession, the Achilles' heel of all dictatorships. Likewise, for the first time the opposition united in a concerted effort to defeat the regime. The opposition victory in the October 1988 plebiscite undermined Pinochet's legitimacy both in terms of his hierarchical authority within the armed forces and his political or "constitutional" legitimacy as chief executive. The probability of a new coup attempt by Pinochet, and a return to violent repression, became progressively less likely, particularly given the changes in national and international conditions since 1973.

The defeat of the military regime in the 1988 plebiscite, in which the majority of the population voted against retaining Pinochet for another eight years, led the armed forces to retreat gradually from political power, while retaining their privileged access to state institutions. Although withdrawing from the direct exercise of state power, the military still managed to retain the loyalty of those civilian sectors that had supported the post-1973 regime (Garretón 1991b). These civilians became the political Right in the future democratic regime.

The democratic opposition, for its part, confronted two fundamental tasks: 1) to seek a new institutional framework that would dismantle the system founded by Pinochet and 2) to secure a democratic government with majority support in the presidential and congressional elections mandated by the Constitution in the event of Pinochet's defeat in the plebiscite. These challenges presupposed constitutional accords with the Right, which amounted to an indirect form of negotiation with the military. These accords transformed the victorious plebiscite coalition into an electoral coalition with a single presidential candidate, a common program, and a congressional pact. To accomplish this, the two leading social and political forces had to become allies. The middle classes and the popular sectors, whose past quarrels had led to the breakdown of democracy, joined forces in the so-called *Concertación de Partidos por la Democracia*.[4] In the political realm, the successful alliance between the centrist Christian Democrats and the parties of the Left (mainly the socialists, with the tacit support of the Communist party) won the December 1989 presidential and congressional elections, thereby avoiding the "Korean syndrome" of a divided opposition.

The Nature of the Democratization Process

The process that began when Pinochet was defeated in the 1988 plebiscite and ended with the inauguration of the new democratic government headed by President Patricio Aylwin on March 11, 1990, was actually an incomplete transition. As a result, the first democratic government faced a major challenge — to complete the transition and initiate democratic consolidation. Completing the transition meant several things: 1) eliminating the institutional remnants of authoritarianism (such as aspects of the Constitution, the organic laws of the Armed Forces and Carabineros, and labor legislation), 2) neutralizing non-democratic actors (pro-Pinochet groups and the authoritarian Right), and 3) resolving the human rights problem inherited from the military regime. Failure to accomplish these tasks would mean that political democracy would not be definitively reestablished. If this were the case, the new civilian government would be weak and unable to fulfill the functions of an authentic democratic political regime and, thus, would remain at the mercy of authoritarian regression.

Moreover, successful democratic consolidation in Chile called for social democratization — reducing inequalities, integrating marginal sectors, channelling the demands of youth — and the modernization of the nation to eliminate the perverse and disarticulating after-effects of the military regime. This involved a redefinition of the development model and of Chile's mode of insertion into the international economy. The basis of the redefinition differed from both the traditional model that collapsed in 1973 and the model imposed by the military regime.

Democratic consolidation also implied overcoming tensions that had emerged in the party system and social movements; for this to happen, the state's leading role in society had to be restored. In this regard, democratic consolidation required a reduction of the pronounced "embeddedness" of parties and social organizations, which prior to 1973 had so fundamentally shaped the identity of social actors in Chile (Garretón 1987; Garretón and Espinosa 1992). Finally, consolidation implied the formation of a permanent social and political majority composed of the Center and the Left, a majority capable of overcoming the confrontation between the middle classes and the popular sectors, on the one hand, and their respective political organizations, on the other.

Contrary to the view promoted by the ruling coalition known as the *Concertación de Partidos por la Democracia* (Coalition of Parties for Democracy), the process initiated in March 1990 should not be defined as a "government of transition." This is not a mere abstract or academic difference; this point has both an intellectual significance and important political effects (Garretón 1991a). In truth, the situation is one of a democratic government operating within a partial democratic regime, one which is not in transition toward anything. By the *Concertación*'s criteria, the Raúl Alfonsín government in Argentina, the Fernando Belaúnde Terry administration in Peru, and the Julio Sanguinetti government in Uruguay could also be defined as "transitional," in the nominal sense that all governments elected after an authoritarian regime are governments of transition.

This conceptual issue has theoretical and methodological consequences that can lead to confusion regarding relevant actors and strategies. In a situation of transition, the central actor is the military, whose rational strategy is to pursue an authoritarian regression, something which hardly fits the Chilean case. In contrast, in partial or highly constrained transitions, an implicit, permanent veto power is granted to non-democratic forces and to the opposition in general. Indeed, governments resulting from this type of transition "self-limit" their capacity to carry out changes indispensable for democratic consolidation. Furthermore, such transitions sharply reduce the capacity of political actors to exercise control over state policies through reliance on democratic procedures, thus limiting the range of options available to the governing coalition.

In August 1991, the government announced the "end of the transition" and several months later promulgated a programmatic document, known as a "navigation chart," which set forth objectives much more closely resembling the agenda of genuine democratic consolidation. Actually, however, if a transition is viewed as a stage defined by the possibility of authoritarian regression, the transition could be said to have ended during 1988 with ratification occurring when the civilian government took power in March 1990. On the other hand, if transition implies the achievement of full democracy, it is erroneous to speak of the "end of the transition" and annulment of authoritarian legacies. By August 1991, when the "navigation chart" was issued, none of the institutional authoritarian enclaves had been eliminated. These considerations lead us to reject the notion of a "government of transition" as a useful concept for the analysis of the redemocratization process in Chile. Instead, we will propose alternative criteria focusing on the goals set forth by the democratic government itself.

The challenges confronting Patricio Aylwin's government and the *Concertación* involved several dimensions. The government and its supporters had to initiate an immediate attack on the authoritarian legacies bequeathed by Pinochet or run the risk that delay would neutralize the pursuit of consolidation, with high costs to the members of the *Concertación*. This entailed elaborating a strategy that would attack the vestiges of authoritarianism as a cluster, establishing priorities and calculating possible trade-offs between one reform and another. The government could radically attack all of the enclaves, or if that were not feasible, adopt a global strategy that, though privileging one or another measure, would permit the government to increase its margins of maneuver. Such a strategy would allow the government to transform its social, political, and electoral majority into an institutional majority. The bedrock of the government's strategy had to be institutional and constitutional reforms that would empower the government to govern. It was necessary to exploit the initial "grace period" of high political legitimacy following the inauguration. This was precisely the strategy conceived by the *Concertación*'s technical and political advisory teams. Nevertheless, between December 1989 and March 1990 this strategy — which required negotiations with the most democratic faction of the Right in order to isolate, neutralize, and/or assimilate it — was modified by the new government's political advisors in ways which will be examined below.

The second aspect of consolidation mentioned above concerns modernization and the democratization of society. Here the problem was one of ameliorating the dire conditions of certain social sectors with an emergency redistributive program (through the payment of the social debt) and of creating the institutional capacity (through state reform) to alter fundamentally the model of social organization and participation, as well as to redefine Chile's model of insertion into the world order. The government could count on a number of factors favoring the pursuit of its strategy vis-à-vis these issues. Adjustment had already been imposed by the military regime, and the short-term costs of redefining the model of insertion into the world economy had already been paid.

There was no immediate, viable threat of an authoritarian regression. In fact, the government could count on a broad-based electoral coalition and majority support among the population. The opposition, in contrast, was torn between nostalgia for the past and finding a place for itself within democracy. Consequently, the major obstacles were the presence of an entrenched authoritarian nucleus *pinochetismo*[5] which had to be isolated or neutralized, and, above all, the existence of institutional enclaves that effectively prevented the Aylwin administration from governing in full exercise of its political majority. This reconfirmed the need for urgent reforms.

The Political Management of the State

This section traces the government's progress in furthering political democratization by overcoming the authoritarian enclaves, and it examines the extent of advances in social democratization and modernization. It also discusses prospects for consolidation and the *Concertación de Partidos por la Democracia*. The evaluation of the performance of the first democratic government can only be characterized as positive from a general, macro perspective, especially in regard to symbolic policies such as human rights and Chile's international relations stance. Public opinion polls confirm the government's strong popularity.[6] Nevertheless, a critical examination of aspects of the government's strategy and leadership, particularly regarding the larger tasks of political democratization, yields a more ambiguous evaluation.

Notwithstanding reservations stemming from the lack of careful studies of these ongoing processes, it can be averred that the Aylwin government lacks a coherent strategy of *political leadership* for overcoming authoritarian enclaves and creating the institutional capacity that would allow it to govern on the basis of its electoral majority. If this were a traditional government, this shortcoming might be insignificant, but this defect is problematic because the Aylwin government is launching a new political regime, one that is inescapably "foundational" in orientation.

The government's first priority was not the political and constitutional reforms that would unblock the instruments of democracy and end the authoritarian institutional enclaves. The government squandered the initial climate of consensus, its unlimited legitimacy, isolation of the hard-line sectors, and an opportunity for initiating broad negotiations with the democratic Right. Initially, the Right would have had no alternative but to support such reforms. In fact, the division of the Right into a democratic sector known as *Renovación Nacional* (National Renovation—RN) and a sector more closely linked to the previous regime, the *Unión Democrática Independiente* (Independent Democratic Union—UDI), granted the RN an excellent opportunity to gain ground by supporting democratizing initiatives that would have isolated the UDI and the hard-line, right-wing opponents of the Aylwin government. Such agreements would have extended earlier accords reached by this moderate sector and the *Concertación* that culminated in the July 1989 plebiscite on constitutional reform. In short, the Aylwin government failed to take full advantage of its "honeymoon" period to deepen democratic reform while the Right was still off balance.

Instead, the government pursued a series of one-shot negotiations without clear strategic objectives, which left it at the mercy of the opposition.

Constitutional reforms prolonging earlier agreements with the Right were not pursued, and the reform of municipal elections was the sole institutional change implemented. Even municipal reforms were quite limited and did not lead to an examination of broader institutional questions outside the electoral arena. As a result, the lines were blurred between basic reform, regardless of the resulting political benefits, and the need to resolve leadership problems within the *Concertación*.

The negotiation of the municipal reform was indicative of a general government tendency to confront single issues tactically. The opposition made these into strategic problems, thereby exposing the government's lack of an overall strategy and revealing the internal tensions within the governing coalition by forcing the government to negotiate its reform agenda on a piecemeal basis. The Right managed to recast the issue of municipal elections in terms of the broader problem of regionalization, decentralization, and the structure of local power (whether it did so as a result of tactical calculations is irrelevant). Despite the undoubtedly democratizing consequences of the municipal reforms, the government, after considerable delay, had to relinquish its position and accept the opposition's proposals. Prolonged negotiations resulted in political erosion, lost time, and the inability to unblock and restructure the institutional system. The municipal reform, which substituted democratic elections for appointments and set elections for June 1992, did not resolve the problem of political power in a democratic framework (a task that corresponds to the incomplete transition). Nor did it resolve the issue of the nature of local power and participation, though it did open the way for potential social democratization and modernization regarding regionalization and decentralization (Garretón and Espinosa 1992).

Something similar occurred in the area of human rights. Again, the issue was a specific problem — political prisoners — which the government addressed without benefit of a long-term strategy, pursuing the approval of the so-called *Cumplido* laws.[7] The opposition seized the initiative, thus forcing the government to accept the type of solution it had avoided: constitutional reform. Constitutional reform in this area was narrowly limited to the modification of the president's prerogative to grant pardons. In contrast, the creation of the *Comisión de Verdad y Reconciliación* (Commission of Truth and Reconciliation), whose report regarding human rights violations during the military regime, as well as legislation to indemnify the victims, had an enormous symbolic value. But limitations restricting consideration to cases involving executions or disappearances, combined with obstacles to pursuing in the courts cases subject to the 1978 Amnesty Law, the continued incarceration of a small number of political prisoners, and the prolonged and uncertain handling of the reform of the judiciary, all led to a perception that the human rights problem had been only partially resolved (Garretón 1993).

The tax, labor, constitutional, and judicial reforms, despite their intrinsic importance, suffered from the same limited conception, from a lack of political leadership, and from the absence of a broader, more coherent strategy of institutional democratization required to complete the transition. Although the *Concertación* initially developed a comprehensive strategy for confronting the authoritarian enclaves, and despite the fact that the Aylwin government enjoyed favorable economic conditions for the strategy's implementation, a broader approach was not followed because to do so would have required negotiations with democratic sectors of the Right, who allegedly would not have lent themselves to such efforts. Negotiations with the Right within the context of such a global strategy were avoided on grounds that such efforts would signal the government's intention to effect changes, something that might have been interpreted by business and, above all, by the military as destabilizing.

The failure to attempt negotiations is surprising since the government's guiding principle of action was said to be a "democracy of agreements" or a "democracy of consensus." If this concept is to have any historical, theoretical, or political meaning, it must refer to basic or fundamental agreements, not transitory project-by-project accords. The "consociational" or corporatist approach to conflict, no matter how narrow or limited, is the very negation of democracy and tends to weaken democratic institutions, such as Congress. This is precisely what occurred with the separation of the municipal issue from other institutional reforms.

In early 1992, the government recognized that it had lost time. Unwilling to be a mere "government of administration," Aylwin presented to Congress a package of political and constitutional reforms to terminate the lifetime tenure granted to the commanders-in-chief of the armed forces, to reform the electoral system, to devolve certain prior prerogatives to Congress, and to effect changes in the Constitutional Tribunal. Nevertheless, by this time the government could no longer count on a sector of the Right to approve the package. Faced with the municipal elections, the RN completed its process of unification with the hard-line sector of the Right, rejecting what supporters of the new coalition called the "dismantling of institutionality," which referred to the authoritarian legacy of the military regime. This was confirmed by the Right's vote against the reform of the electoral system and its declarations that it would reject all of the reforms sent by Aylwin to Congress in mid-1992.

In contrast, the Aylwin government appropriately handled difficulties with the hard-line military leadership, especially *pinochetistas*, by denying them political influence while maintaining smooth relations with the rest of the armed forces. This scenario suggests a possible new model of civil-military relations, even though institutional changes, which are undoubtedly indispensable in the long run, remain to be effected. In any event, it is worth noting some possible shortcomings in this otherwise successful area: weaknesses in handling the defense budget and especially in creating conditions for institutional changes regarding the ministerial control over the national police force, the *Carabineros*; the permanence of the Commanders-in-Chief; and civilian control of upper-level military appointments.

Regarding social democratization and modernization, the government successfully confronted this challenge at the economic level, effecting important redistributive gains in 1990 and advances in growth in 1992. Although progress has been made, a number of problems remain: broad sectors of the population continue to live in poverty, institutional channels for social participation are weak or absent, the debate concerning Chile's insertion into the world economy remains open, and the reform of the state apparatus has yet to be tackled.

Political and Social Actors

As we have seen, the Aylwin government operated in terms of a tactical calculation of resources, using static analyses of the immediate correlation of political forces rather than pursuing negotiations on the basis of fundamental, long-term goals. The result has been negotiations constrained by the prevailing distribution of resources, instead of global policies within a coherent framework for negotiations. The problem with this negotiating strategy is that it leaves the government at the mercy of the opposition's initiative, resulting in an endless succession of small battles over each specific policy question. The typical economic calculus of costs and benefits, incentives, and the distribution of resources is transferred to politics without recognizing the essentially different nature of the political and the economic spheres.

Perhaps the explanation for this strategy lies in the subsuming of the political-party actor that so successfully engineered the termination of the dictatorship: the *Concertación de Partidos por la Democracia*, with its center and left phalanxes. Consequently, there has been little systematic debate among the parties of the governing coalition regarding their principal objectives. Only the moves of the government and the organizational struggles within and between the parties remain. As a result, the democratization of politics has been rudderless. This situation affects the government, which is forced to assume a dual task of political leadership (as government and as political actor), and it particularly affects the direction of the *Concertación* to the extent that the matters left to the *Concertación* are almost purely internal. Struggles for leadership between the component parties of the *Concertación* occur, but there is no sphere of debate regarding a political project nor are there institutional mechanisms to resolve internal disputes.

As a result, the government as a political actor, which subsumes the parties of the *Concertación*, faces only two other types of actors. One is the Right, which displayed considerable political initiative until mid-1992 but has been unable to define a clear democratic stance because of internal competition and its continued ties to extremist sectors of the Right and hard-liners linked to the military regime. The hard-liners within the right-wing opposition won out over more moderate voices advocating the strengthening of the Right within the emerging democratic context. Following the municipal elections that produced a consolidation of the Right opposition, the political opposition as a whole, though particularly its democratic sector, underwent a significant process of decomposition that left the sector generally devastated.[8]

A second major presence consists of those corporate actors — professional groups and business associations — that negotiate specific prerogatives with the state. While the leadership of these corporate actors generally identifies with the government, it has, nevertheless, assimilated a deeply anti-state ideological discourse. No resurgence or recreation of specifically social actors has yet appeared. Public opinion is favorable to the government and supportive of democratic values and practices; however, there is little participation, mobilization, or political representation of the public's problems or conflicts evident in the current phase of postauthoritarian politics. To the extent that the political leadership has not resolved the pending problems of the transition, despite the claim that the transition is over, the political style of a transition persists, thus privileging a mode of political participation concentrated almost exclusively among professionals and upper echelons of party and elite segments of the population. It is here that the ruling coalition, composed of parties capable of expressing public opinion on political issues, reveals its highly problematic side. The political sectors that traditionally represented and mediated social conflict in civil society and who articulated projects of social change are now part of the governing coalition. Thus, civil society, which always expressed itself through political representation, is left without institutional channels for those demands that are not strictly political in the narrowest sense. This frequently means that other social or cultural demands are emasculated and stripped of their content.

Future Tasks and Scenarios

The pending assignment for contemporary Chilean society is to complete the tasks that the transition from military rule initiated but that were left unresolved after the March 1990 inauguration of the Aylwin government. This implies pressing ahead with constitutional reforms that will assure full political democracy and will allow political majorities to govern without facing nondemocratic vetoes (the designated senators, the electoral system, and tutelary civil-military relations). The task also includes deepening and extending reparations for human rights abuses and reforming judicial institutions.

Simultaneously, Chileans must also tackle tasks pertaining to the processes of democratization and modernization, which are specific to democratic consolidation.[9] The first is the elimination of poverty through institutional and structural reforms. An enduring solution to poverty cannot be achieved in an exclusionary manner, as was attempted during the 1960s, by referring solely to property relations; nor, however, can the approach be purely economic, as was the case during the 1980s. The problem of poverty cannot be adequately attacked if it is detached from another pending debate, characterized by complacency regarding the development strategy and the insertion of Chile into a context of inevitable internationalization. It is often thought that because instruments and strategies such as the central role of the market or the open character of the economy have been defined, the problem of a long-term development model has been resolved. Nevertheless, a number of decisions remain: whether to consider alternative forms of cultural and economic insertion in Latin America and the world; how science and technology will be incorporated; what type of education should accompany this model; how the work place and the firm, in their diverse realms and dimensions, should be organized; what model should be implemented to redistribute wealth between rich and poor, modern and marginal, included and excluded; and structural reforms that need to be consensually implemented in the reformulation of the development model.

Another pending problem requiring immediate action concerns reform of the state. The neoliberal illusion, which led to the dismantling of the state's capacity for intervention and thus prevented its transformation and modernization, fails to recognize that not a single development experience during this century has taken place without a strong state presence. This requires a more modern, participatory, and decentralized public sector. It is necessary to downsize some state expenditures, such as those related to defense, and profoundly to transform others, such as those related to the judicial system. Although decentralization is fundamental, municipal reform and regionalization so far have been approached on the basis of a short-term tactical and electoral calculus. Such efforts lack the depth and breadth necessary for a change in the distribution of power and forms of social coexistence that will shape the lives of future generations (Garretón and Espinosa 1992.)

To strengthen the state and its administrative and regulatory apparatus compels the strengthening of the political system, so that society can control the state. Substantial tasks that cannot be avoided include the modernization and democratization of the political parties, the creation of electoral systems and sociopolitical spaces that assure expanded representation, the establishment of institutions that permit the formation of majority governments, and reform of the presidential system (Godoy 1992). Consequently, both reform of the state and the democratization of the political system require reforms in society that will strengthen and augment levels of participation and organization of social actors. Such reforms must modernize social life by allowing people greater access to information and control over matters that affect them. Thus, another pending task is the transformation and modernization of civil society itself.

In terms of political leadership, the chief merit of the Chilean process of democratization has been the constitution of a social, electoral, and governing majority, the *Concertación de Partidos por la Democracia*. To assure the continuity of this leadership, it is necessary to create mechanisms that allow for alternation in positions of authority and the existence of programmatic alternatives without risking the breakup of the coalition. Furthermore, the very existence of the *Concertación* poses questions concerning the future articulation and political representation of emergent social conflicts and demands. The coalition is composed of the two poles — Center and Left — that have historically expressed Chilean social conflicts. How emergent social conflicts and demands will be articulated and represented politically remains to be seen.

The most probable scenario for the final phase of the Aylwin government is a continuation of the traits analyzed here. The substantial tasks required to complete the transition probably will be left for the next presidential term. Fortunately, the municipalities have been democratized, and some advances have been made in reforming the judiciary, although in the latter case, reform has focused more on the efficiency of the administration of justice than on the settling of thorny issues dating from the authoritarian period such as the legacy of human rights abuses. Virtually none of the political reforms have been approved. Having already made a major redistributive effort, the government will probably effect further, though relatively minor, improvements in the economic situation. Nevertheless, in the short-term we cannot expect institutional reforms of the state, strengthening of social actors and their participation, or a redefinition of Chile's economic model for insertion into the world economy.

The core of this scenario is the continued priority given to the economy and the trust placed on the leadership capacity of the governmental elite. This scenario, therefore, privileges the state and the market. The state, which is identified with the incumbent governing team, partially corrects in the social realm the aberrations of the market. In this perspective, there are no social or political actors as such, and the reconstruction of the capacity for social action, in crisis throughout the world, is either postponed or subordinated to the logic of state power or market forces.

Efforts to confront the major tasks discussed here must, in my judgment, strengthen the political leadership capacity of the *Concertación* and its future projection as a government coalition. Although there appears to be agreement on this in theory, institutional mechanisms that reinforce the political commitment of actors to the system (and discipline each sector's tendency to act upon short-term, tactical calculations) do not exist at present. Nevertheless, successes achieved by the first democratic government (public satisfaction and continuing support for the governing coalition, the promising electoral prospects of the leaders of the *Concertación*, the formation of supraparty staffs at various levels of the government, and the programmatic agreement concerning the remaining tasks) make it virtually certain that a representative of the *Concertación* will be elected president of the next democratic government. Despite this, however, the need of each member party to maintain its own distinct profile, the zero-sum game created by the presidential regime, and the absence of space for internal competition and leadership struggle without destroying the alliance constitute future sources of tension within the governing coalition and pose difficulties for the forging of a revamped political pact.

Conclusion: Toward What Kind of Sociopolitical Matrix?

The model of adjustment and structural reform implemented in Chile was instituted during the military regime in the 1970s. This model underwent a deep crisis during the early 1980s, only to experience a successful recomposition (in terms of strictly economic indicators) in the early 1990s. In addition to radical criticisms directed at the political model, in particular regarding the tolerance for violations of human rights and the attempt to institutionalize authoritarian rule on the basis of the 1980 Constitution, initially the principal focus of opposition to the military regime was an attack on the socioeconomic model of modernization imposed by the Pinochet government. That attack highlighted the regime's failure to address issues of equality and social democratization, elimination of poverty, and protection of national autonomy.

At the beginning of the transition, democratic radicalism and demands for respect for human rights were accompanied by progressive moderation in the opposition's criticism of the economic model. By the inauguration of the Aylwin government, criticism was transformed into support for continuation of the economic model (with significant corrections regarding tax reform, labor reform, and redistributive programs directed toward the poorest sectors).[10] Additionally, growing concern emerged regarding the necessity for state reform and policies designed to effect a productive transformation of the economy. By all economic indicators, maintenance of the economic model, albeit with the mentioned corrections, has been extremely successful and has produced high levels of growth and stability. Thus, in contrast to other Latin American processes of democratization, the Chilean case has not been accompanied by an economic crisis. The democratic government's two major priorities were to maintain economic stability and continuity, while attempting to correct perverse social effects and to place state control in the hands of a supraparty governing staff. Given the downgraded role of party leadership and the absence of social actors, government political actions have been guided by economic indicators and public opinion surveys. Like economic indicators, opinion surveys reflect success: throughout Chile there are consistently high levels of satisfaction with the country's performance. There are some signs of frustration: Benefits at the personal level are not perceived, and social goals have not been reached.[11] In other words, the surveys reveal a desire for "more of the same, but for everyone."

This definition of government priorities has resulted in the postponement of pressing social issues. A certain national complacency is expressed in the belief of diverse sectors that Chile is poised to take advantage of a great historical opportunity. This effectively hinders meaningful debate over the major themes and alternatives defining the country's future. Complacency assumes that the choices and strategies followed up until now are, in fact, the only reasonable options available.

As already noted, the model of structural reforms, in the biased and restricted sense of the 1980s, was introduced and largely completed *prior* to the process of political democratization. The continuity of the model, albeit with some changes, has paved the way for a major transformation in the classical sociopolitical matrix of Chilean society. Following a phase of disarticulation, this classical matrix is now undergoing a process of recomposition. The classical Latin American matrix was generally based on an extensive interpenetration or *fusion* among the state, the system of representation, and the social structure, with little autonomy for any of the dimensions. This matrix was partially associated with "inward development" and the "state of compromise." It was also founded on a consensus regarding the active role of the state in the economy and the state's function in social and political organization. As a result, the state was the principal referent of collective action, and politics had a central role. In Chile, more specifically, this matrix involved an extensive imbrication between societal interests and the state, with the party system articulating a fundamental role in the pre-1973 democratic system (Garretón 1987; Garretón and Espinosa 1992).

In the wake of economic, social, political, and cultural transformations in the international context, a new sociopolitical matrixappears to be emerging in Latin America. This matrix is not yet fully crystallized. It contains contradictory elements, but, nevertheless, there is a trend toward an increasingly strong, autonomous, and tense complementary relation among the state, the system of representation, and the socioeconomic base. Within the framework of this emergent matrix, the most significant characteristics of the Chilean case are 1) a technocratic, executive state, very weakened in its capacity to intervene and without a broad reform of its functions, especially its coercive and integrative dimensions; 2) a party system that is accepted and legitimated by society and in which, for the first time, coalitional politics assume preeminence over centrifugal and polarizing tendencies, but with difficulties in establishing firm linkages between the leadership of the state and the articulator of new social issues and demands; and 3) a society in which the autonomy of the market leaves unresolved problems of integration and cohesion, and in which the absence of strong social actors facilitates a narrow corporatism as a form of collective action, along with the marginalization of vast sectors from the sociopolitical game. All of these characteristics coexist in a climate free of crisis, but where the political and cultural space for debating new challenges and alternatives has not yet been generated.

Notes

1. See Garretón (1987) and Garretón and Espinosa (1992) for a discussion of these concepts, which will be elaborated later in this chapter.

2. This section draws on Garretón (1990).

3. For further development of this argument, see Garretón and Espinosa (1992). For an analysis of the Chilean case, see Vergara's chapter in this volume.

4. The *Concertación* was a coalition of seventeen parties. The most important groups within it, however, were the Christian Democrats, the Radicals, the Social Democrats, and the Socialists, which, in turn, were divided into two groups: the PS (Socialist Party) and PPD (Party for Democracy).

5. The loose agglomeration of unconditional supporters, both military and civilian, of former President and Commander-in-Chief of the Army, General Augusto Pinochet.

6. See the regular series of public-opinion surveys published by the Centro de Estudios de la Realidad Contemporánea (CERC) and by Adimark-Centro de Estudios Públicos.

7. This refers to the legislation named after the Minister of Justice, Francisco Cumplido, which comprised the centerpiece of the initial *Concertación* approach to the issue of human rights violations during the military regime.

8. This was precipitated by the episode of telephone espionage that exploded in August 1992 with the public disclosure of a telephone conversation by a senator from *Renovación Nacional*, seeking nomination for the 1993 presidential race. Another presidential pre-candidate, also from *Renovación Nacional*, was involved in publicizing the taped conversation, along with civilians and military personnel.

9. On these topics, see the November and December 1993 documents published by the *Programa de Asistencia Legislativa*, which focus on a *Concertación* program for the next presidential period and the documents and studies published between July 1992 and January 1993 by the Chile Project, organized by the Ministry of Planning and Cooperation (MIDEPLAN).

10. See Pilar Vergara's chapter in this volume for a detailed analysis of these questions.

11. See the CERC and CEP-Adimark surveys cited earlier. Similar trends were also found in two surveys in which the author participated during 1991-1992, one with Marta Lagos and Roberto Méndez for the institution *Participa*, the other in FLACSO, with Irene Agurto and Tomás Moulian.

References

Centro de Estudios de la Realidad Contemporánea (CERC) and Adimark-Centro de Estudios Públicos. Various dates. Public-opinion surveys.

Drake, Paul, and Ivan Jaksi , eds. 1991. *The Struggle for Democracy in Chile. 1982-1990*. Lincoln: Nebraska University Press.

Garretón, Manuel Antonio. 1987. *Reconstruir la política*. Santiago: Editorial Andante.

Garretón, Manuel Antonio. 1989. "La oposición político partidaria en el régimen militar chileno. Un proceso de aprendizaje." In *Muerte y resurrección: Los políticos en el autoritarismo y las transiciones del Cono Sur*, eds. Marcelo Cavarozzi and Manuel Antonio Garretón. Santiago: FLACSO.

Garretón, Manuel Antonio. 1990. "La democratización política en América Latina y la crisis de paradigmas." *Mapocho* 30.

Garretón, Manuel Antonio. 1991a. "Discutir la transición. Estrategia y escenarios de la democratización política chilena." Mimeograph.

Garretón, Manuel Antonio. 1991b. "La redemocratización política en Chile. Transición, evolución e inauguración." *Estudios Públicos* 42.

Garretón, Manuel Antonio. 1993. "Los derechos humanos en los procesos de democratización." FLACSO Working Paper.

Garretón, Manuel Antonio, and Malva Espinosa. 1992. "Reforma del Estado o cambio en la matriz socio-política." *Estudios Sociales* 74.

Garretón, Manuel Antonio, and Tomás Moulian. 1983. *La unidad popular y el conflicto político en Chile*. Santiago: Ediciones Minga.

Godoy, Oscar, ed. 1992. *Cambio de régimen político*. Santiago: Ediciones Universidad Católica de Chile.

Ministerio de Planejamiento y Cooperación (MIDEPLAN). 1993. Studies comprising the Chile Project. January 1992-January 1993.

Programa de Asistencia Legislativa. 1993. Documents setting forth the *Concertación* coalition's program for the next presidential period. November-December.

Valenzuela, J. Samuel, and Arturo Valenzuela, eds. 1987. *Military Rule in Chile*. Baltimore: Johns Hopkins University Press.

Chapter Nine

Market Economy, Social Welfare, and Democratic Consolidation in Chile

Pilar Vergara

Introduction

The current democratic government of Chile, headed by Patricio Aylwin, has repeatedly affirmed its commitment to the consolidation of a free market economy, which is open to foreign interests, based on private enterprise, oriented toward global markets, and governed by imperatives of profitability and international competition. It has also defended the thesis that a capitalist, free market economy is not incompatible with greater social equality, and it has declared balancing economic growth with greater social equity as the fundamental aim of the Aylwin administration. Alleviation of the extreme poverty that affects more than 40 percent of Chileans is considered an inescapable condition for the consolidation and long-term stability of democratic institutions in the country. This chapter questions the ability of the existing free market strategy and the current system of welfare to reconcile the goals of economic growth and greater social equality with the effective democratization of Chilean society.

The first section describes the principal characteristics of the neoliberal socioeconomic strategy imposed by the former military government and assesses its most important results. A preliminary review of both the problematic legacies and the favorable structural conditions bequeathed by General Augusto Pinochet's regime illustrates the scope and significance of continuity under democratic conditions. The second section discusses the current economic and social strategy, its fundamental objectives and challenges, including economic and institutional restrictions. The opportunities the current government inherited for the implementation of a strategy capable of balancing economic growth with greater social equity are also examined. The final section includes some speculation on the role of the state and the market in the Chilean economy and society and on the difficulties and options created by the development and consolidation of democracy in Chile.

The Military Regime and the Neoliberal Experiment
Economic Strategy

The military government headed by General Augusto Pinochet (1973-1989) reversed the socioeconomic tendencies dominant in Chile for several decades. While imposing the supremacy of the free market and the subordination of domestic economic activity to international financial flows, Pinochet drastically reduced the interventionist role of the state, impelled the privatization of the economy, imposed severe restrictions on public spending for social programs, and promoted the liberalization of markets and of foreign trade and exchange rates. At the same time, the military regime also dismantled the political and union organizations which the lower-income classes had used to express their demands and advance their interests.

Reorganization of the economy, successive orthodox stabilization programs during the 1970s, and external shocks that impoverished Chile's economy produced a sharp deterioration of earnings at a time when recessive macroeconomic policies shrank public spending for social programs. Open unemployment and unprecedented levels of poverty were the result. At the beginning of the 1980s, the debt crisis and the resulting transfer of resources abroad, combined with a new regression of macroeconomic and distributive conditions, tempered official optimism that the economy had embarked upon a path of accelerated growth that could have initiated the long-awaited phase of redistribution. The implementation of a policy of restrictive adjustment led to even lower wages, new cuts in social spending, and even higher unemployment rates, as shown in Table 1. A more pragmatic economic policy after 1984 permitted economic recovery and eventually led to sustained growth with moderate inflation. Nonetheless, by the end of the decade, progress in the reduction of poverty and other social maladies was minimal.

Social Policy

Neoliberal reforms were directed not only at the economic structure but also at traditional social institutions such as social security and health care. The free market, viewed as a suitable mechanism for implementing certain economic decisions, was also applied to all sectors and areas of society. It thus became a means of reorganizing society as a whole. The state sharply reduced social spending, and it systematically retreated from the social sector by privatizing services and organizing a new social institution subject to the laws of competition. To that end, in the late 1970s and early 1980s, a broad program of reforms was introduced. Known as social "modernizations," these reforms transferred to the market and the private sector the task of providing goods and social services previously offered by the state, leaving the market in charge of regulating access to these services. These reforms promoted the creation and expansion of a private system of high-quality social services in which those with sufficient means would finance the social benefits they previously received from the state. The state retained responsibility for attending only to sectors with insufficient resources to pay for their benefits.

Table 1
Selected Economic Indicators, 1970–1990

Year	GDP per Capita	Infla- tion Rate	Invest- ment Rate	External Debt (billions of $US)	Unem- ploy- ment Rate	Real Salaries* (1970=100) Average Salaries	Minimum Wage
		(1970=100)					
1970	100	36.1	20.2	3.1	5.9	100.0	100.0
1980	116	17.6	17.6	11.3	16.9	89.4	112.7
1981	121	19.5	19.5	15.6	15.1	97.4	117.9
1982	102	15.0	15.0	17.2	26.1	97.7	116.6
1983	99	12.9	12.9	18.0	31.3	87.0	91.6
1984	104	13.2	13.2	19.7	24.7	81.6	80.1
1985	105	14.8	14.8	20.5	22.0	83.2	74.6
1986	109	15.0	15.0	20.8	17.3	84.9	69.6
1987	113	16.5	16.5	20.7	13.9	84.7	64.0
1988	119	17.0	17.0	19.0	11.0	90.3	66.4
1989	129	18.6	18.6	17.5	8.6	92.0	73.8
1990	130	19.5	19.5	18.6	8.6	93.7	78.8

* Includes emergency employment programs.
Source: Banco Central (various dates) and Instituto Nacional de Estadística (various dates).

The privatization of the health sector was executed through a profound reorganization of the existing national health service and by the implementation of a new system, the *Servicio Nacional de Servicios de Salud* (National System of Health Services — SNSS), comprising twenty-seven competitive regional health providers to be administered according to criteria of private profitability. The old financing system, based on budgetary allotments according to traditional criteria, was replaced by a system of vouchers based on billing for benefits provided. It was expected that the resources received by each establishment would be proportional to the total amount of benefits provided, leading to competition among providers. Other measures gradually transferred the provision of health services to local municipalities.[1]

The social security reform initiated in 1981, which affected only the pension system, substituted the old system of distribution with one of individual capitalization, which is administered by private entities called

Administradoras de Fondos de Pensiones (Administrators of Pension Funds —
AFP). The state's intervention is limited to regulation and supervision of the
system. In the AFP, a worker's old-age pension is determined by contributions
made during his or her working life, plus the return on investments of those
contributions realized by the entity to which one is affiliated. Every active
worker was authorized to choose freely between remaining with the current
provider institutions or switching to the new plans. Those workers who chose
the new system were eligible for fee rates substantially lower than in the old
state institutions; moreover, workers were granted a "bonus of recognition"
for their old fees, which led the vast majority — especially those with higher
incomes[2] — to switch systems. The consequence was the transfer of
substantial public resources to the AFP, definancing previously existing social
security institutions.[3] At the end of 1980s, the resources accumulated in the
AFP were equivalent to 25 percent of the GDP, leading to important
repercussions in the areas of saving and investment.

In addition to the social security reform, the development of private
medicine was promoted by the creation of institutions resembling U.S.-style
Health Maintenance Organizations (HMOs). These *Instituciones de Salud
Previsional*, better known by the acronym "ISAPRES," were private, profit-
making entities offering medical services in exchange for an obligatory
contribution from those enrolled. ISAPRES limit the health risks they are
willing to cover and, as with AFP, require a minimum income for enrollment.
The medical benefits a member receives are proportional to his economic
contribution. The creation of ISAPRES, as with the AFP, entailed the transfer
of substantial public resources to the private sector and a simultaneous
reduction of the already modest funding received by the state health sector.

At the end of the 1980s, the ISAPRES received 50 percent of the financial
resources formerly allocated to public institutions. The resulting definancing
of the public health sector diminished the quality of the services received by
the low-income groups who contributed the majority of the resources. The
institutional reforms aimed at reducing the state's presence and developing
a private market in the health sector led to the coexistence of two health
systems that segmented the services provided according to a member's ability
to pay. Thus, the state's relegation to a subsidiary role and the privatization
of services created a dual system in both social security and health services.

In education, the restructuring of the system transferred the administration of school financing to the municipalities, which, in turn, transferred
responsibilities to private entities. At the same time, the mechanism for
financing education was modified, with the state promising to give a subsidy
for each student attending class, both in the public schools and in the free
private ones that were created. This financial arrangement sought to stimulate

the expansion of private education and, at the same time, to administer public education according to criteria of profitability.

The military government's housing policy followed the same logic seen in health care. The state entrusted the private sector with the task of building public housing. Public institutions were to finance housing for families without sufficient income to obtain even minimal shelter through the market. In addition to contributing financial resources, the state had to choose the beneficiaries and establish norms and procedures. Various direct subsidy plans were put into effect which allowed the beneficiary to acquire a home through the market. The privatization of erstwhile public services limited government assistance to the development of subsidized compensatory and relief programs for households affected by extreme poverty. The distribution of direct subsidies according to need assured access to the most indispensable goods and social services by social groups at the outer fringes of the market.

These programs comprised the so-called "social safety net" implemented by the military government through a series of selective public interventions geared to attend to specific marginalized population groups unable to meet their own basic needs. These interventions sought to focus a substantial part of social spending on these sectors, avoiding improper "diversions" toward other groups. The safety net was defined by the government as its principal instrument for eradicating absolute poverty and constituted, alongside the previously mentioned "modernizations," the second fundamental pillar of the military government's social policy.

The social functions of the state were conceived as a collection of programs, which were established at the end of the 1970s, focused on sectors of extreme poverty. Different social programs were developed: the *Subsidio Unico Familiar* (Family Subsidy — SUF) for segments of the population under 18 years of age with scarce resources and unprotected by social security; the *Pensiones Asistenciales* (Assistance Pensions — PASIS) directed toward extreme poverty among the elderly and invalids; the *Programa de Alimentación Complementaria* (Complementary Nutrition Program —PAC) to meet the nutritional needs of the poor; the *Programa de Alimentación Escolar* (School Nutrition Program —PAE) to serve school-age children; and the *Programa de Jardines Infantiles* (JUNJI), the preschool program run by the Ministry of Education.

These new, focused social programs used innovative and rigorous methods designed to identify the neediest households as the first priority. Among these methods, the Index of Social Stratification (CAS Index) was the most important (Raczynski 1991). The programs were implemented in a decentralized form, leaving to the municipalities the primary responsibility for their application and control (Vergara 1990). Nevertheless, benefits distributed by the safety net were insufficient, both in quantity as well as quality, and they decreased steadily throughout the military period. Efforts to eradicate extreme poverty through the social safety-net programs arose in a context of contraction resulting from economic policies that concentrated revenues, reduced employment, and increased absolute poverty, while maintaining severely depressed levels of public spending. As can be seen in Table 2, social program spending declined sharply, with the sole exception of the social security sector in 1981-1982. At the end of the military period in 1989, spending remained far below levels reached two decades before.

Table 2
Social Public Spending per Capita
(1985 Pesos)

Year	Education	Health	Social Security	Housing	Other	Total	Index (1970=100)
1970	11,773	6,438	24,359	4,941	271	47,782	100
1974	9,401	5,577	14,509	6,416	345	36,248	76
1975	7,441	4,321	14,765	3,662	106	30,296	63
1976	7,955	4,036	14,601	2,707	276	29,576	62
1977	9,290	4,366	16,698	3,034	545	33,934	71
1978	9,774	4,829	19,970	2,836	466	37,865	79
1979	10,695	4,754	22,308	3,541	567	41,865	88
1980	10,441	5,302	23,216	3,519	573	43,051	90
1981	10,844	4,815	26,974	3,482	473	46,587	97
1982	10,953	5,049	31,079	2,442	367	49,890	104
1983	9,276	4,017	28,830	2,022	558	44,703	94
1984	8,967	4,244	28,729	2,362	489	44,791	94
1985	8,899	4,096	26,299	3,241	469	43,004	90
1986	8,371	4,002	25,391	3,036	491	41,291	86
1987	7,418	3,970	24,916	3,333	478	40,115	84
1988	7,690	4,434	25,081	3,727	497	41,429	87
1989	8,727	5,620	26,695	2,523	549	44,113	92

Source: Cabezas (1988).

The military regime's macroeconomic policies also exacerbated distributive inequality. The average unemployment rate during the period was 18 percent, triple the prevailing rate of the 1960s. The average value of wages and salaries always remained below 1970 levels. In 1989, wages and salaries were still 6 percent below what they had been two decades earlier (see Table 1). Information available for metropolitan Santiago presented in Table 3 shows a systematic decline of 25 percent of family income in the lowest-income households while the highest quintile improved its relative standing.

In short, despite the subsidies of the safety net, there was a significant increase in the number of households affected by critical poverty (Raczynski 1992).

Table 3

Consumption Distribution in Households Arranged by Quintiles of Income, Greater Santiago 1969, 1978, and 1988

(percentage of the total)

Quintiles	1969	1978	1988
I (lowest)	7.6	5.2	4.4
II	11.7	9.3	8.2
III	15.6	13.5	12.7
IV	20.6	21.0	20.1
V (highest)	44.5	51.0	54.6
TOTAL	100.0	100.0	100.0

Source: Instituto Nacional de Estadística (1969, 1978, 1988).

Despite all the limitations and the reductions in subsidies, the safety net was, nevertheless, able to compensate partially for declining income and consumption by averting greater impoverishment for some sectors of the population. The welfare network, however, did not in any way point to the eradication of poverty. Moreover, focusing reduced public spending on extremely poor groups came at the expense of the resources and social benefits previously received by middle- and lower-middle income groups. A direct consequence of this was the exclusion and impoverishment of a considerable portion of these sectors, which had neither sufficient income to join the private system and who no longer received essential goods and services previously provided by the state. This strategy was also closely linked to the privatization of social services, which restricted access to the middle- and high-income population and determined the services received by each member according to what he or she paid into the system.

The establishment of the social safety net put the finishing touches on a dual model of social welfare: Chilean society was segmented into a sector protected by the social security system — the vast majority of which came to be affiliated with the private system of social services — and another sector excluded from the system, composed of self-employed workers, the under-employed, the unemployed, and the impoverished middle classes, who saw their lack of social protection accentuated in areas traditionally attended to by the state. The regressive consequences of the dual welfare model were aggravated because private entities were created and expanded by means of a systematic transfer of resources from the public to the private sector. The combination of the transfer of resources and drastic cuts in social spending severely eroded the quality of the goods and services provided and minimized access to benefits by the poorest.

In practice, the dual model of social welfare, with a private system based on market and profitability criteria in coexistence with another state system granting subsidies to those who lack sufficient purchasing power, is a combination of the welfare states that Richard Titmus (1968) classified in his typology as "residual" and "meritocratic." In the residual category, state policies intervene only when market mechanisms fail, with the intent of integrating all those who are excluded because of their salary or employment status. Such interventions are designed to be selective and temporary — although possibly of long duration — and are supposed to be phased out as soon as market mechanisms are able to fulfill their assigned roles. The meritocratic system, in contrast, is based on the individual's position in the labor market. In this system, the social benefits received depend on the merit, effort, and productivity of each individual. Every person chooses in the market the services he or she wants and can afford. By combining both, Chile created a system which further fragmented society and deepened prevailing social inequalities.

Despite their anti-state rhetoric and the primacy granted to the private sector in providing social services, the neoliberals were able only to achieve a partial and selective dismantling of some traditional institutions of the old welfare state. The functional modalities of traditional services were, however, profoundly transformed by submitting their administration to private-profit criteria. Principles of self-financing, fee-for-service systems, and criteria for recovering costs were imposed on social investments. Hence, with the exception of those in extreme poverty, those using state services were obliged to pay for the benefits they received, and these benefits were proportional to payments made by the recipients of services. In this way, important institutional components of the traditional welfare sphere were left intact, although modified by a commercial logic similar to that prevailing in the private sphere; as with the latter, a link was established between the income of the user, his economic contribution to the system, and the benefits received.

The consequences of these policies are evident. The statistics available on poverty in Chile reveal that between 1970 and 1987 the proportion of families whose incomes were insufficient to satisfy their most pressing needs rose from 17 percent to 38 percent, which translated into more than five million people.[4] Illiteracy rates increased significantly during the same period, and academic performance at the elementary level in 1989 was 6 percent lower than twenty years earlier. Some social indicators (such as malnutrition and infant mortality, life expectancy, and preschool enrollment) did improve under the military regime for reasons that will not be analyzed here. This improvement reflects the decision by the military government to concentrate scarce resources in those particular areas with the aim of showing the world successful results in the social arena.[5]

Limited empirical evidence shows an accentuation of structural hetero-geneity which deepened social and economic disparities (Martinez and Tironi 1985). In fact, modernization reached only a limited fraction of Chileans. Rural and urban enterprises survived the structural reforms, and newly created firms raised their productivity and achieved considerable dynamism. Other sectors, such as small producers and self-employed workers, had to make do without state support and faced a twenty-year low in productivity and income levels. Vast segments of the work force remained outside the sweep of moderniza-tion and survived with very low income levels. The same can be said for broad segments of the middle class, whose levels of income and employment were affected by the restructuring of the economy and the implementation of recessive adjustments, in a way that left them unprotected by the social policies of the Pinochet government. This was particularly reflected in a growing "informal" sector. At the end of the 1980s, only approximately 45 percent of the work force contributed to the social security system. At the same time, however, the affiliation of workers to the AFP and the ISAPRES systematically expanded (Arellano 1988).

The Challenge of Growth with Equity in the Democratic Transition
The Free Market Strategy of the Aylwin Government

With the return to democratic rule in 1991, Patricio Aylwin's government did not attempt to change the system of economic organization it had inherited. The open-economy, capitalist strategy denied the state a leading role in the growth process, limited state control over foreign trade, and significantly weakened state capacity to influence private investment deci-sions. State action was largely limited to the formulation of macroeconomic policies and the implementation of general rules governing economic agents and markets.

The neoliberal inheritance did leave behind some structural conditions favorable for growth with stability, which made Chile unique. In contrast to other new democracies in the region, the Aylwin government entered the picture after the implementation of the major structural and institutional reforms advocated by the neoliberal credo. Macroeconomic imbalances were under control, and the country had initiated a path of growth with moderate inflation and balanced fiscal accounts. These economic conditions were due — at least in part — to social spending that had remained repressed for almost two decades, as revealed in Table 4.

Table 4
Pensions, Sole Family Subsidy and Allotment, and Unemployment Subsidy (1970-1989)

Year	Civil Sect. Amt.	Unif. Sect. Payload	Min. Old Age Pens.	Relief Pensions #	Av. Mnth.	Family Allotment Mnth. Av. Force	Unit. Value	Sole Family Subsidy #	Unit. Value	Mnth. Av.	% Unemp. Work
1970	22,678	68,754	12,405	—	—	—	—	—	—	—	—
1974	11,706	59,998	10,501	—	—	—	1,879	—	—	3,7	1.3
1975	11,437	43,185	10,065	27,8	4,175	—	1,781	—	—	29,3	6.0
1976	11,916	52,652	10,621	39,0	5,063	—	1,643	—	—	75,5	13.8
1977	12,993	62,276	11,616	66,0	5,050	—	1,532	—	—	57,0	12.9
1978	14,162	63,339	13,709	91,8	4,865	—	1,490	—	—	60,7	12.6
1979	16,443	71,622	13,280	113,1	4,676	—	1,443	—	—	69,6	14.5
1980	16,937	79,830	13,561	131,7	6,370	—	1,445	—	—	74,3	17.3
1981	17,780	82,632	13,827	156,2	7,102	3,962	1,443	—	818	75,1	19.2
1982	19,042	83,414	13,712	183,9	7,576	3,871	1,404	—	802	130,4	17.5
1983	18,971	82,568	13,268	228,1	7,161	3,929	1,131	527	646	142,5	19.3
1894	20,443	90,432	13,843	278,4	7,562	3,990	1,112	699	634	97,8	14.9
1985	18,426	84,572	12,510	320,8	6,656	4,026	967	967	600	97,3	16.7
1986	18,858	82,236	12,591	324,1	6,552	4,024	810	1,044	502	84,4	16.6
1987	18,493	82,059	12,168	321,6	5,351	4,014	675	955	419	66,0	13.6
1988	—	—	12,461	303,2	—	3,817	589	914	419	52,9	11.5
1989	—	—	12,670	292,2	5,945	3,735	505	—	—	39,2	—

Sources: Arellano (1989), MIDEPLAN (1991), Raczynski (1992), and Vergara (1990).

When the democratic government assumed power, a broad consensus among its advisers legitimated the hegemony of the neoliberal view of the proper functions of the market and the state in the allocation of resources and the importance of maintaining and deepening the economic gains achieved during the military regime (the leading role of the private sector, the liberalization of foreign trade, and so on). These advisers also accepted the need to maintain a stringent macroeconomic equilibrium to avoid inflationary pressures, which hampered investment and growth and resulted in short-term regressive income redistribution that hurt the poor. Departing from convention, however, they believed that the enormous gap between economic successes and social inequalities originated in centralized economic policies combined with exclusionary or inefficient social policies and that these disparities were incompatible with a stable democracy. Without changing this state of affairs and without creating political, economic, and institutional conditions that would make increased economic growth compatible with increasing degrees of social equality, they argued that it would not be possible to consolidate democratic institutions.

The reigning consensus on these issues led the democratic government to maintain the open, competitive, market-oriented strategy inherited from the military: it confirmed its commitment to a free market economy and took a series of steps toward its consolidation. The economy's export orientation was maintained as was liberalization of foreign investment. The globalization of the economy was further advanced by a new tariff reduction, along with free trade agreements and economic integration treaties with other Latin American countries, new incentives for foreign investment, and measures to facilitate Chilean investments abroad. Short-term economic policy continued to grant special priority to controlling inflation and maintaining macroeconomic balances. Concomitantly, income distribution became even more regressive as the government, attempting to address lingering macroeconomic disequilibria, continued the adjustment policies initiated by the Pinochet government.

After two years of democratic rule, the management of the economy produced indisputably positive results. In 1991, production increased more than 5 percent, a figure much greater than the 2 percent registered in 1990, and inflation dropped to 18 percent for the year, from 27.3 percent the previous year. The external sector also had a very favorable year: the trade balance showed a surplus of nearly $500 mullion and international reserves grew to $1.3 billion. Foreign investment continued to arrive in increasing amounts. The unemployment rate was reduced in 1991 to approximately 6 percent.

Social Policy under Democracy

The Aylwin government advocates balancing the free market economic strategy with a distributive effort based on an expansive social policy. Government authorities have repeatedly argued that their first objective is to meet the challenge of reconciling long-term growth with an improvement, albeit slow, in the distribution of income and in the living conditions of the poorest sectors. These distributive proposals depend on the establishment of a concerted strategy among the principal economic, social, and political agents with the aim of seeking negotiated agreements to the problems of employment and wages. Moreover, a similar consensus is required for the passage of tax reform legislation that allocates sufficient resources for the development of a progressive and efficient social spending policy, even if only within margins permitted by the adequate financing of the social effort.

Yet even though the government retained the institutional structure and the methods of operation of the social welfare system imposed by the neoliberal reform — the "modernizations" and the "social safety net" — it failed to introduce major modifications that would end their dual nature and their exclusionary and segmentary impact. The key question facing Chile's civilian government is whether it is feasible to consolidate democracy while simultaneously reconciling the objectives of growth and equity in the context of an open and export-oriented capitalist economy and a dualistic social welfare system.

The new government inherited important economic, political, and institutional restrictions that constrained the battle against poverty and social marginalization. The economic constraints, including the external debt, fiscal shortfalls, reduced social spending, depressed wages, low investment rates, the fragility of macroeconomic balances, and so on, have already been described. Under macroeconomic conditions particularly adverse for low-income sectors, the social tensions that have accumulated and the expectations for improvement are not surprising.

Politico-institutional restrictions also inhibited a more expansive social spending policy. Among these factors, the autonomy of the Central Bank in controlling monetary and exchange policies, and the numerous decrees issued by the military regime shortly before the new government assumed power, merit attention. The sociopolitical context was especially problematic. Employers pushed for a deepening of the free market strategy, demanded a deepening of privatization initiatives, and opposed new taxation for social programs. At the same time, the armed forces retained significant prerogatives that threatened the efforts of the Aylwin government to exert control over the military. This was hardly an ideal environment for the launching of more daring social policies.

In this adverse context, the democratic government adopted four guiding principles to signal its intention to break with the social development strategy of the previous military regime: equity, solidarity, integrity, and social participation. Owing to the constraints, these governing principles operated more at the level of political discourse than on the plane of effective government social action. Tax and labor-legislation reform, however, were given high priority. The approval of these reforms by Congress was possible thanks to a government strategy of coordination between employers, organized labor, and opposition parties and to the consensus in the country regarding the need to improve living conditions in the poorest sectors. By virtue of the negotiations among organized labor, employers, and government, labor reforms recognized the legitimacy of labor unions and led to more equitable legislation concerning minimum wages, pensions, public sector salaries, work contracts, employment stability, and the right to strike. The elimination of the most regressive aspects of the military regime's labor policies, combined with a decline in inflation from 27 percent in 1990 to 18 percent in 1991, boosted workers' wages by almost 6 percent, thereby reversing nearly twenty years of steady erosion in real salaries.

Nevertheless, the undeniable distributive impact of the government's strategy did not benefit all segments of society. The positive effects were mostly concentrated in the participating sectors of organized labor and had little or no impact on those with precarious positions in the labor market, such as the self-employed, the unemployed, and workers in small businesses. These groups were denied participation in negotiations related to matters directly affecting them, such as the minimum wage, employment regulation, and social spending.

The resources garnered from tax reform made it possible to increase social spending without provoking macroeconomic imbalances. Breaking with the tendency prevailing for almost twenty years, fiscal resources generated by the reform permitted an expansive policy of social spending. Even if those resources did not exceed 2 percent of the GDP, they allowed for an increase in the fiscal contribution to social programs by 17.4 percent in 1990 (compared to the spending initially budgeted by the military government for that year) and by 12 percent in 1991. Most of the tax resources collected went primarily to increase subsidies to low-income groups. The minimum wage was also readjusted, and additional resources enabled programs of health,[6] housing, and education[7] to be strengthened. Additional funds were also used to expand primary care and to invest in hospital equipment, an area neglected during the military government. A program was initiated to improve the quality of basic education and expand the coverage of the school nutrition program (PAE). Finally, the benefits of the housing programs were expanded to include extended families. Previously unprotected groups, such as young people, the elderly, and female heads of households, also received benefits.[8]

The democratic government retained another fundamental pillar of the military regime's social policy: the social safety net for the very poor. The safety net has undergone no fundamental changes in its compensatory and ameliorative character, although resources from tax reform have allowed for expansion of some subsidies. Nonetheless, benefits are still insufficient, especially if one considers the magnitude and extent of poverty in Chile. The programs offered through the safety net are woefully inadequate compared to what would be required to raise investment to levels sufficient to break the vicious cycle of poverty in which the poor are trapped.

The *Fondo de Solidaridad e Inversión Social* (Solidarity and Social Investment Fund — FOSIS) was created to finance projects that benefit the neediest groups. FOSIS complements traditional social policies. It funds programs aimed at improving the living conditions of the poorest communities. FOSIS also provides support to urban microenterprise and to small rural producers and small mining artisans so that they can raise their productivity and successfully compete in the market. These resources, however, are fairly insignificant, representing less than 1 percent of total social spending in 1990-1991 (Raczynski 1992).[9] Thus, despite the initiation of many innovative and participatory projects, the FOSIS program is ill-equipped to become the Aylwin government's principal instrument for combatting extreme poverty.

Despite its good intentions, much of the weakness of the Aylwin government's response to poverty stems from the fact that its conception of socioeconomic policy is inherited from the Pinochet regime. The bulk of the previous regime's organizations and methods have been maintained without substantial change. Departing from the premise that the free market economic strategy should continue, some authors (Muñoz 1991; Ffrench-Davis 1991) argue that the democratic government's proposals balance the exigencies of international competitiveness with greater distributive equity. These authors maintain that improvements in wages, employment, and standards of living are feasible if the government meets two basic conditions: 1) implementation of an industrial policy to promote the sustained growth of productivity, with a portion of increased wealth allocated to wages, and 2) adoption of a subsidiary role for the state in seeking to satisfy the basic needs of the most neglected groups by promoting their incorporation into markets and improving their skills so as to open new employment opportunities in the formal sector of the economy.

Underlying this interpretation is the supposition that it is possible simultaneously to promote economic dynamism while pursuing social equality. While quite moderate, this distributive strategy with a subsidiary role for the state has a different orientation from one calling for growth strictly regulated by the market. Each strategy has its own logic, although they reinforce each other. Radical changes in the economic strategy or in the current social welfare system (such as incorporating criteria of equality and solidarity) are not perceived to be necessary by advocates of current policies. Unfortunately, these arguments are not always supported by empirical evidence. Underlying this interpretation, which is implicit in official discourse, is the unmistakable "trickle down" hypothesis which argues that extreme poverty can be eradicated only insofar as economic growth generates new jobs, improves productivity, and increases wages. Unintentionally, this type of analysis reinforces a dualistic strategy of social development: access to a system of high-quality private services combined with efforts to raise real salaries for some on the basis of productivity gains, while perpetuating dependence on state assistance for many who remain on the fringes of the market.

Thus, under the Aylwin government, the preoccupation with equity remains relegated to the collection and allotment of resources destined for social ends and to compensatory programs directed toward extreme poverty. This strategy will entail a coordinated labor-relations policy to negotiate the distribution of the costs and benefits of economic expansion. Nevertheless, these negotiations are restricted to workers in the formal sector, who are protected by the publicly funded social security system (approximately 56 percent of the labor force), while many also have access to privately provided services through the market.

As meritorious as this market-driven distributive strategy may be, eschewing more direct forms of public intervention to promote equity means that the positive impact of governmental policies could be offset by the privatization of the social service system and the even more powerful logic embedded in the economic strategy itself. By the same token, basing the entire distributive strategy on the allocation of social spending and on compensatory programs directed toward the poorest means that social policy will inevitably remain limited to actions of a charitable nature, oriented more toward mitigating the effects of poverty and inequality than to attacking their root causes. This variant of social policy focuses on immediate consumption, with few resources destined to increase the country's productive capacity. Such emphasis serves only to accentuate the contradiction between the objectives of growth and equity.

In short, the current welfare system is plagued by the same contradictions that afflicted the social policies of the Pinochet era. Regressive and exclusionary socioeconomic tendencies will persist if high-income earners are encouraged to rely on private services (with the resulting transfer of public resources to those entities) and if public services catering to the neediest population are allowed to deteriorate. The social security system, for example, has not undergone any of the significant changes that would be required in order to introduce criteria of equity and solidarity. Nor has the ISAPRES system had equity and solidarity criteria incorporated into its operation. Even though state contributions to public health have increased, those resources still represent only approximately 1 percent of GDP. Moreover, a significant number of these resources subsidize the ISAPRES system. The public sector has assumed the responsibility for a series of services that these institutions do not cover. ISAPRES does not finance an integral health plan for all their beneficiary population, nor does it grant maternity assistance, or assume care of the elderly or the chronically ill, or concern itself with prevention and the promotion of health. These tasks must be assumed by state health institutions. Given that public health benefits are determined by the availability of fiscal resources, which continue to be scarce, the quantity and quality of health services are clearly deficient. This constitutes a permanent stimulus for the transfer to ISAPRES of those workers who fulfill income and residence requirements. This, in turn, further erodes the resources available to public institutions, diminishing the quality of the benefits offered and access to those benefits.[10]

Financing for public health services continues to be based on the billing of benefits provided and on tariff systems for the users. Among other things, the latter promotes an allotment of resources that favors benefits for the ailments of the most accommodated groups, at the expense of benefits required by sectors with the least resources.

Elementary preschool financing is still appropriated via state subsidies, although the value of these has been readjusted. In the housing sector, the subsidy policy initiated by the previous government has continued, even though fiscal resources for public housing were increased and modifications to the collection and allotment of housing units were introduced with the intent of attenuating the discrimination affecting those who lacked sufficient resources to accumulate the prior savings required to collect the subsidy. The administration of state social services according to market criteria and private profitability was also maintained.

In sum, at the heart of the social welfare policy, a duality has been maintained between two, not infrequently antagonistic, lines of action: a social institution that ensures access to high-quality private services and free market choice to groups with the highest incomes and a permanent dependence on insufficient state subsidies for the poorest groups. Moreover, far from reinforcing each other, these two lines of action are, in many respects, contradictory because they produce a permanent transfer of state resources toward private entities.

This does not imply, however, that the distribution of income and, in particular, the improvement of salaries and living conditions of the poorest classes are incompatible with an export-oriented growth strategy or, even less, that they would be sustainable only with a contraction of salaries destined to create comparative advantages, as could have been the case in 1979-1980 (Muñoz 1991). On the contrary, economic growth is a necessary — but not sufficient — condition for overcoming extreme poverty in Chile. On a slightly different note, one can hardly criticize the focusing of social spending on the poorest sectors. But targeting the neediest should not excuse the reduction in social spending, nor does it constitute in itself a satisfactory solution to the problem of poverty — especially if the resources destined to those sectors are limited — since its effects are merely absorbed without any lasting positive impact.

Reflections on the Consolidation of Democracy in Chile

The time has come once again to ask ourselves about the prospects for the consolidation of democracy in Chile and about alternative frameworks in which the growth-equity equation may be considered. Issues of stability and democratic consolidation cannot elude questions of social equity and poverty. While it is not possible to finance democracy in Chile without vigorous economic growth that contributes to increasing salaries and employment, most Chileans understand that even long-term dynamic growth requires greater equity. In the words of Richard Solow, the 1987 Nobel Prize Laureate in Economics, "There is no example in the world of successful growth sustained by massive poverty" (*El Mercurio*, July 19, 1992).

Admittedly, other political and institutional forces not addressed in this chapter are relevant to the development of democracy in Chile. But it is still pertinent to question the ability of the Aylwin government to sustain an efficient, dynamic, and internationally competitive market economy while increasing social equality. In other words, is it feasible to reconcile both objectives within the parameters of the existing economic and social framework and thus advance toward an effective democratization of Chilean society?

It is difficult to provide a definitive answer to this question. As things currently stand, it may be naive to expect that the market-oriented strategy will provide satisfactory solutions. It is certain that the current economic system requires incentives for investment, technological innovation, and export development. But it is no less certain that the market, operating without restrictions, is the source of great inequalities. In the current strategy, a distributive logic operates only through the state and the social policy. If substantive improvements in income distribution and reduction of poverty are desired, it is essential to restructure the present welfare system because it relegates the satisfaction of social needs to the laws of a competitive market. Chile's welfare system subordinates the basic needs of the poorest groups — whose purchasing power does not allow them to incorporate themselves into the market — to the fiscal limits of a conservative social policy. This inevitably leads to compensatory relief action which, apart from not eradicating extreme poverty, contributes little to reconciling economic growth with greater social equity and, thereby, to the strengthening of democracy.

Advances have been made toward greater social equity in the work place by means of negotiation and coordination of interests among employ- ers, workers, and the government. In this manner, workers may achieve increases in salaries as a function of increases in productivity, but this does not necessarily result in better living conditions for those who are precariously placed in the labor market or for the unemployed, most of whom are indigent. Unfortunately, those who achieve incorporation into the modern economy are always fewer than those who swell the ranks of the informally employed and the extremely poor. The people marginalized by the free market economy include those employed in activities of low productivity, the self-employed, and unemployed. Due to growth rates in Chile's population and work force, to the requirements of the process of liberalization and restructuring of the economy, and to the increased incorporation of capital-intensive technologies and the already insufficient investment levels, this group is large and may grow even further. Hence, even if the strategy to promote growth and productivity constitutes the only means of overcoming extreme poverty, nothing guarantees an improvement for the poorest groups in a reasonable period of time. Without such an improvement the social stability required to consolidate democracy will be difficult to achieve.

It would also be misleading to suppose that future growth rates of the Chilean economy, as high as they may be compared to those in the authoritarian period, would result in even the gradual incorporation of all the sectors of the population that do not participate productively.[11] Investment rates registered in the country in the last few years, which only recently reached 18 percent, make it impossible to achieve growth rates compatible with a definitive solution to the problems of those who remain marginalized from formal markets.

The Aylwin government's policies effectively depend on "trickle down" theories which claim that income distribution and the solution of the problems of those left behind can only come from growth of the economy and expansion of the modern sectors. This discourse reproduces the neoliberal position that the state should be subservient to the market and that dualism should limit social policy. The critique presented here acknowledges that the Aylwin government initiated programs focusing state social assistance on fighting indigence and that Chilean social policy — through FOSIS — was expanded to enhance physical and human capital assets among some groups of self-employed, underemployed, and small enterprise workers.

To abandon the objectives of macroeconomic growth and stability would pose even greater difficulties in stimulating investment and growth and would, in the short term, provoke even more regressive effects in distributive conditions. Market forces operating freely generate severe distortions, which accentuate the concentration of income and deepen social inequalities, but this should not overshadow their positive attributes as mechanisms for coordinating economic decisions, providing linkages with international markets, and encouraging investment, technological innovation, and economic growth by creating a modern managerial class. Nothing, however, indicates that the market will offer a satisfactory answer to the problems of misery and social disintegration.

Neither should it be expected that a solution will spring from a dual social policy like the one that currently exists, even if social spending were to increase appreciably. In fact, resources allocated for such purposes do not approach the level of the problems they try to resolve. Given the present conditions, government authorities do not anticipate a significant increase in public funds destined for social programs (Molina 1992). The situation is aggravated by the magnitude of the resources needed to finance the social security deficit and pay for the "bonus of recognition" to workers who continue to affiliate with the AFP. The possibility of readjusting services currently offered is, consequently, very limited. In the absence of institutional reforms of the current welfare system, substantial progress in the reduction of poverty and marginality will be difficult to achieve regardless of how much social spending is increased or how efficiently it is targeted. Lamentably, systematic studies do not exist that evaluate the direct and indirect regressive impacts of the operation of the dual welfare system. Undoubtedly, however, the long-term effects of this system on Chilean society are pernicious.

In short, the problem cannot be resolved unless qualitative changes are carried out in the dual system of social protection as it was defined and crystallized during the neoliberal experiment. Needed modifications include the creation of a new host of social policies, as much in the institutional sphere as in the operation of the system, which effectively make equity and solidarity guiding principles of social development and thus reverse the reproduction of inequality derived from existing social institutions. Only the full effect of those principles would eliminate dualistic tendencies and halt the systematic transfer of public resources to private entities. Moreover, mechanisms are needed that require the most affluent members of the system to contribute resources to finance basic benefits for the poorest groups, to ensure to all Chileans access to minimum common benefits regardless of each individual's contribution. The provision of universal basic benefits was achieved in Spain, and success in this area was crucial to the consolidation of democracy in that country (Bresser Pereira, Maravall, and Przeworski 1994).

The need for introducing modifications to the social welfare system has not been a part of the discussions on the tasks of transition. Current debate has centered on problems of economic articulation and on political tasks, such as constitutional reforms to overcome authoritarian legacies (designated sena-tors, military prerogatives, and biased electoral rules, among others). Defining a social welfare model that overcomes those distortions and the deficiencies of dualism, while being compatible with the economic model, lies beyond the current transition agenda. Debate on these matters has focused almost entirely on certain instrumental options related to the efficiency of the concentration of social spending, the relief nature of the subsidies, and the effectiveness of the mechanisms for distributing the subsidies. Discussion of these themes has impeded the open debate of other equally fundamental problems, such as the ones related to the global model of social welfare, to the reorganization and decentralization of services intended to overcome its inefficiencies and discrimination, and to the role of the state, the market, and society.

The discussion of a more just welfare model, which is also compatible with the model of economic organization, is not a simple matter. Too many technical, economic, and political questions come into play, not to mention decisive international factors. Given the scope and complexity of the task, and the resistance that will inevitably appear, reforms tending to produce a radical alteration of the managing principles of the welfare model would not be easy to implement. Neither will it be easy to find viable alternative frameworks capable of reconciling an efficient and dynamic economic system with social and political institutions that assure increasing degrees of equality.

Reforming the state will be required for achieving growth with greater social equity. Changes discussed above would not be possible without 1) modifying current administrative structures; 2) modernizing and making more agile the mechanisms of public administration; 3) decentralizing decision making; 4) redefining the responsibilities of the public apparatus, the private sector, and civil society in providing basic social services; and 5) restoring the state's ability to direct the development process according to its criteria and priorities.[12] A task of such magnitude requires elaborate agreements. These are absolutely essential for securing the governmental capacity to ensure that an acceleration of growth and the maintenance of macroeconomic equilibria do not derail the reform of the social welfare system. Nor should economic exigencies impede the incorporation of principles of equity and solidarity that give society the responsibility for eliminating poverty and social exclusion. In addition to reinforcing the role of the state in the coordination of social policies, a social policy reform is crucial for opening participation to provide an area for society to resolve its problems and to create mechanisms that allow democratic control of markets and societal control of the state. Without advancing along this path and facing the challenges that will inevitably arise, it is difficult to foresee the consolidation of democracy.

Notes

1. It is important to emphasize that it is not my intention to describe the totality of the characteristics and consequences of privatizing reforms but rather to stress the characteristics most relevant to the objectives of this chapter.

2. The taxable incomes of those workers who affiliated with the AFP were substantially higher than those remaining with the old state system. In 1988, the average taxable income in the AFP was 46,700 pesos, while in the old system it was 28,000 pesos, thus giving rise to pensions almost 60 percent higher in the AFP.

3. These reforms did not provide a satisfactory solution to any of the problems that affected the social security system, nor did they help to reduce the federal deficit. The state still had to make the same contributions as previously to the pensions of retirees, who became major recipients of the "bonus of recognition" for those who transferred to the private system. This meant that treasury revenues were drastically reduced because the state no longer received fees from those workers who switched to the new system.

4. CEPAL calculations on the basis of the CASEN survey carried out by ODEPLAN in November 1987.

5. For an explanation of the evolution of social indicators during the military government, see Castañeda (1984), Vergara (1990) and Raczynski (1992).

6. In 1990, the fiscal contribution to this sector increased 7 percent above the amount foreseen by the military government for that year and by 21 percent in 1991.

7. The increase in the fiscal contribution to these sectors in 1990 was 39 percent in the housing sector compared to that initially foreseen by the previous administration and 23 percent in 1991. In the education sector, these percentages reached 23 percent in 1990 and 7 percent in 1991.

8. For a description of the programs and actions developed for these three social sectors, see Raczynski (1992, 100-117).

9. For example, despite an increased percentage of the work force (not less than 25 percent) employed only in small enterprise, total resources allocated for that sector via FOSIS do not exceed 10 percent of the state's relief-subsidy spending.

10. The ISAPRES system, which presently covers about 17 percent of the population and accepts only those workers with the highest incomes while rejecting those likely to require costly treatment, spends an average of $200 per beneficiary. State institutions, in contrast, must attend to the population with the fewest resources, with average expenditures of only $50 per beneficiary. Thus, the ISAPRES averages a 40 percent profit while the definancing of public institutions continues to erode the quality of the services offered to the lowest-income population.

11. For example, a growth rate of 6 percent would be insufficient to achieve substantial progress in reducing poverty. At that level, the economy would only be

capable of generating 90,000 jobs, 80,000 of which would go to the existing work force, thus leaving barely 10,000 vacancies to meet the demand for new jobs. See statements by the Minister of Planning and Cooperation, Sergio Molina (1992).

12. This does not necessarily mean increasing the size of the state, or imposing indiscriminate bureaucratic restrictions, or granting control of social services to the state. On the contrary, it is an attempt to give the state the political and technical ability to define the fundamental direction of the strategy of economic and social development.

References

Altimir, Oscar. 1971. "La dimensión de la pobreza en América Latina." *Cuadernos de la CEPAL*. Santiago: ECLAC.

Arellano, José Pablo. 1988. *Políticas sociales y desarrollo. Chile 1924-84.* Ediciones Santiago: CIEPLAN.

Arellano, José Pablo. 1989. "La seguridad social en Chile en los años 90." *Colección Estudios CIEPLAN.* Santiago: CIEPLAN.

Banco Central. Various dates. National Accounts data.

Bresser Pereira, Luiz Carlos, José María Maravall, and Adam Przeworski. 1994. "Economic Reforms in New Democracies: A Social Democratic Approach." In *Latin American Political Economy in the Age of Neoliberal Reform: Theoretical and Comparative Perspectives,* eds. William C. Smith, Carlos H. Acuña, and Eduardo A. Gamarra. Coral Gables, Fla.: North-South Center, University of Miami.

Cabezas, Mabel. 1988. "Revisión metodológica y estadística del gasto social en Chile: 1970-86." *Notas Técnicas CIEPLAN* 114 (May).

Castañeda, Tarciso. 1984. "Contexto socio-económico del descenso de las tasas de mortalidad infantil." *Estudios Públicos* 16. Santiago.

Castañeda, Tarciso. 1990. *Para combatir la pobreza. Política social y descentralización en Chile durante los ochenta.* Santiago: Centro de Estudios Públicos.

Ffrench-Davis, Ricardo. 1981. "The Monetarist Experiment in Chile: A Critical Survey." *World Development* (November).

Ffrench-Davis, Ricardo, and Dagmar Raczynski. 1990. "The Impact of Global Recession and National Policies on Living Standards: Chile, 1973-89." *Notas Técnicas CIEPLAN* 97.

Ffrench-Davis, Ricardo. 1991. "Desarrollo económico y equidad en Chile: herencias y desafíos en el retorno a la democracia." *Colección Estudios CIEPLAN* 31, March 31. Santiago: CIEPLAN.

Faño, N. 1991. "El Fondo de Solidaridad e Inversión Social. ¿En qué estamos pensando?" *Colección Estudios CIEPLAN* 31 (March).

Foxley, Alejandro. 1982. *Latin American Experiments in Neo-Conservative Economics.* Los Angeles and Berkeley: University of California Press.

García, Alvaro. 1991. "Las orientaciones de la política social." *Colección Estudios CIEPLAN* 31 (March).

Garretón, Manuel Antonio. 1987. *Reconstruir la política. Transición y consolidación democrática en Chile.* Santiago: Editorial Andante.

Gurreiri, Adolfo, and Edelberto Torres Rivas, eds. 1990. *Los años noventa: ¿Desarrollo con equidad?* San José: FLACSO-CEPAL.

Haindl, Erik, and C. Weber. 1986. "Impacto redistributivo del gasto social." *Serie de Investigación.* Depto. de Economía, Universidad de Chile.

Haindl, Erik, et al. 1989. *Gasto social efectivo. Un instrumento que asegura la superación definitiva de la pobreza crítica.* Santiago: ODEPLAN-Universidad de Chile.

Iglesias, A., et al. 1991. *Diez años de historia del sistema AFP. Antecedentes estadísticos 1981-1991.* Santiago: AFP Habitat.

Instituto Nacional de Estadística. 1969. Survey of Family Budgets.

Instituto Nacional de Estadística. 1978. Survey of Family Budgets.

Instituto Nacional de Estadística. 1988. Survey of Family Budgets.

Instituto Nacional de Estadística. Various dates. Data on unemployment and salaries.

Larrain, Felipe, ed. 1987. *Desarrollo económico en democracia.* Santiago: Ediciones Universidad Católica de Chile.

Marcel, Mario. 1989. "Privatización y finanzas públicas: el caso de Chile, 1985-88." *Colección Estudios CIEPLAN* 26 (June).

Marcel, Mario. 1991. "El financiamiento del gasto social." *Colección Estudios CIEPLAN* 31 (March).

Martínez, Javier, and Eugenio Tironi. 1985. *Las clases sociales en Chile, cambio y estratificación, 1970-1989.* Santiago: SUR.

Martínez, Javier, and Arturo León. 1984. "La involución del proceso de desarrollo y estructura social." Materiales para Discusión, CED.

Mercurio (El). 1992. July 19.

MIDEPLAN. 1991. *Un proceso de integración al desarrollo. Informe Social 90/91.* Santiago: Ministry of Planning and Cooperation.

Molina, Serio. 1992. Statements to *La Epoca,* March 13.

Muñoz, Oscar. 1991. "Estado, desarrollo y equidad: algunas preguntas pendientes." *Colección Estudios CIEPLAN* 31 (March).

ODEPLAN. (various years). *Informe Social,* Republic of Chile, Santiago.

Raczynski, Dagmar. 1991. "La ficha CAS y la focalización de programas sociales." *Notas Técnicas CIEPLAN* 141.

Raczynski, Dagmar. 1992. "Políticas sociales en Chile: origen, transformaciones y perspectivas." CIEPLAN. Unpublished manuscript.

Riveros, Luis. 1984. "Distribución del ingreso, empleo y política social en Chile." *Documento de Trabajo* 25, CEP.

Sánchez, H. 1990. "Análisis del subsistema de ISAPRES — período 1891-1989." In *Eficacia y calidad del sistema de salud en Chile,* ed. M.I. Romero. Santiago: CPU.

Stallings, Barbara, and R. Kaufman, eds. 1989. *Debt and Democracy in Latin America.* Boulder, Colo.: Westview Press.

Tironi, Eugenio. 1988. *Autoritarismo, modernización y marginalidad. El caso de Chile 1973-89.* Santiago: Editorial Puerta Abierta.

Titmus, Richard. 1968. *Essays on the Welfare State.* London: Allen and Ubwin.

Torche, Arístides. 1987. "Distribuir el ingreso para satisfacer las necesidades básicas." In *Desarrollo económico en democracia,* ed. Felipe Larrain. Santiago: Universidad Católica de Chile.

Valenzuela, Arturo, and Samuel Valenzuela, eds. 1986. *Military Rule in Chile: Dictatorship and Oppositions.* Baltimore: The Johns Hopkins University Press.

Valenzuela, Arturo. 1977. *Political Brokers in Chile: Local Government in a Centralized Polity*. Durham, N.C.: Duke University Press.

Vergara, Pilar. 1985. *Auge y caída del neoliberalismo en Chile*. Santiago: FLACSO.

Vergara, Pilar. 1990. *Políticas hacia la extrema pobreza en Chile, 1973-1988*. Santiago: FLACSO.

Mexico

Selected Macroeconomic Indicators for Mexico

	1982	1983	1984	1985	1986	1987	1988	1989	1990	1991	1992p
Real Gross Domestic Product	*(Percent Average Annual Growth Rates)*										
Total GDP	-0.6	-4.2	3.6	2.6	-3.8	1.7	1.2	3.5	4.4	3.6	2.6
Manufacturing	-2.7	-7.8	5.0	6.1	-5.3	3.0	3.2	7.2	6.1	4.0	1.8
Agriculture	-2.0	2.0	2.7	3.8	-2.7	1.4	-3.8	-2.2	5.9	1.0	-1.4
Construction	-7.1	-19.2	5.4	2.7	-10.3	2.8	-0.4	2.1	7.0	2.4	7.8
Gross Domestic Investment	*(As a Percent of GDP)*										
	26.4	20.2	20.7	22.2	18.3	18.8	21.2	21.7	23.0	23.7	—
Non-Financial Public Sector	*(As a Percent of GDP)*										
Current Revenue	28.9	32.9	32.2	31.2	30.3	30.5	30.2	29.1	29.3	26.2	25.9
Current Expenditures	33.4	33.0	32.1	32.6	37.9	39.1	35.0	30.1	26.7	22.1	20.1
Financial Balance (-Deficit)	-16.9	-8.6	-8.5	-9.6	-15.9	-16.0	-12.4	-5.6	-3.9	1.8	3.4
Prices, Salaries and Unemployment	*(Percent Average Annual Growth Rates)*										
Consumer Prices	59.7	101.6	65.5	57.7	86.2	131.8	114.2	20.0	26.7	22.7	15.5
Real Wages in Manufacturing	0.7	-22.8	-7.1	-2.7	-5.9	-1.9	-1.3	9.0	2.9	4.0	4.3
Unemployment	4.2	6.8	6.0	4.4	4.3	3.9	3.6	3.0	2.8	2.6	—
Real Effective Exchange Rate	*(Index 1980 = 100)*										
	115.2	125.4	102.9	99.1	144.6	157.5	130.1	118.9	118.7	108.0	101.7
Balance of Payments	*(Billions of Dollars)*										
Current Account Balance	6.3	5.4	4.2	1.1	-1.7	4.0	-2.4	-4.0	-7.1	-13.3	-22.8
Trade Balance	6.8	13.8	13.0	8.5	4.6	8.4	1.7	-0.6	-4.4	-11.1	-20.7
Exports	21.2	22.3	24.2	21.7	16.0	20.7	20.6	22.8	26.8	27.1	27.5
Imports	14.4	8.6	11.3	13.2	11.4	12.2	18.9	23.4	31.3	38.2	48.2
Capital Account Balance	9.5	-2.4	-1.1	-2.1	1.1	-1.0	-1.4	1.4	8.5	20.4	26.0
Change in Reserves (- Increase)	3.6	-2.0	-2.2	2.7	0.0	-5.6	6.6	-0.2	-2.3	-8.0	-1.2
Total External Debt	*(Billions of Dollars)*										
Disbursed Debt	86.0	93.0	94.8	96.9	100.9	109.5	100.8	95.4	97.4	101.7	101.1
	(In Percent)										
Interest Payments Due/Exports	47.6	37.5	39.2	37.2	38.3	29.7	29.9	28.3	24.1	21.2	18.7

p = preliminary

Sources: Inter-American Development Bank, *Economic and Social Progress in Latin America*, 1992 and 1993 Reports, and the International Labor Organization.

Chapter Ten

Making Economic Reform Politically Viable: The Mexican Experience

Blanca Heredia

Introduction

Over the last two decades and largely in response to major fiscal and balance-of-payments crises, many developing countries initiated ambitious experiments in market-oriented reform. Beyond their broadly similar roots and their common orientation toward a greater reliance on market mechanisms and toward increasing the financial solvency of the state, these experiments have tended to vary significantly in scope, sustainability, and success.

In accounting for such variance, analysts have increasingly turned their attention to the political and institutional dimensions of economic policy change (Haggard and Kaufman 1992; Nelson 1990; Perkins and Roemer 1991). In spite of avowed attempts to move beyond economic explanations, the rapidly expanding literature on the politics of stabilization and adjustment has tended, with few exceptions, to regard economic cleavages as the main determinants of political action and, therefore, as the single most important variable in accounting for policy outcomes. Especially among those approaches that emphasize social structures (Frieden 1991), but also among those that focus on state institutions, politics often appears to be a mere reflection of underlying social struggles organized around the pursuit of competing economic interests. Such an image explains most of the literature's emphasis upon the balance of power between economic winners and losers in accounting for cross-national differences in policy orientation and effectiveness, as well as the generalized tendency to view political institutions as filters that simply mitigate or magnify the underlying conflicts of interest that ultimately determine economic policy change.[1]

Mexico's stabilization and adjustment experience challenges many of the expectations derived from these widely held assumptions. Extremely costly and far-reaching changes in economic policy failed to elicit an organized response on the part of losers. Winners extracted personal rewards rather than pushing for greater reform. Coalitions underwent continuous shifts in the course of economic reform and systematically failed to correspond fully to changes in the balance of forces among competing economic groups. This lack of correspondence can be partly explained by the structure of the Mexican private economy, by policy sequencing and policy design. Most of the explanation, I will argue, lies in the nature of the Mexican political system.

This chapter examines the political conditions that allowed successful implementation of stabilization and structural adjustment in Mexico, and it analyzes some of the effects of such processes upon the country's political system. The main argument developed in this chapter is that economic liberalization was made possible largely by a structure of political authority based on hierarchical patronage networks that cut across classes and sectors and by the unprecedented degree of elite cohesion that characterized the implementation of economic policy change. More generally, this chapter suggests that the relative causal weight of economic cleavages in the process of economic policy making, rather than being constant across space and time, is itself determined by the nature of the formal and informal institutions through which political power is generated and reproduced in different periods and national settings.

The clientelistic structures upon which Mexico's government has historically rested systematically inhibited collective action organized around common economic interests and made discretionary exercise of state power and elite cohesion pivotal to the operation and reproduction of authoritarian rule. In the course of economic reform, such structures limited the ability of losers to resist economic reform collectively, while they simultaneously provided state officials with capacity to distribute selectively its benefits and costs. High levels of elite cohesion, which derived from the marginalization of developmentalist currents within the state apparatus after 1982 and from the monopolistic power-sharing arrangements that have long governed relations within the political elite, allowed policy reformers to recast radically the institutional makeup of the Mexican economy without compromising political stability or regime continuity.

The exclusionary effects of extreme elite cohesion, along with reduced space for the discretionary enforcement of legal and administrative rules associated with economic liberalization, however, have introduced significant tensions in the basic structure of the Mexican political system. Traditional forms of consensus building at the intra-elite level are proving increasingly incompatible with the exigencies of administrative rationality. Sectoral and regional networks of patronage are breaking down and the attempts to generate new mediations between society and government — such as those represented by the *Programa Nacional de Solidaridad* (National Solidarity

Program — PRONASOL) — have still to prove their effectiveness. Political parties, in spite of increased visibility, remain weak, and advances in citizen-based forms of political interaction occur in a highly fragmentary and unequal fashion. In sum, traditional forms of governance are severely stressed, while alternatives still remain very much in the making.

The first section of this chapter provides a brief overview of the basic structure of the Mexican political system. Section two examines the specific political conditions that made the implementation of economic liberalization possible as well as some of the most important effects of such process upon the organization of Mexican politics. The final section offers a tentative assessment of the balance between continuity and change in the recent evolution of the Mexican political system.

Power and Policy: Governance in a Fragmented Polity

Through legislation, direct intervention, and rationing of various sorts, governments affect prices and in so doing, strongly condition both the relative distribution of income and wealth and the aggregate outcomes of individual economic choices. In a world of scarce resources, economic policy making is bound to be an intensely contested process. Groups and individuals will seek to influence government policy so as to further their absolute and relative economic gains. Government officials, in turn, will tend to favor those decisions and courses of action that maximize their ability to retain effective command.

The relative sensibility of state authorities to competing interests and demands tends to be powerfully influenced by the nature of political institutions (North 1990). Institutions shape the strategies through which groups and individuals acquire, and maintain the ability to acquire, their preferred economic objectives. They condition the ways in which interests are defined, structured, and represented in the political realm, thereby critically affecting the relative political costs and benefits to policy makers derived from meeting or failing to meet alternative pressures and demands (Bates 1990; Alt and Shepsle 1990).

This section examines the institutional context of economic policy making in Mexico. The analysis focuses on the interest-aggregation effects of an authority structure premised on the operation of hierarchical and segmented networks of patronage and on the particular ways through which the reproduction of such networks came to be historically reconciled with elite cohesion and with effective economic governance (Bates 1990, 31-54; Alt and Shepsle 1990).

The Structure of Mexican Politics:
The Centrality of Fragmentation

Government in Mexico has historically rested upon the coordination of segmented and hierarchical patronage networks that cut across classes and sectors, rather than upon a configuration of power among classes. The critical importance of patron-client relations in Mexican politics historically lay in the centrality of political fragmentation. Existing originally as the result of a juxtaposition between an urban, Spanish-dominated political order and a vast hinterland inhabited by a variegated collection of indigenous groups, political fragmentation survived due to the persistent weakness of a sense of shared membership within a common political order (Escalante 1992).

In polities where actors fail to recognize themselves as bound by common rules, the state's authority to issue norms and commands must be regularly compromised to ensure effective capacity for governance (Escalante 1992). The legal order must be systematically violated to allow the reproduction of authority relations premised on the widespread social acceptance of differential, rather than equal, rights and obligations. Where all groups demand and expect special treatment and where all recognize each others' claims as valid, government must operate through the continuous negotiation of the legal order.[2]

Under a setting of this nature, interests tend to aggregate vertically rather than horizontally.[3] This is so because the most rational course of action in the pursuit of interests and values, whose realization depends upon protection against equal legal treatment, is to develop privileged links with those willing and able to provide such protection. In the economic realm, the salience of vertical over horizontal political bonds produces situations in which income and profit maximization tend to be strongly associated with the ability to insure privileged access to government or largesse in the enforcement of legal and administrative rules. To the collective action dilemmas that the pursuit of common economic interests generally entails, clientelism adds a different and often insurmountable one: the competition for the divisible benefits that allow everyone to further his or her economic gains.

In a fragmented polity, governance as a whole tends to rely primarily upon hierarchical and segmented networks of patronage whose reproduction is critically contingent upon the discretionary exercise of state power. Power relations tend to be grounded in hierarchical ties that insure loyalty and obedience in exchange for protection against equal legal treatment. The centrality of vertical and segmented bonds reduces the political value of collective goods and turns the pursuit of divisible benefits into the basic stuff of politics. Collective action around shared economic interests is systematically discouraged, thus limiting politicians' sensitivity toward the costs and benefits that policy imposes upon those similarly situated in the economy.

The Sources of Stability: Centralization and Elite Cohesion

The constraints that clientelism puts on the development of horizontal forms of interest aggregation have granted Mexican state officials considerable autonomy vis-à-vis collective economic interests in the making of public policy. Such autonomy historically has been balanced, however, by acute dependence upon cooperation or acquiescence of political, social, and economic elites whose power derives from their ability to grant or obtain particularistic benefits for themselves and their clients.

Elite cohesion is a critical condition of effective domination in any political system. In clientelistic polities, however, the unbinding quality of formal rules makes cooperation among elites particularly difficult because common principles for assessing competing claims to political power tend to be in short supply. Thus, the propensity of excluded elites to resort to force is especially high, and political instability often becomes the key means through which to allocate state power among rival claimants.

Throughout most of this century, Mexico has avoided instability associated with the reproduction of clientelistic power relations. This accomplishment has largely been achieved through power-sharing arrangements that allowed for the orderly distribution and redistribution of the right to use state authority in the pursuit of private and particularistic goals (González Graf 1986, 33-40). Critical to the development of cooperative arrangements among Mexican elites were the high costs of more than ten years of revolutionary violence and the new distribution of power that resulted.

By the end of the 1920s, though no single revolutionary faction fully controlled Mexico, one group had enough power to make it too costly for rivals to attempt further to alter by force the prevailing distribution of power. A system was thereby established in which the members of the revolutionary family agreed to share, rather than to compete for, political power (Knight 1992, 113-145). Through restricted electoral competition and the creation of the *Partido Revolucionario Institucional* (Institutional Revolutionary Party — PRI) — a central political machine controlled by government — public posts came to be regularly distributed according to the relative power positions of different factions. On the other hand, the machine's capacity periodically to ensure electoral majorities for the government granted the added benefit of providing democratic legitimation to decisions arrived at through non-democratic means.

Once in control of the state apparatus, the ability of political elites to exercise effective national rule still faced a number of extremely important obstacles. The destruction of the Porfirian order had strengthened regionally based political and military bosses. Without their cooperation or acquiescence, elites could scarcely govern; yet, in exchange for loyalty and support regional elites demanded the right to use state authority in ways that systematically undermined effective national rule. In addressing this problem, the state created and controlled functionally based national organizations. Through the PRI's sectoral corporations, the government was able to check the power of regionally based elites, while simultaneously using local and regional bosses as a means to control sectoral party leaders (Kaufman 1988, 191-216; Eisenstadt and Lemarchand 1981).

Restricted electoral competition and the centralized political machine have allowed for remarkably high levels of elite cohesion, political stability, and regime continuity. The incorporation of popular sectors through corporatist institutions, which act as national (as opposed to regional) networks of patronage directly managed by the executive, have significantly reduced the costs that regional fragmentation tends to impose upon effective national rule in clientelistic settings. Both factors have greatly facilitated the overall tasks of governance. Since the private use of state authority often breeds administrative inefficiency, however, additional factors account for Mexico's long decades of relatively high levels of effectiveness and continuity in the making of economic policy.

Clientelism and Economic Governance: Managing the Tensions

Numerous examples testify to the potential for conflict that arises between political and administrative rationality in political systems organized on the basis of patron-client relations. Clientelistic ties tend to undermine bureaucratic coherence because patrons tend to colonize state institutions, turning them into weakly connected islands of privatized public authority (Evans 1989). Under those conditions, state officials have little capacity to define goals and pursue them effectively. If unchecked, clientelism reduces the political value of access to government itself, thus eroding the central premise upon which ultimately rest all forms of power in fragmented polities.

In Mexico, two key mechanisms appear to have been pivotal in mitigating the high administrative costs of patronage networks on effective economic governance: the constitutional prohibition against presidential reelection and the development of technocratic policy making institutions relatively insulated from the political process. The first mechanism substituted absolute expansion of the political elite for high levels of elite mobility and circulation.[4] Rather than continuously expanding through the growth of state intervention the pool of power resources available for distribution through the growth of state intervention, that pool was expanded by placing strict temporal limits upon tenure in office. Through presidential non-reelection, a relatively constant or, at best, moderately expanding resource base could be distributed and redistributed among a large political class. The perverse administrative effects associated with the absolute growth of shares of political power were significantly reduced, ensuring the value of those shares.

Accommodation between technical and political rationality was also facilitated by the creation of a set of policy making institutions relatively insulated from electoral politics and, thus, relatively more protected from the particularistic demands that pervaded other parts of the state apparatus. The most prominent of these institutions were the Central Bank and the Finance Ministry (Maxfield 1990). Access to them did not primarily depend upon the kinds of resources that allowed sectoral elites in the official party to insure electoral majorities. Neither did such access exclusively depend upon clientelistic networks centered around the president himself. Though good relations with incumbents occupying higher echelons in the executive branch were certainly helpful for a successful career in public financial institutions, technical competence and merit were also crucial.

The hegemonic position that public financiers attained within the economic policy making apparatus was largely the result of their superior administrative capabilities vis-à-vis other government agencies, as well as their traditionally close ties with private financial elites. While simultaneously ensuring coherence and continuity in macrolevel policy, these characteristics were a brake on potential explosive budget growth often present in clientelistic political systems.

Throughout the postrevolutionary era, discretionary enforcement of the law was pervasive and constituted a key resource in the reproduction of the fragmented networks of patronage upon which political domination effectively relied. Discipline, however, was achieved by a hierarchical structure that vested ultimate discretionary power in the president and by a series of formal and informal arrangements that mitigated the administrative costs of discretionary power itself.

Rapid and sustained economic growth from 1940 up to the early 1970s enhanced the effective operation of the formal and informal arrangements upon which orderly relations at the intra-elite level depended. Economic growth provided opportunities for social mobility and significant resources to sustain and reproduce the patronage networks that supported the edifice of government. As economic conditions deteriorated and as effects of social and economic modernization became evident, traditional political structures and institutions were caught between growing demands and reduced resources. The reconciliation between administrative and political rationality became increasingly difficult. Serious strains also appeared in the previously functional relationship between the two main tasks of the electoral system: the distribution of power shares among political elites and the democratic legitimation of the regime.

From 1970 to 1982, highly liquid international financial markets provided resources which were augmented by the huge oil revenues that became available toward the end of that period. The multiple tensions derived from economic instability and the emergence of more vocal demands for new forms of political participation were basically met by the expansion of the political elite. New groups were incorporated into the political system through the expansion of direct state intervention in economic and social life and through the partial liberalization of electoral competition (Bazdresch and Levy 1991; Dornbusch and Edwards 1991).

The availability of low-cost foreign financial resources loosened fiscal discipline. Government agencies such as the Finance Ministry and Central Bank, which had traditionally managed to impose a relatively orthodox fiscal and monetary policy, lost ground while developmentalists in sectoral ministries and state firms advanced. Since the developmentalists were never fully able to break the control of fiscal conservatives in the Finance Ministry and the Central Bank, a war of attrition ensued which eroded policy coherence and effectiveness.[5] The extraordinarily swift expansion of the public economy as a whole diminished the executive's ability to manage its own administrative structure and exacerbated tensions with private economic elites.[6]

Although instrumental in defusing opposition to the regime, the partial liberalization of the electoral process enhanced the importance and visibility of elections and made it progressively more difficult for the official party to reconcile its functions in the realm of intra-elite relations with its legitimizing tasks. Rather than a source of democratic legitimacy, electoral contests became the privileged means by which to question the regime's democratic credentials (Loaeza 1989, 273-285).

Sharp deterioration of administrative competence caused by the formidable growth of the public economy, extreme economic dependence upon oil revenue, and continued access to foreign credit made the economic system particularly vulnerable to the extremely adverse international economic conditions of the early 1980s. Rising interest rates and shrinking oil prices marked the end of the attempt to reproduce authoritarian rule by means of an economic growth strategy premised on the rapid expansion of state intervention in economic life.

Economic Crisis and Institutional Reform:
The Political Logic of Structural Adjustment
The Political Conditions of Policy Effectiveness

The explosion of the debt crisis in 1982 marked the beginning of the worst economic crisis in Mexico since the 1930s. During that year, GNP experienced a negative growth rate of -0.5 percent, inflation reached 98.9

percent, the value of the peso was devaluated 466 percent, and the government increased its foreign debt by almost $6 billion. By the end of 1982, total foreign debt amounted to $84 billion (89.9 percent of GNP) and interest payments absorbed 43.6 percent of total export value.[7]

For government finances, 1982 was equally stark. After several decades of relatively small fiscal deficits[8] — especially compared to other countries in the region — the budget deficit jumped from 6.5 percent of GNP in 1980 to 15.6 percent in 1982 (NAFINSA 1989). Since the deficit exceeded total public investment, its rise indicated that the government's foreign loans were financing not only investment but also current expenditures.[9]

When Miguel de la Madrid (1982-1988) assumed power in December 1982, he faced a chaotic economic situation and a political system beset by growing strains and tensions at various levels. Almost from the beginning, the new administration stressed the need to use the crisis as an occasion to transform the country's economic structure. For the president and his economic advisers, the crisis provided the opportunity to overcome obstacles to promote growth through the elimination of the conditions that had made possible the "excesses" of the two previous administrations. At first the nature of this transformation was only vaguely defined. By 1986, due both to the very limited success of initial fiscal retrenchment and to the additional external shock produced by the sharp drop in oil prices that year, the structural adjustment program acquired its distinctive promarket orientation and began in earnest.

Overall, the program had two basic dimensions: macroeconomic stabilization and structural adjustment. It encompassed three major phases (Lustig 1992): From December 1982 through 1985-1986, economic policy addressed price stabilization and relied heavily upon both fiscal and monetary retrenchment. During the second phase from 1985 to 1987, advances toward structural adjustment — especially in the area of foreign trade — were made along with efforts to mitigate the recessionary effects of orthodox stabilization measures. The third phase, from December 1987 to the present, began with the launching of the Economic Solidarity Pact, which incorporated both an orthodox (fiscal discipline) and a heterodox (incomes policy) component as well as a decisive move toward trade opening.[10] The third phase was also marked by the deepening of privatization and deregulation and entailed a more integrated approach to fiscal and structural dimensions of economic reform.

In carrying out what proved to be an extremely complex, risky, and costly process, certain key features of the political system were extremely important. Particularly significant were the coincidence between the explosion of the crisis and the beginning of a new presidential term, the wide array of formal and informal discretionary faculties with which the Mexican presidency is endowed, the historical hegemony of public financial institutions in the definition of macropolicy, and the PRI's virtually monopolistic control over the electoral process.

The beginning of a new presidential term was important because in Mexico non-reelection has made it possible for the system to adjust periodically to new correlations of forces. Non-reelection has guaranteed the coexistence of a very strong presidency with considerable elite mobility. For those who feel inadequately represented under a given administration, knowing that non-reelection brings the possibility of changing relative power positions reduces incentives to exit the system. By increasing tolerance to what are perceived as short-term rather than permanent costs, non-reelection acted as a critical buffer between the behavior of particular presidents and the power of the presidential institution as such.

In the case of President de la Madrid, the political turnover usually associated with the inauguration of a *sexenio* was particularly important because it entailed a major transformation of the ways in which new presidents traditionally coped with the need to assure renovation while at the same time ensuring the continued representation of major political forces and policy trends (Smith 1979). One of the most salient features of de la Madrid's administration was the severe reduction of pluralism within the upper echelons of government and the virtual monopolization of the "commanding heights" of the executive branch by technocratic elites drawn from public financial institutions (Kaufman 1988, 83). Almost half of the new ministers came from the Ministry of Budget and Planning, which was headed by de la Madrid from 1979 to 1981, and the rest came mostly from the Finance Ministry or from the Central Bank (Hernández Rodríguez 1987).

The close ties between the president and his ministerial officials, along with the unprecedented degree of professional and ideological homogeneity, constituted one of the de la Madrid administration's most valuable political resources. The acute costs of the war of attrition between rival policy currents within the state's economic bureaucracy under José López Portillo (1977-1982) and the virtually complete loss of prestige of statist and developmentalist policy orientations during 1982 were crucial to the creation of this resource. Those events paved the way for a radical redefinition of the balance of power within government and for the forceful comeback of those groups associated with the state's most powerful policy making institutions: the Central Bank and the Finance Ministry.

The return of public financial institutions to the center of policy formulation was bolstered by acute financial scarcity and the need to reestablish relations with international creditors. Ascendancy of institutions, which were traditionally much less open than developmentalist agencies to the particularistic demands of large numbers of societal groups, made it possible to introduce sharp cuts in government spending. The centrality of these institutions goes a long way toward explaining the administration's ability to reduce total government expenditures from 44.5 percent of GNP in 1982 to 41 percent in 1983 and to sustain an orthodox fiscal stance throughout the whole *sexenio* (Banco de México 1984).

Private economic elites' close ties to public financial institutions were also instrumental in reestablishing cooperative relations with major business groups. Those relations had been seriously injured by de la Madrid's predecessor's decision to expropriate private banks in September 1982. Support of this group was critical to the pursuit, as well as the success, of the government's market-oriented reform strategy.

The large array of both legal and informal presidential powers, along with the extensive systems of control developed over decades, gave the president space for political maneuver despite extremely stringent macroeconomic constraints. Discretionary executive power was crucial, for instance, in recuperating or maintaining the support of key social groups through particularistic negotiations and concessions. Along with benefits from privatization that accrued to dominant economic groups, federally subsidized foreign exchange eased the burden of repayment of private foreign debt and constitute good examples of presidential manipulation in relation to private economic elites. Largesse in the application of controls over the financial management and employment policy in *Petróleos Mexicanos* (PEMEX) — Mexico's largest earner of foreign exchange — is yet another example of the usefulness of presidential discretionary powers.[11]

The highly fragmented quality of political relations and traditional power-sharing arrangements that had long provided cooperation at the intra-elite level proved vital in allowing the political system to cope with the acute tensions associated with crisis and adjustment. Political fragmentation imposed often insurmountable obstacles to resistance organized on the basis of shared economic interests. Potential allies were pitted against one another in their desperate pursuit of particular benefits. Such obstacles were magnified by the highly unequal impacts of the economic crisis and adjustment measures at the regional, sectoral, and subsectoral levels, as well as by the progressive marginalization from the centers of decision making within those political elites most responsive to the interests of economic losers.

In the case of industrialists, for example, collective action against the government proved extremely difficult to organize and sustain because government policy tended to exacerbate — intentionally or not — differences that naturally exist among private firms due to size and sectoral or regional location. A long history of particularistic negotiations with the state apparatus and a set of interest-based, private sector organizations — along with the crosscutting and often contradictory effects of different economic policy measures — further limited the ability of badly hurt economic sectors or politically active business elites to forge opposition coalitions and alliances. Deep mistrust of the effectiveness and uniformity of enforcement of legal and administrative rules — and the equally entrenched expectations of privileged concessions — finally turned business' weak credibility into an asset for carrying out economic reform. Lack of credibility was important because it reduced incentives to oppose policy change actively. Discretionary executive power and hope of preferential treatment were critical because they made individual negotiation the most reasonable course of action for private economic elites (Elizondo 1993; Heredia 1992).

For labor as a whole, crisis and adjustment entailed enormous costs in terms of both wages and employment. From 1983 to 1988, real wages fell between 40 percent and 50 percent and employment grew by an average annual rate of only 0.4 percent (Lustig 1992). In spite of this, labor in Mexico exhibited considerable quiescence, especially when compared to the militant behavior of the working class in other Latin American countries during the same period.

Table 1
Strikes in Brazil, Chile, and Mexico

Year	Brazil	Chile	Mexico
1983	312	41	216
1984	534	38	427
1985	843	42	159
1986	1492	41	312
1987	2369	81	174
1988	1954	72	132
1989	4189	101	118

Source: ILO (various years).

In accounting for the relatively low levels of labor unrest in Mexico, unequal allocation of the costs of economic adjustment among different segments of the working class and especially the continued loyalty of union elites to the government proved crucial. As indicated by the evolution of minimum versus manufacturing wages from 1982 on, salaries of unionized workers tended to suffer less than those of unorganized ones. From 1982 to 1990, minimum wages fell by 47.7 percent, while those in the manufacturing sector experienced a fall of "only" 19.8 percent.[12] Union elites, who supported government policy containing minimum wages as a key ingredient of stabilization, avoided heavy political costs because maneuvering room was available in their private contractual negotiations with individual firms.

Not all unionized workers did as "well" in terms of wages during the 1980s. Real wages of central government employees, for instance, fell 52.5

percent between 1982 and 1988.[13] In this case, direct state control over public employees' unions, along with the compensation provided by an 18.1 percent growth of public employment from 1982 to 1988, helps explain why overt resistance was low.[14] Equally important in accounting for the political quiescence of public employees during this period is the considerable leeway that bureaucrats in Mexico have long enjoyed in the use of public authority as a source of private gain. Though figures on this issue are unavailable, interview data suggests that corruption tended to increase during these years, thus acting as a "spontaneous" adjustment mechanism for the sharp drop in public sector wages.

Even where sharp wage cuts took place — as in the case of public sector employees — unions tended to remain loyal to the government. The nature of union-government relations in Mexico explains this phenomenon. Networks of reciprocity that connect workers, labor elites, and government officials operate on the basis of long-term relations. Short-term costs of supporting the government during periods of stress are assumed by unions in the expectation that compensation will be forthcoming once better times arrive. Rather than being dependent on the outcome of any given round of the game, relations between unions and the government are premised upon the longevity of the game itself. Equally important is the fact that transactions involved in the relationship comprise much more than just wages. They include both legal and illicit economic and political benefits for union elites, as well as various compensations for the rank and file.

The highly unequal regional distribution of the costs of crisis and adjustment also proved instrumental in making stabilization politically viable. Though rates of growth from 1982 to 1988 were overall either very moderate or negative, some states fared better than others. During that period, GDP in Baja California Norte, Tabasco, and Tamaulipas decreased by over 6 percent; in Chiapas and Baja California Sur, GDP fell by more than 10 percent, while Puebla's economy was stagnant (-0.8 percent). The picture was somewhat more positive in stages such as Jalisco and Michoacán, which did manage to eke out some growth, and in some less populous states, such as Quintana Roo, where the economy grew a cumulative 11.9 percent.[15]

Also revealing is the change in states' allocation of federal public investment from 1983 to 1988, especially when compared to corresponding allocations during the preceding administration. As shown in Table 2, for most states the share of federal public funding during the 1983-1988 period fell in relation to that of 1977-1982. Only one-third of Mexico's states experienced some positive redistribution. Among them was the Federal District, whose share of total federal public funding increased from an annual average of 22.5 percent during 1977-1982 to 26.6 percent in the period from 1983 to 1988.

Table 2
Federal Public Investment by State
(Annual Average % Share by Presidential Period)
Presidential Period

State	1977-1982 100.00	1983-1988 100.00	Deviation
Aguascalientes	0.39	0.58	+0.19
Baja California	2.20	1.84	-0.36
Baja California Sur	0.97	0.71	-0.26
Campeche	2.38	5.44	+3.06
Coahuila	3.33	1.93	-1.40
Colima	1.01	1.04	+0.03
Chiapas	4.82	1.73	-3.09
Chihuahua	1.98	1.57	-0.41
Distrito Federal	22.48	26.61	+4.13
Durango	0.99	0.88	-0.11
Guanajuato	1.93	1.29	-0.64
Guerrero	1.84	1.82	-0.02
Hidalgo	2.03	1.80	-0.23
Jalisco	2.41	2.40	-0.01
México	3.33	3.14	-0.19
Michoacán	3.01	5.95	+2.94
Morelos	0.66	0.59	-0.07
Nayarit	0.82	0.54	-0.28
Nuevo Leon	2.89	2.14	-0.75
Oaxaca	2.52	2.31	-0.21
Puebla	1.41	1.50	+0.09
Querétaro	0.87	0.76	-0.11
Quintana Roo	0.80	0.71	-0.09
San Luis Potosí	1.15	1.28	+0.13
Sinaloa	2.53	1.75	-0.78
Sonora	2.18	1.94	-0.24
Tabasco	7.77	2.53	-5.24
Tamaulipas	5.32	2.47	-2.85
Tlaxcala	0.41	0.37	-0.04
Veracruz	14.01	7.71	-6.30
Yucatán	0.80	0.88	+0.08
Zacatecas	0.77	0.54	-0.23

Sources: For the 1977-1982 period, Juan José Palacios (1989), Table 1, p. 270. Figures for the 1983-1988 period based on the author's own data.

As with business and labor, the highly differential regional impact of crisis and adjustment expanded the government's room for maneuver by dispersing costs and, thus, dividing losers. In mitigating resistance and crafting political support for economic policy change, however, the elitist nature of the political system and the multidimensional and long-term character of elite-client relations were absolutely central in allowing policy reformers to manipulate the highly unequal costs of crisis and adjustment effectively.

Following the impressive showing of the *Partido Acción Nacional* (PAN) in the municipal elections of the states of Chihuahua and Durango in 1983, the political reform process initiated during the López Portillo administration was postponed to allow the government to recover control of the electoral sphere and to continue using the distribution of electoral posts as a key means to retain the loyalty of sectoral party elites. In exchange for their cooperation with adjustment measures, labor, peasant, and popular sector leaders gained continued representation within the government. Access to power positions allowed these elites to reproduce, in turn, ascendancy over their rank and file by doling out particularistic benefits for selected clients.

The removal or marginalization from the centers of economic decision making of previously important members of the political elite deprived their clients of their only true source of unity and of the single most important lever to resist economic policy change effectively. Widespread expectation for renewed access to government power during the subsequent presidential administration mitigated the incentives for defection among disfavored elites. Finally, the continued discretionary enforcement of legal and administrative rules for those directly involved in government facilitated the reproduction of significant levels of intra-elite cohesion.

In sum, the combination of a fragmented polity and an executive endowed with formidable discretionary powers made it possible for the Mexican government to carry out a very severe process of economic adjustment without having to incur the costs of widespread social and political mobilization. The successful implementation of stabilization and adjustment itself allowed regime elites to recuperate control over the state apparatus and major economic forces reinforcing the political system's capacity to provide both stability and effective governance.

The Political Consequences of Stabilization and Adjustment

Substantive economic policy reform also entailed important political costs: increasing conflict at the intra-elite level, mounting problems in the electoral sphere, and growing tensions in the management of relations between federal and regional authorities. Economic liberalization magnified the opportunities for intra-elite conflict accumulated over the long decades of rapid social and economic change. To the strains introduced by the growing importance of technical versus mass-based elites, and the tensions from the rapid expansion of the political class during the 1970s, economic policy change added a rapid reduction of the power shares available for distribution and a radical reduction of pluralism.

Toward the end of the de la Madrid administration, what had initially appeared as a temporary recomposition of the political class and a short-term reduction of the political resources available for distribution increasingly became perceived as more permanent. When Carlos Salinas was nominated in 1977 as the PRI presidential candidate, this perception widened. What had been taken as temporary setbacks were now viewed as an imminent threat of permanent political exclusion. Carlos Salinas's highly visible role in the economic reform, along with his technocratic background, alienated important segments of the political class. His nomination precipitated the worst intra-elite crisis since the 1930s. Prominent members of the revolutionary family headed by Cuauhtémoc Cárdenas, the son of Lázaro Cárdenas, one of the PRI's founders, defected from the ruling party and organized a large, left-of-center coalition that managed effectively to challenge the PRI's hegemonic electoral position for the first time since its creation. Conflict among political elites overflowed the bounds of party and state and spilled into the electoral sphere (Reding 1988). As in other non- or semi-competitive electoral contexts, Mexican elections have historically had two main functions: 1) to provide democratic forms of legitimation to decisions arrived at through nondemocratic means and 2) to organize elite consensus through the periodic distribution and redistribution of power shares among its members.[16] The first function is carried out during the actual casting of votes; the second one is performed during the internal negotiation process through which official party candidates are nominated.

Since the creation of the ruling party — and especially from 1940 to 1970 — the PRI's monopolistic hold over the electoral terrain and the electoral efficiency of its corporatist structure made elections simultaneously functional both to legitimation and to the regulation of intra-elite relations. While "automatically" ensuring — via sectoral elite control over popular sectors — the translation of consensus within the elite into majority votes for the PRI, the inclusiveness of corporatist arrangements, the absence of electoral competition, and the benefits derived from long decades of rapid and sustained economic growth turned the intraparty candidate selection process into the most important aspect of elections.[17]

As Mexican society became more complex and diverse, the balance of power among social groups within the party and outside it underwent significant transformations. Rapid industrialization, and an even faster process of urbanization, diminished first the relative weight of the PRI's peasant sector and, later, the position of the labor sector vis-à-vis the heterogeneous popular sector (Pacheco Méndez 1991, 7-31). Increasing electoral and political importance of cities, and the attendant growth of groups excluded from corporatist structures, placed additional burdens upon both the labor and the popular sectors of the PRI. In addition to the strains associated with the internal recomposition of the balance of forces within the party itself, groups located outside the PRI gained importance, and changes in traditional patterns of political recruitment became more costly. Critical, in this sense, were the costs imposed upon party elites by the mounting importance of bureaucratic and technocratic careers for gaining access to power positions within the state apparatus.

In combination, these trends gradually eroded the ability of the government's political machine to ensure the reproduction of intra-elite consensus and provide democratic legitimation to intra-elite agreements and decisions. As a result, after 1970, the ruling party experienced gradual and steady electoral losses. In an effort to cope with these mounting electoral challenges, regime elites introduced changes in electoral legislation and, beginning in the 1970s, began implementation of a highly regulated process of electoral opening (Molinar Horcasitas 1991). Opportunities for competition were thereby moderately increased and the risks of non-institutionalized forms of mobilization and participation significantly reduced.

It has been persuasively argued, however, that the increase in electoral competition heightened the significance and visibility of elections and, thus, heightened the tension between the official party's role as an electoral machine and its role as provider of order at the intra-elite level (Gómez and Bailey 1990, 57-87). The government's need to respond to the demand for competitive and credible elections became increasingly incompatible with the need to insure elite consensus through power-sharing arrangements unrelated or insensitive to electoral competition as such.

Crisis and adjustment throughout the 1980s magnified the social and political challenges generated by long-term socioeconomic modernization and exacerbated tensions within the ruling party. Six years of zero growth, along with the social costs of stabilization and structural adjustment, imposed a heavy toll on an electoral machine that relied on the government's ability to provide goods and services in exchange for votes. The extensive use of corporatist controls to contain popular sector demands and to repress growing social discontent further debilitated corporatist elites — especially in the cities — reducing their capacity to assure continued electoral support for the PRI.[18]

Large income losses in the middle class were also important in eroding the PRI's electoral strength. Many in this sector became independent voters.[19] Formal representation within the PRI has largely excluded middle sectors, for whom the growth of independent civic and political organizations has been particularly important. Middle sectors now constitute the bulk of the PAN's

electoral base, and their vote tends to respond either to ideological considerations or to short-term cost-benefit calculations.

Finally, cleavages within the national political elite further damaged the
government's electoral machine and placed added competitive demands
upon it. In clientelistic political systems, competition tends to strengthen
clients and magnify pressures on government resources as the means to
ensure electoral majorities.[20] Competition erodes deferential clientelistic ties,
favoring instead more strategic ones that pressure budgetary resources. Thus,
the budgetary discipline required to ensure macroeconomic stability is not
easily reconciled with the needs of a political system based upon patronage.

To the costs that crisis and adjustment imposed upon intra-elite relations
and the government's electoral machinery, one must add the costs of managing
the relations between central state authorities and local power elites. In this
realm, crisis and adjustment also acted as catalysts of longer-term processes of
social transformation and translated into heightened degrees of electoral
conflict and competition at the regional level, while increasing tensions in the
overall relationship between federal and local levels of government.

Regional diversity has long made the coordination of local power
arrangements in Mexico a vital ingredient of effective governance (Meyer
1983, 131-147; Palacios 1988). One of the greatest achievements of the
postrevolutionary political system was its ability to provide a highly flexible
and resilient framework for managing center-periphery relations. This framework rested upon a flexible and heterogeneous collection of practices and
institutions that allowed for variable degrees of regional autonomy, while
simultaneously ensuring significant levels of coordination and centralization.

Political centralization associated with stabilization and structural adjustment, the reduction of the resources to shape social and economic relations
at the local level (produced by state retrenchment), and the heavy costs these
processes exacted on the corporate electoral machinery accelerated the
potential for tension in center-periphery relations accumulated over years of
rapid socioeconomic development. Governors, trapped between local political and economic elites, who were strengthened by reduced state intervention
and increasingly tight controls from the center, found it more and more
difficult to broker the relationship between federal and local power structures
adequately. Erosion of traditional sectoral identities made regional solidarities
— mostly defined in anti-centralistic terms — into a vehicle for collective
action. As a result, in the course of the 1980s, intraparty and electoral conflict
increased in many states. Opposition parties, particularly the PAN, obtained
important wins in regional electoral contests, and the need for overt
intervention by the president in regional affairs became more frequent.

Increasing problems in the effective and stable management of center-
periphery relations are revealed in the cases of Mexican governors who failed

to complete their mandate. From 1988 to 1992, eight out of twelve of these governors were directly removed by the center to ensure governance at the regional level or subordination to the center. Not since the Miguel Alemán *sexenio* (1940-1952) had so many governors been forced out of office (Anderson 1971; Camp 1982). The rise of direct presidential intervention in regional politics suggests that the traditional mechanisms for reconciling relative regional autonomy and federal coordination are increasingly unable to function spontaneously. Overall then, along with the significant gains that stabilization and structural adjustment entailed for continued political stability and the recuperation of regime elites' governing capacity, crisis and adjustment also imposed important political costs. Particularly affected were order and cooperation at the intra-elite level in the operation of the government's electoral machinery and in center-periphery relations.

Continuity and Change in Contemporary Mexican Politics

When Carlos Salinas de Gortari assumed the presidency in December 1988, he inherited both the successes and the costs of the economic policy of his predecessor. Major advances in the realm of stabilization and structural adjustment facilitated the continuation and deepening of market-oriented reform. A manageable fiscal deficit, the endurance of fiscal austerity, and the removal of many of the initially very strong political and bureaucratic constraints operating against economic liberalization provided the new administration with important assets in the further restructuring of the Mexican economy.

These conditions allowed the Salinas administration to complete the privatization and deregulation processes and the tax reform efforts initiated during the de la Madrid administration. Between 1989 and 1990, 132 out of the 412 parastatal entities that still existed in 1988 were privatized (Quintana 1991), and from 1990 to 1992, the nationalized banking system was resold to the private sector.[21] Through an exceptionally rigorous and uniform enforcement of taxation laws, important advances were made in the elimination of loopholes, the expansion of the tax base and the radical reduction of tax evasion.[22]

Salinas also had to deal with the political and social costs associated with six years of adjustment. First and foremost were the costs imposed by the 1988 electoral process on presidential authority. With only 50.1 percent of the vote (by official counts), widespread allegations of fraud, and the unprecedented challenge by a left-of-center opposition, which won 30 percent of the presidential vote, the most urgent initial task faced by the new administration was to reassert the authority of the chief executive.

While Salinas' political skills and decisiveness were certainly very important, the recuperation of presidential authority was made possible by the maneuvering room provided by the policy achievements of the previous administration and by the new correlation of social and political forces generated by such achievements. One of the first important moves in the reassertion of presidential authority was the ousting and incarceration of the leader of the most powerful union in the country, the *Sindicato de Trabajadores Petroleros de la República Mexicana* (Petroleum Workers Union of the Mexican Republic) (Loyola Díaz 1990, 263-297). The sharp reduction of oil's share of total exports brought on by the export diversification facilitated the move against the oil workers' union. Equally relevant in this regard was the Salinas administration's management of electoral affairs. As mentioned earlier, crisis, stabilization, and structural adjustment dealt a heavy blow to the ability of corporatist party elites to deliver electoral victories. The weakening of these elites also changed the operation of the government's electoral machine. Macroeconomic stability and healthy public finances were also extremely important in making adjustments possible.

Changes in the electoral and partisan arenas included two basic components, the incorporation of opposition parties — most notably, the *Partido Acción Nacional* (PAN) — and the subordination of the official party to the executive in the provision of goods and services to popular sectors. The inclusion of the PAN in the electoral game proceeded through a series of negotiations between PAN leaders and top-level government officials and has resulted in what amounted to a virtual market-sharing arrangement. It was, however, a sharing arrangement that excluded the president, assured a majority for the PRI in Congress, and was premised on negotiation of electoral results rather than on the vote totals.[23]

The incorporation of *Acción Nacional* into the electoral game was not the result of the government's generosity. Over a long period of time, the PAN consolidated a strong presence among urban middle classes in a number of regions. For the government, refusing to recognize the PAN's strength, especially after July 1988, would have been costlier than accepting it. *Acción Nacional* proved to be both a loyal player and a relatively non-threatening contender in what remained an essentially one-prize-only political system.[24]

The limitations on PAN's strengths as a national contender in presidential elections are due to its historical inability to consolidate its linkages with large business groups more than its allegedly unsurmountable difficulties in expanding its social base (Gibson 1991). Arguments that focus on the PAN's relations with corporations are supported by two facts: the growth of the party during times of serious stress in state-big business relations and the advances made by *Acción Nacional* in those states where it has managed to obtain the firm backing of local business elites (Barraza and Bizberg 1991). Experience suggests, therefore, that once such support has been consolidated, membership numbers are not a major impediment.

The Salinas administration's negotiation of the PAN's incorporation into the electoral arena as a subordinate partner of government was, in many ways, the result of both successes and costs of economic policy making during President de la Madrid's government. For the government, the most important cost in this area was the ability of *Acción Nacional* to capitalize on widespread discontent generated by economic reform among small and mid-size regional entrepreneurs. The costs that stabilization and structural adjustment entailed for large numbers of these firms accelerated and consolidated a process of politicization which began in the 1970s. As a vehicle for such discontent, *Acción Nacional* acquired a crucial asset in regional electoral contests and a major bargaining chip with government.

Negotiations with the PAN were also decisively influenced by the reconciliation between big business and the state. This reconciliation — well advanced by the time Carlos Salinas entered office — deprived the PAN of the one constituency it required to become an effective national contender. In short, the costs of economic restructuring for mid-size regional entrepreneurs and urban middle classes gave the PAN the power to negotiate a larger slice of the electoral pie. The government's ability to reestablish cooperative linkages with major economic groups placed a formidable limit upon the PAN's further growth at the national level, thus making its *subordinated* incorporation into the electoral system possible.

The most significant change in recent years in the relationship between the executive and the official party has been the launching of the *Programa Nacional de Solidaridad* (PRONASOL). The Salinas administration used PRONASOL to address some of the accumulated costs of the crisis for the poorest sectors of Mexican society and also managed to refurbish the government's capacity to manage the electoral front. The PRI's impressive electoral rebound in the 1991 congressional elections indicates that PRONASOL provided the government with an extraordinarily powerful, flexible, and relatively cheap electoral weapon.[25] Rather than investing in high-cost, general welfare programs whose electoral benefits are uncertain, PRONASOL allowed the government to maximize electoral profits by directing government resources into targeted regions and social groups.[26] Financial costs were thereby reduced and political benefits insured.

The executive's direct control over the program has proved crucial to the program's political and electoral effectiveness. Endowed with its own administrative structure and placed under the firm financial and political control of the executive, PRONASOL turned into a strategic instrument for generating new patronage networks directly responsive to the executive. Though the program's relationship with local authorities and party structures varied significantly among regions, its very flexibility allowed it to adjust to different political and electoral contexts, while simultaneously creating new channels and networks of political incorporation, social control, and electoral support that have become an asset for the president in dealing with uncooperative regional or corporate elites.

Though innovative in a number of respects (including its active community participation, municipal involvement, and targeted nature), PRONASOL reproduces many of the electoral practices that have long characterized Mexico. For instance, PRONASOL guides the exchange of publicly provided goods and services for votes, and it maintains the highly discretionary process through which such public goods and services are allocated. However, PRONASOL replaced the sectoral and regional corporatist and clientelistic relations, upon which the government's electoral machine operated prior to the 1980s, with networks based primarily upon the reciprocal exchange of material and political concessions. Such networks are less resilient to short-term losses than traditional ones.

Assessing the effects of the subordinated incorporation of *Acción Nacional* into the electoral game and the creation and operation of PRONASOL is not easy. In the short run, both efforts appear to have expanded the state's range of maneuver. However, they expand the number and weight of political actors whose continued political loyalty and support for the regime tend to be more instrumental than that of regional and sectoral party elites. In the medium term the capacity of the regime to reproduce itself is diminished by 1) the erosion of traditional authority relations, 2) the expansion of more purely instrumental clientelistic networks in the electoral terrain, 3) the growth of independent voters produced by long-term socioeconomic change, and 4) heightened levels of electoral competition.

To these potential costs to regime stability, one must add the potentially corrosive effects of economic liberalization (and tax reform, in particular) upon the operation of basic mechanisms by which political order has been historically generated and maintained in Mexico. Three of those potential effects are particularly relevant: 1) the reduction of available funds and power positions to be shared and distributed among members of the political elite; 2) the increasing salience and importance of private circuits of political power in which economic or regional elites become less dependent upon central state authorities and acquire virtually full control over their sectors, regions, and constituencies; and 3) the emergence or expansion of "islands of equality" in a polity that continues to be marked by high levels of social heterogeneity and political fragmentation.

The first of these consequences may significantly affect traditional power-sharing arrangements through which order and cooperation within the political elite has been historically maintained. As rewards shrink, loyalty and discipline are likely to erode. As direct state intervention diminishes and as administrative rules are either simplified or eliminated, the opportunities for rent-seeking, and the use of discretionary power in the construction of political support and mobilization of collective resources for general economic and political goals, will be reduced.

The second potential effect is already visible in many areas of the economy and in various regions of the country. It is also critically associated with the highly unequal nature of Mexican society. As water flooding over an uneven terrain, the power "liberated" by the contraction of the state apparatus tends to concentrate in pockets. State retrenchment from key areas of social and economic interaction further magnifies preexisting power and income differentials, while simultaneously depriving of state protection those least endowed, thus subjecting them more fully to the influence of local or economic dominant elites. Political order under this new set of conditions is likely to lead to the replacement of brokers by relatively more independent allies whose cooperation in ensuring desired outcomes and behavior will be crucial.

The third likely consequence of economic change and, particularly, of tax reform is the growth of "islands of equality" whose impact upon political stability and change is likely to be decisive, even if, at this point, highly uncertain. Growing equality of condition before the law constitutes, perhaps, the single most important potential source of a full-fledged transition to democracy in Mexico. As with any major social change involving the emergence and consolidation of new political identities and new regularized forms of political interaction, the expansion of citizenship likely to be promoted by far-reaching tax reform will not take place overnight. Whether or not such reform acts as an effective catalyst for the development of citizenship-based forms of political governance, however, will depend upon numerous variables. Critical among them will be timing itself: the extent to which, during the lapse required for the consolidation of citizenship, gradual adjustments to traditional forms of governance are introduced that are simultaneously compatible with the emergence of liberal democratic procedures and able to provide anchors for effective governance. Only if such conditions are met will governability and democracy in Mexico cease to be polar opposites and will the prospects for an effective transition toward more civilized and less uncertain forms of political coexistence increase (Camou 1992, 55-65).

Conclusions

I must confess that politicians were smarter than the political scientists, because they took the stuff as weaponry, while we took it as science. We swallowed economics before subjecting it to political analysis.

Theodore Lowi, president's address to the American Political Science Association (Lowi 1992, 5)

Professor Lowi's statement rings particularly true for the study of economic policy making. In few other areas of political science, in fact, has the language of economics so fully displaced the language of politics. Borrowing of methods, questions, and values from economic theory, however, has often made politics vanish from political analysis. This chapter has argued for the primacy of the political, while analyzing how states go about creating markets. Rather than denying the importance of market constraints and economic cleavages in the making of economic policy, what I have suggested here is that the political salience of such constraints and cleavages is itself conditioned by the nature of political institutions. Where power and authority are generated and maintained through the continuous negotiation of the legal order, individuals placed in similar economic positions are likely to regard each other as competitors rather than allies. As a result, the costs and benefits that stabilization and adjustment impose on economic actors cannot be easily translated into collective action, thereby reducing state-elite sensitivity toward them. In patronage-based political systems, distributive conflicts among sectors and classes tend to be less central politically than in polities in which the greater salience and validity of general rules and mandates increase the level of aggregation at which interests become politically significant.

State officials' considerable autonomy vis-à-vis organized collective interests in patronage-based polities entails an acute dependence upon those who head and manage the clientelistic networks upon which government relies. Rather than focusing on distributive conflicts organized around economic cleavages, the study of the politics of economic liberalization in these settings should award greater attention to intra-elite dynamics — especially the mechanisms through which access to the state is allotted among rival claimants — as well as to the effects of clientelism upon administrative efficiency (Schneider 1992). This chapter has argued that it is precisely in those two realms, not in the balance of power between economic winners and losers, where the explanation for Mexico's often-noted exceptionality can be found. The clues for the country's political future also lie along the dimensions of elite dynamics.

Notes

1. The same applies to the work on institutional engineering and policy design.

2. On illegality as a *sine qua non* condition for the operation of clientelistic authority relations, see José Varela's masterful study (1977) of the Spanish political system during the Restoration.

3. On the relationship between political institutions and the process of interest aggregation, see Guillermo O'Donnell (1994).

4. According to Smith's empirical analysis (1979,180) of elite mobility and circulation in Mexico, there is a continuity rate of only 30 percent to 35 percent within the upper echelons of government across presidential administrations, which places Mexico among the political systems with one of the highest elite turnovers in the world.

5. On the policy orientations of the two currents, see Cordera and Tello (1981, Chapter 3). On the policy effects of the mounting confrontation between them, see Teichman (1988, Chapter 5).

6. From 1971 to 1982 total government spending grew from 24.8 percent to 42.7 percent of GNP; and the budget deficit jumped from 2.5 percent of GNP in 1970 to 15.8 percent in 1982 (Newell and Rubio 1984, 281-283). The number of state firms, on the other hand, went from 491 in 1970 to 845 in 1976 and to 1155 in 1982 (Secretaría de Gobernación y Presidencia de la República 1988, 15). As far as subsidies are concerned, and as shown by a recent study on public sector pricing during the 1977-1982 period, subsidized public prices in oil products, electricity, and water supply in Mexico City generated, by themselves, a welfare cost of 2 percent of GDP in 1982. The study also indicates that "the amount of foreign borrowing the country had to incur in order to meet the additional consumption of energy induced by subsidies to these products including foregone governmental income, was approximately $101 billion when carried forward to 1984.Together, by 1984, the absence of these subsidies would have wiped out Mexico's total foreign debt" (Gil Díaz 1986, 4).

7. Presidencia de la República (1982-1988, 19-25).

8. During the latter half of the 1960s, annual fiscal deficits averaged around 2 percent of GNP. During the 1970s, deficits grew reaching 10 percent of GNP during 1975 and 1976 (Banco de México 1984, 22).

9. Presidencia de la República (1982, 4).

10. Of the three major stabilization plans (PIRE, 1983; PAC, 1986; and PSE, 1987) carried out during this period, only the last one was truly successful. Twelve months after its launching (December 1988), inflation, which had been running at 15.5 percent in January of that year, had been brought down to 2 percent. In annual terms that meant a reduction of the rate of inflation from 159.2 percent in 1987 to 51.7 percent in 1988 and 19.7 percent in 1989. In December 1988, the plan was renamed (*Pacto de Estabilidad y Crecimiento Económico*) and has been periodically renewed ever since.

11. From 1984 to 1989, PEMEX's expenditures on wages and salaries rose from 14 percent to 22 percent of total expenditures (*Proceso* 1992a, 9).

12. Banco de México, October 1991.

13. Calculated on the basis of figures provided by INEGI as reported in NAFINSA (1990, 637).

14. Figures on public sector employment (*NAFINSA* 1990, Table 13.30, 633-4).

15. Comprehensive studies of economic performance at the regional level are difficult to find (Palacios 1988, 7-37; 1989, 265-279).

16. Noncompetitive elections also tend to perform important socialization and communication functions. On the role of elections in noncompetitive systems in general, see Hermet 1986, 18-53; Loaeza 1989, 273-285; and Segovia 1987, 13-23.

17. Beginning in 1946 — when the official party got the name it has today and the structure it retained until the late 1980s — the three sectors of the party — Peasant, Labor, and Popular — agreed to a sharing arrangement whereby each sector was allotted a quota of the total electoral districts on the basis of the relative power of each sector in different states and regions (Medina 1978).

18. During the 1988 elections, in approximately 85 percent of total urban districts, PRI candidates faced strong competition and sixty-six PRI congressional candidates (out of three hundred) were defeated by opposition parties. The largest losses were experienced by labor-sector candidates, followed by the subgroup incorporated within the popular sector of the party (Pacheco Méndez 1991, 23-24).

19. According to the results published by INEGI in the last *Encuesta nacional de ingresos y gastos de los hogares* (1989), the only income categories that suffered *relative* losses during the 1977-1989 period were those included in deciles XVIII and XIX.

20. Scott (1972, 109-113).

21. As a result of tax reform, the number of registered taxpayers increased by one million between 1988 and 1990, and total tax revenue rose from 8.5 percent of GDP in 1987 to 10.8 percent in 1991 (Elizondo forthcoming, 41).

22. A revealing indicator of the radical novelty of the government's attitude and behavior in fiscal affairs is the treatment of tax evaders. From 1921 to 1988, only two tax evaders ended up in prison; in 1988, the government prosecuted seven; in 1989, fifty; and in 1990, nearly four hundred, including a number of businessmen (Elizondo forthcoming, 38). Also see the statements by the undersecretary of finance Francisco Gil Díaz (1990).

23. A clear example can be found in the 1992 election in the state of Guanajuato where widespread allegations of fraud resulted in the resignation of the PRI gubernatorial candidate just before assuming office. A good showing on the part of Acción Nacional led to what appears to have been an arrangement between the government and the party whereby the PAN mayor of the state capital was appointed by the local Congress as interim governor.

24. In spite of its limited share of the presidential vote in most elections, including 1988, the PAN has steadily increased its gains in congressional elections and,

especially, in those at the municipal and the gubernatorial level. As of 1992, the PAN holds two elected governorships (Baja California and Chihuahua), one interim governorship (Guanajuato), and it controls a number of regional capitals (such as Mérida in the state of Yucatán).

25. During the 1991 congressional elections, the PRI got 61.5 percent of the total vote, whereas in 1988 its share had been only 50.7 percent. The absolute number of votes for the official party increased 46.6 percent from 1988 to 1991, and in 40 electoral districts the growth amounted to over 100 percent (Alcocer and Morales 1991, 27-40).

26. A clear example of the flexibility provided by PRONASOL was the management of the program in recent gubernatorial and local congressional elections in the state of Michoacan where the Partido de la Revolución Democrática obtained majority votes for its presidential candidate in 1988 and where the party has its most important base of political support. During 1992, 12 percent of total PRONASOL funds were invested in Michoacan. In 1991, 60 percent of the resources were channeled to the state and concentrated in the 25 municipalities where the PRI obtained over 60 percent of the vote during the national congressional elections (*Proceso* 1992b, 14).

References

Alcocer, Jorge, and Rodrigo Morales. 1991. "Mitología y realidad del fraude electoral." *Nexo* 14:166 (October).

Alt, James E., and Kenneth A. Shepsle, eds. 1990. *Perspectives on Positive Political Economy.* New York: Cambridge University Press.

Anderson, Roger. 1971. *The Functional Role of Governors and their States in the Political Development of Mexico, 1940-1964.* Ph.D. dissertation, University of Wisconsin.

Banco de México. 1984. *Informe Anual: Indicadores Económicos.* México, D.F.: Banco de México.

Barraza, Leticia, and Ilán Bizberg. 1991. "El Partido Acción Nacional y el regimen político mexicano." *Foro Internacional* 123:3 (January-March).

Bates, Robert. 1990. "Macropolitical Economy in the Field of Development." In *Perspectives on Positive Political Economy,* eds. James E. Alt and Kenneth A. Shepsle. New York: Cambridge University Press.

Bazdresch, Carlos, and Santiago Levy. 1991. "Populism and Economic Policy in Mexico, 1970-1982." In *The Macroeconomics of Populism in Latin America,* eds. Rudiger Dornbusch and Sebastian Edwards. Chicago: University of Chicago Press.

Camou, Antonio. 1992. "Governabilidad y democracia." *Nexos* 15:170.

Camp, Roderic A. 1982. *Mexican Political Biographies, 1935-1981.* Tucson: University of Arizona Press.

Cordera, Rolando, and Carlos Tello. 1981. *México: La disputa por la nación.* México: Siglo XXI.

Dornbusch, Rudiger, and Sebastián Edwards, eds. 1991. *The Macroeconomics of Populism in Latin America.* Chicago: University of Chicago Press.

Eisenstadt, Samuel N., and Rene Lemarchand, eds. 1981. *Political Clientelism, Patronage and Development.* Beverly Hills: Sage Press.

Elizondo, Carlos. 1993. *Property Rights in Business-State Relations: The Case of the Bank Nationalization.* Ph.D. dissertation, Oxford University.

Elizondo, Carlos. Forthcoming. "In Search of Revenue: Tax Reform in Mexico under the Administrations of Echeverría and Salinas." *Journal of Latin American Studies.*

Escalante, Fernando. 1992. *Ciudadanos imaginarios.* México: El Colegio de México.

Evans, Peter. 1989. "Predatory, Developmental and Other Apparatuses: A Comparative Political-Economic Perspective on the Third World State." *Sociological Forum* IV (4).

Frieden, Jeffry A. 1991. *Debt, Development and Democracy: Modern Political Economy and Latin America, 1965-1985.* Princeton, N.J.: Princeton University Press.

Gibson, Edward. 1991. *Conservative Parties and Democratic Politics: Argentina in Comparative Perspective.* Ph.D. dissertation, Department of Political Science, Columbia University.

Gil Díaz, Francisco. 1986. *Debt Accumulation and Distorted Growth Through Subsidized Public Sector Prices.* Unpublished manuscript.

Gil Díaz, Francisco. 1990. Press conference. January.

Gómez, Leopoldo, and John Bailey. 1990. "La transición política y los dilemas del PRI." *Foro Internacional* 121 (July-September).

González Graf, Jaime. 1986. "La crisis de la clase política." *Nexos* 136 (April).

Haggard, Stephen, and Robert Kaufman, eds. 1992. *The Politics of Economic Adjustment: International Constraints, Distributive Conflicts and the State.* Princeton, N.J.: Princeton University Press.

Heredia, Blanca. 1992. *Mexican Business and the State: The Political Economy of a "Muddled" Transition.* Kellogg Institute Working Paper. University of Notre Dame.

Hermet, Guy. 1986. "Las elecciones en los regimenes autoritarios: Bosquejo de un marco de analisis." In *Para que sirven las elecciones?* eds. Guy Hermet, Alain Rouquié, and Juan Linz. México: Fondo de Cultura Económica.

Hermet, Guy, Alain Rouiqué, and Juan Linz, eds. 1986. *Para que sirven las elecciones?* México: Fondo de Cultura Económica.

Hernández Rodríguez, Rogelio. 1987. "Los hombres del presidente de la Madrid." *Foro Internacional* 109 (July-September).

Higley, John, and Richard Gunther, eds. *Elites and Democratic Consolidation in Latin America and Southern Europe.* New York: Cambridge University Press.

INEGI. 1989. *Encuesta nacional de ingresos y gastos de los hogares.* México, D.F.

ILO (International Labor Office). Various years. *Yearbook of Labor Statistics.* Geneva, Switzerland: International Labor Office.

Kaufman, Robert. 1988. *The Politics of Debt in Argentina, Brazil, and Mexico: Economic Stabilization in the 1980s.* Berkeley: Institute of International Studies, University of California, Berkeley.

Knight, Alan. 1992. "Mexico's Elite Settlement: Conjuncture and Consequences." In *Elites and Democratic Consolidation in Latin America and Southern Europe,* eds. John Higley and Richard Gunther. New York: Cambridge University Press.

Loaeza, Soledad. 1989. *El llamado de las urnas.* México: Cal y Arena.

Lowi, Theodore. 1992. "The State in Political Science: How We Become What We Study." *American Political Science Review* 86 (1).

Loyola Díaz, Rafael. 1990. "La liquidación del feudo petrolero en la política moderna, México 1989." *Mexican Studies/Estudios Mexicanos* 6 (2).

Lustig, Nora. 1992. *Mexico: The Remaking of an Economy.* Washington, D.C.: Brookings Institution.

Maxfield, Sylvia. 1990. *Governing Capital: International Finance and Mexican Politics.* Ithaca, N.Y.: Cornell University Press.

Medina, Luis. 1978. *Evolución electoral en el México contemporáneo.* México, D.F.: Ediciones de la Gaceta Informativa de la Comisión Federal Electoral.

Meyer, Lorenzo. 1983. "México en el siglo XX: La concentración del poder político." In *La unidad nacional en América Latina: Del regionalismo a la nacionalidad,* ed. Marco Palacios. México: El Colegio de México.

Molinar Horcasitas, Juan. 1991. *El tiempo de la legitimidad: Elecciones, autoritarismo y democracia en México.* Mexico: Cal y Arena.

NAFINSA (Nacional Financiera S.A.). 1989. *La economía mexicana en cifras, 1988.* México, D.F.: Nacional Financiera S.A.

NAFINSA (Nacional Financiera S.A.). 1990. *La economía mexicana en cifras, 1990.* México, D.F.: Nacional Financiera S.A.

Nelson, Joan, ed. 1990. *Economic Crisis and Policy Choice: The Politics of Adjustment in the Third World.* Princeton, N.J.: Princeton University Press.

Newell, Roberto G., and Luis F. Rubio. 1984. *Mexico's Dilemma: The Political Origins of Economic Crisis.* Boulder, Colo.: Westview.

North, Douglas. 1990. *Institutions, Institutional Change and Economic Performance.* New York: Cambridge University Press.

O'Donnell, Guillermo. 1994. "The State, Democratization, and Some Conceptual Problems (A Latin American View with Glances at Some Post-Communist Countries)." In *Latin American Political Economy in the Age of Neoliberal Reform: Theoretical and Comparative Perspectives,* eds. William C. Smith, Carlos H. Acuña, and Eduardo A. Gamarra. Coral Gables, Fla.: North-South Center, University of Miami.

Pacheco Méndez, Guadalupe. 1991. "La disfuncionalidad de las máquinas electorales." *Argumentos* 12 (April).

Palacios, Juan José. 1988. "Las inconsistencias de la política regional en México, 1970-82: El caso de la asignación de la inversión pública y federal." *Estudios Demográficos y Urbanos* 7 (January-April).

Palacios, Juan José. 1989. "Descentralización en medio de la crisis?" *Estudios Demográficos y Urbanos* 11 (May-August).

Perkins, Dwight, and Michael Roemer. 1991. *Reforming Economic Systems in Developing Countries.* Cambridge, Mass.: Harvard Institute for International Development.

Presidencia de la República. 1982. *Criterios Generales de Política Económica 1983.* México, D.F.: Presidencia de la República.

Presidencia de la República. 1982-1988. *Las Razones y las Obras.* Crónica del Sexenio. Sexto Año. México: Unidad de la Crónica Presidencial/Fondo de Cultura Económica.

Proceso. 1992a. México, D.F. March 16.

Proceso. 1992b. México, D.F. May 4.

Purcell, Susan Kaufman. 1981. "Mexico: Clientelism, Corporatism, and Political Stability." In *Political Clientilism, Patronage, and Development,* eds. S.M. Eisenstadt and René Lemarchand. Beverly Hills, Calif.: Sage Press.

Quintana, Enrique. 1991. "Cuando el proceso termine, no habrá más." *Este País* 9 (December).

Reding, Andrew. 1988. "The Democratic Current: A New Era in Mexican Politics." *World Policy Journal* 2 (Spring).

Schneider, Ross Ben. 1992. *Politics within the State: Elite Bureaucrats and Industrial Policy in Authoritarian Brazil.* Pittsburgh: University of Pittsburgh Press.

Scott, James. 1972. "Patron-Client Politics and Political Change in Southeast Asia." *American Political Science Review* LXVI:1 (March).

Secretaría de Gobernación y Presidencia de la República. 1988. "Restructuración del Sector Paraestatal." *Cuadernos de Renovación Nacional 4.* México: Fondo de Cultura Económica.

Segovia, Rafael. 1987. "El fastidio electoral." In *La vida política mexicana en la crisis,* eds. Soledad Loaeza and Rafael Segovia. Mexico: El Colegio de México.

Smith, Peter. 1979. *Labyrinths of Power: Political Recruitment in Twentieth -Century Mexico.* Princeton, N.J.: Princeton University Press.

Teichman, Judith A. 1988. *Policymaking in Mexico: From Boom to Crisis.* Boston: Allen & Unwin.

Varela, José. 1977. *Los amigos políticos: Partidos, elecciones y caciquismo en la Restauración (1875-1900).* Madrid: Alianza Editorial.

Chapter Eleven

On the Political Economy of Market and State Reform in Mexico

Jaime Ros

Introduction

Mexico has been moving in recent years toward a more outward-oriented development strategy that gives greater scope to market forces and a larger economic role to the private sector. It has done so faster and farther than many other developing countries in Latin America. Since 1983, and especially after 1985, Mexico has fully applied the market-reforms package urged by the "Washington Consensus": radical liberalization of trade and industrial policy, large-scale privatization of state-owned enterprises, and massive deregulation of foreign investment flows and domestic economic activities. These institutional and policy changes have taken place under severe macroeconomic stress, following massive external and fiscal shocks and successive attempts at macroeconomic stabilization involving dramatic changes in the economy's rate of accumulation, external competitiveness, and public finances.

Mexico's path to macroeconomic stabilization and structural adjustment can be summarized briefly: In the wake of the 1982 debt crisis, a very orthodox, stabilization-first strategy was adopted with the aim of rapidly restoring price and balance-of-payments stability. This was to be followed by gradual structural adjustment which would promote an incremental process of resource reallocation in a stable and growth-oriented macroeconomic framework. This "high-growth, slow-structural adjustment strategy" — which prevailed as a policy stance during 1984 and part of 1985 — was soon abandoned in favor of radicalization of market-reform measures. Contrary to conventional wisdom and advice, these market-reform measures were implemented within the highly adverse macroeconomic environment created by the 1986 oil-price shock. In late 1987, following the failure of successive orthodox attempts at inflation control, macroeconomic policy shifted to a more heterodox approach to stabilization, embodied in the "Economic

Solidarity Pact." This plan aimed at rapid disinflation through the combination of wage and price controls, an exchange-rate freeze, and tight fiscal and monetary policy. Despite the high priority given to price stabilization in this period — or perhaps because of it, as argued below — structural adjustment measures have been accelerating since then.

Despite almost a decade of stagnation and macroeconomic instability, the virtual absence of political tensions and resistance to change has made the Mexican transition remarkably rapid and smooth, in contrast to the experience of more reluctant reformers, such as Brazil, which experienced similar macroeconomic difficulties. Compared to other Latin American countries well advanced in the reform process, such as Chile and Bolivia, the dislocation and adjustment costs for Mexico appear to be strikingly small. Moreover, Mexico's recent economic trends — positive per-capita growth for three consecutive years, successful inflation stabilization, and massive capital inflows since 1989 — provide an adjustment model to be emulated by less eager reformers.

After a brief overview of why adjustment has been so difficult in debtor countries, this chapter develops two arguments. First, precisely because it is unique, Mexico's smooth and comparatively successful experience should be attributed to a number of singular features. The analysis suggests that these features go well beyond policy management, political structure, or geopolitical advantages. They are firmly rooted in the country's macroeconomic structure. Secondly, structural reforms are considered as a set of nontraditional instruments to overcome the macroeconomic adjustment process itself. It is the costs of adjustment, as suggested by a "political economy model" of the reform process developed in the third section, that explain the acceleration of the reform drive in the late 1980s. And it is the very particular nature of macroeconomic policy trade-offs, rather than the intrinsic merits of market reforms for the allocative and dynamic efficiency of the economy, that explains the sustainability of the reform package so far. One implication of all this is that there may be little in this adjustment model worthy of emulation by others.

Credit Rationing, Policy Ineffectiveness, and Macroeconomic Instability[1]

As emphasized by the recent literature on three-gap models and the internal transfer problem,[2] the external shocks of the 1980s created imbalances in both the balance of payments and the fiscal accounts of Latin American debtor countries. Closing these external and fiscal gaps involves two separate problems. First, for the country as a whole, it was necessary to generate a sufficient foreign exchange surplus to meet the increased debt service and to compensate for terms-of-trade losses, given the sharp reduction in external financing. This is the external transfer problem. Its magnitude was determined by several factors: the initial level of external debt, the amount of external financing received in the post-crisis period, the size of terms-of-trade losses suffered during this period, and the degree of trade openness of the economy as well as the composition of its exports and imports. The first two determined the size of financial transfers abroad. The third accounted for the additional real resource transfers (i.e., at constant pre-crisis terms of trade), while the pattern of foreign trade affected the size and effectiveness of the exchange-rate adjustment required to close the external gap.[3]

In addition, an internal transfer problem arose when the government appropriated domestic savings needed to effect the external transfer, since most of the debt is either owed or guaranteed by public sectors and terms-of-trade losses often curtailed public sector revenues. This is the internal transfer problem which — given the severe credit rationing that public sectors faced in domestic and external financial markets — turns into a fiscal adjustment problem, giving rise to the emergence of a "third gap," the fiscal constraint in three-gap models. For it meant that in order to carry out the external transfer efficiently — i.e., without an excessive reliance on domestic output losses and the inflation tax — traditional expenditure-reducing and expenditure-switching policies (absorption cuts and currency depreciation) were not enough. A non-inflationary mobilization of the transfer also required a redistribution of savings from the private to the public sector, i.e., not merely an increase in domestic savings but, more specifically, an increase in public sector savings.

The magnitude of this internal transfer problem was partly determined by the size of the external transfer itself. The bigger the external shock, the larger the fiscal effort required to effect a non-inflationary mobilization of the transfer, again because the initial fiscal shock was generally equivalent in size to the external shock and was also due to the increased default risk which, through capital flight, added to the external-transfer burden and made domestic credit rationing even more severe. Yet, this is so only to the extent that other things are equal, and two other factors were generally not equal across debtor countries.

First, the exchange rate adjustment required to close the external gap had important fiscal impacts that depended on 1) the state of the public sector foreign exchange balance (approximately the difference between government export revenues and the net external transfer, i.e., debt service minus external financing received by the government) and 2) the internal/external currency composition of public debt that affected the sign and size of debt-related effects of devaluation (i.e., the increase in real debt service on external debt and the offsetting decline in the real value of domestic debt service). Indeed, the total fiscal effort can be seen as the initial fiscal shock — at pre-devaluation exchange rates — plus the depreciation-induced loss in real government disposable income.

Second, along with the more or less destabilizing (or stabilizing) effects of currency depreciations on public finances, the inflationary complications of the external and fiscal shocks were also determined by the degree of indexation in the wage/price and tax systems as well as by the state of domestic financial markets, often referred to as "fiscal rigidities" in the literature on default risk (see, in particular, Ize and Ortiz 1987). High wage/price indexation and long fiscal lags exacerbated the inflation acceleration required to effect a given real exchange rate adjustment, while a low demand for domestic financial assets constrained the possibilities for a redistribution of domestic savings through money and bond seignorage.

Before considering the implications of the above in the Mexican experience, it is convenient to visualize the main forces that, as a result of the fiscal and external dimensions of the shocks of the past decade, created a potential vicious circle of macroeconomic instability and stagnation (see Diagram 1).

Diagram 1

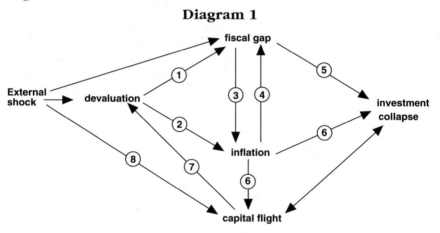

1) Depreciation-induced real wealth loss

2) Wage/price indexation

3) Monetization of fiscal deficits

4) Olivera-Tanzi effects

5) Fiscal constraints on public investment

6) Uncertainty and resource misallocation effects

7) Increased current account adjustment

8) Default risk and fiscal rigidities

This vicious circle was set in motion, to some degree, in all the major debtor countries in Latin America, and the process perpetuated itself well after the elimination of the initial external gap created by the shocks themselves. As a common characteristic of adjustment processes, the cycle led to a sharp reduction in the effectiveness of traditional macroeconomic policy instruments. Given the size of the external and fiscal shocks and the severity of credit rationing faced by governments, macroeconomic policies operated between the Scylla of a liquidity trap in the market for foreign assets and the Charybdis of an internal debt trap in the domestic bonds market (see Ros 1991a). Fanelli, Frenkel, and Rozenwurcel (1990) illustrate the problem with an illuminating comparison to the Keynesian concept of a liquidity trap:

> When the entrepreneurs' expectations regarding the future evolution of the economy are pessimistic, this same pessimism induces them to allocate funds in financial assets and away from productive investment. In such a situation, as Keynes has shown, monetary policy is either inefficient or ineffective and cannot reverse pessimistic expectations. And this is so because the economy's problems lie in the state of the entrepreneurs' animal spirits. This analogy with the Keynesian liquidity trap, however, ends here. Traditional Keynesian medicine would not work in an open economy with the characteristics of Latin American economies.... In the present Latin American situation, the agents facing a highly unstable macroeconomic environment show an increased liquidity preference for foreign assets, and consequently, the demand for domestic financial assets is very low, a few percentage points of GDP in many Latin American countries. So, if the government sought to finance even a small increment in its deficit in the domestic financial market (its only possible choice since the foreign credit market is rationed), the pressure on the demand for the increased supply of financial assets would be so strong that it would induce a disequilibrium in the market which would ultimately foster capital flight.

There is another aspect to the ineffectiveness of conventional macroeconomic policies, which emerged whenever the vicious circle or spiral looped into a high inflation period. As illustrated by Diagram 1, high-inflation regimes are characterized by multiple interactions between inflation, public finances, and monetary growth. Not only do inflationary pressures acquire a momentum of their own, as indexation mechanisms become more and more entrenched in the wage and price formation systems, but they come to influence fiscal deficits strongly —through a myriad of effects depending on tax-collection lags, public price adjustment rules, effects on real government spending, and real wage and exchange rate effects — as well as their finance by affecting money demand and the composition and term structure of the public debt. Under these conditions, the money supply process becomes endogenous, i.e., jointly determined with the rate of inflation and largely escaping the control of the monetary authority. Due to these interactions and the resulting inertia, any single-sided approach to price stabilization — based on monetary, fiscal, exchange rate, or any other single policy instrument — is bound to be inefficient and very likely also to be ineffective. This is the basic insight of the heterodox literature on inflation and stabilization, and it is the case for incomes policy in the task of bringing high inflation under control.

Overcoming the ineffectiveness of conventional policy instruments in the post-1982 period has been the central problem faced by Latin American governments. It is a problem that remains thus far unsolved by many of them. The following section looks at the Mexican experience from this perspective: Why and how did Mexico eventually escape from the vicious circle of macroeconomic instability and stagnation?

Some Singular Features of Mexico's Adjustment Process
Oil Rents and the Absence of a Wage Constraint

The first point to be emphasized is that the strength and perversity of the mechanisms and feedback effects described in the diagram, and the resulting constraints on domestic policies, were lessened by a number of specific-country features which made Mexico's macroeconomic adjustment problem very different from that of other large debtors. To be sure, Mexico's problem combined two features: a very severe external transfer burden — as in other major debtors, but aggravated by the oil price collapse and the initial inelasticity of its exports — and a relatively minor internal transfer problem, whose solution was greatly facilitated by the existence of a sizeable foreign exchange surplus in the government's income and expenditure accounts, an initially moderate inflation rate, a low degree of indexation and demonetization, and the relative absence of policy constraints on the wage front.

Let us begin with the latter, the internal transfer problem. First, the fiscal effects of currency depreciations have been positive in the Mexican experience due to the existence of massive oil export revenues in the fiscal accounts which more than offset interest payments on external debt, even after the oil price declines of the second half of the decade. Just as copper revenues in Chile and coffee export tariffs in Colombia, oil revenues in Mexico (as in Venezuela) turned the exchange rate adjustments required to close the external gap into an automatic mechanism of fiscal adjustment. The importance of this feature can hardly be exaggerated: the 1982 devaluations almost fully explain the increase in Mexico's public savings in that year, as a consequence of the real revaluation of the government's external surplus by 2 percent GDP. In Argentina and Brazil, without similar export/fiscal revenues, the fiscal effects of currency depreciations in that same year determined, respectively, a 5 percent and 2 percent expansion of the fiscal deficit as a proportion of GDP.[4]

Second, the initial conditions in product, labor, and financial markets — a tradition of moderate inflation, a low degree of indexation in the wage/price system, and large room for maneuver in wage policy — were rather favorable to a noninflationary mobilization of the transfer, certainly much less unfavorable than in high inflation countries with entrenched indexation mechanisms and relatively demonetized financial systems. On the eve of the 1982 crisis, for example, Mexico was still under a yearly system of wage settlements, while in Brazil the frequency of wage adjustments had already become semestral and Argentina was moving from quarterly to monthly settlements.[5] No less important, wage adjustments during the critical 1983 year fell to less than half of past price increases and remained, on average, below past inflation since then. Financial disintermediation and demonetization were also far less advanced: cash balances in the first quarter of 1982 were 10 percent of GDP, compared to 5.8 percent in Brazil and 4.9 percent in Argentina (Reisen and van Trotsenburg 1988, Table I.14).

These features had profound implications for fiscal adjustment and explain why Mexico's record in this respect appears so outstanding in the aftermath of the debt crisis. The large public sector operational deficit in 1981 (10 percent of GDP) turned into a small surplus (0.4 percent of GDP) as early as 1983, largely due to a 5.5 percent contraction in public investment, a 2.3 percent real revaluation of oil export revenues (net of interest payments) in the fiscal accounts, and a fall in real salaries of public employees which accounts fully for the 1.5 percent decline in public consumption expenditures (Banco de México 1989). The internal transfer solution was thus facilitated; besides the public investment collapse (the dirty and unsustainable component of the adjustment), it was largely achieved through the depreciation- and wage-policy-induced transfers of real income from the private to the public sector.

In contrast, exchange rate adjustments and fiscal imbalances interacted perversely in other large debtors, such as Brazil and Argentina: as the domestic currency depreciated, the higher exchange rate hurt the fiscal accounts and exacerbated the size of the inflation tax required to close the fiscal gap in real terms. Combined with high indexation, increasing demonetization of the domestic financial system, and Olivera-Tanzi effects, this difference accounts for what is the most striking contrast in the adjustment experiences of those countries and Mexico: much higher inflation rates in the former, by far more remarkable than any difference in growth performance. In fact, it is not necessary to go much beyond the destabilizing impact and stabilizing of exchange rate adjustments to explain the much faster acceleration of inflation and, eventually, the hyperinflation episodes in Brazil and Argentina.

Oil, however, was Mexico's mixed blessing for it exacerbated an already severe external transfer problem. Just as did all other large debtors (with the exception of Chile), Mexico effected large financial transfers abroad, of the order of one-third of total export revenues, between 1983 and 1989. These debt-related transfers were compounded with one of the largest terms-of-trade losses in the Latin American region; as result of the oil price declines, especially after 1985, the terms-of-trade deterioration amounted to a 40 percent decline between 1981 and 1990. Moreover, the dominant position of oil in the export structure (over 70 percent at its peak in 1982-1983) reduced the supply elasticity of overall exports and exacerbated the contractionary effects of devaluation on private expenditures. Currency devaluation eased fiscal adjustment in the presence of oil export revenues accruing to the state, but, by leaving their foreign currency value unaffected, the required adjust-ment in the non-oil current account was exacerbated. For a given real exchange rate adjustment, so too was the overall reduction in domestic expenditure required to achieve a given current account adjustment.[6] It is not surprising, therefore, to find that the external gap was largely closed through a sharp import contraction in the period preceding the 1986 oil price shock and was accompanied by one of the largest declines in the investment/GDP ratio in Latin America.[7]

Analogous reasoning also explains why, when oil revenues were severely curtailed by the 1986 crisis, external and fiscal adjustments had to be very different from those in the preceding period. Since both the private sector trade deficit and the public sector trade surplus were now smaller, so too were the contractionary effects of devaluation on absorption. With a more elastic response of non-oil exports — resulting from past devaluations and an exceptionally high real exchange rate in 1986-1987 — and a lesser degree of external credit rationing, the balance-of-payments adjustment was made less severe and much more efficient, relying on export expansion rather than import contraction. And with smaller positive fiscal effects of devaluation — as a result of reduced oil revenues — and already very low levels of public investment, fiscal policy had no option but to rely on an increase in domestic public savings.

Nevertheless, the collapse of public and private investments that took place in the wake of the debt crisis and the increase in domestic public savings to compensate for the loss of foreign exchange revenues after the 1986 oil shock had a longer term cost besides the stagnation of productive activity and the contraction of the population's real incomes: the sharp decline in the domestic private savings rate. The fiscal and foreign exchange constraints restricted economic growth to such low levels and for such a long period of time that they ended up shifting the savings constraint well below its original levels. By the end of the decade, the foreign exchange and fiscal gaps that were opened by the debt crisis and the oil shock had, indeed, been closed but at the cost of exacerbating the savings constraint. We shall return to this problem later because it is one of the central problems that economic policy has been trying to overcome since the mid-1980s.

The Role and Efficiency of Incomes Policy

The Mexican labor market, or rather the formal labor market which plays a leading role in wage determination, is highly organized, with a number of "institutional rigidities" constraining labor mobility and reallocation. At the same time, the labor market shows a high degree of real wage flexibility, largely as a result of a centralized and corporatist system of wage determination, strongly conditioned by government policies. Minimum wages are fixed in a national tripartite commission — involving the government (the single largest employer), the confederation of labor unions, and business organizations — and are determined by both economic factors (mainly, past inflation) and policy objectives, which greatly influence formal and informal indexation rules.[8] The influence of political factors and policy objectives goes, however, beyond the institutional determination of minimum wages and its influence on the "basic wage." Although "contractual" wage settlements (at the firm or sectoral level) are decentralized, sectoral wages tend to follow the official guidelines (either for the minimum wage or, sometimes, more specific ones). Several factors guarantee this outcome, including, in particular, the fact that the overwhelming majority of labor unions belong to the dominant government party, the location of the stronger and larger unions in the public sector (such as the petroleum and electrical workers unions), and a sui generis bargaining process very often involving economic and political threats and the exchange of wage losses or gains for bureaucratic concessions and power. This process of wage determination gives the government remarkable room for maneuver in its wage policy, a feature rooted since the 1920s in the relationship of the Mexican working class movement to the state and the fact that labor unions are weak at their base with official paternalism providing their general orientation (on the subject, see Noyola 1956).

The absence of a "wage constraint," i.e., the comparatively large room for maneuver in the government's wage policy, has been one important factor in softening the difficult policy trade-offs that other debtors faced in correcting external and fiscal imbalances. It also had other important implications, as we shall now see.

Although fiscal constraints were less severe and indexation mechanisms less entrenched than in many other Latin American countries, Mexico could not avoid a period of high inflation. With the 1982 devaluations, inflation accelerated sharply from its initial rate of 25 to 30 percent in 1981. In spite of the massive fiscal turnaround following the debt crisis — which brought the public sector operational balance into surplus by 1983 — the very orthodox stabilization strategy of this period failed to bring inflation down to target. Price increases stabilized at a high rate of around 60 percent per year in the second semester of 1985. The ensuing oil shock left no option but to keep a very high real exchange rate and thus temporarily sacrifice price stabilization objectives. The cost was, however, a higher rate of inflation, which was running at 160 percent in 1987. Increasing financial fragility and two financial shocks, followed by a new exchange rate crisis in December,[9] eventually led to renewed priority for price stabilization and also an attempt at a different approach to anti-inflation policy.

What followed confirmed the insights of the heterodox approach to stabilization — and its case for incomes policy under high inflation — and simultaneously illustrates how the efficiency of incomes policy was enhanced by Mexico's old corporatist and centralized system of wage determination. In December 1987, while facing the prospect of further inflation acceleration, a new foreign exchange crisis, generalized wage demands, and the threat of a further increase in the frequency of wage adjustments (which by then were taking place every quarter compared to every year in 1981), the government launched the *Pacto de Solidaridad Económica*. The *Pacto* was a tripartite agreement. It comprised an initial freeze on the exchange rate and public prices, together with further fiscal adjustment (the government's contribution to the program), wage restraint (including an initial wage freeze on the part of labor unions), and a radicalization of the import liberalization program, initiated in 1985, which was introduced in the *Pacto* negotiations as the business sector's main contribution to the counter-inflation policy, together with voluntary price restraints and guidelines.[10]

The *Pacto*, unlike previous stabilization attempts, fully achieved its targets; in fact, it reached its goal of 1 to 2 percent monthly inflation for the end of 1988 within the first few months of its implementation. From 160 percent in 1987, the annual inflation rate was down to 20 percent by 1989 and, after a temporary flare-up in 1990, dropped to 18.8 percent in 1991. Disinflation took place without deepening the contraction of labor's real earnings and even within the context of a surge of consumer spending and business investments. The ensuing recovery of economic activity, moderate at first, has been gaining momentum in the past two years. The success of the program has been such that, in spite of the continuous real appreciation of the Mexican peso, the government has been able to reduce, over time, the preannounced rate of daily devaluations (down to a 2 percent annual rate at present).

The role of incomes policy in these developments should not be underestimated, as is often the case in orthodox views. In orthodox views, incomes policy is seen as a useful auxiliary component of a disinflation package, but not really as a necessary condition for its success.[11] In principle, fiscal and monetary policy — the "fundamentals" — are the only necessary and sufficient conditions for curing inflation, even though, without the anesthetic provided by incomes policy, the cure may indeed be painful. The Mexican experience does not fit well with these views and suggests that incomes policy was far more than a convenient and, indeed, very effective anesthetic.

In fact, the *Pacto* is a rare case of inflation stabilization without fiscal adjustment. From 1988 to 1991, the operational budget deficit was on average higher than in 1987 by about 2 percentage points of GDP. Despite an increase in the government's primary surplus (the budget excluding all interest payments on public debt), the higher operational deficit was a consequence of the high real interest payments on domestic public debt that the government transferred to the private sector in 1988 and 1989. But even after the recent decline in real interest rates, the operational budget surplus in 1991 had improved by only 0.7 percentage points of GDP with respect to 1987, less than can be accounted for by the effects of lower inflation on tax collection (the Olivera-Tanzi effect operating in reverse).[12] The basic reason for this lack of fiscal adjustment is that the effects of the *Pacto*'s fiscal measures — which, indeed, contributed to rising domestic public savings — were fully offset by declining external public savings resulting from the real appreciation of the peso and its effects on the domestic currency value of oil export revenues.[13]

If incomes policy was a necessary condition — and surely far more necessary than a nonexistent fiscal adjustment — this does not mean that it was a sufficient condition for the success of the *Pacto*.[14] Lack of fiscal adjustment means the fall in the inflation tax on aggregate demand (of the order of 3 percentage points of GDP) was not compensated for by an equivalent reduction of government spending or an offsetting increase in noninflationary public revenues. The expansionary effects of incomes policy — which led to a rapid growth of private spending at rates of 4 percent in 1988 and 6 percent in 1989 — were absorbed by the current account of the balance of payments, which turned rapidly from surplus to deficit during 1988. The current account deficit led, in turn, to a severe loss of international reserves — close to $7 billion in 1988, or 3.4 percent of GDP, about the size of the reduction in the inflation tax — which could not have continued for much longer without compromising the *Pacto*'s exchange-rate policy rules and, with it, the sustainability of the stabilization attempt as a whole. At this point, other non-macroeconomic instruments were about to be introduced to soften the policy trade-offs and overcome the ineffectiveness of macroeconomic policy.

A Political Economy Model of Structural Reforms
The Model

As mentioned in the introduction, Mexico's reform process has gone through several phases, with each successive wave of market reforms often accelerating well beyond the original intentions of policy makers. In addition, the timing and sequence of policy reform were counter to established orthodox principles.[15] Many price controls were removed before trade liberalization began, and thus world prices could not serve as a guideline for domestic prices. Trade policy reform, in turn, took place in the midst of a severe external shock which magnified foreign exchange constraints, high inflation which distorted price signals, and an economic slowdown which exacerbated adjustment costs. Before price stabilization was consolidated, financial liberalization was undertaken at a time of high real interest rates.

This section develops a model of the reform process which attempts to explain those two characteristics: the snowball effects in the process sequence and the apparent irrationality of policy makers in the timing of policies. The model incorporates the growing realization by some economists that the explanation must draw from the field of political economy. In discussing trade policy reform, Dani Rodrik has asked: "If a period of macro-instability is the worst time to undertake a trade reform, why are so many countries doing it?" After discarding as an insufficient explanation the growing influence of some academic economists on policy makers, he offers the following reasons:

> First, a time of crisis occasionally enables radical reforms that would have been unthinkable in calmer times. That it takes the prospect of a severe denouement to bring a nation to its collective senses is the aggregate version of an insight due to Samuel Johnson: "When a man knows he is to be hanged in a fortnight, it concentrates his mind wonderfully." The quip seems to apply with equal force to nations in severe crisis, as some of the key cases of radical trade reform illustrate: Bolivia in 1985, Mexico since 1987, Poland 1990, Peru 1990. In all of these cases, a macroeconomic crisis of unprecedented proportions has led the leadership to embrace a wide range of reforms, of which trade liberalization was one component.
>
> The second reason has to do with the role of foreign creditors, and of the IMF and World Bank, in particular. The 1980s were a decade of great leverage for these institutions vis-à-vis debtor governments, especially where poorer African countries are concerned. The trade policy recommendations of the World Bank were adopted by cash-starved governments frequently with little conviction in their ultimate benefits. This accounts for the high incidence of wobbling and reversal on the trade front, once again especially in Africa. It also indicates that we ought not to be too optimistic on the sustainability of reform in many of these countries (Rodrik 1992, 89).

I believe, however, that there is more to it than these useful insights and that a good explanation should also clarify some unconventional links between macroeconomic adjustment and market reforms to account for the very different pace of reform in countries with policy makers of similar convictions.[16]

The model comprises a relationship showing the proximate determinants of the reform process and two reaction functions, one for policy makers and the other for foreign lenders and investors:

(1) $R = R\,(w_{pm}, O, T_p)$

(2) $w_{pm} = w_{pm}\,(C, w_f)$

(3) $w_f = w_f\,(R, i, C)$

R = stage of the reform process

w_{pm} = willingness of policy makers to reform

w_f = willingness of foreign lenders to lend

T = policy trade-offs between stabilization and structural reform

O = domestic opposition to market reforms

i = market interest rate

C = costs of not obtaining external finance

Equation 1 expresses the stage of the reform process, or the degree of implementation of structural reforms, as a function of the willingness of policy makers to reform and of the political obstacles they face (the extent of domestic opposition to reforms), as well as the objective policy trade-offs between stabilization and market reform. A well-known example of the latter refers to the exchange-rate dilemmas faced by a trade liberalization program in conditions of macroeconomic instability: the price stabilization objective is likely to require a real appreciation of the domestic currency, while the trade program pulls the real exchange rate in the other direction to avoid an unsustainable expansion of imports. In the absence of a sufficient number of policy instruments, the package is inconsistent, and one or both of its objectives will not be achieved. The sharper these trade-offs, the greater the likelihood that trade liberalization will have to be reversed, or slowed down, no matter how eager the policy makers are to undertake it. The "trade liberalization cum tablita" experiments in the Southern Cone during the late 1970s are often referred to as an illustration. They also illustrate, incidentally, the role of domestic opposition, or rather its suppression by authoritarian regimes, in the implementation of reforms.

The willingness of policy makers to reform is determined by the expected net benefits of reform as perceived by them. In regard to equation

2, the incentives faced by policy makers are, in turn, a function of the costs of not obtaining external finance and the willingness of foreign lenders to lend, given those costs. Since at least part of the potentially available external funding from multilateral and commercial bank creditors is made conditional on the adoption of market reforms, the costs of not obtaining foreign credit are a great incentive for policy makers to reform. Those costs may take the form of economic stagnation, high inflation, or an unmanageable degree of conflict introduced by other policy options. Given these costs, the benefits of reforming are also enhanced by a greater willingness of foreign lenders to lend, which as shown by equation 3 is essentially the same as the response of foreign lenders to the implementation of reform, other things being equal. One could add to this function the size of the allocative and dynamic efficiency gains expected from the reform process. These expected benefits — which have been present in the Mexican experience, as we shall see later — are excluded for the time being in order to emphasize that, even if these benefits are not perceived, other conditions may end up inducing policy makers to accelerate the reform process. An alternative justification for not including these gains in the net benefit function would be to assume that policy makers are short-term maximizers (no heroic leader here). Since those gains are likely to take a long time to materialize and make a difference, short-term maximizers will discount them with such a high rate as to make them negligible.

Foreign lenders, on the contrary, are long-term maximizers and apply, say, the market interest rate to discount the long-term benefits of reforms. The repayment of their loans or the profitability of their investments depends on the long-term economic viability of the recipient country, and they perceive market reforms as enhancing this viability. Their willingness to lend thus depends on the stage of the reform process and, inversely, on the market interest rate which affects the discounted value of the future benefits of policy reform, as illustrated by equation 3. The expected viability of a given country is also affected by lenders' perceptions of the country's long-term growth potential and economic and political stability. Since these "country risks," in banker's jargon, are strongly correlated with the costs of not obtaining external finance as perceived by the policy makers, we use the latter as a proxy for the former (and simply to avoid a proliferation of variables).

Taking the policy trade-offs, the costs of not obtaining external finance (C), internal opposition (O), and the market interest rate (i) as exogenous variables, the three-equation model can be solved for R, the stage of the reform process, and the willingness to lend and to reform (w_f and wpm). In this form, the model can be further simplified in two relationships: the foreign lenders function as shown in equation 3 below, and, substituting from equation 2 into equation 1, the stage of reform (R) as a function of the willingness to lend and other exogenous variables, as shown in equation 4.

(3) $w_f = w_f(R, i, C)$

(4) $R = R^* (w_p, C, O, T_p)$

which determine simultaneously w_f and R. Both of these relationships are likely to be strongly nonlinear as shown in Figure 1. In the case of the foreign lenders function (the w_f (R) curve), because a critical mass of reforms may be necessary before foreign investors are convinced to step up their lending, and because beyond a certain point the country in question already qualifies as a "market economy," no further significant benefits are expected from additional reforms (the willingness to lend, viewed as a permanent flow of foreign savings, may even decline at that stage). Similarly, the reform process-function (the R (w_f) curve corresponding to equation 4) is likely to speed up slowly before a critical level of foreign lending makes it worthwhile to undertake reforms. It will then accelerate at intermediate levels of foreign lending and become inelastic again at even higher levels because the marginal benefits of further reforms for policy makers diminish when the availability of foreign credit is already very abundant.[17]

Figure 1

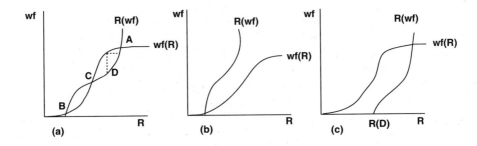

Figure 1 shows the determination of foreign lending and policy reforms in three different situations. In Figure 1.a, the particular form of the model has some similarities with the "critical mass" model of Schelling.[18] There are three equilibria, two stable (a high one at point A and a low one at point B) and one unstable, the intermediate one at point C. The latter represents a critical mass of both foreign lending and domestic reforms, beyond which the reform process will accelerate toward the high equilibrium at A. To visualize this, consider a point such as D. At this point, the stage achieved by the reform process R (D) is such that lenders consider it worthwhile to step up their lending beyond w_f (D) and toward their foreign lending function. This positive response induces policy makers in turn to accelerate policy reforms beyond R (D), triggering a further response on the part of lenders, and so on. This process stabilizes at A where the absence of further benefits for lenders and policy makers justifies no additional policy reforms. Analogous reasoning would show that any departure of the reform process below C would trigger successive responses on the part of lenders and policy makers tending to reverse policy reforms toward the low-level equilibrium at A.

The critical mass of reforms is determined by the shape and position of the two curves, and it will thus be reduced by any shift to the left of the foreign lenders function or any shift to the right of the policy makers and the reform-process functions.[19] In particular, a weaker internal opposition (-DO) or a softening of policy trade-offs (-DT$_p$) reduces the critical mass of reforms by shifting the policy makers function (and, thus, the reform-process function) to the right, while a drop in the market interest rate has a similar effect by shifting the lenders function to the left. The effect of an increase in the costs of not obtaining external finance (DC) is, at first sight, ambiguous by shifting both curves to the right: these greater costs make policy makers more willing to reform but also make foreign investors more reluctant to lend. The first effect is, however, likely to predominate under most conditions as lenders spread these costs over a longer time horizon than policy makers. The critical mass of reforms will thus be reduced.

Multiple equilibria need not be the only possible outcome. Figures 1.b and 1.c show a unique equilibrium at a low and high level, respectively. In Figure 1.b, reluctant policy makers — facing a strong internal opposition, sensing difficult policy trade-offs, or perceiving small costs in not obtaining external finance — will undertake a minimal amount of reforms. There is then no critical mass of reforms that will convince foreign investors to lend, and the process remains stuck at a low level of both foreign lending and policy reform. In Figure 1.c, enthusiastic reformers — facing little opposition at home and soft policy trade-offs — will undertake a large number of reforms even in the absence of foreign lending (R[0]), but this, in turn, will trigger a positive response from lenders, and the reform process will accelerate well beyond the policy makers' minimal intentions, stabilizing at a high level of foreign lending.[20]

The Unconventional Macroeconomic Role of Structural Reforms

The model can now be applied to explain the timing and sequence of the reform process in Mexico. Initially, market reforms were, in fact, reversed during the 1982 crisis: foreign exchange controls were introduced, and direct import controls, fully re-established in 1981, were kept almost intact until mid-1985. This reversal was the consequence of the sharp contraction in foreign lending (a shift to the right in the foreign lenders function) which prevailed until 1985 despite the massive fiscal adjustment that took place in 1982-1983.

Thus, notwithstanding President de la Madrid's intentions to reform — comprehensively stated in the 1983 National Development Plan — the reform process proceeded at a slow pace throughout 1983 and 1984.

Several new developments took place in 1985-1986. On one hand, the Baker Plan was seen as an increase in the foreign lenders' response to reform and, thus, as both an exogenous shift to the left in the foreign lenders function and an increase in the expected net benefits of reform for debtors (a shift to the right in the policy makers function) since a major player was announcing the need to step up foreign lending in exchange for the adoption of market reforms. On the other hand, the mid-1985 foreign exchange crisis — and even more so the oil shock in early 1986 — had two other important effects. By forcing macroeconomic policy to provide unprecedented levels of "exchange-rate protection" in 1986-1987, the highly adverse external environment had the paradoxical effect of softening the policy trade-offs involved in trade liberalization by facilitating the adjustment of industrial firms to a more open economy. For this reason, and also because the high exchange rate and domestic recession subsumed the specific costs of trade liberalization into the broader and more apparent costs of overall macroeconomic adjustment, the oil shock also lessened resistance to change. This is a major reason for the smoothness, both economic and political, of the Mexican transition toward a liberalized trade regime.[21]

The second effect of the oil shock was to increase the costs for the policy maker of not obtaining external finance, thus adding to previous incentives to accelerate the reform process. By cutting in half the foreign exchange revenues of the country's main export product, it also made foreign creditors more reluctant to lend. Nevertheless, President de la Madrid's dilemma in early 1986 was eventually resolved in favor of keeping on course toward structural reform. Throughout 1986 and 1987, a large number of privatizations (although not the major ones) were undertaken. In particular, the radicalization of the trade liberalization program, announced in August 1985, was followed to the letter, and deregulation of foreign investment flows, unimpressive since 1984, gained momentum.

A further acceleration of the reform process has taken place since 1988. As we have seen, a comprehensive incomes policy was essential to recover price and financial stability, but the other roots of policy ineffectiveness were still in place. Even if private investments had recovered, it was soon apparent that the sharp decline in private savings rates could make an economic recovery unsustainable. Without external finance, the sustainability of stabilization itself was in doubt as the reserve losses of 1988 may remind us. To avoid the "stabilization without growth" scenario or, even worse, a return to high inflation, the government had to compensate the legacy of the macroeconomic adjustment process (i.e., the severely depressed rates of investment and domestic savings) with a substantial increase in foreign savings. Under these circumstances, external finance was less dispensable than ever before.

At the same time, all other incentives were in place for a big leap forward in the reform process. The Brady Plan, just as the Baker Plan before it, was soon to offer a reduction in external transfers in exchange for further reforms, now in the more attractive form of debt relief, thus increasing the net benefits of reform. The real exchange rate was at or near peak levels by the end of 1987 and, as recent experience had shown, could provide a cushion for the dislocation costs of a radicalization of trade reform. The latter did indeed take place in the context of the stabilization program in late 1987, as already seen. In May 1989, an overhaul of foreign investment regulations was introduced — all but a repeal of the 1973 law on foreign investment — opening new areas of the economy to foreign capital and establishing automatic approval of 100 percent foreign ownership for investment projects fulfilling a number of conditions. Financial liberalization and, more generally, a comprehensive deregulation of tertiary activities, including road transportation and telecommunications, has been undertaken since 1989. Privatization entered its major and more complex phase involving the sale of some the largest state enterprises. The two airline companies, *Mexicana de Aviación* and *Aero Mexico*, were sold in mid-1989, and the two largest copper-mining parastatals, *Compañía Minera de Cananea* and *Mexicana de Cobre*, along with the telecommunications company *Teléfonos de México* (TELMEX), were sold to a group of domestic and foreign investors in 1990. The commercial banks, nationalized in 1982, went to local financial groups in 1991-1992. It is worth noting that the official case for reduced state participation has not been based on microeconomic efficiency. It is a macroeconomic argument, ultimately based on policy ineffectiveness, which makes reference to the very special conditions of the 1980s: a government rationed in credit markets, unmet social needs, and a private sector with ample financial resources abroad ready to be invested in previously state-dominated activities that do not have a high social priority. Under such conditions, a clear comparative-advantage argument can be made for privatization even if public enterprises had absolute efficiency advantages over private firms since society as a whole would clearly gain from a reallocation of public investments from areas where social returns and private returns do not differ greatly to activities yielding a higher differential in social/private returns.

Two other factors contributed to the acceleration of the reform process. So far, the analysis has assumed that the costs of not obtaining external finance are exogenous, that is, independent of the reform process itself. Yet, some policy reforms may have the effect of increasing these costs. Import liberalization, combined with the real peso appreciation since 1988, appears to be one such case: the import boom that followed has been one of the main factors behind the exploding trade and current account deficits that exacerbated the need for further external finance. In fact, the sequence of events clearly suggests that the acceleration of reforms in other areas — in particular, the reprivatization of the banking system — were triggered as a means to alleviate, through capital inflows, a balance-of-payments position that was otherwise unsustainable, partly as a result of recent trade and exchange-rate policies.[22] The other factor, also related to trade reform, was the smoothness of the transition itself during 1985-1987. This had a feedback effect on the reform process. It created what appears to be a mistaken evaluation, on the part of policy makers, of the role of trade policy reform in the manufacturing exports boom up to 1987 (see, on the subject, Peres 1990; Ros 1991b). Thus, it also generated exaggerated expectations about the long-term benefits of trade liberalization and that contributed to the further acceleration of trade reform in late 1987. (I am departing here from the assumption that policy makers are cynical and short-term maximizers.)

The model has other interesting applications, which also clarify some particular features of the Mexican experience. For example, it could explain the sudden shift away from gradualist sequencing of reforms, in the recent "big bang" experiences of Peru and Venezuela. In the early 1990s, the costs of not obtaining external finance, partly as a result of past adjustments and failures, have become unbearable and are more fully perceived by policy makers; unlike previous periods, many other incentives are now fully in place. Taken together, these factors can cause a sudden acceleration of reforms, a shift from Figure 1.b to 1.c.[23]

On the other hand, the slower pace of reform in Brazil can be seen, in part, as a consequence of sharp trade-offs between stabilization and market liberalization. Unlike Mexico (or Venezuela) with a small internal transfer problem, in Brazil traditional exchange-rate dilemmas are exacerbated by a large internal transfer problem. To the extent that trade liberalization increases the exchange rate necessary to reconcile internal and external balance, it adds to the required fiscal adjustment. This is probably why the short-lived stabilization episodes in Brazil's experience (as well as in Argentina with its similar internal problem) have been consistent only with highly overvalued currencies. And it can also explain the high degree of real exchange-rate variability in this adjustment process. An accelerated transition in the trade policy regime would then only increase the fiscal burden and could make the policy reform unsustainable unless the fiscal accounts had initially overadjusted. As long as this harsh precondition is not met and/or a massive reversal of external transfers does not take place, gradualism emerges as the only viable option in an already fiscally strangled economy. Similarly, with less history of capital flight (in comparison to Mexico and Argentina) on which to draw, the macroeconomic advantages of privatization become less obvious.

Conclusion:
Long-Term Consequences of Adjustment and Market Reforms

With low investment and domestic savings rates, Mexico's economic growth in the early 1990s was half what it was during the oil boom. Based on present trends (around 4 percent per year), growth would remain significantly below the long-term rate of the postwar period (6.5 percent per year). Despite a foreign savings rate well above historical levels, the economy invests today a lower proportion of its output than at any time in the two decades before 1980 and thus expands its productive capacity at a slower pace than in the past. The economy, in sum, emerges weaker, rather than stronger, from the years of crisis and adjustment.

At the same time, a "great transformation" has taken place in between, if I may appropriate Polanyi's expression for events of a different scale. This massive reform process raises two central questions: Are market reforms likely to affect significantly the economy's productivity growth rate and external competitiveness so that, despite lower rates of accumulation, the economy may recover some of the growth potential lost during the crisis? Can the shift in the market/state balance bring about a permanently higher flow of external savings, significantly greater than historical rates, that would allow an increase in the rate of accumulation, despite the sharp decline of the domestic savings rate? Unfortunately, it is too early to answer the first question fully and too difficult to answer the second. Thus, I address these questions in a very tentative and speculative way (Ros 1991a).

Some policy reforms — especially those affecting the domestic regulatory framework — were long overdue and were clearly desirable on both efficiency and equity grounds. These were exemplified most strikingly by the regulations in road transportation. Adverse impacts have been rather limited or even absent. A case in point is the continued decline of interest rates after the financial liberalization measures in 1989. Benefits of deregulation in many areas have largely exceeded its costs. These have not been, however, the most radical reforms, nor those from which the greater benefits were to be expected.

The case for greater selectivity in state participation in the economy and, indeed, for state disengagement in a number of productive activities is also extremely powerful. But this is so, as already mentioned, for macroeconomic reasons related to the special conditions of the 1980s. This argument has less significance for long-term economic growth beyond the promise, which so far largely remains just that, of a considerable expansion in human capital investments and the provision of public goods. On the other hand, the microeconomic efficiency gains and performance improvements of the newly privatized enterprises are yet to be seen in most cases.

The state is smaller but not necessarily more efficient. To be sure, some recent trends on the revenue and transfers sides of fiscal accounts are encouraging: the efficiency of tax collection has improved, the tax base has expanded, several inequitable subsidies have been eliminated, and the inflation tax has practically disappeared. But many other changes on the expenditure side have been far less positive. Overall, Mexico's fiscal adjustment has not encouraged a greater internal efficiency of the public sector, despite or perhaps because of its massive character. Before 1985, it probably was less efficient than in many other countries, as manifested by the incapacity of fiscal policy to increase public disposable income beyond the depreciation-induced gains in fiscal revenues. As already discussed, fiscal adjustment in this period was largely achieved through deep cuts in public investment and in the real salaries of public employees, hardly a useful means to improve the efficiency of the state and its bureaucracy. Despite some positive recent trends in social spending, state disengagement has not served its main purpose: the expansion of social infrastructure. Privatization revenues primarily support (very effectively, no doubt) recent stabilization efforts by temporarily compensating for the fall in inflation tax and strengthening the capital account of the balance of payments, through the private sector's financial assets brought back home to purchase the public enterprises.

The results of trade policy reform are also controversial. Despite the smoothness of the microeconomic processes of resource reallocation, and probably for related reasons, the dynamic effects of trade liberalization on productivity performance have been mixed and, overall, are not very encouraging. Since 1986, labor productivity remains below the historical rate and, despite some moderate improvement compared to the 1980-1985 period, five out of the nine broad components of manufacturing recorded a productivity growth decline in the recent period. Current trends in the trade pattern and industrial structure are, with no major exceptions, an extrapolation of the past, probably as a result of the effectiveness of past import-substitution policies in changing the economy's pattern of comparative advantages in favor of manufacturing and what were then infant industries. Certainly, the economy is now more open on both the import and export sides, but the structural deficit in non-oil trade is rapidly expanding, especially as the real exchange rate returns to historical levels. Finally, by abandoning trade and industrial policy instruments without an effective replacement, the economy runs the risk of freezing, or of changing too slowly, its present structure of comparative advantages. The danger of getting stuck in the relatively unskilled and low-paid tasks of the production processes of capital-intensive industries is a far-from-desirable prospect for a country that needs to grow fast and to increase living standards rapidly for its nearly 90 million people.

If market reforms show little in terms of significantly improving the economy's dynamic efficiency, what about their effects on external capital inflows? Since 1989, the reform process has brought into the treasury huge capital inflows in the balance of payments and, from privatization revenues, billions of dollars (sixteen billion dollars, to be precise, since 1989, some three-quarters of which arrived in 1991, representing 4 percentage points of GDP). Its overall impact on business confidence has been clearly positive. In fact, it has seemingly created a new beginning among the local entrepreneurial class as well as with foreign investors. This had a practical positive response, as witnessed by the large quantity of capital repatriation since 1989 and, at another level, the financial restructuring of some leading Mexican conglomerates, whose outlook was anything but bright immediately after the 1982 crisis.

Reform has reached its climax, at least symbolically: new legislation for the land tenure system and the enactment of the North American Free Trade Agreement (NAFTA) with the United States and Canada in January 1994. Privatization concluded in 1992, with the sale of the remaining banks and the insurance company as well as parts of the operations of CONASUPO (the food distribution company) and of SIDERMEX (the largest steel producer). This means that a substantial portion of recent capital inflows is likely to disappear in the near future. Those inflows related to privatization revenues were clearly temporary in nature and will begin to disappear unless PEMEX were to be put on sale. All this leads us to a most important aspect of the overall reform process. Does the alluded change in entrepreneurial attitudes and behavior reflect a temporary euphoria or, rather, a long-lasting revival of animal spirits that, in the future, could be seen as the major positive outcome of the reform process? This question falls outside the scope of this chapter and of the judgment of its author. But on its answer depends the size of the macroeconomic adjustment problem that lies ahead in the medium term.

Notes

1. This section and part of the following one draw on two recent papers by the author (Ros 1992a, 1992b).

2. See Bacha 1990; Carneiro and Werneck 1988; Fanelli, Frenkel, and Winograd 1987; Fanelli, Frenkel, and Rozenwurcel 1990; Ros 1991a; Taylor 1991, as well as the literature on the external and internal transfer problems (in particular, Ortiz and Noriega 1988; and Reisen and van Trotsenburg 1988).

3. The smaller and less diversified a country's tradable sector and the higher the share of primary exports and complementary imports in foreign trade, the larger was likely to be the real currency depreciation required to effect a given external transfer. Country size, resource endowments, and past success in industrialization and trade policies were, in turn, among the main determinants of these characteristics of foreign trade.

4. The estimates for Brazil and Argentina are in Reisen and van Trotsenburg (1988) and correspond to the depreciation-induced increase in the real value of external interest payments.

5. Macroeconomists with experience in inflation projections are very familiar with the implications: broadly speaking, the inflation acceleration caused by a given shock doubles with each halving of the interval between two consecutive wage adjustments.

6. Reduction of domestic spending was, in fact, *induced* by devaluation. Under these conditions the exchange rate was certain to affect external balance through Hirschman and Díaz Alejandro effects, i.e., through contractionary effects on private income and spending which are nothing else but the stabilizing effects on fiscal accounts.

7. This is similar to the case of Venezuela, precisely the other country that was also most dependent on oil export revenues. Brazil, in contrast, with its larger and more diversified manufacturing export base, achieved a more efficient external adjustment — in terms of output losses and given the required current adjustment — than any of the oil exporting countries, especially before inflation went out of control and brought with it a more severe reduction of domestic investments. Argentina, in this respect, represented the worst of all possible worlds. It combined a relatively rigid export structure — with a large share of primary exports as in the oil exporting countries — without the benefit of the stabilizing effects of devaluation. The result was the deepest collapse of the investment process — more than 11 percentage points decline in the investment/GDP ratio — and the most prolonged period of economic decline and high inflation. For a more detailed analysis, see Ros (1992a).

8. See on the subject, Casar and Márquez (1983) and Márquez (1981) on the role of the minimum wage as a "basic wage," i.e., the lowest general wage for unskilled labor on which the whole structure of relative earnings differentials is based.

9. For a less cryptic account of these events, see Beristain and Trigueros (1990) and Ros (1992b).

10. It should be noted that, although import liberalization did not contribute significantly to disinflation (Ize 1990), import tariffs policy was fine-tuned for a couple of years in accordance with the *Pacto* price guidelines for the private sector.

11. See Williamson 1990, among many others.

12. The Oliviera-Tanzi effect was estimated at 0.9 percent of GDP in 1987. If other effects of inflation on the operational deficit — on financial subsidies and the composition of the public debt — are included, the sum adds up to 1.2 percent of GDP (see Banco de Mexico 1989). On the other hand, the financial deficit — the budget with no inflation adjustments at all — dropped sharply from 16 percent of GDP in 1987 to 1.3 percent in 1991, but this reduction is fully attributable to the decline in the inflation rate (and, in particular, its effect on nominal interest rates).

13. This analysis could be objected to on the grounds that *past* fiscal adjustment, leading to a sizeable primary since 1987 and before, contributed to reduce the government solvency problems and thus to relax credit rationing and the initially tight capital account of the balance of payments. But this is, at most, a complementary remark. Without income policies, the turnaround of the capital account would not have taken place (as the experience of the second semester of 1987 clearly suggests). In any case, the point remains: there was no additional fiscal adjustment (adjusted for inflation) after 1987.

14. Unless one takes the view that the turnaround of the capital account since 1989 was itself a consequence of successful price stabilization (which, in my opinion, has an element of truth). If this is so, then Mexico's macroeconomic structure was featuring in recent years a multiplicity of equilibria and, under such conditions, the coordination of wage and price decisions by incomes policy becomes not only a necessary but also a sufficient condition to move the economy from high inflation to low inflation equilibrium.

15. See, for example, Corbo and Fischer (1990): "The importance of the sequence reforms — reforms oriented mainly to reduce severe macro imbalances first and to improve resource allocation and restore growth later — has become increasingly clear with experience." Along the same lines, it has even been stated that the "broad characteristics of any realistic sequence of reforms are no longer in doubt" (Blanchard et al. 1991).

16. Note also that the two reasons offered cannot be applied to some countries at the same time: reform is either embraced by a heroic leadership which has finally come to its senses or undertaken with little conviction by cash-starved governments as a result of IMF and World Bank leverage. While the author probably did not mean to apply both reasons to the same case, an explanation of the Mexican experience along these lines would have to rely on the first reason only. This would, in my view, be a poor explanation.

17. The strongly nonlinear nature of the policy makers function, and thus of the reform-process function, was pointed out to me by Samuel Valenzuela in discussing an earlier version of the model.

18. And some important differences, too. A point on either of the two curves reflects an optimizing behavior on the part of either foreign lenders or policy makers. Schelling's model of the "dying seminar," one of the two curves is the 45-degree line stating the condition that in equilibrium, expectations are fulfilled. The underlying reasons for the S shape of the other curve are also completely different.

19. The irony was unintended.

20. In Figures 1.b or 1.c, the curves could cross again at negative levels of foreign lending and reform, but such an intersection (not shown in the figures) would be unstable. Any positive departure from it would make policy makers and lenders realize that it is to their mutual advantage to move toward the higher level (and the only stable) equilibrium.

21. The other major reason, besides the general lack of domestic opposition, is probably Mexico's successful import-substitution experience in the past — in the sense that this strategy effectively modified the economy's pattern of comparative advantages in favor of manufacturing and the initially infant industries. This feature reveals itself in the fact that current trends in the trade pattern and industrial structure are with no major exceptions and are an extrapolation of the past. For further analysis, see Ros 1992c.

22. I say partly because the large current account deficits in recent years also reflect the decline of the private savings rate, a consequence not of trade policy reform but of the past macroeconomic adjustment.

23. This was, in fact, one of the original motivations for the model. In a conference session last year on Peru and Venezuela, I asked why Fujimori and Pérez had turned from gradualist candidates to "big bang" presidents. One participant's response, in an overwhelmingly structuralist audience, was provocative. He gave me, as he said, "a neoclassical answer: they are optimizing under constraints."

References

Bacha, Edmar. 1990. "A Three-Gap Model in Foreign Transfers and the GDP Growth Rate in Developing Countries." *Journal of Development Economics* 32 (2):279-296.

Banco de México. 1989. *Informe Anual.* México, D.F.: Banco de México.

Beristain, Javier, and I. Trigueros. 1990. "Mexico." In *Latin American Adjustment: How Much Has Happened?* ed. John Williamson. Washington, D.C.: Institute for International Economics.

Blanchard, O.R., et al. 1991. *Reform in Eastern Europe.* Cambridge, Mass.: MIT Press.

Casar, María Amparo, and C. Márquez. 1983. "La política de salários mínimos legales: 1934-1982." *Economía Mexicana* 5. México: CIDE.

Carneiro, Dionísio, and Rogério Werneck. 1988. *External Debt, Economic Growth, and Fiscal Adjustment.* Texto Para Discussão 202, Departamento de Economia, Pontifícia Universidade Católica do Rio de Janeiro.

Corbo, Vittorio, and Stanley Fischer. 1990. "Adjustment Program and Bank Support: Rationale and Main Results." World Bank (November). Mimeo.

Fanelli, José María, Roberto Frenkel, and Carlos Winograd. 1987. *Stabilization and Adjustment Policies and Programmes. Country Study 12. Argentina.* Helsinki: WIDER.

Fanelli, José María, Roberto Frenkel, and Guillermo Rozenwurcel. 1990. "Growth and Structural Reform in Latin America: Where We Stand." Report prepared for UNCTAD. Buenos Aires: CEDES.

Ize, A. 1990. *Trade Liberalization, Stabilization, and Growth: Some Notes on the Mexican Experience.* Washington, D.C.: International Monetary Fund.

Ize, A., and G. Ortíz. 1987. "Fiscal Rigidities, Public Debt, and Capital Flight." IMF Staff Papers 34 (June).

Márquez, C. 1981. "Nivel de salario y dispersión de la de la estructura salarial, (1939-1977)." *Economía Mexicana* 3. México: CIDE.

Meller, Patricio. 1991. "Review of the Chilean Trade Liberalization and Export Expansion Process (1974-1990)." Paper presented at the WIDER Conference on Trade and Industrialization Reconsidered, Paris, September.

Noyola, Juan. 1956. "El desarrollo económico y la inflación en México y otros países latinoamericanos." Reprinted in *La Economía Mexicana* 2, ed. L. Solis. *México: Lecturas de El Trimestre Económico* 4, Fondo de Cultura Económica.

Ortíz, G., and C. Noriega. 1988. *Investment and Growth in Latin America.* Washington, D.C.: International Monetary Fund.

Peres, Wilson. 1990. "From Globalization to Regionalization: The Mexican Case." OECD Technical Papers 24. Paris: OECD.

Reisen, H., and A. van Trotsenburg. 1988. "Developing Country Debt: The Budgetary and Transfer Problem." Paris: OECD Development Centre.

Rodrik, Dani. 1992. "The Limits of Trade Policy Reform in Developing Countries." *The Journal of Economic Perspectives* 6:1 (Winter).

Ros, Jaime. 1991a. "Movilidad de capital y eficacia de las políticas ante una corrida del crédito." *El Trimestre Económico* LVIII (3).

Ros, Jaime. 1991b. "The Effects of Government Policies on the Incentive to Invest, Enterprise Behavior, and Employment: A Study of Mexico's Economic Reforms in the Eighties." Working Paper 53. Geneva: International Labor Organization.

Ros, Jaime. 1992a. "Domestic Macroeconomic Instability and Integration in the World Economy: Latin America in the 1980s and Prospects for the 1990s." Paper presented at the workshop on "Latin American Integration and the World Economy: Confronting the Choices." Washington, D.C.: Inter-American Dialogue (December).

Ros, Jaime. 1992b. "Ajuste macroeconómico, reformas estructurales y crecimiento en México." Work for the project on "The Role of the State in Latin America," with support from the CEDEAL Foundation.

Ros, Jaime. 1992c. "Mexico's Trade and Industrialization Experience Since 1950: A Reconsideration of Past Policies and Assessment of Current Reforms." Prepared for the project on "Trade and Industrialization Reconsidered." Helsinki: WIDER.

Schelling, T. 1991. *Micromotives and Microbehavior.* New York: W.W. Norton & Co.

Taylor, Lance. 1991. *Income Distribution, Inflation, and Growth: Lectures on Structuralist Macroeconomic Theory.* Cambridge, Mass.: MIT Press.

Williamson, John. 1990. "What Washington Means by Policy Reform." In *Latin American Adjustment: How Much Has Happened?* ed. John Williamson. Washington, D.C.: Institute for International Economics.

Index

A

COMIBOL (Corporación Minera de Bolivia) 130, 136
Comisión de Verdad y Reconciliación 225
Compañía Minera de Cananea and Mexicana de Cobre 314
comparative advantage 317
Complementary Nutrition Program 241. *See also* PAC
Concertación de Partidos por la Democracia 221, 222, 223, 224, 225, 226, 227, 228, 230, 231
CONDEPA (Conciencia de Patria) 118, 119, 120, 133
Confederación de Trabajadores Mexicanos 19. *See also* CTM
Confederación Nacional Campesina 19. *See also* CNC
Constitution, 1988 (Brazil) 154, 155, 166, 173
Convertibility Plan 12, 45, 46, 48, 49, 86, 87, 88, 90, 92
cordobazo 76
corruption 115, 116, 120
counter-narcotics 123
Cruzado Plan 15, 202, 203. *See also* Plano Cruzado
CTM (Confederación de Trabajadores Mexicanos) 19
Cumplido laws 225
CUT (Central Unica dos Trabalhadores) 157, 158

D

de la Madrid, Miguel 273, 274, 275, 280, 283, 285, 313
debt crisis 1, 5, 6, 8, 18
Decree 21060 (Bolivia) 105, 106, 112
Decree 22407 (Bolivia) 106, 112, 132
delegative democracy 9
Delfim Netto, Antônio 189, 191, 202
democratic consolidation 1, 2, 4, 6, 16, 18, 20, 21, 26, 27, 28, 221, 222, 229, 253
deregulation 220
developmentalist state 153, 160, 175
dirigismo 153, 154

dual legitimacy 108, 111
dualistic democracies 19
Due Obedience Law 43

E

economic elites 269, 272, 275, 276, 282
economic growth 271, 272, 280
Economic Solidarity Pact 298
economic strategy 237, 238, 248, 250, 251
elections 106, 107, 108, 109, 110, 116, 117, 118, 119, 121, 122, 272, 279, 280, 281, 284, 285
elite-client relations 279
empleomanía 108, 122
employment 275, 276, 277
Enterprise for the Americas (EAI) 114
Erman González, Antonio 88
exclusionary democracy 5, 6, 13, 18, 20
external gap 299, 301, 302, 304
external shock 298, 299, 308

F

Falkland Islands 76. *See also* Malvinas
Family Subsidy 241. *See also* SUF (Subsidio Unico Familiar)
Fernández, Max 118, 119, 120
Figueiredo, João 202
fiscal crisis 152, 159, 160, 161, 163, 166, 167, 169, 170, 172, 174
fiscal deficit 273, 283, 300, 301, 303
fiscal disequilibrium 84
fiscal paralysis 160, 161, 164, 172, 173
FONAMA 114
foreign debt 79, 80, 81, 83, 85, 86, 88, 89, 90, 273, 275. *See also* debt crisis
foreign investment 106, 112, 114
FOSIS (Fondo de Solidaridad e Inversión Social) 250, 254. *See also* Solidarity and Social Investment Fund
fragmentation 268, 270, 275, 286
Franco, Itamar 15, 152
free market strategy 237, 245, 248
Frondizi, Arturo 78
Fujimori, Alberto 14

About the Publisher

The mission of the North-South Center is to promote better relations among the United States, Canada, and the nations of Latin America and the Caribbean by providing a disciplined intellectual focus for improved relations, commerce, and understanding in the hemisphere, wherein major political, social, and economic issues are seen in a global context. The Center conducts policy-relevant research and programs of education, training, cooperative study, and public outreach and engages in an active program of publication and dissemination of information on the Americas. The North-South Center fosters linkages among academic and research institutions throughout the Americas and acts as an agent of constructive change in the region.

Ambler H. Moss, Jr.
Director, North-South Center

Robin Rosenberg
Deputy Director, North-South Center

Richard Downes
Director of Communications

Kathleen A. Hamman
Editorial Director

Mary M. Mapes
Publications Director

Jayne M. Weisblatt
Editor

Production Notes

This book was printed on 60 lb. Cougar Natural text stock with a 10 point CIS cover stock.

The text of this volume was set in Garamond for the North-South Center's Publications Department, using Aldus Pagemaker 5.0, on a Macintosh Centris 650 computer. It was designed and formatted by Stephanie True Moss.

The cover was created by Mary M. Mapes using Quark XPress 3.2 for the composition and color separation. The cover photo was taken by Eduardo A. Gamarra in 1987, in Potosí, Bolivia, showing three of 23,000 unemployed miners on the day they were fired.

This book was copy edited by Jayne M. Weisblatt, Vanessa Gray, Erik Bridoux, and Mariela Córdoba.

Printed in the United States of America by Thomson-Shore, Inc., of Dexter, Michigan.